STATE AND LOCAL GOVERNMENT AND POLITICS:
ESSENTIAL READINGS

STATE AND LOCAL GOVERNMENT AND POLITICS:

ESSENTIAL READINGS

Edited by

Harry A. Bailey, Jr. *Temple University*

Jay M. Shafritz *University of Pittsburgh*

 F. E. PEACOCK PUBLISHERS, INC.
ITASCA, ILLINOIS

Copyright © 1993
F. E. Peacock Publishers, Inc.
All rights reserved
Library of Congress Catalog Card No. 92-061960
ISBN 0-87581-372-0
Printed in the United States of America
10 9 8 7 6 5 4 3 2 1
1997 1996 1995 1994 1993

CONTENTS

Contents

LIST OF CONTRIBUTORS

Glenn Abney, Department of Political Science, Georgia State
    University
Charles G. Bell, Department of Political Science, California State
    University, Davis
John T. Carnevale, Staff Member, Economics and Government
    Division, U.S. Office of Management and Budget
Robert S. Erikson, Department of Political Science, University of
    Houston
James L. Garnett, Division of Business and Public Management, West
    Virginia College of Graduate Studies Institute, West Virginia
Henry R. Glick, Department of Political Science, Florida State
    University
Dennis O. Grady, Department of Political Science and Criminal
    Justice, Appalachian State University, Boone, North Carolina
Albert K. Karnig, Department of Political Science, University of
    Wyoming
Thomas P. Lauth, Department of Political Science, University of
    Georgia
David C. Long, Attorney, Long and Silverstein, P.C., Washington,
    D.C.
David B. Magleby, Department of Political Science, Brigham Young
    University
John P. McIver, Department of Political Science, University of
    Colorado, Boulder
Huey L. Perry, Department of Political Science, Southern University,
    Baton Rouge
Paul E. Peterson, Department of Political Science, Harvard University

William T. Pound, Executive Director, National Conference of State
Legislatures, Denver, Colorado

Bella Rosenberg, Assistant to the President, American Federation of
Teachers, New York, New York

Alan Rosenthal, Eagleton Institute of Politics, Rutgers University, New
Brunswick

Barry M. Rubin, School of Public and Environmental Affairs, Indiana
University, Bloomington

Larry Sabato, Department of Political Science, University of Virginia

Carl W. Stenberg, Executive Director, Council of State Governments,
Lexington, Kentucky

Alfred Stokes, Department of Political Science, Xavier University, New
Orleans

David B. Walker, Department of Political Science, University of
Connecticut

B. Oliver Walter, Department of Political Science, University of
Wyoming

Elder Witt, Independent Journalist and Deputy Publisher, *Governing:
The Magazine of States and Localities,* headquartered in Washington,
D.C.

Gerald C. Wright, Jr., Department of Political Science, Indiana
University, Bloomington

C. Kurt Zorn, School of Public and Environmental Affairs, Indiana
University, Bloomington

PREFACE

With libraries bulging from thousands of new books acquired each year and the ever-increasing concern for the wanton destruction of forests to make paper, nowadays one should have a solid explanation for bringing a new book into the world. As socially responsible editors we plead that we saw a need—a need for a comprehensive reader in state and local government dealing with the myriad changes in this field that have occurred during the last two decades.

"Laboratories of democracy" was a phrase first coined by Louis Brandeis (1856–1941), associate justice of the U.S. Supreme Court (1916–1939), to refer to state governments that develop innovative policies to deal with social and economic problems. The implication was that if the policies succeeded, they would be adopted by other states or by the federal government. Brandeis wrote in a dissenting opinion to *New State Ice Co.* v. *Liebmann* (1932):

> It is one of the happy incidents of the federal system that a single coura-
> geous State may, if its citizens choose, serve as a laboratory; and try novel
> social and economic experiments without risk to the rest of the country.

One hesitates to contradict Brandeis, but conditions have changed. The states (as well as localities) no longer have the option to be innovative. Because of increased federal mandates, decreased federal funding, and constituent demands for increased services and lower tax rates, the states have had no choice but to probe the utmost depths of innovation. Unlike the federal government, state and local governments must balance budgets each year—and must make the hard policy choices necessary to achieve this. Thus it is increasingly true that policy analysts, public administrators, and elected officials now look locally for the kind of innovative vigor that was once more expected of the national government.

A major impetus for this turn of events was the *New Federalism* of Presidents Ronald Reagan and George Bush. Beginning in 1981, they sought to return power and responsibility to the states and to dramatically reduce the role of the federal government in domestic programs. This had two phases: first, President Reagan's economic recovery program included reductions in the federal domestic spending (meaning nonmilitary) budget, the use of new *block grant programs** to give states greater flexibility in using federal monies, the reduction of the volume of new federal regulations, and tax reductions to stimulate the economy. Phase two was the return from the federal to state governments of some authority to tax, thereby increasing the revenue capacity of state governments. These goals have had a mixed success. The main problem is that federal funding has been cut at the same time as the states have been mandated to undertake hundreds of new functions relating to health, the environment, factory safety, and education, among others. The massive budget deficits run up by these two presidential administrations have made it almost impossible for the federal government to even consider a return to previous levels of federal funding. The states and their local governments consequently have had no choice but to cope as best they can.

All this is by way of asserting the newly claimed importance of studying state and local government. It is a subject of enhanced importance for those interested in politics, administration, and every aspect of the policy sciences. This collection designed for introductory courses in state and local government covers all the core areas: the intergovernmental framework (fiscal federalism), citizen participation, governors, legislatures, courts, taxation, education, and economic development. Included are representative pieces from many of the best-known writers in political science and public administration as well as selections from those whose reputations are still emerging. Our first criterion was naturally significance—a selection had to deal with a major continuing or newly evolving issue. But equally important was readability. We made every effort to select and edit items to make them accessible to a student

---

*A block grant is one distributed in accordance with a statutory formula for use in a variety of activities within a broad functional area, largely at the recipient's discretion. For example, the community development block grant program administered by the Department of Housing and Urban Development funds community and economic development programs in cities, on Indian reservations, and in U.S. territories. The nature of the block grant allows these jurisdictions to allocate the funds to supplement other resources in ways they choose.

audience. State and local government is the one subfield of political science that most crosses departmental boundaries. Indeed, it is often a required course for journalism and education majors as well as for government majors. The subject itself delves heavily into sociology, law, education, and economics as well as all of the expected concerns of political science and public administration. Thus for this multifaceted topic we offer this multifaceted text—one that we hope will bring a large measure of clarity to a sometimes confusing world of state and local government and politics.

We are indebted to many individuals who contributed to this book. First, we thank all of the authors and publishers for permission to reprint their fine materials. Second, valuable research assistance was furnished by David Dillard of Temple University's Paley Library and Meltem Muftuler, now a professor of political science at Bogazici University in Turkey.

Still others were generous with their time, expertise, and energy in our behalf. The reviewers and the editor commissioned by F. E. Peacock Publishers were uniformly helpful in their critiques; they were Professors William K. Hall of Bradley University, Kim Q. Hill of Texas A & M University, David G. Houghton of Western Michigan University, James Sheffield, Jr., of Wichita State University, Norman R. Luttbeg of Texas A & M University, and David Suffell of Ohio Northern University. We are especially grateful to Robert J. Cunningham of Lake Forest, Illinois, who edited our manuscript. His careful attention to important details and his helpful suggestions in the writing undoubtedly made this a more readable book.

Finally, we thank Mary L. Bailey and Luise A. Shafritz for their continuing support of all our work. They are the wind beneath our wings.

Harry A. Bailey, Jr.
Temple University
Philadelphia, Pennsylvania

Jay M. Shafritz
University of Pittsburgh
Pittsburgh, Pennsylvania

CHAPTER I

THE INTERGOVERNMENTAL FRAMEWORK FOR STATE AND LOCAL POLITICS

INTRODUCTION

An understanding of the constitutional framework within which the fifty states and over eighty thousand local governments operate is fundamental to the study of American state and local government.

Intergovernmental relations include the entire range of interactions among all the levels and types of governments. The formal relationships between the federal government and the states, to be sure, are considerably different from those between the states and their respective local governments. The federal-state relationship is based upon an association between sovereign entities. However, local governments are not sovereign. They are not legally equal to their states because they are essentially creations of their states.

Intergovernmental transfers of money, especially transfers of money from the federal government to the state governments and from the state government to the local governments, have been fundamental to the intergovernmental relationship.

Federal *grant-in-aid programs* to the states—that is, money granted to state or local governments for particular purposes—began as early as the Republic itself. Programs awarding funds directly to the localities began in earnest in 1932 and mushroomed during President Franklin D. Roosevelt's New Deal. The federal-local relationship continued to grow during President Lyndon B. Johnson's Great Society and into the mid-1970s.

During the 1980s, under President Ronald Reagan's New Federalism, the flow of dollars from the federal government to the state and local governments was reduced considerably. Recent figures indicate that the federal portion of state and local government expenditures peaked in 1978 at 26.5 percent, dropped to 20 percent in the mid-1980s, and has remained at around 18 percent ever since.[1] As a result, state and local governments must now rely more on their own in-house resources.

How the relationship among the federal, state, and local governments works in practice, especially the fiscal relationship, is the subject of the selections in this chapter. In Reading 1, "Intergovernmental Relations," Carl W. Stenberg provides a brief history of intergovernmental fiscal relationships in the United States. Next, David B. Walker, in his article "The State-Local Connection: Perennial, Paramount, Resurgent," examines federal-state linkages from the 1930s to the present.

NOTE

1. See Ann O'M. Bowman and Richard C. Kearney, *State and Local Government* (Boston: Houghton Mifflin, 1990), p. 54.

Reading 1

INTERGOVERNMENTAL RELATIONS

Carl W. Stenberg

According to Carl W. Stenberg, intergovernmental relations in the United States have been undergoing dramatic change as a result of the shift from a national to a more subnational (state- and local-oriented) federal system.

Stenberg notes that mounting federal deficits have caused the federal government to cut back on the spending which once made up a considerable part of state and local budgets. Thus future federal grant programs are not likely to play a considerable role in activities considered to be basically state or local.

An additional by-product of the federal government's fiscal condition, Stenberg suggests, is that it will increasingly focus only on matters, such as *entitlement programs* (for example, Social Security, Medicare, and food stamps), that transcend subnational boundaries and call for substantial expenditures on an equitable basis among the states. Thus the federal government will likely play a much diminished financial role in state and local affairs. Nevertheless, it will continue to intervene in subnational affairs by mandating state and local action without providing compensatory funding.

It appears to Stenberg that this new state- and local-oriented federalism has raised the concern that the states are incapable of filling the policy and financial gap left by the federal government. He argues to the contrary that states are much more capable now of effective and equitable governance, pointing to newly reformed state governments and the initiatives they have taken in a number of policy areas. Stenberg notes further that *states* have taken action to raise sufficient funds to maintain service levels and to fund the new initiatives necessitated by federal cutbacks.

While the national government has given the states and localities more autonomy in determining their own priorities, obstacles remain in the way of enlarged local government. Federal courts, for example, have made decisions in a number of policy areas that have resulted in reducing local autonomy and discretion. Among such decisions are those reaffirming that local governments are but creatures of the state legislature, and that federal regulators can preempt local authority on wages and working conditions.

Although state aid to local governments has grown, much of this increase went to school districts rather than to general purpose units. Local governments which rely most heavily on property taxes find that these revenues are inadequate to meet growing citizen demands for needed services. Importantly, several other sources of revenue may be tapped by local government only with permission of its state. Thus local government is restricted in the discretion it has and in its capacity to look after its own needs. Stenberg concludes that how well the states respond to local needs will heavily influence the federalism of the future.

Intergovernmental relations have been in a period of dramatic and rapid change, unparalleled in recent history. As the pendulum swung over the past few years from a national to a more state and local-oriented federal system, the powers and responsibilities of all three levels of government were—and continue to be—"rebalanced."

The nature and effects of these shifts are not well understood, widely recognized or generally accepted. This article attempts to sort out some of the reality from the rhetoric surrounding the federalism debate of the 1980s. Key events and developments at each level are put into perspective and their longer-term significance is assessed.

THE FEDERAL ROLE IN FLUX

The federal budget has been the chief instrument of rebalancing intergovernmental relationships. The domestic program-cutting concerns of the early 1980s have been superseded by deficit-financing fears. The "guns versus butter" debate of an earlier decade has been reopened and recast. Questions have been raised not only about the amount and pace of the defense buildup, but also now about the entitlement buildup, especially in the areas of income support and medical care.

Intergovernmental fiscal positions have shifted as well. The rate of state and local spending, which since the Korean War had grown faster

---

Source: Carl W. Stenberg, "Intergovernmental Relations," *The Book of the States, 1984–85* (Lexington, Kentucky: Council of State Governments, 1984), pp. 15–17. Copyright © by the Council of State Governments. Reprinted with permission.

than that of the federal government, was braked sharply in the late 1970s by the recession, Proposition 13–type fiscal limits and federal aid cuts. Austerity measures, tax hikes and the national economic recovery have improved the fiscal condition of many states and turned budget deficits into surpluses. In contrast, the federal government has become the big spender as well as the big borrower in the public sector. Mounting federal deficits have bolstered efforts to discipline federal fiscal decision-making through a balanced budget amendment to the Constitution and other means.

The intergovernmental significance of these developments is at least four-fold:

• First, the role of federal grant programs in state and local affairs will not be as great as during the last two decades. The growth rate of federal aid as a percentage of state and local expenditures began to taper off during the Carter administration. The pressures from the deficit, defense and entitlement sides of the federal budget and the presence of surpluses in several states make substantial reversal of this trend unlikely.

• Second, despite these changes, congressional entrepreneurs will not refrain from launching new program initiatives aimed toward essentially state or local matters. Quite the contrary, as underscored by recently enacted surface transportation, drunk driving, and employment and training laws, national responses to highly visible subnational problems will continue; however, they will be more difficult to pass. Moreover, while federal budget constraints may make Congress less inclined to play the role of city council or county board of supervisors, there may well be a strong temptation to demonstrate its concern by mandating state and local action without providing compensatory funding.

• Third, even though there has been a 25 percent reduction in the number of categorical programs, the basic shape of the federal aid system has not changed much. Despite the enactment of 10 block grants since 1980 and the renewal of general revenue sharing, approximately four-fifths of all federal aid is delivered through categorical programs— about the same percentage as in the late 1970s. As a result, while in certain programs recipient flexibility has increased, the system overall has not become more discretionary.

• Fourth, the drive to reduce federal deficits through such revenue enhancing strategies as raising tax rates, closing loopholes or levying new taxes will have major intergovernmental implications. For example, proposals calling for the federal government to dip into state or local tax wells, such as consumption levies, or to end preferred fiscal positions, such as the tax-exempt status of state and local bonds, will create tension and conflict.

Given these developments, in the years ahead we can expect to see greater congressional reluctance to shoulder financial responsibilities for activities considered to be basically state or local, more willingness to enact mandates without providing money, and continued desire to hold on to the categorical program reins. One by-product of these responses, noted by the Advisory Commission on Intergovernmental Relations, might well be movement toward a *de facto* sorting out of responsibilities. The federal domestic role may focus increasingly on national issues or problems that clearly transcend state boundaries, require a nationwide minimum level of effort, call for substantial expenditures, and involve equity between states. Many entitlement programs would qualify under these standards.

The failure of President Reagan's plan to trade federalization of Medicaid and food stamps for state assumption of welfare as well as takeover of a number of smaller programs has been viewed by some observers as a rare historic opportunity that was missed. Yet the aborted "great swap" of 1982 did put federalism on the front pages of the nation's newspapers and did cause public officials to think more seriously about who does what. If nothing else, the attempt helped sow the seeds for a sorting out effort driven by fiscal pragmatism rather than political philosophy.

STATES UNDER THE SPOTLIGHT

The prospects of a state and local-oriented federalism, with the states in particular being expected to assume previously federal or federally assisted responsibilities, have caused some consternation among members of Congress, the federal bureaucracy, interest groups and the private sector. Often these individuals believe the states to be incapable and insensitive, and they doubt that the states will move to compensate for cuts in federal domestic programs or to assume leadership in meeting citizen needs.

Recent research suggests a different conclusion—that the states are more capable now than ever before of effective and equitable governance. The reformers' checklist has been achieved in most states: constitutions have been simplified; governors and legislatures have been strengthened; executive branches have been streamlined; and court systems have been modernized.

At the same time, it remains to be seen if the states' institutional capacity will be translated into a commitment to take action. There are, however, encouraging signs:

- Most states have taken painful austerity measures and have bitten the fiscal bullet to raise sufficient revenues to maintain service levels and meet new needs. A significant amount of these funds have been used for state aid to local governments and school districts.
- The states have taken the initiative in a number of high priority areas—industrial policy, job creation, drunk driving, enterprise zones, educational quality—well in advance of congressional interest or action.
- The states have compiled an impressive record in managing the recently enacted block grant programs.

Despite these examples, the jury will be out for some time on the states' response to the intergovernmental issues of the 1980s. Stereotypes are not easily overcome, and the philosophical, political and practical reasons for doing business in Washington rather than 50 state capitals cannot be overlooked. Therefore, while the states' early performances have been impressive, they will continue to be under the spotlight.

GREATER GRASSROOTS GOVERNMENT

Some observers of the recent decentralizing thrust of intergovernmental relations have noted that the units of government closest to people and their problems—localities—will have greater latitude over and more autonomy in determining priorities and finding ways to meet them. Certainly the Reagan administration and the Congress have taken significant steps in this direction through block grants and regulatory relief. However, at least three obstacles lie in the path of greater grassroots government:

- The often overlooked members of the intergovernmental partnership—the courts—have done much in recent years to call attention to their role and powers. Federal courts have been particularly active in the grant law, anti-trust and official immunity areas. Decisions often have had the effect of reducing local autonomy and discouraging the exercise of discretionary authority. The *Boulder* decision and other franchising cases, for instance, have reaffirmed that local governments are creatures of their states and derive their authority and protection from the legislature. Similarly, the courts have widened the authority of federal regulators to preempt local decisions, such as wage, hour and working conditions in non-traditional functions. And, policy-makers and program administrators have become gun-shy after judicial narrowing of the scope of public official immunity and widening of the circumstances under which officials may be held personally liable for their own or their subordinates' actions or inactions.

- A second factor to be considered here is the "intergovernmentalization" and "privatization" of functions below the state level. Austerity conditions have put pressure on localities to contract for the provision of services with their neighboring jurisdictions or private firms. While these actions may well save money, sharing means a loss of control and independence.
- The third grassroots government consideration has to do with the states. As noted above, recent court decisions have underscored the historic position of local governments *vis-à-vis* the states, as well as the need for state authority to act on a day-to-day basis in some areas. Legal and fiscal constraints are coupled. While the states' fiscal picture has brightened, this has not been the case in localities heavily dependent on property taxes. State aid has risen overall, but much of the increase goes to school districts rather than general purpose units.

So, a number of localities are squeezed in a fiscal vise. Their existing revenues are inadequate to meet citizen needs and service demands. Local governments must go to the state for more money or more authority to tap new sources or raise existing rates. The states' response to requests for local revenue diversification and enhancement will be a litmus test of their readiness to play a significant role in the rebalanced federalism of the 1980s.

To sum up, the federal system will be in a state of flux for some time to come. Shifts in functional and financial responsibilities will be accompanied by friction and uncertainty. For state governments in particular, the developments that have occurred or are underway provide excellent opportunities and real challenges for states to demonstrate that they can serve as "laboratories for democracy," and to take the lead in forging a genuine intergovernmental partnership for the years ahead.

THE STATE-LOCAL CONNECTION: PERENNIAL, PARAMOUNT, RESURGENT

David B. Walker

Although significant federal-state linkages date from the 1930s and enormous federal-state-local linkages date from the 1960s, David B. Walker argues that the state-local relationship is becoming paramount in the federal system.

The irrelevance of the state-local connection was evident in the 1960s and 1970s by virtue of certain actions of the federal government. These actions included the federal government's bypassing states to go directly to local entities in federal aid allocations; the federal government's granting all categories of subnational governments eligibility status for grant programs; the propensity of the federal government to treat the major categories of subnational governments as equal providers of public goods and services; the practice of federal aid programs to assign equal status to different jurisdictions in the same governmental grouping; and the tendency of the federal government to treat most local issues as if they were national ones.

The federal government's view of state-local relations as irrelevant had several roots. First, state legislatures were based on badly malapportioned legislative districts and thus incapable of truly representing the people. Second, state constitutions hobbled state governors with long ballots which made gubernatorial leadership of the executive branch extremely difficult. Third, states had extremely cumbersome procedures for getting legislation passed. Fourth, states utilized mostly regressive fiscal resources to meet their programmatic responsibilities. And, fifth, states were often very slow to address pressing civil rights questions.

Meanwhile, state governments were themselves undergoing considerable transformation during the past two decades. First, legislatures are, today, regularly and equitably apportioned. Second, legislative committees are now fewer in number and must have open meetings announced in advance. Third, the majority of the legislatures have a process for reappropriating some or all federal grants to the state and local governments. Fourth, all states now have legislative reference libraries to better equip the legislatures to perform their functions. Fifth, states now have a more diversified revenue base to include personal income, corporate income, and sales taxes. Sixth, the governor is now better equipped to lead the state government as a result of the shortening of the executive ballot, the provision for gubernatorial budget, the granting of reorganization authority to the governor, and the authority to appoint a sizeable increase in staff. Finally, states are now more sensitive to civil rights issues than at any time in the last century.

The full resurgence of the state-local nexus began as federal budget deficits grew and federal aid to the states and localities tapered off in 1979 and 1980. In particular, ten new federal-state block grants were enacted in 1981–82; these merged more than forty federal-local grants into ten programs. The reduction of categorical grants and the curbing of federal regulatory activity were the largest indicators that the reemergence of the significance of the states and of the state-local relationship was underway.

The state governments have now achieved a pivotal intermediary role in the intergovernmental system in their capacity as the prime recipients of federal grant funds and as channelers of federal aid to their localities. On the downside, Walker notes that a particularly nagging problem in the state-local connection remains: there has been a dramatic increase in state-mandated programs without commensurate increases in expenditures by the states, thus leaving the local governments to pick up the costs. Walker concludes that, despite some distrust of state governments by county and city governments, the state-local connection should increase in vitality in the years ahead.

The state-local relationship traditionally has been the paramount American intergovernmental connection. Significant federal-state linkages date mainly from the 1930s, and widespread federal-state-local and direct federal to local grant and regulatory contacts were pretty much a product of the past two decades. The state-local relationship, then, has been and, if certain trends continue, will again become paramount in the system.

Source: Reprinted with permission from David B. Walker, "The State-Local Connection: Perennial, Paramount, Resurgent." Reprinted with permission from the February 1984 issue of NATIONAL CIVIC REVIEW, 73:2, pp. 53–63. National Civic League Press, 1601 Grant Street, Suite 250, Denver, CO 80203.

For over 200 years, the states have been the chief architects, by conscious and sometimes unconscious action or inaction, of the welter of servicing, financial, institutional and jurisdictional arrangements that form our 50 different state-local systems, and provide the means by which most domestic American governance is conducted and nearly all domestic policies are implemented.

SIGNS OF SLIPPAGE

This elemental fact of intergovernmental relations appeared at times to be forgotten or overtly challenged during the 1960s and 1970s. Evidence of this change was apparent in many of the actions of the national government.

- The increasing "bypassing" of the states in federal aid allocations was one manifestation (rising from 8 percent of $7.1 billion in 1960, to 12 percent of $20 billion in 1968, to 24 percent of $40 billion by 1974, to about 25 percent of $94.7 billion by 1981 and less than that now).
- The parallel development at the national level of a "panoramic partnership principle" wherein practically all categories of subnational governments were accorded eligibility status under an ever-expanding number of grant programs (from 132 in 1960 to 537 by 1980) was yet another sign.
- The accompanying tendency of Washington policymakers to treat the various major categories of subnational governments as separate, disconnected, and sometimes even equal providers of public goods and services and as contesting supplicants for the federal aid largesse was still another bit of evidence of national hostility to state-local fiscal, functional and jurisdictional relationships (and of the willingness of some of the subnational governmental groups to help foster this animosity).
- The parallel inclination in federal aid programs to assign equal status to very different jurisdictions in the same local governmental grouping (i.e., towns and townships as well as counties under General Revenue Sharing and metropolitan counties under community development) ...further underscores Washington's disdain for the differences among the 50.
- The ever-increasing blurring of private and public issues during these two decades along with the mounting habit of the media, the public, and many elected officials at all levels to treat almost any state, substate regional or local issue as a national one, subject to national allevi-

11

ation (usually via a grant-in-aid or a regulation), were major indicators of the seeming irrelevance of the state-local connection.

- Finally, the nearly monolithic focus on intergovernmental fiscal transfers and regulations as the chief means of mounting a response to many challenges confronting local governments inevitably led to ignoring the structural and functional components of local governmental reform—components that only the states in collaboration with their localities can address.

WHY THIS APPARENT NATIONAL UNAWARENESS?

These and other developments suggest a shifting of the eyes of the electorate and of state and local elected officials toward the nation's capital, and the nation's decision makers found it difficult to resist the attention. But how could this come to pass? How could the array of legal, fiscal, functional and political linkages, which in all of the states combine differently to form 50 distinct and diverse polities, be ignored?

In one sense, of course, this fundamental fact of American federalism was not overlooked. The expanding state-local linkages belie the claim that all were oblivious. But certainly there was a broad trend toward treating this inevitable and sometimes impossible relationship in a cavalier or contemptuous fashion. Moreover, the federal government was looked to by more and more citizens and organizational groups as the prime instrumentality for expressing their respective social, economic or moralistic goals. But, again, the question arises: Why?

The national image of most state governments in the 1950s and the mid-1960s is one part of the answer. Caustic critics pointed to their archaic constitutions. Rube Goldberg–like governmental structures, and badly malapportioned and amateurish legislatures as evidence that the states were poorly prepared to cope with pressing public and local needs. They derided the states' cumbersome procedures, their generally regressive and anemic fiscal resources, their semi-closed political systems, their generally unsympathetic treatment of their own localities, and their often deplorable record on civil rights as further signs of deficiencies. These castigations helped nurture a tendency to focus on the national capital and to view the states with contempt.

Optimistic assumptions in the 1960s about the resourcefulness and progressivity of the federal revenue system also were part of this shifting toward Washington. Equally sanguine assumptions about the productivity, management acumen, competitiveness and rich resource bases of the nation's economy reinforced the belief that the federal fisc was and would be the fruitful provider of whatever was needed to help fill funding gaps at the state and local levels.

Not unrelated to these centralizing tendencies was the erosion of the political parties as mediating and moderating institutions within the federal system. The steady decline in state and local party influences over nominating and electoral processes at all levels as well as in the legislative process nationally cannot be ignored as a factor here. When this development was coupled with the simultaneous advent of an increasing array of interest groups located in and focusing sometimes exclusively on Washington, the centralization trend became even more pronounced.

Buttressing all this were overall popular attitudes favoring an expansionist national government role and believing in the capacity of the central government to solve and resolve basic and mundane societal and economic problems. Not to be overlooked was a general unawareness among the citizenry of the structural and functional differences among the 50 systems. These trends prompted a steady watch on Washington and a parallel posture of downgrading the state-local relationship.

THE RESURGENCE OF THE CRUCIAL CONNECTION

By the late 1970s, however, popular and political faith in the capacity of the federal government began to fade, and with good reason. Much of it, after all, was misplaced to begin with.

Moreover, the optimism regarding federal revenues and the national economy began to evaporate as early as the winter of 1973–1974. Federal aid to states and localities began to taper off by 1979 and 1980; budget deficits continued throughout the decade; and the indexation of various entitlement programs in the early 1970s really began to take a budgetary toll as inflation soared in the latter part of the decade. Meanwhile, defense outlays again began to rise beginning with FY 1979, even as some regulatory curbs were being imposed and new block grants proposed. The latter, of course, indicated a growing awareness of the need for correcting some of the earlier excesses of national interventionism.

All of these later Carter trends continued and were greatly accelerated under President Reagan. Federal aid declined from nearly $95 billion in FY 1981 to $88 billion by FY 1982, up to nearly $94 billion by FY 1983, prospectively to over $98 billion for FY 1984. Ten new federal-state block grants were enacted in 1981–1982, including the merger of some primarily separate 77 grants (more than 40 of which had been federal-local grants) into 10 programs. At least 60 largely small grants received no funding in 1981, producing with the block grant mergers an overall reduction in the number of operating grants of roughly 25 percent by early 1982.

Curbing federal regulatory activity was and is another facet of Reagan federalism, leading to the Vice President's Task Force, the slowing down of new regulatory issuances, the administration's revision of some of the more onerous earlier rules (bilingual education, access for the handicapped, Davis-Bacon, etc.), and a more authoritative oversight role assigned to the Office of Management and Budget.

These undertakings, along with the recision of OMB Circular A-95 and the thrusting of prime responsibility for the structure of its review and comment process onto state governments, underscore the emergence of a less extended, more frugal and somewhat diminished regulatory (the federal courts excepted) role on the part of the national government. The failure of the historic effort in 1982 to effectuate a "Big Swap," however, means that a national role, though moderately reduced, remains in most program areas. The interest groups concerned with the programs involved in that effort at intergovernmental disengagement (Medicaid, AFDC, food stamps and about 34 other programs) are still active and assertive in the Washington political arena. Having said this, the earlier myth of Washington's boundless resources, skill at problem solving, and needed concern for practically all public endeavors now is recognized by most for what it was—a myth.

Despite the goals of Reagan federalism, however, there has been no revolution in intergovernmental relations. Nonetheless, some retrenchment, some reduction in the number of federal grants, some revising and reducing of regulations have occurred—all part of a reaction to the excesses of the 1970s that directly or indirectly reemphasizes the crucial significance of the states and of the state-local relationship.

THE SILENT REVOLUTION

Even with this heavy focus on Washington, the states during the past 20 years were undergoing a major transformation, the most dramatic of any two decades in their more than 200-year history. In practically every state, efforts were made to promote greater efficiency, economy and accountability in all branches of their governments. Hence, during this period:

• Eleven state constitutions were totally overhauled and all but a few others were partially modified. The trend in most cases was toward curbing excessive constitutional detail, strengthening individual rights, enhancing the capacities of all three branches of state government, broadening the suffrage and extending local home rule.

- Legislatures today are periodically and equitably apportioned, thanks in large part to Supreme Court decisions; 36 now are formally required to meet annually and the rest do as a practical matter; 16 states do not restrict the length of sessions, and 22 (compared to 36 in 1960) do not curb the legislature's power to call special sessions; and nearly half now organize early.
- The number of legislative committees has been greatly reduced and about two-thirds have uniform rules of procedure that apply to all committees; advance notice of hearings is required in most states; and all require open committee meetings.
- All states have legislative reference libraries now; 32 staff out all of their committees and over 80 percent provide assistance to most of their legislative committees; presiding officers in all states have clerical assistance, and over 80 percent have professional aides as well; and a comparable number now name the state auditor and have responsibility for the auditing process.
- Some form of "sunset" review process exists in 35 legislatures; 38 have authority to review proposed administrative rules and regulations; and 37 have established a process for reappropriating some or all federal grants to state governments.
- Turning to the governors, 46 now have four-year terms, compared to 19 in 1960; gubernatorial appointment authority has broadened somewhat with the decline in the number of elected administrative officers; 47 have the authority to prepare an executive budget (as against 42 in the late 1950s); reorganization authority has been assigned to 16, as against seven in the earlier period; governors' salaries overall, like the legislators', have not kept abreast of inflation, but their staffing, again like the legislatures', has improved considerably.
- Twenty-three states underwent major executive branch reform during the period 1964–1979; the number of multimember boards heading line agencies and departments was reduced; 35 have government-wide merit systems, and three-quarters of all permanent state employees are under such systems.
- With the state judiciaries, all save one now have a court administrative office; all but seven require legal training for appellate and trial judges, compared to 33 a quarter of a century ago; special disciplinary and removal commissions exist in 41 states (only one existed in 1960); and about three-quarters today have most of the features of "reformed" integrated state-local systems, compared to 18 in the late 1960s.
- Fiscally, states now have much more diversified revenue systems; 40 have a broad-based personal income tax; and 45 have broad-based sales and a corporate income tax; states overall have been the senior

partners with respect to combined state-local expenditures for nearly a decade now.[1]

These and other current indicators certainly buttress the claim that reform, not standpatism, has dominated the recent state institutional and fiscal record; that more managership, greater professionalism and more unshackling were the dominant goals of this remarkable effort; and that state capacity—whether defined in administrative, fiscal, or programmatic terms—was enhanced as a result.

At the same time, some of the facts relating to contemporary legislatures suggest that the traditional ideal of the "citizen" legislature by no means was replaced totally by the "professional" norm. With executive reorganization, political, economic, administrative and sometimes historic factors combined to modify the full application of the orthodox administrative principles. Thus, education departments or boards, attorneys general offices, other constitutional posts, and quasiregulatory boards and commissions rarely have been touched by executive reorganization plans. Furthermore, about a third of the reorganizations achieved during this period were of the "traditional type," in that they involved a *"reduction of the number of agencies—to some degree within the existing pattern of agencies headed by elected officers, boards, and commissions"* (George A. Bell, "State Administrative Organization Activities 1972–1973," *Book of the States, 1972–73*, Lexington, Kentucky, Council of State Governments, 1972, page 138).

Similarly, while judicial reform proceeded more uniformly and at a faster pace than changes in the other branches of state government, all or most of the judicial officers in 27 states are elected, and in 10 instances on a partisan ballot. All this suggests that the older state values of representativeness, administrative pluralism, achieving accountability through severe institutional constraints, and hostility to concentrated gubernatorial power have not disappeared. Instead, these values still compete with the newer managerial and professional ones to greater or lesser degrees within each state.

Despite these caveats, however, the statement still can be made that there were more changes on more state structural fronts during the past 20 years than in any other period since the drafting of the first state constitutions.

---

1. These findings are drawn from *The States Transformed: Expanded Roles, New Capabilities*, written by Mavis Mann Reeves for the U.S. Advisory Commission on Intergovernmental Relations (forthcoming).

THE STATES' NEWLY REVITALIZED SYSTEMIC ROLES

What do these institutional, procedural, and fiscal changes have to do with the states' position in the federal system? The answer, it would seem, is that without them the present systemic role of the states would be inconceivable.

In traditional legalistic terms, the states' systemic role flowed from the fact that they were the repositories of the reserved powers under the U.S. Constitution. Hence, they served as a source of constraint on efforts to expand national power; as the prime guardians of their respective citizens' public health, safety, welfare and order; and as the constitutional source of all local governmental authority.

In policy terms, the states were the paramount arena for devising innovations throughout the 19th century and well into the 20th. They also served as the foremost instruments of popular choice in nearly all policy areas during the first half of the last century, in most such areas from 1865 to 1932, and in fewer but still significant areas in the early 1960s. These policy areas included public education; regulation of insurance, other businesses, public utilities, professions and intrastate transportation; and most criminal justice functions, to cite only a few.

As administrators of federal aid programs, the states' role was minimal in the last century and involved only 15 relatively minor grant programs by 1930. Some 30 years later, the number of these collaborative undertakings had risen to 132. Over 90 percent of the federal dollars went to the states, but only four state departments and agencies were heavily affected.

In political terms, state parties traditionally possessed what cohesion and strength there was in the nation's party system. They played a pivotal role in selecting national officeholders, and they exerted a strong noncentralizing influence on national policymaking.

For at least 140 years, then, the states were far more than middlemen. They were paramount political and policy actors and innovators, the exclusive legal architects of local government, which at the time provided most of the public services available, and effective restrainers of national governmental activism.

From Roosevelt through Eisenhower, the scope of the states' police powers lessened somewhat; their performance as policy innovators was severely eroded; and their involvement with national program goals through federal grants expanded, but in comparatively modest terms. Meanwhile, their political influence in Washington remained potent; their involvement with and their aid to their localities grew; their paramount position in the nation's electoral processes for the most part went unchallenged; and the 50 state-local fiscal and servicing systems they engineered provided the overwhelming bulk and funding of domestic governmental services. Thus, as recently as the early 1960s, the states still served as key instruments in certain significant policy areas. They clearly performed with continuing vigor their role as powerful representatives of 50 different sets of geographic interests, and had assumed an important administrative and funding role in the comparatively small and inexpensive package of federal grants then extant.

Since the mid-1960s, the states' role in the federal system has undergone major changes, and the states themselves have acquired new responsibilities, even as their traditional ones were revitalized. One major authority has contended that, in contrast to their earlier basic functions, the current state role basically is to assume two main responsibilities: planning and controlling big and frequently intergovernmental programs, and using their position as the major intermediate level of government and of politics to mobilize political consent for these programs (Samuel H. Beer, "The Modernization of American Federalism," *Publius*, Fall 1973, page 81). In this assessment, the forces of modernization—growing interdependence, scientific and technological advances, the concomitant rise of centralizing coalitions and of professional-bureaucratic complexes, and the continuing national effort to respond to public demands for more and better services—transformed the national government into the paramount vehicle for achieving social goals. Yet, these forces also led to new intergovernmental functions being assigned to the states.

This intriguing intergovernmental interpretation of the states' adaptation to modernization is borne out by many of the fiscal, funding and structural developments since the mid-1960s affecting the states and their de facto role in the federal system. As the prime recipients of federal grant funds and as channelers of federal aid to their localities (20 percent of all state aid in 1976–1977), states have assumed a pivotal intermediary role. They plan, supervise, partially fund and sometimes directly execute large, costly and socially significant intergovernmental programs. These shifts, of course, are emphasized in all of the 10 new block grants enacted in 1981–1982. Moreover, as the major financiers from their own revenue sources of primary, secondary and higher public education; primary and secondary local public highway systems; and health and hospital functions, the states have carved out still another dimension of this important intergovernmental role wholly apart from federal initiatives. The dominance of fiscal and "matching money" issues in state politics over the past 10 years or more, along with strong state involvement in environmental programs, Medicaid, social services and special education—to cite the major examples—clearly demonstrate that the states are forums of political debate for their newly assigned intergovernmental programmatic role.

Alongside these new intergovernmental roles, there is a cluster of traditional ones. Through their political and independent policymaking processes, the states reflect differing approaches to taxes, servicing preferences, social legislation and governmental accountability. They exhibit differing degrees of devotion to the older governmental values of fully representative institutions, administrative pluralism, and accountability through institutional constraints, as was noted earlier. They also demonstrate varying commitments to the reform values of management professionalism and "unshackling," again as earlier discussion highlighted.

The states also revitalized their earlier function as experimental laboratories within the overall system. Witness their pioneering efforts over the past decade and a half in consumer protection, campaign finance, "sunset" legislation, coastal zone management, hospital cost control and enterprise zones.

Out of this broad, differentiated representative role also flow 50 differing functional assignment, taxing and funding patterns. Finally, each state addresses differently its historically strong responsibilities regarding its local governments.

POSITIVE ASPECTS OF THE STATE-LOCAL CONNECTION

As significant as the new federal-state intergovernmental role and the states' revitalized political, representational and experimental functions is the current state-local relationship. Both the new intergovernmental and the revised traditional roles subsume it, and, for some, the acid test of whether either of these systemic responsibilities is fully and effectively performed in the years ahead depends on how this relationship evolves.

On the positive side of the ledger, most states in recent years have moved to establish at least some of the bases for a better state-local partnership. Witness the following:

• In the procedural area, nearly nine-tenths of the states by 1980 had enacted broad legislation authorizing interlocal servicing agreements, as against three-fifths in 1960, and these became an increasingly popular device for handling servicing problems that arise because of the mismatch between local jurisdictional boundaries and program needs; specialized or general state statutes pertaining to voluntary transfers of functions between and among local units also increased, and the use of transfers by cities and counties rose markedly during this period; and 35 states sanctioned municipal use of extraterritorial powers.

- Regarding basic local authority and discretion, all but a few states have formally granted broad structural or home rule authority to their municipalities, and nearly three-fifths, as against eight in 1960, have given their counties the same type of authority; in addition to lessening the constraints of Dillon's rule, 22 states by 1979 had granted residual powers to some, but rarely all, of their general units of local government.

- With reference to diversifying and strengthening local revenues, some 36 states now permit some or all of their counties, cities or both to use either a local sales or income tax; transfers of heretofore local functions to the states also picked up during the last decade, most notably in the public welfare area; state aid to local governments increased by 40 percent in noninflated dollars between 1970 and 1980; four-fifths of the states had provided more than half of local school costs by 1981 and half the states had revised their school aid formulas during the 1970s, chiefly in the direction of achieving greater fiscal equity between and among school districts; finally, well over four-fifths of state-local welfare costs and more than half of their health and hospital outlays were borne by the states by 1981.

LINGERING LOCAL SUSPICIONS

Despite these signs of greater state involvement and concern, local governments in many states still harbor old suspicions. On the crucial fiscal front, they stress that only 14 states have authorized any significant use of local sales or income taxes. They point out that state enactment of property tax rate and levy limits as well as expenditure lids increased during the 1970s, with 14 states acting during 1970–1977. Following California's passage of Proposition 13 in June 1978, 16 states enacted such limits during the first eight months of 1979 alone. All these actions, they stress, undermine efforts to grant greater local discretionary authority.

Local officials also complain about the dramatic increase in the use of state mandates since the mid-1960s. One survey of the 50 states, some note, found that in 77 potential mandating areas, 22 states had enacted 39 or more direct orders or grant conditions requiring additional local expenditures. And, although they concede that over 40 states now have a "fiscal note" procedure, only 13 states provide anything in the way of reimbursements for the mandates they impose. Arbitrary mandates and the move toward greater home rule, local officials maintain, are wholly incompatible.

Many local leaders acknowledge the significant rise in state aid, especially to schools. But they also emphasize that general units of local government, particularly municipalities, have not been major recipients, and that state general revenue sharing programs that do focus on cities and counties are excessively fragmented, insufficiently equalizing and inadequately funded (about 10 percent of all state aid in any year). They maintain that effective targeting of state aid frequently appears to be as great a political problem for the states as it is for the national government. In serving as channelers of federal aid, many local governmental leaders concede that the states' handling of the new block grants has gone fairly well, although the state propensity to add conditions has not disappeared.

CONCLUSION

To sum up, it seems certain that the state-local connection will become an increasingly important one in the years ahead. Current and prospective trends at the national level suggest persisting pressures on the federal fisc and seemingly inevitable hikes in defense outlays, yet only minor abatements in federal regulatory and preemptive intrusions. Above all, perhaps, the deeply troubled fiscal state of the Medicare program and the federal retirement system, and by the early 1990s probably social security, cannot be ignored by national decisionmakers. These prospective developments suggest only modest future rises in federal aid, but continued federal regulatory thrusts, and a kind of "sorting out" of certain clearly national responsibilities from those of the states and localities—Medicare, social security, federal pensions and defense, after all, are totally federal responsibilities—not contemplated by those engaged in such efforts in 1982.

These developments, it would seem, push the state-local relationship even more prominently to the center of the domestic servicing, funding and administrative scene. Thanks to their recent transformation, the states are better prepared to assume these roles than they would have been a generation ago. Yet, their policies vis-à-vis their localities to date have both negative as well as positive sides. Thus, the time has come to place the state-local relationship on a more productive, partnership-like basis. Each level needs the other and both need to form a common front as they face the vicissitudes, ambivalences and intrusions of national politics, policies and court decisions.

The emergence of state advisory bodies on intergovernmental relations in some 19 states is, it would seem, a good omen. A neutral institution, serving no one party, level, or branch of state or local government can, if properly funded, adequately staffed and skillfully led, probe the tension points in state-local relations, develop viable proposals, and even muster some of the necessary political support for their implementation. Institutional innovations like these, as well as some basic shifts in attitudes among officials at both levels, are needed to convert what currently, in many cases, are forced and fearful patterns of interdependence into a future partnership composed of tested and trusting members.

CHAPTER II

CITIZEN INFLUENCE AND PARTICIPATION IN STATE AND LOCAL GOVERNMENTS: BALLOTS AND INTEREST GROUPS

INTRODUCTION

Citizen participation in state and local governments refers to individual and/or group activity which seeks to influence the selection of public officials and/or the policy positions and actions these officials take.

Citizen participation takes a variety of forms. People can join a political club, give money to a candidate or party during an election campaign, attend political meetings, contact local government officials about some problem, actively work for a party or candidate during an election, or work with others to solve community problems. However, the most common form of citizen participation in government is voting. Moreover, the standard measure of citizen participation in government is the percentage of eligible voters who turn out on election day.

Voting behavior studies indicate, basically, that who turns out to vote is closely related to socioeconomic status. Voter turnout is greater among the better-educated, those with higher incomes, and those with higher-status occupations.

Political scientists have found, also, that several factors other than socioeconomic status affect voter turnout from one election to another. First among these is the region of the country. Voter turnout is generally lowest in southern and border states because, historically at least, these states have had fewer well-educated and affluent persons in their populations.[1]

Second, the turnout rate varies by age with older citizens being more likely to vote than younger citizens. One study found that people in their forties tend to be the most politically active. The most apathetic voters are the young, especially the eighteen- to twenty-one-year-olds.[2]

Third, voter turnout is affected by the way in which states administer registration procedures. Difficult registration procedures mean fewer registered voters and lower voter turnout.[3]

Fourth, differential voter turnout occurs by level of government election. National elections, especially presidential elections, because of their high profile media status and important issues, usually engender higher voter turnout than do state and local elections.[4]

Finally, elections in which attractive candidates are running a close race increase voter turnout. Few local elections fall into this category. Albert K. Karnig and B. Oliver Walter, in "Municipal Voter Turnout during the 1980s: The Case of Continued Decline," an article reprinted here as Reading 3, report their latest findings and conclusions for local election turnout.

Interest groups are a channel of participation through which a citizen can affect public policy at the state and local levels. *Lobbyists* are professionals hired by interest groups to represent their views before government. Lobbyists attempt to influence officials by making campaign contributions, retaining the officials or their law firms as legal counsel, providing the officials with honoraria for speeches, utilizing the officials or their allies as consultants, educating officeholders and the public about the value of the goals and programs of the pertinent interest group, and, of course, by supporting candidates for office at election time. Government officials pay attention to interest groups which have money and votes and the organizational sophistication to mobilize these and other resources for maximum effectiveness.

Interest groups want state government to enact policies in their interest; at the very least interest groups do not want state government to enact policies at odds with their interests. Lobbyists for the interest groups pressure both the legislative and state agencies which usually have considerable rule-making functions.

Lobbyists active on behalf of interest groups at the state level represent, among others, business, labor, agricultural, professional, and good government groups; ideological and religious groups; and consumers. Business interest groups tend to be most powerful and influential at the state and local level. However, the neighborhood-based organization is increasingly influential at the local level. And in large, formerly great industrial cities like Philadelphia and Pittsburgh, organized labor still exercises great influence over public policy.

Charles G. Bell, in his "Legislatures, Interest Groups, and Lobbyists: The Link beyond the District," reprinted in this chapter as Reading 4, notes some of the changes occurring in legislative relationships with interest groups, especially at the state level.

NOTES

1. Richard H. Leach and Timothy G. O'Rourke, *State and Local Government: The Third Century of Federalism* (Englewood Cliffs, N.J.: Prentice-Hall, 1988), p. 103.

2. See Nicholas Henry, *Governing at the Grassroots: State and Local Politics,* 3rd ed. (Englewood Cliffs, N.J.: Prentice-Hall, 1987), p. 35.

3. Robert S. Lorch, *State and Local Politics: The Great Entanglement,* 3rd ed. (Englewood Cliffs, N.J.: Prentice-Hall, 1989), pp. 49–51.

4. See Ann H. Elder and George C. Kiser, *Governing American States and Communities* (Glenview, Ill.: ScottForesman, 1983), p. 87.

Reading 3

MUNICIPAL VOTER TURNOUT DURING THE 1980s: THE CASE OF CONTINUED DECLINE

Albert K. Karnig and B. Oliver Walter

As the authors of this reading aptly observe, "One of the basic tenets of American conservatism is that local government is closer to the people and more responsive to the electorate...." Paradoxically, they note that voter participations in municipalities over 25,000 in population has decreased steadily at least since the 1930s.

Karnig and Walter collected questionnaire data in 1986 and 1987 from city clerks in 881 cities with over 25,000 in population; the response rate was 94 percent. Comparing these data with data collected in previous years, the authors then examined some correlates of city voter participation. They found that a downturn in municipal voter turnout has occurred despite such trends as increasing educational levels and the enactment of less restrictive registration laws that are presumed to increase voter participation.

The authors conclude that socioeconomic factors were only of marginal importance, in the aggregate, in municipal voter turnout. Neither registration laws nor level of voter registration had much to do with municipal voting. Citizens, they argue, register to vote with state and national elections in mind and thus the extent of voter registration does not have a significant impact on municipal voter participation. The authors observe that over time a strong and consistent pattern of regional differences in turnout rates does exist. The East has the highest participation rate while the South has the lowest.

Since the above factors don't fully explain the decrease in voter turnout, the authors probed further. They found that virtually all cities in their study had instituted independent elections, separating local elections from those at the state and national levels. Consequently, voter turnout in such elections was significantly lower than in concurrent elections. They also found that government reforms, such as nonpartisan elections and council-manager governments, tended to remove incentives to participate by insulating administrators from the electoral process. Another reason for declining municipal voter turnout has to do with the fact that policy and revenue control has shifted from the local to higher levels in the political system. Congressional and presidential balloting tends to become more important than municipal balloting.

Finally, the authors point out that suburbanization may have had an impact on municipal voter turnout. Since World War II there has been an increasing mismatch between where citizens reside and the focus of the news. TV and the big newspapers concentrate on central city news. Thus suburban municipal voters tend to be less interested in elections for which they are eligible to vote and more interested in elections for which they are ineligible.

One of the basic tenets of American conservatism is that local government is closer to the people and more responsive to the electorate, if not more efficiently managed, than the federal government. And judging by public opinion data, citizen confidence in local government is quite high. For example, CBS/*New York Times* (Plissner, 1986) reported the findings of a national survey that asked which level of government was doing the best. More respondents (32 percent) believed local government was doing the best job; smaller fractions viewed state (26 percent) or the federal government (21 percent) as doing best. However, despite apparently higher levels of trust, voter participation in local elections has decreased steadily at least since the 1930s.

Declining voter turnout is, of course, not limited to local elections. Presidential races provide the most visible data on declining participation—as turnout has plummeted from 62.8 percent in 1960 to 53.3 percent in 1988. Less visible, though well recognized by political scientists, is the diminishing off-year congressional turnout, which has largely paralleled presidential trends—with decreases over the past several decades. Voter turnout at the local level has been comparatively invisible during this period, because of the absence of routine data collection on local races and a lack of interest by political scientists.

In this paper we report results from a recently completed survey of American cities, compare recent elections to local elections in previous decades, and examine some of the correlates of city voter participation.

Source: Albert K. Karnig and B. Oliver Walter, "Municipal Voter Turnout during the 1980s: The Case of Continued Decline," (Paper delivered at Annual Meeting of Midwest Political Science Association, Chicago, April 13–15, 1989), pp. 1–21. Copyright by the authors. Reprinted with their permission.

The reduction of electoral participation at all levels is among the most clearly documented trends in post-1950s U.S. politics. However, the downturn is somewhat paradoxical because it has occurred despite several major trends that might well have increased participation, e.g., enactment of less restrictive registration laws, enfranchisement of southern blacks, increasing politicization of women, and rising educational levels. Ruy Teixeira (1987) has found, for instance, that the net impact of socioeconomic variables on presidential voter turnout between 1960 and 1984 was, in fact, positive.

Not merely has turnout been decreasing in the United States, Bingham Powell (1986) has also shown that turnout in the United States is lower than in other developed democracies. Indeed, the general decline in U.S. voting since 1960 has occurred while the average turnout in other democracies has been stable at approximately 80 percent. Powell concludes that although American attitudes remained "favorable to citizen participation of all kinds, including voting, though less so than in the early 1960s," the American legal and institutional environment impedes voter participation more in the United States than in other democracies.

Powell's conclusion is congruent with the thesis developed by Kelley, Ayres, and Bowen (1967), who demonstrated the overwhelming explanatory power of registration rates on turnout. Specifically, they found that "78 percent of the variance in the percentage of the population of voting age that voted [in the Kennedy-Nixon presidential election] could be accounted for by variations in the percentage of the population that was registered to vote" (p. 362). Using state election data from Texas, Shinn (1971) uncovered strong support for the registration hypothesis at the subnational level. In their widely cited book on voter participation, Wolfinger and Rosenstone (1980) also argue that registration laws have reduced American voter turnout. The authors display data revealing that if every state had registration laws in 1972 as permissive as those in states with the most permissive legislation, turnout would have increased by about 9 percent in the 1972 presidential election. Finally, Frances Piven and Richard Cloward (1988) make essentially the same argument and demonstrate that American voter turnout is not substantially different from other Western democracies if one compares the percentage of registrants voting. Nonetheless, declines have generally continued. Even the 1982 off-year congressional election and 1984 presidential election turnouts were only small increases; by and large, since 1960 turnouts have decreased despite increasingly permissive registration laws.

But are registration rates as important an explanatory variable in municipal elections as in presidential contests? Although the relationship between registration and voting at the municipal level is positive, it is much weaker than at the presidential level. For example, Karnig and Walter (1974a) found that the percent registered to vote explained only 24 percent of the variance in adult voter turnout in early 1960s municipal elections—much less in the presidential contests.

It would be a mistake, however, to conclude that the falloff in voting rates is solely the result of registration rules. The decay of partisanship also has been shown to help account for declining voter turnout (Abramson, Aldrich, and Rohde, 1986). And Teixeira argues persuasively that diminishing levels of political efficacy and interest in politics are important causes of ebbing voter participation. He demonstrates that 62 percent of the difference in voting turnout between 1960 and 1980 could be explained alone by changes in newspaper reading habits and the overall changes in political efficacy.

The primary objective of nonpartisan elections is to lessen the influence of political parties. Although party activity at the local level is sporadic, party competition can increase interest in elections because party conflict increases the psychological stakes of party identifiers in the election's outcome. The negative link between nonpartisan elections and voter participation has been demonstrated with data from the 1960s and the 1970s (Alford and Lee, 1968; and Karnig and Walter, 1983). It is of interest to determine whether the presence of nonpartisan elections has continued to depress turnout in the 1980s.

Another structural factor shown to have an impact on municipal voter participation is the form of government. Those favoring the city manager form of government believe that municipal administration should be based upon professional standards and should be largely separated from the hurly-burly of politics. Clearly, the manager form of government tends to reduce interest in politics because administration by professional bureaucrats, more often than not, lacks the zest of a political struggle. Professional administration both reduces the role of political parties and lowers the intensity of political debate.

Nonpartisan elections and manager government may also reduce political efficacy. Political parties can be used as mechanisms to influence government, and with nonpartisan elections the role of the party is reduced. Moreover, the basic ethos of the manager form of government is that many, if not most, decisions are administrative—which means they should not be influenced by political considerations. Thus the citizens' ability to have an impact on decisions may also be reduced.

Whether municipal elections are held independently or at the same time as other elections is also related to interest and involvement. Some cities hold elections independent of all others; a second set of cities schedule municipal elections concurrently with other local races; and a third group of cities hold elections simultaneously with contests for state

29

and/or national office. Alford and Lee (1968) and Karnig and Walter (1974a, 1977) found that elections concurrent with state or national balloting have higher turnouts than elections that are held independently. Because state, and particularly national, offices are viewed by most citizens to be more important, they tend to trigger greater voter turnout. When elections are held independently, as off-year congressional races are independent of presidential voting, participation decreases. In simultaneous elections, once at the polls, the great majority of voters cast ballots in races at all levels. Consequently, a concurrent election normally improves turnout in the races deemed to be less important, but has some positive spin-off benefit for the more important races by drawing at least some voters to the polls who are interested in the lower-order contests. By expanding the attractiveness of voting on election day, concurrent elections stimulate higher turnout. Whatever their other merits may be, independent elections have had a dampening effect on electoral participation.

Finally, previous studies have also found considerable regional variation in municipal voting turnout (Alford and Lee, 1968; Karnig and Walter, 1974b, 1983). At least since the 1930s, voter participation in the Northeast has outdistanced that in all other areas of the United States. The West, which normally has the highest participation in presidential elections, has had municipal turnouts only slightly higher than that in the South. Regional variation may simply be the result of differential distributions of those variables discussed above. For instance, only 1 percent of the western cities had partisan elections, compared with 57 percent in the Northeast. Fourteen percent of the western cities had the mayor-council form of government, as opposed to 75 percent in the Northeast. We have argued, however, that to some extent regional turnout variation is related to the political culture of that region (Karnig and Walter, 1974b). For instance, in earlier studies, we found turnout lower in the South even when other factors were controlled.

These findings suggest three hypotheses: First, institutional arrangements which interfere with the link between organized political parties and the decision to vote will likely lead to lower voter participation. Second, institutional rules which serve to dampen interest in politics will also lead to a decrease in voter turnout. Finally, regional political cultural characteristics will influence the level of turnout.

DATA

Our information was collected from a variety of sources. The primary focus of this paper is on data collected in 1986 and 1987. Questionnaires were sent to city clerks in cities over 25,000. Three follow-up contacts were made by mail and, finally, those clerks who did not respond were contacted by phone. Frankly, our questionnaire was too complicated, and following the compilation of data, we found it necessary to contact a large percentage of the cities for additional information or to correct obvious mistakes. This process lasted for over one year. Nearly all of the elections for which we have data were held between 1985 and 1987. In all, we have complete information on 881 cities—a 94 percent response rate.

One of the most frustrating aspects of working with Census data is the lack of continuity in reporting data by the Census Bureau. In previous work, we found that percent foreign stock and percent of city residents in the same dwelling during the past five years correlated strongly with city voter participation. These variables do not appear in the 1980 *County and City Data Book*. Therefore, it was impossible for us to make comparisons between the 1980s data and earlier periods.

We correlated the most common socioeconomic variables such as percent minority population, median income, and average years of education with our dependent variables. The highest correlation obtained was between education and turnout. However, it was a modest .20. Thus, in this analysis, we will assume that socioeconomic factors are of marginal importance, at least at the aggregate level.

Information on municipal elections in the 1930s was gathered from the 1935 and 1937 *Municipal Yearbooks*. The 1960s data were also collected by the International City Management Association (in 1962). We collected the 1975 information from mailed questionnaires. With the exception of the 1935–37 data sets, all municipalities over 25,000 in population were surveyed.

The two dependent variables in this paper are (1) percent turnout of all citizens twenty-one years of age or older in the first two sets of elections, and eighteen years of age or older in the final two elections; and (2) percent turnout of eligible persons registered to vote. These variables are, of course, highly correlated, but there are exceptions. For instance, in the 1930s the percent of registrants voting in the South was comparable to registrants voting in the remainder of the nation. However, because blacks were largely disenfranchised, the percentage of all adults voting in the 1930s was significantly lower in the South than in any of the other regions.

RESULTS

The municipal-election data reflect a unidirectional decline in voter participation (see Figure 1). Beginning with the 1935–37 turnout of 40.5 per-

FIGURE 1   Municipal Voter Turnout from 1934 to 1986

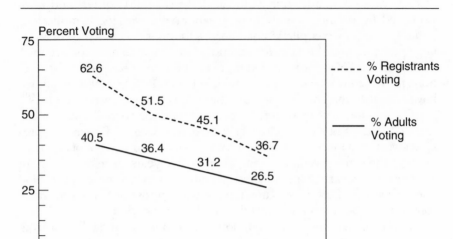

cent, there was a municipal turnout drop to 36.4 percent in 1962; a further diminution to 31.2 percent in 1975; and rather than displaying a bottoming-out effect, there was yet another decline, to 26.5 percent, in 1986. Municipal turnout in 1986 was lower than in any other measured year. The overall decline between the mid-1930s and 1986 was 14 percent for the percent of adults voting and a remarkably high 25.9 percent for the percent of registrants voting. Viewed somewhat differently, the 1986 percent of adults voting in municipal elections would have to increase by over 50 percent in order to reach the mid-1930s level, and the percent of registrants voting would have to increase by a staggering 70 percent to approximate the rate in the mid-1930s. Without question, when compared to presidential and off-year congressional turnout, municipal turnout has diminished enormously.

In an earlier article (Karnig and Walter, 1983), we presented data from surveys conducted in the 1930s, 1960s, and 1970s. That study demonstrated the suppressing impact of nonpartisan elections. Although political science research literature is replete with research showing the deterioration of political affiliation, the partisan-nonpartisan difference

TABLE 1 Municipal Voter Turnout by Electoral and Governmental
Characteristics

	% Adults voting	% Registrants voting
Election type		
Partisan (191)	30.9	45.2
Nonpartisan (651)	25.2	33.9
Government type		
Mayor (321)	30.9	43.5
Manager (508)	23.4	31.9
Concurrent elections		
Yes (159)	42.1	55.3
No (692)	22.9	32.3

remains much the same as in previous years. Partisan cities have an average turnout level nearly six percentage points higher than nonpartisan municipalities. And the difference is even greater, nearly twelve percentage points, if percentage of registrants voting is used as the dependent variable.

The difference between manager and mayoral cities also remains intact. Mayoral cities have an average turnout over seven percentage points higher than manager cities and eleven points greater for the percent of registrants voting.

Independent elections also had significantly lower turnouts than concurrent elections; however, we were surprised by the magnitude of the differences. The percent of registrants voting in strictly independent city elections was 32.3 percent, whereas the rate in cities holding elections concurrently with state or national contests was 55.3 percent. The percent of adults voting in independent elections was 22.9 percent, while the turnout in cities holding elections simultaneous with state or national races was 42.1 percent (see Table 1).

As discussed above, the level of voter registration has been shown to have a major effect on the level of presidential voting but much less impact in municipal elections. Table 2 reveals that, according to the 1980s data, there are astonishing differences between the effect of registration rates on presidential elections and the effect of such rates on municipal turnout. Kelly and his associates (1967), as noted, have demonstrated that registration rates accounted for 78 percent of the variance in turnout in the 1960 presidential race. In an earlier study employing 1962 municipal data (Karnig and Walter, 1974a), we showed that there was not nearly

TABLE 2 Correlations between Percent Registered to Vote and Adult Turnout over Time

	Correlations	Variance explained
Presidential elections	+ .88	78%
Municipal elections		
1962	+ .49	24
1975	+ .28	8
1986	+ .27	4

such impact of registration on municipal turnout. Indeed, registration rates were found to account for only 24 percent of the variance in 1962 local electoral participation. As Table 2 indicates, registration explained a mere 8 percent of the difference in municipal voter turnout in 1975 and about 4 percent in 1986. The differences are profound—between a nearly deterministic situation in presidential elections and one in which registration rates are of limited influence at the municipal level. The implication here is simple: substantial increases in registering voters are not apt to dramatically affect municipal turnout.

In Table 3, we assess regional differences in turnout. Examination over time suggests a strong and rather consistent pattern of regional differences in turnout rates. In the 1930s, 1960s, and 1970s for both adult and registrant turnout, the East had the highest participation rates while the South was lowest. This pattern holds using our 1980 data.

We have discussed three types of explanatory variables: extent of voter registration, city institutional characteristics, and region. We have noted how institutional and regional characteristics are correlated. Therefore, in the final section of this paper, we will employ multivariate procedures to determine, first, the extent of explanatory overlap and,

TABLE 3 Municipal Voter Participation by Region

Regions	% Adults voting	% Registrants voting
East (152)	32.2	48.6
South (219)	21.2	31.0
Midwest (257)	25.0	32.4
West (230)	29.4	38.9

TABLE 4 Multiple Regression for Municipal Voter Turnout by Level of Registration, City Structure, and Region

Variables entered	Multiple R	Increase in R	Final Beta
Percent registered	.07	.07	.29
Structural	.35	.28	
Partisanship			.07
Type of government			.21
Independent elections			.41
Region	.39	.04	
East			−.03 (ns)
South			.16
Midwest			.18

second, the overall impact of the these variables upon municipal voter participation.

As was noted earlier in this paper, municipal voter turnout can be partially attributed to the extent of voter registration. And we will argue that whether or not an individual registers to vote is seldom the result of factors related to the institutional characteristics of a community. More likely, registration is related to interest in the national and state election, the sense of civic duty, and socioeconomic factors. For this reason hierarchical multiple regression is used to control the extent of municipal voter registration, and this variable is entered into the multiple regression equation first. The structural characteristics are entered prior to the region because, as we reasoned above, regional differences may simply be an artifact of distributional differences in structural variables. Dummy variables were used to represent the region. The dependent variable used is the percentage of adults voting (see Table 4).

Based on Table 4 we can draw the following conclusions: First, institutional characteristics, particularly independence of elections, are very important determinants of voter participation. There may be very good reasons for adopting nonpartisan, independent elections and a city manager form of government. But those making the decision should do so with the clear knowledge that voter participation will decrease. Second, citizens obviously register to vote with state and national elections in mind. The extent of voter registration simply does not have a great impact upon municipal voter participation. Finally, regional differences do exist even after we control for structural characteristics. It is unclear whether the significance of this variable is due to variables we have not considered or whether cultural factors are at work.

DISCUSSION AND CONCLUSIONS

The evidence displayed in this paper demonstrates a clear trend toward decreasing voter turnout in municipal elections. The dimensions of this decline are, in fact, remarkable. If we use presidential and off-year congressional elections as benchmarks, we find that municipal turnout sank at a rate acutely faster than that of national elections. For example, fifty years ago municipal turnout was roughly the same as off-year congressional turnout, but by 1986 it was only about three-fourths of the congressional rate. Similarly, in the 1930s municipal turnout was 80 percent of the presidential rate, but by 1986 it was only roughly one-half.

Several factors probably have contributed to the overall decline: the introduction of eighteen-year-old voting, Watergate and voter alienation, and decaying parties. All have had an impact. Still, the effects of these factors should have been felt equally at the national level—even more so with respect to partisan decay. The enfranchisement of millions of southern blacks had, we believe, a positive impact on adult voter turnout and negative effects on registration turnout. Again, however, the consequences should have been felt in national contests as well. Moreover, we do not believe that registration laws—or rates for that matter—have much to do with municipal turnout. As we have noted, registration accounted for a mere 7 percent of the variance in 1986 turnout of adults in city elections. Indeed, for this reason voter registration drives are not apt to trigger much change in local voter participation.

If the factors outlined above do not fully explain the stark decrease in municipal voter turnout, what does? We would suggest four reasons. First, as we have noted, the growing adoption over time of government reforms has served to impede local turnout. Nonpartisanship and particularly council-manager government have tended to sanitize local politics by removing important party cues and transferring policy-making authority to nonelected administrators who are comparatively insulated from the electoral process. Thus, reform has stripped voters of both informational mechanisms and incentives to vote (see Karnig and Walter, 1983). Second, a very large percentage of all cities separate local elections from those at the state and national levels. Most cities have instituted independent elections. Without the stimulus of state and national races, local elections become multimillion dollar exercises which are "separate and unequal" (Karnig, 1977). In fact, turnout in elections held concurrently with state and national contests is nearly twice as high as turnout in independent races. Adopting simultaneous elections is probably the single most instrumental step that cities can take to promote local turnout, reduce unnecessary costs, and probably even increase turnout in higher-level races as well. Nonetheless, since local officials are inevitably fearful of bringing new—and unpredictable—voters to the polls, we doubt this step will be taken.

Third, policy and revenue control has shifted from the local to higher levels in the political system. As Peterson (1981) has shown, there has been a fundamental diversion of decision-making and financial control to the national government. In the period under review, the ratio of local to federal spending fell from 1.37 in 1932 to .48 in the middle 1970s. As the federal government has become predominant, the electorate may well see local votes as less meaningful than in the past and as less important than presidential or congressional balloting.

Finally, suburbanization may have had an impact on local turnout. With the mushrooming development of incorporated suburban enclaves, especially in the post–World War II era, there has been an increasing mismatch between where citizens reside and the focus of local news. In part this may be a consequence of television, the source of news for most voters, which concentrates attention on events in the central city. It may also be due to many local newspapers becoming cost-ineffective and closing. In either case, suburban voters receive less media stimulation about their cities' politics. Hence, they may tend to be more informed about and interested in the elections for which they are ineligible to vote, while being less knowledgeable about and interested in the suburban elections for which they are eligible to cast ballots.

REFERENCES

Abramson, Paul, and John Aldrich. 1982. "The Decline of Electoral Participation in America." *American Political Science Review* 76 (March): 502–21.

Abramson, Paul, John Aldrich, and David Rohde. 1986. *Change and Continuity in the 1984 Elections.* Washington, D.C.: Congressional Quarterly Press.

Alford, Robert, and Eugene Lee. 1968. "Voting and Turnout in American Cities." *American Political Science Review* 62 (September): 796–813.

Cassel, Carol, and D. Hill. 1981. "Explanations of Turnout Decline," *American Politics Quarterly* 9 (April): 181–95.

Karnig, Albert. 1979. "Local Elections: Separate and Unequal," *National Civic Review* 66 (April): 182–185.

Karnig, Albert, and Oliver Walter. 1974a. "Registration and Voting: Putting First Things Second." *Social Science Quarterly* 55 (June): 159–66.

Karnig, Albert, and Oliver Walter. 1974b. "Voting Turnout in American Cities."
R.M. Social Science Journal 15 (April): 55–71.

Karnig, Albert, and Oliver Walter. 1977. "Municipal Elections." *Municipal
Yearbook*. Washington, D.C.: ICMA, pp. 65–72.

Karnig, Albert, and Oliver Walter. 1983. "Decline in Municipal Voter Turnout:
A Function of Changing Structure." *American Politics Quarterly* 11
(October): 491–505.

Kelly, Stanley, Richard Ayres, and William Bowen. 1967. "Registration and
Voting: Putting First Things First." *American Political Science Review* 61
(June): 359–77.

Peterson, Paul. 1981. *City Limits*. Chicago: University of Chicago Press.

Piven, Frances Fox, and Cloward, Richard A. 1988. *Why Americans Don't Vote*.
New York: Pantheon Books.

Plissner, Martin. 1986. "State of the Union." CBS/*New York Times* Poll, January
27, 1986.

Powell, Bingham. 1986. "American Voter Turnout in Comparative
Perspectives." *American Political Science Review* 80 (March): 17–43.

Reiter, H. 1979. "Why Turnout Is Down." *Public Opinion Quarterly* 43 (Fall):
297–311.

Teixeira, Ruy. 1987. *Why Americans Don't Vote*. Westport, Conn.: Greenwood
Press.

Shinn, Allen. 1971. "A Note on Voter Registration and Turnout." *Journal of
Politics* 33 (November): 1120–29.

Wolfinger, Raymond, and Steven Rosenstone. 1980. *Who Votes?* New Haven,
Conn.: Yale University Press.

Reading 4

LEGISLATURES, INTEREST GROUPS, AND LOBBYISTS: THE LINK BEYOND THE DISTRICT

Charles G. Bell

This article describes the growth of interest group activity in the law-making process in state legislatures. Interest groups hire lobbyists to represent their respective positions to the state legislators. Because legislators have constituencies outside their district constituencies, lobbyists function as the linkage between the legislators and the larger groups they represent.

Professor Bell notes several recent changes in lobbyist-legislator relationships. First, legislators increasingly turn to lobbyists for campaign contributions in order to pay for the legislators' campaigns. Second, the growth of large legislative staffs has resulted in two things: lobbyists spend more time with legislative staff than they do with legislators, and key staff often leave the legislature to become lobbyists. Third, court-ordered reapportionment altered the urban-rural balance in the states' upper legislative chambers. As a result, upper-house legislators now devote more time to urban interests. The result is that rural lobbyists spend more time attempting to persuade upper-house legislators to their point of view. Finally, the development of strong governors has proved to be a counterbalance to interest group/lobbyist influence with state legislators.

Lobbyists play an indispensable role in the legislative process, providing a crucial link between legislators and various organized groups which often exist outside the lawmaker's district constituency. Indeed, a legislator's publics comprise not only his or her district constituency, but virtually any organization concerned with state policy. And as states develop increasingly complex economic, demographic, and social systems, legislative district boundaries become less meaningful in defining policy-relevant publics for most lawmakers.

Research by several political scholars has shown that lawmakers often do not act as district delegates.[1] Frequently legislators find their electoral constituencies are either irrelevant to the policy under consideration, uninformed, or not interested. Legislators often act as a "trustee" and, hence, turn to information sources outside their electoral districts—the governor or other executives, the bureaucracy, legislative staff, or lobbyists.

TASK, TRADITIONAL VIEWS, AND CONTROLS

Not very many years ago, states were considered the backwater of American politics, their governments incompetent at best and often corrupt. But the states have changed dramatically. Constitutions have been modernized, legislatures professionalized, and governors' powers enhanced. Major reforms in administrative processes and fiscal controls have been put in place. And reapportionment reforms have given urban citizens an effective voice in their state's legislature.

Not surprisingly, due to the growth and professionalization of state government, interest groups and their lobbyists have become more involved in the state policy process. Yet essentially their tasks remain unchanged. Most observers would list the following as major lobbyist-legislative activities:

- Provide client group with legislative process expertise;
- Develop or transmit client legislative proposals (draft bills) for introduction by friendly legislators;
- Supply information on pending legislation to lawmakers;
- Provide information to client(s) on legislation of interest;

Source: Charles G. Bell, "Legislatures, Interest Groups, and Lobbyists: The Link beyond the District," *Journal of State Government* 59 (Spring 1986), pp. 12–17. Copyright © by The Council of State Governments. Reprinted with permission.

- Transmit client group attitudes on pending legislation to lawmakers;
- Engender grass roots support for client legislative goals;
- Develop working coalitions in support of, or in opposition to, pending legislation; and
- Provide campaign assistance to legislators supportive of, or potentially supportive of, the client's policy goals.

Traditional views about legislator-lobbyist relations, however, are not consistent. Some political scientists see interest groups taking advantage of a status quo bias in the legislative process to protect the established and the elite. Others view the legislature as essentially a neutral referee of the group struggle—ratifying the victories, defeats, and compromises in the form of statutes. Still other political analysts argue that the legislature has a mind and will of its own, playing a significant role in making public policy and acting as an agent of change when interest groups petition the legislature to either codify or change the results of private conflict.

Controlling excesses of interest group power has always been a concern of both legislators and political scientists. James Madison argued that such controls could be found in two mechanisms. One was structural: a republican form of government in which popularly elected public officials respond to their constituents rather than various factions. The second was the policy process itself: a large diverse nation would generate a pluralist dynamic, and the conflict of interests would moderate the influence of any particular one.

Most American political scientists have a substantial bias in favor of a strong two-party system as a means of controlling interest group influences. Indeed, many view interest groups and political parties as natural enemies. However, in New York and Michigan the close relationship between organized labor and the Democratic Party makes that party stronger. Similarly, the close relationship between farm interest groups and the Republican Party in Alabama, Connecticut, Iowa, and other states, is well known. But, given the generally weak condition of most states' political parties, there are precious few instances in which they serve as effective counterweights to interest group power.

More recently, other institutional mechanisms were touted to control interest group excesses. In the mid-60s, many political scientists and legislators decided the "professionalized" legislatures could provide the appropriate counterweight to undue interest group influence. In the 1970s, a wave of post-Watergate state reforms established lobbyist registration and reporting requirements, as well as expenditure limits designed to curb interest group influence. Some states have tried public campaign finance to reduce interest group influence in elections.

RECENT CHANGES IN LOBBYIST-LEGISLATOR RELATIONSHIPS

While popular attention focuses largely on lobbyist campaign contributions and their asserted effects on legislators' behavior, other factors affecting lobbyist-legislator relations are probably more significant. These changes are both institutional and contextual. Consider four primary institutional changes.

First, professionalized state legislatures have produced the new lawmaker—typically young, with no other adult experience except those in the political arena. Often these young lawmakers went directly from school into legislative staff positions and then were elected to public office. Their views of government, policy, and process have not been tempered by any other experiences. Lacking substantial community roots in their district, they increasingly turn to lobbyists for campaign contributions in order to pay for the media campaigns which have replaced earlier grassroots organization and community-based efforts.

Second, the development of a large staff in professionalized legislatures has had, and will continue to have, a significant impact on lobbyist-legislator relations. These legislatures have become training schools for lobbyists. In California, committee consultants and other key staff often leave the legislature to become contract.[2] Ex-consultants offer their policy expertise to appropriate clients, fulfilling the lobbyist's traditional knowledge function. Others, who have worked for the legislature in a managerial function—as a member's administrative aide or with the Rules Committee—have little policy expertise. Instead, they offer their clients contacts and process expertise.

In states with large legislative staffs, more time is spent by lobbyists with staff than with legislators. An examination of California lobbyists' expense reports reveals that lobbyists more frequently breakfast or lunch with a staff member than with a legislator. Frequent contacts with staff in the capitol building also occur. Much, if not all, of the negotiations involving a legislator's bill may be handled by a staff member.[3]

Third, court-ordered reapportionment significantly altered not only the urban-rural balance in states' upper chambers, but also significantly modified the tactics of both rural and urban interest groups. As a result, upper house legislators not only devote more attention to urban interests, but have become as vigorous in that attention as have lower house legislators—reducing urban interest group dependence on the lower house. Concomitantly, rural interests now lobby both houses with equal intensity.

Finally, the development of strong governors has altered legislator-lobbyist relations. A governor's ability to run for reelection, existence of an executive budget and item veto, and four-year term have a substantial impact on the legislative process and, as a result, the role and effectiveness of lobbyists.[4] Some recent research has shown the governor to be among the most effective counterweights to interest group influence in the states.[5]

Parallel to these developments, there have been several important contextual changes:

- Significant reduction in federal government activity in several important policy arenas;
- Substantial growth in multistate and international business enterprises;
- Growth in political awareness and activity by several previously uninvolved segments of the population;
- Increase in the number of states within which the two major political parties seriously contest offices;
- Increase in the proportion of voters who have no strong party affiliations;
- Increase in ideological politics;
- Substantial growth in PAC activity; and
- Increased use of the initiative in several states.

Growing state policy activity flowing from both federal cut-backs and the continuing growth in multistate and international business activity has impelled more local governments, business firms and other organizations toward the states' capitals. Toxic dump sites, uniform and unitary tax issues, and public education reform are recent state policy issues that have engendered substantial lobbying efforts.

Growing political awareness and activity among previously uninvolved segments, such as the United Farm Workers in California and environmentalists in Maine, have had a substantial impact on the legislative process. Established groups have lost influence and policies have been changed.

The decreasing number of one-party states requires that interest groups closely allied with one party begin to work with the "other" party. Traditional alliances have been loosened, and floating coalitions produce a more fluid legislative process.

Citizens' decreasing party loyalty and increasing ideological voting further reduce the relevance of party to policy. Legislators, aside from narrowly defined leadership issues, may find information and voting cues in floating coalitions.

Growing PAC activity accounts for part of the increase in campaign money spent every two years, contributing to the arms race mentality of election spending. It also indicates the growing number of people who are involved in interest group politics.

Increased use of the initiative and referendum reflects a significant tactic which interest groups are using to either avoid the traditional legislative process or to recoup losses in the legislature. In those states permitting the initiative, interest groups are increasingly resorting to the ballot to achieve by media blitz what they couldn't secure in the legislative process. In 1984, gambling issues were on the ballot in Arkansas, California, Colorado, and Oregon. There appears to be some association between extensive use of initiatives and the existence of strong interest groups in the states.[6]

THE LOBBYING INDUSTRY IS GROWING, CHANGING

Numbers are up. While the number of lobbyists decreased in California from 777 in 1981 to 738 in 1985 (–5%) the number of registered interest groups increased from 777 to 1212 (+56%). Montana has experienced an explosion of lobbyists—from an average of slightly more than 200 lobbyists throughout the 1960's, to 538 in 1981 and more than 800 in 1983.[7] In Wyoming, the number of registered interest groups grew from 250 in 1979 to 325 in 1983 (+30%).[8] In New York, the number of lobbyists grew from 1,294 in 1979 to 1,488 in 1983 (+15%), while the number of clients grew from 580 to 625 (+8%).[9] In New Hampshire, the number of lobbyists grew 47% between 1975 and 1983 (from 122 to 179).[10] In Oregon, the growth rate was a staggering 99% between 1975 and 1984.[11]

There are at least two exceptions to this trend. In Vermont, the lobbyist corps grew only slightly, from 198 to 202 (+2%) between 1977 and 1984, while in Idaho the number of registered lobbyists actually dropped by 13% (from 298 in 1977 to 258 in 1983). Moreover, the amount spent by Idaho lobbyists (excluding campaign contributions) declined from $264,143 to $137,925 (–48%) in the same period.[12]

More contract lobbyists are appearing in several states. In California, the latest data shows 206 contract lobbyists (30% of the total) who have anywhere from 2 to 30 clients. This is a 31% increase (from 157) since 1979. In Oregon, the number grew from 45 to 62 (38%) between 1975 and 1984. In New Hampshire there was a slight growth, from 22 to 26 (18%), between 1975 and 1983. However, the contract lobbyist growth rate in Oregon and New Hampshire was less than for the lobbying corps as a whole.

It may well be, based on the California experience, that when an organization decides to lobby state government, it initially sends one of its own employees to the capital (often someone from the legal or public relations department) to represent its position. But given the often full-time nature of lobbying, the long commute and nights away from home, and the skills required in every state, such employees soon recommend the hiring of a professional lobbyist—and a contract lobbyist has another client!

Different kinds of people are joining the lobbyist corps. In California, the 1981 lobbyist corps was 81% white male, but by 1985 that proportion dropped to 74%, with women comprising 21% of the group (Blacks, Hispanics, and Asians accounted for the balance of 5%). In Oregon, the percentage of women lobbyists grew from 10% in 1975 to 17% in 1984. In New Hampshire, the proportion of women lobbyists grew from 6% in 1975 to 22% in 1983; in neighboring Vermont the proportion increased from 12% in 1977 to 18% in 1984. A few years ago, women lobbyists typically represented reform and community improvement groups, occupational groups largely made up of women (nurses) and, quite often, public employee groups. Today, women represent a much wider range of interests.

Significant changes in the types of interest groups are appearing. Analysis of lobbyists' registration data from California, 1979–1985, shows some significant changes in the number and kinds of interests being represented in Sacramento. Overall, the number of registered interest groups grew by 49%, with the greatest growth in health groups (126%), education (95%), local governments (68%), and public utilities (58%). In contrast, the number of organizations representing finance, insurance, labor, and legal groups grew very little.

Government agency lobbying is now a significant component of the "swirl of interests" in every state's capital. Some states require both local and state government entities to register, others exempt one or both. A few local governments registered in 1984 in Georgia, but no state agencies. Washington state registers both local and state government entities, but they accounted for only 10 out of 502 (2%) of the registered interests in 1984. But in neighboring Oregon, 124 state agencies and nine local entities accounted for over 20% of the total number of registered lobbyists. In California, local governments are registered but state agencies are exempt. Local entities (149) accounted for 12% of the total in 1984. If state agencies had been required to register, at least another 71 (listed in an unofficial guide of state agency "legislative coordinators") would have brought the total to 220 out of 1,282 interests (17%) in the golden state.

Resident lobbyists dominate their capital corps regardless of the state's location or legislation session length. With its relatively isolated capital, massive economy, and long sessions (over 200 days per year), California has very few out-of-state registered lobbyists (six out of 738 in 1985). In nearby Washington, only 27 out of 704 lobbyists were from out-of-state, even though Washington's legislature is limited to 90-day sessions per year. Across the nation, in Vermont, only 17 out of 209 lobbyists were from out-of-state in 1984.

Interstate-lobbyist organizations may be developing. A prominent California contract lobbyist, Donald K. Brown, also appears on the 1984 Washington State list of registered lobbyists, as do three others from California. Northwest General Telephone Co. was represented by the same lobbyist in both Washington and Oregon. Another firm, Cascade Rehabilitation Counciling, Inc., is similarly represented in both states by the same lobbyist. Safeway Stores' Washington lobbyist also represents them in Oregon. A major California contract lobbyist firm, A-K Associates, maintains affiliate offices in most of the other large states.

RE-EVALUATING TRADITIONAL VIEWS OF THE "GROUP STRUGGLE"

Recent research into interest group-legislative relations in three states— California, Iowa, and Texas—suggests that Madison's "pluralist" view of the legislative process is essentially in error.

Low levels of interest group conflict were found in each of the three states. Examining a large number of randomly selected bills introduced into the three states' legislatures, the study revealed that from 67% to 77% of them engendered no group conflict.[13] No doubt, much of this "non-conflict" legislation was of a minor or technical nature, but lawmakers looking to the dynamics of group conflict for a better understanding of these bills would have been disappointed. Interest groups faced off against one another in the legislative arena on only 25% to 33% of these bills.

The impact of group conflict varied in the three states, but even in California, where interest groups enjoyed more success than in Iowa or Texas, their impact was marginal for the 738 sample bills examined. The balance of group conflict had some impact on the outcome of bills concerned with civil, family, and individual rights; local government; state administration; taxation; and crime and corrections. Equally important, the balance of group conflict had no impact on determining welfare, labor, public employee, occupational regulation, election, and public safety bills.[14] Examining the same policy areas in Iowa revealed that the balance of group conflict had an impact only on business regulation; while in Texas, the group struggle affected only legislation on crime and corrections, elections, and occupational regulation.

Clearly, the interest group struggle was limited to a minority of bills in the three states, and had relatively little impact in Iowa and Texas and only modest impact in California.

REFLECTING ON THE CHANGES

Lobbyist-legislator relations have changed in the past few years due to: (1) increased legislative professionalization, (2) the growing number of lobbyists and PACs, (3) the expansion of contract lobbying, and (4) the changing characteristics of the lobbyist corps. Registration requirements and restrictions provide much better information about lobbyists and interest groups, but probably have not had much effect on their activities.

Legislators, looking for more or better information and independent analysis, have developed significant staff resources in several states. These staff persons make legislators less dependent on lobbyists (and agency personnel), but they have also significantly altered the past patterns of direct lobbyist-legislator communications.

The growing number of interest groups and lobbyists could be a blessing in disguise—legislators may become less dependent on any one interest group or cluster of groups. As the number of lobbyists and interest groups increases, each particular group or lobbyist becomes relatively less significant as a source of information or campaign support.

It is worth noting that while the number of interests represented in the states' capitals is growing, levels of voter participation have been decreasing. The two patterns may not be associated, but an argument can be made for some relationship.

PAC fund-raising may contribute to reduce citizen involvement in other forms of campaign participation—door-to-door or telephone voter contact work, volunteer work at a local election headquarters, voter registration drives, etc. Legislators may find themselves increasingly dependent on interest group campaign support for both reasons.

Clearly, legislator-lobbyist relations are changing. While these changes are most obvious in their effect on the day-to-day legislative process, their greatest significance can be found in the fact that they reflect significant changes in the demography, economics, and politics of the states.

NOTES

1. John Wahlke et al. *The Legislative System* (New York: John Wiley & Sons, 1962); see also Charles G. Bell and Charles M. Price, *Legislative Socialization.* (Newbury Park, Calif.: Sage, 1975). These findings cover California, New Jersey, Ohio, and Tennessee. In contrast, legislators in Pennsylvania appear to more often perform as delegates, according to Frank J. Sorauf, *Party and Representation.* (New York: Atherton Press, 1963).

2. Jerry B. Briscoe and Charles G. Bell, "The New Sacramento Lobbying Corps," *Data Brief.* (Berkeley, Calif.: Institute of Governmental Studies, University of California). *Pending.*

3. Michael J. BeVier, *Politics Backstage: Inside the California Legislature.* (Philadelphia: Temple University Press, 1979); Paul Sabatier and David Whiteman, "Legislative Decision Making and Substantive Policy Information." *Legislative Studies Quarterly* (August, 1985).

4. Larry Sabato, *Goodbye to Good-time Charlie.* (Washington, D.C.: CQ Press, 1983).

5. Charles W. Wiggins, Keith E. Hamm, and Charles G. Bell, "Interest Group and Party Influence Agents in the Legislative Process" (Presented at the 1984 annual meeting of the American Political Science Association).

6. Charles M. Price, "The Initiative: A Comparative State Analysis..." *Western Political Quarterly* (June 1975); and David B. Magleby, *Direct Legislation.* (Baltimore: Johns Hopkins Press, 1984).

7. Thomas Payne, "Interest Groups in Montana" (Presented at the 1984 annual meeting of the Western Political Science Association).

8. Janet Clark and B. Oliver Walter, "Wyoming Interest Groups" (Presented at the 1984 annual meeting of the Western Political Science Association).

9. New York Temporary State Commission on Lobbying, "1983 Annual Report" (Albany, N.Y.: Commission, 1984), p. 4.

10. Based on lobbyist registration data supplied by the Department of State, State House, Concord, N.H. 03301.

11. Based on lobbyist registration data supplied by the Oregon Government Ethics Commission, Salem, Oreg. 97310.

12. Vermont data from the Secretary of State, Montpelier, Vt. 05602; Idaho data from Gary Moncrief, "Interest Groups in Idaho," (Presented at the 1984 annual meeting of the Western Political Science Association).

13. Keith E. Hamm, Charles W. Wiggins, and Charles G. Bell, "Interest Group Involvement, Conflict, and Success in State Legislatures..." (Presented at the 1983 annual meeting of the American Political Science Association).

14. Charles G. Bell, Keith E. Hamm, and Charles W. Wiggins, "The Pluralist Model Reconsidered:..." (Presented at the 1985 meeting of the American Political Science Association).

CHAPTER III

CITIZEN INFLUENCE AND PARTICIPATION IN STATE AND LOCAL GOVERNMENTS: POLITICAL PARTIES, PUBLIC OPINION, AND DIRECT DEMOCRACY

INTRODUCTION

Citizen influence and participation in state and local governments take place not only through voting and interest groups but also through political parties, public opinion, and the instruments of *direct democracy* (the *initiative,* the *referendum,* and the *recall*).

Public opinion can be viewed as a variable concept, i.e., public opinion can be both passive and active.[1] Opinion that we keep to ourselves is passive; opinion that we make known to decision makers is active. Even so, the question we must ask is: Does public opinion have a significant effect on the policies of the states? The answer is an emphatic yes. As early as 1976, Robert S. Erikson found that state policies do reflect public opinion.[2] Subsequently, in 1985, Gerald C. Wright, Jr., Robert S. Erikson, and John P. McIver reported that public opinion had a greater impact on public policy than did economic variables.[3]

Thomas R. Dye does not place as much trust in public opinion as an influencer of public policy as do Robert Erikson and his colleagues. After reviewing studies which examined the impact of public opinion on public policy, Dye concludes: "[I]t is not really the opinions of the general public that influence public policy, but rather the opinions of state and community leaders inside and outside of government."[4] John A. Harrigan, however, notes that recent research has shown that public opinion has a much greater impact on public policy than previously thought.[5] According to Harrigan, researchers have found a consistency between preferences expressed in public opinion polls and public policies on about two-thirds of all public opinion preferences.

The political party is the device through which people nominate candidates for public office, help those candidates win elections, and organize the government once the election is over. The political party, accordingly, is an important route to participate in and influence state and local governments. As Richard H. Leach and Timothy G. O'Rourke have observed: "It is impossible to refer to citizen participation in general or to voting and elections in particular without discussing political parties."[6]

Despite the important role which parties apparently perform or should perform in our democracy, contemporary American political parties have been described alternately as in a state of decay, decline, or demise.[7] However, recent observers reject the notion that the parties are dying.[8] At the state level, Malcolm E. Jewell and David M. Olson point out that "state parties are being strengthened and party cohesion maintained in the state legislatures."[9] And at the local level, a recent study indicates that local parties have held their own during the last twenty

years.[10] Nicholas Henry writes that perhaps the most significant development in state parties is their dramatically increasing professionalism.[11]
State party organizations have larger budgets, employ full-time professionals as party chairs, employ larger and increasingly more specialized
staffs, and utilize party-centered advertising and get-out-the-vote campaigns.

Robert S. Erikson, Gerald C. Wright, Jr., and John P. McIver, in their
article "Political Parties, Public Opinion, and State Policy in the United
States," which is reprinted in this chapter as Reading 5, indicate that
there is a clear consistency between political parties, public opinion, and
public policies in the states.

Citizen influence and participation in state and local governments
take place also through the instruments of direct democracy—the initiative, the referendum, and the recall.

Nicholas Henry writes that "most states and cities allow their citizens to vote on policy matters and to eject officials who have overstayed
their welcome in ways that the federal government has never considered."[12] And Michael J. Ross avers that via the instruments of direct democracy "some of the most explosive issues in American politics can be
presented for consideration by the voters."[13]

Opponents of direct democracy argue that it should not replace representative democracy.[14] They maintain that there should be no recall of
the executive and the legislator once we have elected them. Only at the
next election should the citizenry have an opportunity to make new
choices. They argue, also, that the citizenry should not be using the initiative or the referendum to have the opportunity to vote directly on public policy questions. This, opponents say, is the responsibility of our duly
elected representatives.

Advocates of direct democracy, on the other hand, argue that the
"three devices of direct democracy provide a safety valve with which the
voters can bypass legislative inaction, challenge governmental policies,
and rid themselves of unsatisfactory elected officials.[15]

In "Taking the Initiative: Direct Legislation and Direct Democracy in
the 1980s," which is reprinted in this chapter as Reading 6, David B.
Magleby examines the use of the referendum, the initiative, and the recall in American state and local governments.

NOTES

1. Ann H. Elder and George C. Kiser, *Governing American States and Communities: Constraints and Opportunities* (Glenview, Ill.: ScottForesman, 1983),
p. 95.

2. See Robert S. Erikson, "The Relationship between Public Opinion and State Policy: A New Look Based on Some Forgotten Data," *American Journal of Political Science* 20 (February 1976).

3. See Gerald C. Wright, Jr., Robert S. Erikson, and John P. McIver, "Measuring State Partisanship and Ideology with Survey Data," *Journal of Politics* 47 (May 1985).

4. Thomas R. Dye, *Politics in States and Communities*, 4th ed. (Englewood Cliffs, N.J.: Prentice-Hall, 1981), p. 89.

5. See John A. Harrigan, *Politics and Policy in States and Communities*, 3rd ed. (Glenview, Ill.: ScottForesman, 1988), p. 106.

6. Richard H. Leach and Timothy G. O'Rourke, *State and Local Government: The Third Century of Federalism* (Englewood Cliffs, N.J.: Prentice-Hall, 1988), p. 76.

7. See Ann O'M. Bowman and Richard C. Kearney, *State and Local Government* (Boston: Houghton Mifflin, 1990), p. 144; Gerald L. Houseman, *State and Local Government: The New Battleground* (Englewood Cliffs, N.J.: Prentice-Hall, 1986), p. 196.

8. See Joseph A. Schlesinger, "The New American Political Party," *American Political Science Review* 79, No. 4 (December 1985), pp. 1152–69.

9. Malcolm E. Jewell and David M. Olson, *American State Political Parties and Elections* (Chicago: Dorsey Press, 1982), p. 293.

10. See James J. Gibson, Cornelius P. Cotter, John F. Bibby, and Robert J. Huckshorn, "Whither the Local Parties? A Cross-Sectional and Longitudinal Analysis of the Strength of Party Organizations," *American Journal of Political Science* 29, No. 1 (February 1985), pp. 139–61.

11. Nicholas Henry, *Governing at the Grassroots: State and Local Politics* (Englewood Cliffs, N.J.: Prentice-Hall, 1987), p. 92.

12. Ibid., p. 53.

13. Michael J. Ross, *State and Local Politics and Policy: Change and Reform* (Englewood Cliffs, N.J.: Prentice-Hall, 1987), p. 68.

14. Ibid., p. 74. See also Robert S. Lorch, *State and Local Politics: The Great Entanglement*, 3rd ed. (Englewood Cliffs, N.J.: Prentice-Hall, 1989), pp. 69–70; and David C. Saffell, *State and Local Government: Politics and Public Policies*, 3rd ed. (New York: Random House, 1987), p. 106.

15. David R. Berman, *State and Local Politics*, 4th ed. (Boston: Allyn & Bacon, 1984), p. 68. See also Russell W. Maddox and Robert W. Fuquay, *State and Local Government*, 4th ed. (New York: Van Nostrand and Reinhold, 1981), p. 175.

POLITICAL PARTIES, PUBLIC OPINION, AND STATE POLICY IN THE UNITED STATES

Robert S. Erikson, Gerald C. Wright, Jr., and John P. McIver

The authors ask: How much do partisan elections contribute to the effective representation of state public opinion? They observe that while it makes sense theoretically for parties to provide the electorate with a clear choice of policy options, state policy research seems to indicate that political parties do not make a difference with respect to policy directions in the states. The authors found that while state public opinion is strongly correlated with state policies, liberal and conservative states do not differ in their tendencies to elect Democrats or Republicans to state office, thus suggesting that the impact of state opinion on state policy would seem to bypass the electoral process.

In order to find the role that political parties do play in state policy, the authors first postulated a theory of state electoral politics. According to this theory, state parties are motivated to win elections. Assuming this is so, they should also respond to state public opinion. To the extent that parties do respond to such opinion, they should achieve electoral success. Accordingly, the most conservative parties should be found in the most conservative states and the most liberal parties should be found in the most liberal states. In actuality, however, state parties are pushed toward the median voter position by electoral considerations and away from that position by the party activists.

The authors argue that where state elections are decided by ideology, *electoral success should go to the party that is ideologically closest to the state electorate.* Accordingly, Republican state parties should be most successful when they move toward the liberalism of the Democratic opposition and Democratic state parties should, likewise, be most successful when they move toward the conservatism of the Republican opposition. The authors conclude that it is this ideological flexibility that obscures the relationship between state political party control and public policy.

The authors postulate also a model of electoral representation. According to this model, centrist parties are rewarded at the ballot box.

Thus Democrats move in a conservative direction; Republicans move in a liberal direction. This flexibility of the political parties accounts for the reportedly low correlation between party control and public policy.

While Democratic and Republican legislators differ in their ideological values, their electoral motivations cause them to make ideologically similar decisions when in control of state legislatures. Thus state public opinion can influence state public policy even though party control is statistically uncorrelated with either state opinion or state policy. This is so because state political parties respond to state public opinion, and state voters respond to political party positions.

The authors assembled four separate indicators of the ideological preferences of Democratic and Republican party state elites. The four indicators were the ideological position of each (1) congressional candidate, (2) state legislator, (3) local party chairman, and (4) national convention delegate. These indicators were combined into a comprehensive measure of elite opinion. State policy liberalism was based on its score on eight policy issues, including education and consumer protection. Erikson and his colleagues found a significant responsiveness of the Democratic and Republican parties to public opinion. They noted particularly that parties modify their positions in response to state public opinion to avoid penalties in the election booths.

The authors observe also that state political parties select ideological positions that attempt to preempt electoral sanctions. That is, the voters elect Democrats who are liberal personally but once in office tilt to the right, or they elect Republicans who are conservative but once in office tilt to the left. In sum, party control of the legislature is not a sufficient predictor of state public policy.

One central question about modern democracies is, How much do partisan elections contribute to the effective representation of public opinion? In theory, programmatic parties provide the electorate with a clear choice of policy options, and election results are followed by predictable policy consequences. But empirically, does it matter which party (or coalition) governs? Most recent cross-national comparisons of Western democracies answer affirmatively. Socialist or leftist party participation in the national government is associated with a high inflation-to-unemployment trade-off (Hibbs, 1977), growth of the governmental sector (Cameron, 1978; Lange and Garrett, 1985), high public expenditure (Tufte, 1978;

Source: From *American Political Science Review* 83 (September 1989), pp. 729–750. Copyright © 1989 by the American Political Science Association. Reprinted by permission.

Castles, 1982), welfare spending (Castles, 1982; Hicks and Swank, 1984), quality-of-life (Moon and Dixon, 1985), and income equality-redistribution (Tufte, 1978; van Arnhem, Corina and Schotsman, 1982; but see also Jackman, 1975, 1980). In sum, nations where leftist parties are most influential also tend to have the kinds of policies and policy consequences with the greatest appeal to leftist constituencies. Time series analyses for individual nations also show policy consequences resulting from party control (Alt, 1985; Hibbs, 1977, 1987). Party control does matter.

It may be the case, however, that party control matters only in terms of the sharp divisions between European Socialist parties of the Left and parties of the Right. In the U.S. context, it is by no means clear that major policy differences flow from variation in Democratic versus Republican control. At the national level, while some time series find policy consequences from party control of the presidency or Congress (Hibbs, 1977, 1987; Kiewiet and McCubbins, 1985), the role of parties remains in some dispute (Beck, 1982; Browning, 1985; Lowery, 1985). At the state level (our focus here) the policy relevance of party control has been viewed with particular skepticism.

In state policy research, the apparent irrelevance of political parties has been a persistent puzzle. Presumably, Republican states would have the most conservative policies and Democratic states the most liberal policies. But this is not the case. The relative strengths of the Republican and Democratic parties in state politics appear to be statistically unrelated to policy directions in the states even after the imposition of rigorous controls (Dye, 1966; Plotnick and Winters, 1985; Winters, 1976). Only time series analyses show any evidence of the expected party effects, with welfare spending responsive to party control in some states but perhaps not in others (Dye, 1984; Garand, 1985; Jennings, 1979).

The nonrelationship between party control and state policy appears to deny common, seemingly informed, stereotypes of how politics in the United States works. Most observers would agree that Democratic and Republican elites differ ideologically in their values and in certain manifestations of behavior, such as roll call votes. Could this be an illusion? Perhaps in state politics, the two parties have become indistinguishable on policy substance—just what spatial models of party competition predict should happen for electorally driven parties (Downs, 1957).

Or perhaps the seeming irrelevance of parties is confirmation of the general theory that policy outcomes are determined by environmental, rather than political, variables (Dye, 1966, 1979). Indeed, the failure of party control to predict policy may be the strongest evidence available in support of the environmental theory. Although Republican and Demo-

FIGURE 1 A Simple Model of State Public Opinion and Policy

State opinion liberalism	$\rightarrow$	Democratic party control	$\rightarrow$	Policy liberalism

cratic candidates diverge in their campaign rhetoric and even in their personal values, perhaps Republican and Democratic politicians ultimately enact the same policies when given the responsibility of governing. By this scenario, politicians in office respond to the social needs and economic constraints of the state at the expense of campaign pledges or other ephemeral political considerations.

A BROKEN ELECTORAL LINKAGE?

Does electoral politics in the states really not matter? Recently we reported evidence that challenges the economic determinism interpretation of state politics (Wright, Erikson, and McIver, 1987). We discovered that despite the apparent strength of economic variables as predictors of state policies, state public opinion is strongly correlated ($r = .80$) with state policies and is a much stronger predictor than economic variables considered individually or as a group.

Clearly, the ideological preferences of state electorates play an important role in determining the ideological tone of state policies. Partisan elections would seem a likely conduit for this flow of causality, with liberal states electing Democrats who enact liberal legislation and conservative states electing Republicans who enact conservative legislation. This simple model is diagrammed in Figure 1.

But our data do not fit this simple model.[1] Echoing earlier findings, we find Democratic party control of state legislatures unrelated ($r = -.22$) to an eight-item measure of state policy liberalism. Moreover, even if party control could account for policy, the linkage between opinion to policy via parties would be broken at the front end. The correlation between the liberalism of state publics and Democratic control is only .07. Thus, liberal and conservative states do not differ in their tendencies to elect Republicans or Democrats to state office. The strong effect of state opinion on state policy would seem to bypass the electoral process.

Not only are the ideological preferences of state electorates uncorrelated with the partisan composition of state elected officials but they are also unrelated to the electorate's partisan preferences. The mean liberalism of state public opinion correlates only .01 with mean Democratic party identification. State party identification, however does correlate with party control ($r = .86$), as one would expect.

Democratic states do elect the most Democrats to state office. But the most Democratic state electorates are not unusually liberal. And the Democratic legislatures they elect do not enact unusually liberal legislation. All this would seem to deny the presence of much policy representation. But we must remember that the most liberal state electorates do elect legislators who enact the most liberal legislation, even with the absence of any obvious partisan linkage.

Are political parties as irrelevant to the representation process as this analysis suggests? Perhaps political parties do play an important role, but the linkage is more complicated than has been presented so far. But to pursue this possibility, one needs a theory of how partisan elections fit into the representation process in the states.

A THEORY OF STATE ELECTORAL POLITICS

A theory of state electoral politics must take into account the wide variation in the ideological orientations of state political parties. To take an obvious example, the Democratic party of Mississippi is far more conservative than the Democratic party of New York and perhaps than the New York Republican party as well. With the Democratic and the Republican parties each differing ideologically from one state to the next, the potential exists for serious confounding of our understanding of how parties contribute to the policy representation in the states. This ideological variation of state parties sometimes appears to be chaotic and idiosyncratic to particular state political cultures. But there is good reason to suspect some order and predictability in both the source of the variation and its electoral consequences.

To develop some propositions about state party ideology, party electoral strength, and state policy, let us take the role of elections in the policy process seriously. Suppose that state electorates actually reward and punish the parties on the basis of their policy positions and specifically on the basis of their placement of the left-right continuum; that is, suppose that state electorates tend to reward the party that best reflects their ideological viewpoints. Suppose also that state parties are motivated (at least in part) to win elections. Then, to the extent that parties are electorally motivated, they should respond to state opinion. To the extent that parties respond effectively to state opinion, they should achieve electoral success.

When state parties respond to state opinion, the most conservative parties would be found in the most conservative states and the most liberal parties would be found in the most liberal states. Of course, we do not expect state parties' ideologies to be driven *entirely* by state opinion. If they were, state parties would always converge to the position of the state's median voter. In actuality state parties, like national parties, are pushed toward the median voter position by electoral considerations and away from the median voter position by the preferences of their activists (Aldrich, 1983; Calvert, 1985; Poole and Rosenthal, 1984; Wittman, 1983).

To the extent that state elections are decided by ideology, state electoral success should go to the party that is ideologically closest to the state electorate. Thus, Republican state parties should be most successful when they move toward the liberalism of the Democratic opposition. Democratic state parties should be most successful when they move toward the conservatism of the Republican opposition. These policies could backfire, but only if the parties move too far, as when the Democrats get so conservative that the Republicans outflank them on the left. But this does not happen with state parties.

To summarize, it is the ideological flexibility of the Democratic and Republican parties in the states that obscures the linkage between state party control and public policy. But this is not to say that the partisan electoral process in the states is unimportant. As we will show, ideologically flexible parties can respond to state public opinion and in turn, be electorally rewarded and punished based on how well they represent state opinion.[2]

Our argument can be recognized as a variation of the familiar Downsian theme that electoral rewards lie in the political center (Downs, 1957)....We now explore the implications for estimating the role of party control in the representation process in the states.

A MODEL OF ELECTORAL REPRESENTATION

According to our model, centrist parties are electorally rewarded. This means that the Democrats are rewarded for movement in the conservative direction and the Republicans for movement in the liberal direction.[3] In short, liberal parties (Democratic or Republican) negatively affect Democratic success. Figure 2 introduces party positions to the model of state electoral representation. We label this variable party elite liberalism. Note how electorally responsive parties can account for the absence of correlations between opinion liberalism and Democratic success and between Democratic success and policy liberalism.

FIGURE 2   Representation Model with Party Elites

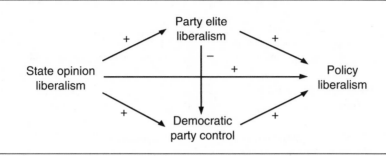

In our model, liberal opinion causes liberal parties. However, when state electorates respond to party positions, liberal parties hinder Democratic success. This makes a negative indirect path from opinion liberalism to Democratic control. At the same time, the model shows a positive direct effect of opinion liberalism on Democratic legislative strength. The net effect of the combined indirect and direct paths could well be a low-bivariate correlation between state opinion and party control.

The model also accounts for the low correlation between party control and policy. According to the model, party ideology suppresses the positive relationship between party control and policy; liberal parties work against Democratic control but for liberal policies. This source of spurious negative correlation obscures the posited positive effect of Democratic control on liberal policy.

Figure 2 also shows how parties' responsiveness to state opinion contributes to representation in a rather straightforward fashion. Liberal state opinion causes liberal state party elites, which results in liberal policies. Finally, the model allows for the direct effect of opinion on policy independent of partisan variables.

The model can be complicated further. Figure 3 adds two more variables: state party identification and the liberalism of the state legislature. Figure 3 also adds specificity to the meaning of party control by redefining it in terms of Democratic legislative strength.

This new model places party identification as an intervening variable between opinion liberalism and Democratic legislative strength. Partisanship provides a mechanism for translating public opinion into legislative power: liberal states tend to identify with the Democratic party, which increases the number of Democratic state legislators. Surprisingly,

FIGURE 3 Full Representation Model

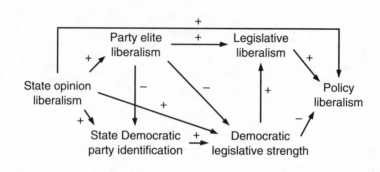

as we reported, the correlation between opinion liberalism and Demo-cratic party identification in the states is quite weak. But the role of party elites can explain this anomaly: liberal states cause liberal parties, which over time contribute negatively to Democratic partisanship. This effect hides the expected relationship between public opinion and partisanship in which liberals tend to identify with the Democratic party.

The liberalism of the legislature is introduced as an intervening vari-able caused by the degree of liberalism among the two major parties' elites and the partisan division of the legislature: the more liberal the parties and the more Democrats in the legislature, the more liberal the legislature should be. The inclusion of legislative liberalism provides an additional subtlety to the model. Electing Democrats should liberalize the legislature, which leads to liberal policies. But as Figure 3 suggests, with legislative liberalism and public liberalism held constant, the resid-ual direct effect on policy liberalism of electing Democrats could be negative.

The ceteris paribus condition is crucial for this proposition. We do not seriously speculate that electing Republicans is the way to get liberal policies (although speculation of that sort can be found in the literature: see Goodin, 1983). Rather, under identical political circumstances and with identical ideological values, Republican and Democratic legislators should respond in different directions to electoral motivations: Republi-cans should find more votes by moving left and Democrats should find more votes by moving right. Of course Republican and Democratic legis-lators tend to differ in their ideological values. But conceivably, electoral motivations could be so strong that conservative Republicans and liberal

Democrats make ideologically similar decisions when in control of the state legislatures.

In summary, the model of Figure 3 shows how state opinion can influence state policy via a variety of indirect electoral pathways. These pathways are based on the assumptions that state parties respond to state opinion and that state electorates respond to party positions. If this theoretical development is correct, electoral politics can be crucial for policy representation in the states, even though party control is statistically uncorrelated with both state opinion and state policy.

One important omission from this model is the governor's role in state policy. This omission is due largely to measurement considerations rather than to disregard for the governor's role in the legislative process. When the dependent variable is a set of policies cumulated from years of legislative decision making, it makes little sense to include the governor's party affiliation for the short term as an independent variable. And partisan control of governorships over the long term bears little relationship to other indicators of partisanship. Where unusual long-term success for a party is found at the gubernatorial level (e.g., the Democratic in Utah, the Republican in Michigan), this may result precisely because of gubernatorial leadership that is ideologically atypical for the party. We are far more reluctant to assume that governors share the ideological positions measured for their party's elite than we are that, on the average, state legislators do so.

While we do not include the state's chief executive in our model for measurement reasons, this decision should not significantly distort the model we present. Much has been made in recent years of the increasing formal authority of governors. Yet little evidence exists that demonstrates an empirical link between the powers of the executive and actual policy direction. For instance, state representatives rarely see the governor as playing a significant role in the state legislature. Legislators rank the governor last among thirteen potential decision cue sources: less than 2% of all state legislators choose the governor as the principal informant for their decisions (Uslaner and Weber, 1977, 34).

MEASUREMENT

To put the theory to use, it is necessary to operationalize each of the component parts. Most critical is the measurement of the one "brand-new" variable: party elite liberalism. In all, we were able to assemble four separate indicators of the ideological preferences of Democratic and Republican state elites, which we combined into a comprehensive measure of elite opinion. The four indicators are:

1. *Congressional candidates' conservatism-liberalism.* Using the 1974, 1978, and 1982 CBS-*New York Times* surveys of congressional candidates, we ascertained the ideological position of each congressional candidate who ran in these three election years. First, the issue responses to these surveys were summed to create ideological scores (Erikson and Wright, 1989; Wright, 1986; Wright and Berkman, 1986). Second, ideological scores were standardized across the election years using the scores of the incumbents who served throughout the period. Third, means were calculated by party and state. The result is the measurement of the mean ideological position for each party's candidates in each state over three elections.

2. *State legislators' conservatism-liberalism.* For the more than a thousand state legislators surveyed by Uslaner and Weber in 1974 for their state legislative decision-making study (Uslaner and Weber, 1977), we constructed factor scores to measure their ideological positions. These were calculated at the individual level using the legislator's stands on the death penalty, abortion, pollution regulation, gun control, teachers' unions, and legalization of marijuana. Factor scores were averaged for the legislators of each state party.

3. *Local party chairmen's conservatism-liberalism.* As part of their study of state and local party organizations, Cotter and his colleagues ascertained the ideological identifications of county party chairs in 1979-80 (Cotter et al., 1984). We use the mean ideological position of Republican and Democratic county chairs in each state as a third measure of party elite liberalism.

4. *National convention delegates' conservatism-liberalism.* Ideolgoical self-identification of delegates to the Democratic and Republican national conventions in 1972, 1976, and 1980 has been collected by Miller and Jennings (1987; also see Farah, Jennings, and Miller, 1981). Here we use the mean ideological identifications of the state party delegations over these three convention years.

For many analytic purposes, these four indicators could be treated separately, as distinct measures of different phenomena. Here, we are interested in the general ideological positions of state party elites, especially as they might be viewed by the attentive electorate. For this purpose, we combine the four indexes. Each of the four is an imperfect measure of party positions. By combining them into one composite index, we strengthen the instrument as a measure of party elite position.

These eight (four sets for two parties) sets of ideological scores correlate strongly with each other. We could choose any of several methods for combining these scores in a grand index, and the exact procedure makes little difference. In the present analysis, we used the following procedure: Each set of scores was standardized over the 92 separate parties (for 46 states, with Alaska, Hawaii, Nebraska, and Nevada excluded). The four sets of Republican elite scores and the four sets of Democratic elite scores were then summed to produce composite Republican and Democratic indices. For much of the analysis we simplify further by employing the average (or midpoint) ideological position of the two state party elites.[4]

Operationalization of other variables can be described more briefly: The liberalism of *state opinion* is measured as the mean ideological identification (conservative-moderate-liberal) in the pooled CBS–*New York Times* surveys over the 1976–82 period. These state estimates, some based on pooled state samples larger than the typical national survey, are reliable at .82 or above (Wright, Erikson, and McIver, 1985). *State party identification* is measured as the mean party identification (Republican-Independent-Democrat) in the CBS–*New York Times* pooled samples (Wright, Erikson, and McIver, 1985).

Democratic state legislative strength is measured as the average of the Democratic strength for each legislative chamber over the 1977–84 period. Upper and lower chambers are weighted equally. *Legislative liberalism* is measured indirectly as the weighted average of the Democratic and Republican elite liberalism scores, where the weights are determined by the parties' relative legislative strength (weighing the two chambers equally). In other words, we assume that the average liberalism of a state's Democratic legislators is the mean composite liberalism score for the state's Democratic elite; and we assume that the average liberalism of a state's Republican legislators is the mean composite liberalism score for the state's Republican elite. Democratic and Republican composite liberalism scores are then combined in proportion to the two parties' average legislative strength.

State policy liberalism is the standardized sum of state policy scores on eight separate issues: education, Aid for Families with Dependent Children, criminal justice, gambling, consumer protection, progressive taxation, and Equal Rights Amendment ratification. These items form one common dimension, with an estimated reliability (alpha) of .89 for the composite measure (Wright, Erikson, and McIver, 1987).

The following sections report on the empirical fit of the causal model presented above in Figure 3. For handy reference for these sections, Table 1 reports the correlation matrix for the variables; Table 2 shows the results of the standardized regression equations; Figure 4 shows the causal model with the estimated standardized path coefficients (betas) included. . . .[5]

TABLE 1 Correlations among Variables for Model of State Policy Process

Variables	Opinion liberalism	Party elite liberalism	Democratic party identification	Democratic legislative strength	Legislative liberalism	Policy liberalism
Opinion liberalism		.69	.01	.07	.79	.80
Party elite liberalism			−.48	−.42	.79	.85
Democratic party identification				.86	.01	−.33
Democratic legis- lative strength					.19	−.22
Legislative liberalism						.78
Policy liberalism						

Note: Alaska, Hawaii, Nebraska, Nevada are excluded.

TABLE 2 Standardized Regressions for Path Model of Policy Process

Independent variables	Dependent variable				
	Democratic elite liberalism	Democratic party identification	Democratic legislative strength	Legislative liberalism	Policy liberalism
Opinion liberalism	.69* (.11)	.66* (.17)	.18 (.13)		.41* (.11)
Democratic elite liberalism		−.92* (.17)	−.17 (.14)	1.05* (.04)	
Democratic party identification			.78* (.10)		
Democratic legis- lative strength				.63* (.04)	−.35* (.07)
Legislative liberalism					.52* (.11)
Adjusted R^2	.47	.46	.74	.95	.81

Note: Alaska, Hawaii, Nebraska, Nevada are excluded. Standard errors are in parentheses.

*$p < .001$, two-tailed test.

FIGURE 4 Path Model of the State Policy Process (46 States)

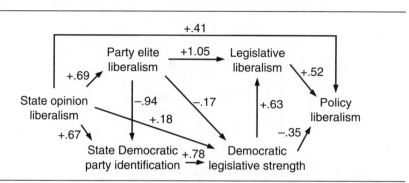

PUBLIC OPINION AND PARTY ELITES

First, we consider the relationships between state opinion and the positions of the Democratic and Republican party elites. The correlations are .54 for Democratic elites and .72 for Republican elites. The average of the two party positions (or the midpoint) correlates at .69 with state opinion.

These correlations suggest a healthy responsiveness by parties to opinion. Part of this responsiveness is merely that state party elites reflect to some extent the ideology of the general publics from which they are drawn (the "sharing" model: Erikson, Luttberg, and Tedin, 1988). A second contributing factor—and for electoral politics a more interesting one—is that state parties deliberately modify their positions in response to state opinion, from fear of electoral sanctions.

But while state parties respond to public opinion, they certainly are not the centrist electoral machines of Anthony Downs's model. State parties clearly represent the ideological predilections of their activists. Figure 5 shows how the state parties vary as a function of state opinion but remain ideologically distinct from one another. The unusual dimensions of this figure represents an attempt to scale state parties and state opinion on a common metric. The horizontal axis of this scatterplot is the liberalism of state opinion, scaled as a standardized measure. The vertical axis represents the liberalism of party elites. The scale for the vertical axis is set so that the expected midpoint between the two party positions equals state opinion. In other words, this scaling procedure assumes that on average neither party is more representative than the other and that the relative representativeness of the two parties is unrelated to state opinion.

FIGURE 5 Party Elite Liberalism by State Opinion

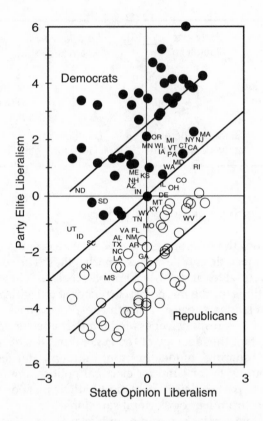

Note: Solid dots represent Democratic elites; hollow dots represent Republican elites. State labels are placed at the midpoint between the Democratic and Republican elite positions.

Figure 5 illustrates how state parties position themselves relative to state opinion and their partisan opposition. In every state, the Democratic elite is more liberal than the Republican elite. And given the scaling assumptions, each Democratic party is more liberal than state opinion, and each Republican party is more conservative than state opinion. In most states, the divergence of the two parties is considerable: typically, the divergence between the state's Democratic and Republican positions exceeds the entire range of mean state opinion between the most conservative and the most liberal states.

Clearly, Figure 5 does not present a picture of ideological convergence, with political parties mimicking the ideological stance of the state's median voter. The considerable within-state divergence of the two parties' ideological positions suggests a strong ideological pull by the parties' activists. But this tendency toward ideological extremism is not reason to ignore the responsiveness of the parties to state opinion. Figure 5 shows how state party positions vary in response to state opinion: the more liberal the state, the more liberal the Democratic party and the more liberal the Republican party. On the one hand activists push state parties away from the center; on the other hand, electoral considerations push state parties back toward the center.

STATE OPINION, STATE PARTY POSITIONS, AND PARTY STRENGTH

We argued that party positions should influence state partisanship, with liberal parties hurting the Democrats. We see in Figure 4 that the estimated path coefficient confirms our theoretical expectation. The liberalism of party positions (summarized as the party midpoint) shows a quite dramatic negative effect on Democratic party identification (beta = $-.94$). The control for party positions also confirms another important theoretical expectation: the initial opinion-party identification correlation was only .01; but now, with party positions controlled, we find the expected positive influence of state opinion on state party identification (beta = .67).

The responsiveness of state party identification to party elite ideology is shown in Figure 6. This figure shows the scatterplot of the relationship between state party positions, measured as the relative deviation of the party midpoint from the midpoint predicted from state opinion, and state party identification. Clearly, parties that are liberal relative to state public opinion push state electorates toward the Republicans, and parties that are conservative relative to state public opinion push states toward the Democrats.

It may seem dissonant to see state electorates respond to ideological positions of state parties in terms of party identification. This finding conflicts with two supposed axioms of U.S. politics—that party identification is unmoving and that state politics is largely invisible to voters. The so-clearly observed pattern, however, does not dictate that state electorates frequently change their partisan character in response to short-term ideological maneuvering by state parties. Much more plausibly, it

FIGURE 6   Party Identification by Party Elite Liberalism

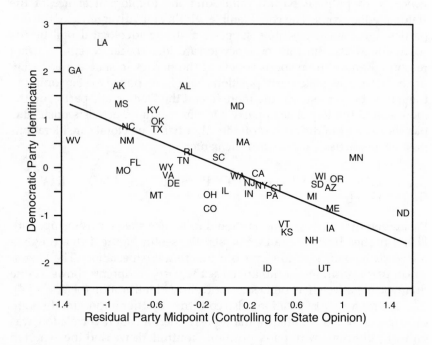

represents the influence of state party positions over the long haul, with the long-term ideological tendencies of state parties accumulating a long-term influence on the party identification of the state's electorate.

State party identification takes on importance because it is the most important direct cause of state legislative partisanship (beta = .78). Thus, via their influence on state party identification, state opinion and state party positions indirectly influence legislative partisanship. Direct effects are also present. Although the coefficients are not statistically significant, state opinion appears to influence legislative partisanship positively (beta = .18) while the ideologies of state party elites appear to influence legislative partisanship negatively (beta = −.17), as predicted. In other words, the relative ideological positions of state opinion and party positions may influence legislative elections directly, even beyond the predominant paths via party identification. This may represent aggregate evidence of "issue voting" in state legislative elections beyond the long-term component channeled through state party identification.

We see now how public opinion influences legislative party strength even though state opinion does not correlate strongly with legislative party strength as the simplest model would predict. Liberal electorates do cause Democratic legislatures; but liberal state electorates also result in liberal state parties, which works to the electoral advantage of the Republicans. Both processes are surprisingly strong statistically when the appropriate controls are imposed. But they are not ordinarily visible because they cancel each other out.

STATE OPINION, STATE PARTIES, AND THE LEGISLATURE

Legislative policy preferences should reflect the policy positions of the two state parties and the two parties' relative legislative strength. Indeed, that is how we measure legislative preferences: as the sum of the state's Republican and Democratic elite positions, each weighted according to the party's average legislative strength. Figure 4 shows these linkages from state party positions and Democratic legislative strength to legislative liberalism, in the form of the large beta coefficients (1.05 and .63, respectively) that can be observed. Of course, these coefficients must be interpreted modestly since legislative preferences are defined in terms of party positions and the legislative party division.

Recall that party positions, summarized as the party midpoint, correlate at .69 with state opinion. Now, with the parties reweighted according to their legislative strength, the measure of legislative preferences correlates at an even higher .79 with state opinion. The working of partisan elections accounts for this increase: the more liberal the parties relative to state opinion, the more the electorate will choose the more conservative Republican party over the more liberal Democratic party.[6] Figure 7 presents the scatterplot of the .79 correlation between state opinion and legislative liberalism.

So far, the data show a pattern that comfortably matches our theoretical expectations. State parties select ideological positions that in part are responses to anticipated electoral sanctions. Then, the state electorates' enactment of these sanctions result in a mix of Democratic and Republican legislators that enhances further the representation of state public opinion. The final task is to observe the translation of legislative preferences into public policy.

FIGURE 7 Legislative Liberalism by State Opinion

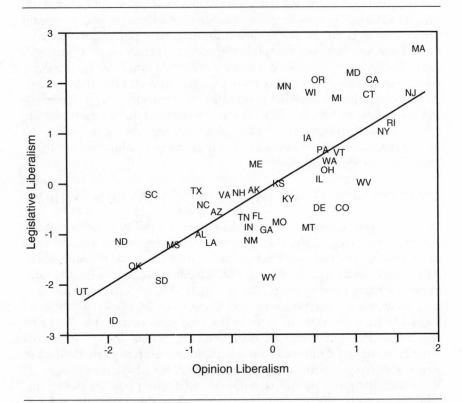

LEGISLATIVE ELECTIONS, LEGISLATIVE PREFERENCES, AND STATE POLICY

We posit three variables to influence state policy directly: legislative liberalism, Democratic legislative strength, and state opinion. The coefficients for these variables can be seen in Figure 4 and Table 2. As Table 2 shows, the three independent variables together account for a large 81% of the variance in policy liberalism.

As expected, the liberalism of the state legislature helps determine the direction of state policy but with a beta coefficient of only .52, suggesting that other variables also contribute.[7] One of these variables is state public opinion, which exerts a direct effect (.41) on policy liberalism. This effect presumably represents responsiveness by the state legislature to pressures of public opinion independent of legislative preferences. The most provocative influence is the negative coefficient (-.35) for the effect of Democratic legislative control on policy liberalism.

A negative coefficient for Democratic legislative strength is not entirely unexpected, given that legislative preference and state opinion are adequately controlled. As we have observed, even with the evident influence of state opinion, state parties tend to stand quite distant from the center of state opinion. Therefore, we might expect each party to moderate further when translating its positions into policy.

From the coefficients in Figure 4, legislative partisanship influences policy in two ways. Obviously, the more Democrats the voters elect, the more liberals they elect. And liberal legislatures lead to liberal policies. We see this from the indirect path of about .32: .63 from Democratic strength to legislative liberalism times .52 from legislative liberalism to policy liberalism. The second way is the direct path (-.35) from Democratic legislative strength to policy liberalism. Once again we have two processes that evidently cancel out. The results suggest that the partisan division of the legislature is of little relevance after all, as if, once in office, Democrats and Republicans start acting so much like each other that one cannot tell the difference![8]

Admittedly, some question must remain concerning the accuracy of the estimated negative impact of Democratic legislative strength on policy liberalism. On the one hand, the coefficient for Democratic legislative strength has the strongest t-value (-5.18) of the three predictors of policy liberalism. Assuming correct specification of the model, the negative coefficient is highly significant. On the other hand, one can suspect possible bias from misspecification of the model.

Southern regionalism is a natural suspect as a confounding influence. To the extent that the South's history of Democratic success but conservative policies is due to the unique southern culture, it is necessary to control for southern regionalism. Indeed, inclusion of a simple dummy variable for the eleven former Confederate states reduces the coefficient from Democratic legislative strength to policy liberalism from -.35 down to -.23. Removing the eleven former Confederate states entirely from the analysis pushes the coefficient down to -.20. . . .

Under these and alternative model specifications, the negative path from Democratic legislative strength to policy liberalism can be pushed toward statistical insignificance.[9] Yet the coefficient does not go to zero nor does its sign change. Thus the net effect of party control on policy remains somewhat ambiguous. The state electorate's choice for state legislature seems to be to elect Democrats who are liberal personally but in office trim to the right or to elect Republicans who are conservative personally but in office trim to the left. The results with the regional control suggest that on balance, Democrats may make more liberal policies but that the statistical evidence must be viewed with caution.[10]

DIRECT DEMOCRACY

So far, we have ignored the direct effect of state opinion on state policy (beta = .41) independent of the electoral paths discussed. Even with the ideological and partisan composition of the state legislature held constant, state opinion exerts an independent influence on state policy. At first glance, this "direct" effect of opinion on policy may seem to reflect sources of representation that are independent of the electoral process. But let us consider how the electoral process may underlie this "direct" effect as well.

Conceivably, when legislatures follow public opinion over their own collective judgment, they do so because legislators believe that they should play the role of instructed delegates. But a more likely reason for following public opinion is the fear of electoral sanctions when they do otherwise. To some extent, the "direct" effect of state opinion may also reflect the unmeasured role of state governors in the representation process: state electorates presumably tend to elect governors with whom they agree politically and who try to respond to the voice of state opinion. Finally, the "direct" effect of state opinion can reflect direct democracy, in the form of referendum voting.

To a degree that should not be ignored, citizens can participate directly in state policy making. About three hundred referenda and initiatives come before state voters during every legislative biennium. Perhaps the best-known recent example of direct citizen input into state government was the 1978 wave of tax and spending limit votes in 15 states following the passage of Proposition 13 in California. But many other issues came before state electorates in the late 1970s and early 1980s (Magleby, 1984; Ranney, 1978; for specific issues and outcomes, consult *Congressional Quarterly Weekly Reports*). In various states, voters made policy decisions on gambling laws (from casinos to horseracing to lotteries), bottle bills, utility regulation (with specific emphasis in many states on nuclear power regulation), public smoking, anticrime measures (death penalty, handgun control, bail reduction, and prison construction), teacher homosexuality, "right-to-work" laws, state funding of abortion, voluntary prayer in schools, and state equal rights amendments. In sum, state electorates had the opportunity to alter a number of policies, including many that compose our measure of state policy liberalism.

CONCLUSION

We have helped to explain why party control of the state legislature is not a particularly good predictor of state policy. The answer is not that electoral politics is unimportant but precisely the opposite. We have seen strong evidence that (1) party positions respond to state opinion, (2) state elections reward and punish state parties based on their responsiveness to public opinion, and (3) Republican and Democratic legislators moderate their positions when making policy. Ironically, although state Republican and Democratic parties tend to represent ideological extremes, they also respond to state opinion—perhaps even to the point of enacting similar policies when in legislative control. This is, of course, exactly what the Downsian model of the electoral process says that electorally responsive parties should do. It is just that this result is achieved by a circuitous process.

We suggest a new way of thinking about state politics. At the state level, the Democratic and Republican parties offer an ideological choice but also respond to state opinion. How well they respond helps to determine their electoral success at the legislative level and also the content of state policy. State politics—in the sense that term is usually understood—does matter.

NOTES

1. Four states have been eliminated from the analysis. Three of these—Alaska, Hawaii, and Nevada—were eliminated due to limitations in our measurement of public opinion (Wright, Erikson, and McIver, 1985). Nebraska is excluded because of its nonpartisan legislature.

2. This argument may apply to cross-national comparisons as well. The U.S. Democratic party is more ideologically centrist than European parties of the Left, and more successful electorally. One may wonder, therefore, whether the relative electoral success of the left, but nonsocialist, U.S. Democrats (and also the Canadian Liberals) disturbs the cross-national relationship between leftist party success and policy. However, cross-national studies do not code the nonsocialist U.S. Democrats and Canadian Liberals as parties of the Left. The Leftist designation is reserved for explicitly socialist or social democratic parties. If cross-national studies were to code the U.S. Democrats and Canadian Liberals as successful leftist parties, cross-national relationships between party control and policy would become seriously attenuated.

3. We speak somewhat loosely about movement to the political center. Strictly speaking, attempting to observe whether parties are at the political center would require a common metric for parties and the electorate. In actuality, the location of the center is irrelevant, since each party should be electorally re-

warded for moving toward the ideological position of its opposition, whatever side of center. . . .

4. The party midpoints for the four indicators of party elite liberalism correlate among themselves in a range from .71 (state legislators and county chairs) to .83 (congressional candidates and local chairs). The midpoints correlate with the composite tally in a range from .87 (county chairs) to .93 (state legislators). Within party, the correlations range from .52 to .73. A principal components analysis of the eight state-level indicators of elite ideology yielded two distinct factors. As expected, these components identify the ideological constraint within parties as well as philosophical distinctiveness of the Democrats and Republicans. The rotated principal components are as follows:

Party elites	F1	F2
Republican		
State legislators	.87	.19
National delegates	.64	.35
Congressional candidates	.84	.20
State and local party officials	.81	.27
Democratic		
State legislators	.35	.77
National delegates	.32	.72
Congressional candidates	.56	.72
State and local party officials	.06	.91

5. Certain arrows (e.g., from state party identification to legislative liberalism) are deleted from Figure 4, on the grounds that the expected direct effect is zero. Technically speaking, therefore, Figure 4 presents an *overidentified* model. Inclusion of the omitted effects would be of little consequence other than to clutter the analysis with small, theoretically meaningless coefficients. One possible exception, however, is a persistent negative relationship between state party identification and policy liberalism when other variables are controlled (see n. 9). Still another alternative specification would be to separate the indicator of party elite liberalism into separate variables. When all four indicators (based on legislators, congressional candidates, convention delegates, and county chairs) are used as separate independent variables, in each case the adjusted R-squared goes down, a clear diagnostic sign that the decomposition is ill advised. Division into two separate variables representing candidates (congressional candidates and state legislators) and party leaders (delegates and chairmen) has some appeal. However, the correlation of .82 between these separate two-indicator composites results in too much multicolinearity to disentangle any separate effects.

6. Testing this proposition directly requires the measurement of state party positions and state opinion on a common scale. Suppose we assume the metric that we used for party positions for the construction of Figure 5. Using this scale, we should find the least Democratic success when the midpoint between the parties is more liberal than state opinion. Indeed, the correlation between the

party midpoint-state opinion difference and Democratic legislative strength is strongly negative (−.63). In 38 of the 46 states, whether the midpoint between the parties is to the left or to the right of state opinion predicts whether the Democrats win more or less than their average percentage of the legislative seats.

7. For an alternative demonstration that bypasses the measure of legislative liberalism, consider the regression of state policy liberalism on party elite liberalism, state opinion, and Democratic legislative strength. From this equation, the coefficient for Democratic legislative strength is a negligible −.02. Thus, holding constant both state opinion and the positions of the state parties, Democratic legislative strength does not predict more liberal policies.

8. Just as we have a measure of legislative liberalism, based on weighting state party positions by their legislative strength, so, too we can measure the ideological positions of *losing* legislative candidates, weighting party positions by the legislative strength of their opponents. Gratifyingly, when this variable is added to the policy equation, it yields a coefficient of only .01. The ideological positions of state parties matter only in proportion to their electoral strengths.

9. Apart from controlling for region, the one other specification found to reduce the negative coefficient for legislative liberalism appreciably was to control for state party identification. Democratic party identification is somewhat negatively related to policy liberalism, even outside the South. This oddity suggests the possible presence of some unmeasured variable that accounts for both Democratic strength and policy conservatism, causing these two variables to covary.

10. The effect of party control on policy conceivably varies across states, with party control being most important in states where parties approximate the ideal of programmatic, disciplined parties. Perhaps in such states we would find that Democratic legislative success has a direct positive effect on policy liberalism. Accordingly, we reexamined the party effect after sorting on several measures of state party characteristics. We sorted on party competition (Ranney, 1971), legislative party cohesion (LeBlanc, 1969), state party strength (Cotter et al., 1984), party diversity (Garand, 1985), interparty policy differences (using our own measures), and polarization of party identification based on ideology (from our state opinion data). When examining the top scoring states on each of these variables, we still found in each instance the estimated direct impact of Democratic legislative strength on policy liberalism to be negative.

REFERENCES

Aldrich, John H. 1983. "A Downsian Spatial Model with Party Activism." *American Political Science Review* 77:974–90.

Alt, James E. 1985. "Political Parties, World Demand, and Unemployment: Domestic and International Sources of Economic Activity." *American Political Science Review* 79:1016–40.

Beck, Nathaniel. 1982. "Parties, Administrations, and American Macroeconomic Outcomes." *American Political Science Review* 76:83–93.

Browning, Robert X. 1985. "Presidents, Congress, and Policy Outcomes: U.S. Social Welfare Expenditures, 1949–77." *American Journal of Political Science* 29:197–216.

Calvert, Randall L. 1985. "Robustness of the Multidimensional Voting Model: Candidate Motivations, Uncertainty, and Convergence." *American Journal of Political Science* 29:69–95.

Cameron, David C. 1978. "The Expansion of the Public Economy: A Comparative Analysis." *American Political Science Review* 72:1243–61.

Castles, Francis G. 1982. "Politics and Public Policy." In *The Impact of Parties on Public Expenditures*, ed. Francis G. Castles. Newbury Park, Calif.: Sage.

Cotter, Cornelius, James Gibson, John Bibby, and Robert Huckshorn. 1984. *Party Organizations in American Politics*. New York: Praeger.

Downs, Anthony. 1957. *An Economic Theory of Democracy*. New York: Harper.

Dye, Thomas R. 1966. *Politics, Economics, and the Public: Political Outcomes in the American States*. Chicago: Rand McNally.

Dye, Thomas R. 1979. "Politics vs. Economics: The Development of the Literature on Policy Determinism." *Policy Studies Journal* 7:652–62.

Dye, Thomas R. 1984. "Party and Policy in the States." *Journal of Politics* 46:1097–1116.

Erikson, Robert S., Norman R. Luttbeg, and Kent L. Tedin. 1988. *American Public Opinion: Its Origins, Content, and Impact*. 3d ed. New York: Macmillan.

Erikson, Robert S., and Gerald C. Wright, Jr. 1989. "Voters, Candidates, and Issues in Congressional Elections." in *Congress Reconsidered*, 4th ed., ed. Lawrence C. Dodd and Bruce I. Oppenheimer. Washington: Congressional Quarterly.

Farah, Barbara G., M. Kent Jennings, and Warren E. Miller. 1981. "Convention Delegates: Reform and the Representation of Party Elites, 1972–1980." Presented at the Conference on Party Activists, Williamsburg, Va.

Garand, James C. 1985. "Partisan Change and Shifting Expenditure Priorities in the American States, 1945–1978." *American Politics Quarterly* 13:355–91.

Goodin, Robert E. 1983. "Voting through the Looking Glass." *American Political Science Review* 77:420–34.

Hibbs, Douglas A. 1977. "Political Parties and Macroeconomic Policy." *American Political Science Review* 71:1467–87.

Hibbs, Douglas A. 1987. *The American Political Economy: Macroeconomic Politics in the United States*. Cambridge, Mass.: Harvard University Press.

Hicks, Alexander, and Duane Swank. 1984. "On the Political Economy of Welfare Expansion." *Comparative Political Studies* 17:81–119.

Jackman, Robert W. 1975. *Politics and Social Equality: A Comparative Analysis*. New York: John Wiley.

Jackman, Robert W. 1980. "Socialist Parties and Income Inequality: A Comparative Analysis." *Journal of Politics* 42:135–49.

Jennings, Edward. 1979. "Competition, Constituencies, and Welfare Policies in the American States." *American Political Science Review* 73: 414–29.

Kiewiet, D. Roderick, and Mathew D. McCubbins. 1985. "Congressional Appropriations and the Electoral Connection." *Journal of Politics* 47:59–82.

Lange, Peter, and Geoffrey Garrett. 1985. "The Politics of Growth: Strategic Interaction and Economic Performance in Advanced Industrial Democracies." *Journal of Politics* 47:792–827.

LeBlanc, Hugh L. 1969. "Voting in State Senates: Party and Constituency Influences." *Midwest Journal of Political Science* 13:33–57.

Lowery, David. 1985. "The Keynesian and Political Determinants of Unbalanced Budgets: U.S. Fiscal Policy from Eisenhower to Reagan." *American Journal of Political Science* 29:428–60.

Magleby, David B. 1984. *Direct Legislation: Voting on Ballot Propositions in the United States.* Baltimore: Johns Hopkins University Press.

Miller, Warren E., and M. Kent Jennings. 1987. *Parties in Transition: A Longitudinal Study of Party Elites and Party Supporters.* New York: Russell Sage.

Moon, Bruce E., and William J. Dixon. 1985. "Politics, the State, and Basic Human Needs: A Cross-national Study." *American Journal of Political Science* 29:661–94.

Plotnick, Robert D., and Richard F. Winters. 1985. "A Politico-economic Theory of Income Redistribution." *American Political Science Review* 79:458–73.

Poole, Keith T., and Howard Rosenthal. 1984. "The Polarization of American Politics." *Journal of Politics* 46:1061–79.

Ranney, Austin. 1971. "Parties in State Politics." In *Politics in the American States,* ed. Herbert Jacob and Kenneth Vines. Boston: Little, Brown.

Ranney, Austin. 1978. "United States of America." In *Referendums: A Comparative Study of Practice and Theory,* ed. David Butler and Austin Ranney. Washington, D.C.: American Enterprise Institute.

Tufte, Edward R. 1978. *Political Control of the Economy.* Princeton, N.J.: Princeton University Press.

Uslaner, Eric M., and Ronald E. Weber. 1977. *Patterns of Decision Making in State Legislatures.* New York: Praeger.

van Arnhem, J., M. Corina, and Geurt J. Schotsman. 1982. "Do Parties Affect the Distribution of Income? The Case of Advanced Capitalist Democracies." In *The Impact of Parties on Public Expenditures,* ed. Francis G. Castles. Newbury Park, Calif.: Sage.

Winters, Richard F. 1976. "Partisan Control and Policy Change." *American Journal of Political Science* 20:597–636.

Wittman, Donald. 1983. "Candidate Motivation: A Synthesis of Alternatives." *American Political Science Review* 77:142–57.

Wright, Gerald C., Jr. 1986. "Elections and the Potential for Policy Change in the U.S. House of Representatives." In *Congress and Policy Change,* ed. Gerald C. Wright, Jr., Leroy N. Rieselbach, and Lawrence C. Dodd. New York: Agathon.

Wright, Gerald C., Jr., and Michael Berkman. 1986. "Candidates and Policy in United States Senate Elections." *American Political Science Review* 80:567–88.

Wright, Gerald C., Jr., Robert S. Erikson, and John P. McIver. 1985. "Measuring State Partisanship and Ideology with Survey Data." *Journal of Politics* 47:469–89.

Wright, Gerald C., Jr., Robert S. Erikson, and John P. McIver. 1987. "Public Opinion and Policy Liberalism in the American States." *American Journal of Political Science* 31:980–1001.

Reading 6

TAKING THE INITIATIVE: DIRECT LEGISLATION AND DIRECT DEMOCRACY IN THE 1980s

David B. Magleby

David Magleby examines the ways in which direct legislation—the initiative, the popular referendum, and the recall—is increasingly used at the state level. The constitutions and/or statutes of twenty-three states contain provisions for the initiative. The initiative process permits registered voters to write or sponsor a proposal, and if the appropriate number of valid signatures on a petition are gathered, the proposal is placed on the ballot.

There are two general kinds of initiatives: the direct initiative and the indirect initiative. The *direct initiative* provides that a proposal can be placed directly on the ballot by the voters without any intervening process except for a state official, usually the secretary of state, certifying to the qualifying signatures on the initiative petition. The *indirect initiative* means that a proposal which has received the appropriate number of qualifying signatures must first go before the state legislature for its consideration. The legislature has the opportunity to vote into law the measure as is, modify or amend it, or reject it. If the legislature does not satisfy the sponsors of the initiative, the sponsors may gather additional signatures and place their proposal on the ballot.

Forty-nine states provide that major constitutional revisions must be submitted to a general referendum vote of the people. Magleby notes, however, that while only twenty-five states provide for the popular referendum, the use of this device has been growing. The *popular referendum* provides for voters filing petitions with sufficient signatures to vote on actions taken by state legislative bodies.

Recalls of statewide officials are permitted in only fifteen states. Recall provisions are much more popular at the local level; forty states provide for this device in some of their local jurisdictions. The *recall* device permits petitioners with a specified number of signatures to call for an election for the specific purpose of voting yes or no on the removal of an official from public office.

Magleby found that there has been a notable increase in the frequency of initiatives and popular referendums throughout the states; this increase has been most apparent in California. The initiative is a powerful agenda-setting tool. The initiative campaign focuses the public's and the politicians' attention on the issue. Indeed, even if the initiative loses, it will often serve as a check on special interests and/or the state legislature. The initiative is also powerful in that it can help to "nationalize" a local issue. How initiative issues such as tax reduction, toxic wastes, nuclear power, etc., fare in one state often have great impact in other states and on the national government.

The dramatic increase in initiative politics is reflected in the development of an issue industry. Professional signature-gathering firms have emerged and have applied the campaign technology of direct mail and computers in circulating petitions, polling, and raising money. Magleby concludes that the availability of direct legislation significantly enlarges the role of voters in the American states.

The last decade has seen a resurgence in interest in three direct democracy devices—the initiative, the popular referendum and the recall.[1] These processes reflect the Progressive Era reformers' aim of enlarging the role of citizens and voters as well as restricting or checking the power of intermediary institutions such as state and local legislatures, political parties, and elected executives. The focus of this article is to examine the increased use of the initiative and popular referendum at the state level as well as how the process actually works.

STATEWIDE PROVISIONS FOR INITIATIVE, POPULAR REFERENDUM AND RECALL

The initiative process permits petitioners to write and, if a sufficient number of valid signatures are gathered, place those proposals on the ballot. The initiative can be placed directly on the ballot (the direct initiative); or before the legislature. If the legislature does not enact the measure or otherwise satisfy the sponsors of the initiative, the sponsors can gather additional signatures and place their proposal on the ballot (the indirect initiative). Five times as many states have the direct initiative as

Source: From *PS* 21 (Summer 1989). Copyright © 1989 by the American Political Science Association. Reprinted by permission.

the indirect and, in states that permit both, proponents typically prefer to go directly to the ballot.

The popular referendum permits voters to petition to vote on actions taken by legislative bodies if they can gather sufficient signatures, but often within a more constricted time frame than is the case with the initiative. It is important to distinguish the popular referendum from referendums in general. For instance, every state except Delaware requires major constitutional revisions to be submitted to a vote of the people, but only half of the states provide the popular referendum. Many states also permit advisory referendums and statutory changes to be placed on the ballot by local governments or the state legislature. Table 1 lists the states that provide for statewide initiative, popular referendum, and recall as well as the year in which one or more of these processes was first adopted and the type of initiative permitted by state. The bottom part of Table 1 summarizes the number of states having each of the processes.

The initiative, popular referendum, and recall are all products of the Progressive Era. In the two decades between 1898, when South Dakota was the first state to adopt the initiative and popular referendum,[2] and 1918, when Massachusetts adopted the indirect initiative and popular referendum, all but four of the states which now have the direct legislation adopted it. As Table 1 also shows, the process is distinctively western (Price, 1975). Only Arkansas and Florida provide for direct legislation in the South, and only Maine, Massachusetts and Maryland in the North-East. Initiative, popular referendum, and recall are much more extensively permitted at the local levels; only three states do not have one of these processes in at least some units of local government (National Center for Initiative Review, 1983).

The recall experienced a similar history and regional slant. Of the 15 states which provide for a recall of statewide officials, 10 placed these provisions in their constitution during the first two decades of this century; and, as with the initiative, the most recent statewide recall activity has been in western states (Cronin, 1981). Western states, as Table 1 demonstrates, are also the most likely to have adopted all three devices— initiative, popular referendum and recall. In 40 states there are provisions for recall at the local level in at least some jurisdictions (National Center for Initiative Review, 1983).

RENEWED INTEREST IN AND USE OF DIRECT LEGISLATION

There has been a dramatic increase in frequency of initiatives appearing on statewide ballots. The 1980s have seen a dramatic growth in the num-

TABLE 1   Statewide Provisions for Initiative, Popular Referendum and Recall

Region, state, and year adopted	State provisions			Type of initiative	
	States having the:			Direct, indirect, or both	Constitutional, statutory, or both
	Initiative	Popular referendum	Recall		
East					
Maine (1908)	X	X		I	S
Maryland (1915)		X			
Massachusetts (1918)	X	X		I	B
South					
Arkansas (1909)	X	X		D	B
Florida (1978)	X			D	C
Georgia (1978)			X		
Louisiana (1914)			X		
Midwest and Border					
Illinois (1970)	X	X		D	C
Kansas (1914)			X		
Kentucky (1917)		X			
Michigan (1908)	X	X	X	B	B
Missouri (1908)	X	X		D	B
Nebraska (1912)	X	X		D	B
N. Dakota (1914)	X	X	X	D	B
Ohio (1912)	X	X		B	B
Oklahoma (1907)	X	X		D	B
S. Dakota (1898)	X	X		D	B
Wisconsin (1926)			X		
West					
Alaska (1959)	X	X	X	D	S
Arizona (1910)	X	X	X	D	B
California (1911)	X	X	X	D	B
Colorado (1910)	X	X	X	D	B
Idaho (1912)	X	X	X	D	S
Montana (1906)	X	X	X	D	B
Nevada (1904)	X	X	X	B	B
New Mexico (1911)		X			
Oregon (1902)	X	X	X	D	B
Utah (1900)	X	X		B	S
Washington (1912)	X	X	X	B	S
Wyoming (1968)	X	X		I	S
Total	23	25	15		

States with initiative, popular referendum and recall, 11
States with initiative and popular referendum only, 11
States with initiative only, 1
States with popular referendum only, 3
States with recall only, 4
Initiative provisions: Direct or indirect initiative
          Direct only, 15
          Indirect only, 3
          Both direct and indirect, 5
        Constitutional or statutory initiative
          Constitutional only, 2
          Statutory only, 6
          Both constitutional and statutory, 15

Source: Summary of Statewide Provisions of Initiative, Popular Referendum and Recall.

FIGURE 1   Statewide Initiatives on Ballot and Adopted by Decade

On ballot	25	269	186	246	146	117	85	120	191
Adopted	17	98	49	96	59	39	39	44	81
	1900	1910	1920	1930	1940	1950	1960	1970	1980
	–09	–19	–29	–39	–49	–59	–69	–79	–87
					Decade				

The data points for the preceding figure are as follows:

Decade	On ballot	Passed
1900–1909	25	17
1910–1919	269	98
1920–1929	186	49
1930–1939	246	96
1940–1949	146	59
1950–1959	117	39
1960–1969	85	39
1970–1979	120	44
1980–1987	191	81

Sources: Sue Thomas, "A Comparison of Initiative Activity by State." *Initiative Quarterly* 3 (1984): 8–10; Virginia Graham, "A Compilation of Statewide Initiative Proposals Appearing on Ballots through 1976." Washington, D.C.: Congressional Research Service.

ber of popularly initiated (by petition) propositions appearing on statewide ballots. Figure 1 summarizes the number of initiatives on state ballots since 1900.

If present trends continue, the initiative will experience greater use in the 1980s than at any time since the 1930s, and in terms of initiatives adopted by voters, the 1980s could set an all-time high. The initiative was widely used in the 1910s through the 1930s but dropped off in the 1940–69 period. Even more dramatic than the rise in numbers of initiatives on the ballot is the number of proposed initiatives which have been officially titled and begun the circulation process. Measures are titled when the proponents submit their proposal to the state election officials with a modest filing fee. The trend is most pronounced in California, where 181 measures began the petition circulation process in the 1970s, surpassing the number of measures titled in all of the previous four decades combined, and more than tripling the previous high for a single decade. So far in the 1980s, 194 measures have been titled, meaning that more initiatives have begun the petition circulation process than in any other decade. Since 1898 the subject matter of initiatives nationwide is fairly uniformly distributed over such issue categories as health, welfare, housing, business negotiation, revenues and taxes, and public morality.

The popular referendum has also recently experienced renewed use in Idaho, Nebraska, South Dakota and North Dakota. However, issue activists often prefer to overturn legislative acts with the initiative because the requirements for qualifying a referendum are often more stringent than for an initiative; in states with the constitutional initiative, proponents can place their proposal directly in the state constitution.[3]

WHO USES THE PROCESS? HOW? AND WHY?

States that provide for the initiative, popular referendum and recall have adopted a wide variety of procedural rules. Among the most important rules are those that relate to ballot access. In order to qualify an item for the ballot, the campaign for the proposition must collect a sufficient number of valid signatures and, in some cases, also meet geographic distribution conditions or other requirements. The most stringent law for signature validation is probably found in Richmond, Virginia, where each signature for city-wide initiatives must be independently notarized. At the other end of the stringency continuum is North Dakota, which presumes each signature to be valid, a necessary consequence of the fact that North Dakota does not have voter registration. In addition, North Dakota also has the lowest signature threshold of any state, requiring only 2% of the 1980 census. The number of signatures required to qualify a petition in all other states is either a percentage of the total vote cast in the preceding general election or a percentage of votes cast in a previous election for a particular office, usually the governor. Making signature requirements a percentage of the vote rather than a fixed number, as in the Swiss constitution, has meant that ballot access has not become easier with time.

Where a state sets its signature threshold is a significant factor in determining the extent to which the propositions make it to the ballot. All three states with the most initiatives and popular referendums on the ballot since 1950 (North Dakota—75; California—74; Oregon—76) have comparatively low signature thresholds for statutory initiatives—2, 5, and 6%. The signature requests in each of these three states are higher for constitutional initiatives—North Dakota 40%; California 8%; and Oregon 8%—but in all cases these fall below the median for initiative states. Wyoming, on the other hand, has a signature threshold of 15% and has had only one initiative qualify for the ballot.

Both conservative and liberal groups have used the initiative and both have won some victories (Ranney, 1978). The general pattern has been to vote conservatively on life-style, moral and racial issues and more liberally on economic questions. Even more important than ideology, however, is the way the issue is simplified in the campaign.

By using the initiative device, issue activists have a powerful agenda-setting tool. Just getting on the ballot allows sponsors to attempt to focus public attention on their issue. The campaign is often a contest to see which side can define the ballot issue in terms best suited to their electoral objectives. Because a vote in a single state is often seen has having national implications, the incentive to go to the ballot is even greater. Politicians, whom the process was designed to check, have also discovered that advocating and using the initiatives can be politically useful. In states without the process, gubernatorial candidates such as Albert Quie in Minnesota and William Clements in Texas have in the last decade run a platform to establish the initiative. In states that already have the initiative, candidates often support and even sponsor initiatives as part of their campaign strategy. California Governor George Deukmejian made the "Victims Bill of Rights" initiative part of his campaign for the Republican nomination in 1982, just as previous Democratic Governor Jerry Brown had pushed a campaign reform initiative in 1974. In some instances, otherwise obscure persons, such as California tax reformers Howard Jarvis or Paul Gann, have become important state or even national figures by leading an initiative fight.

While initiatives can be isolated occurrences—the result of the political environment in a particular state or locality—they have increasingly become regional or even national in importance as proponents in one state form issue networks across state boundaries. The nuclear freeze, nuclear power, tax reduction, and spending limitation initiatives are all examples of this phenomenon (Zisk, 1987, pp. 218–21).

Initiative campaigns have also grown in importance in the 1970s and 1980s because of the sheer volume of advertising for and against some measures. In 1978, for instance, over $7 million was spent on the Clean Indoor Air initiative campaign in California, mostly by tobacco companies opposing the measure. This amount exceeded the expenditures of most statewide candidate general election campaigns, including the gubernatorial election. In the 1984 Missouri election more was spent on Proposition A, the Nuclear Power Plant proposition, than in the candidate contests for governor, lieutenant governor, secretary of state, and all state house and state senate races combined (Magleby, 1986). In 1984, 42 ballot measure campaigns nationwide cost over $73 million. On a single 1986 California ballot measure limiting public employee compensation, nearly $8 million was spent, but as is often the case far more money was spent on the "no" side, 85%, and the measure was defeated.

THE INITIATIVE INDUSTRY

It is not surprising that given the level of expenditures on direct legislation, an initiative industry has developed. Signature gathering firms have long been in the business of helping groups qualify their measure for the ballot. But during the 1970s and 1980s the industry has expanded and applied the new campaign technology of direct mail and computers in circulating petitions, raising funds, and polling. For instance, Howard Jarvis' tax reform propositions that have appeared on the California ballot since Proposition 13 in 1978 were qualified with signatures gathered entirely through the mail. Campaign contributions were solicited in the same mailers, and returns more than met the $1 million fee charged by the direct mail firm.

But getting measures on the ballot is only part of what the initiative industry provides its clients. Polling, media production, direct mail, campaign management, and legal services are other areas where initiative politics have become more professionalized. With the growth in professionalization of the process has come an increase in expenses. It now costs between $1.25 and $5.00 per signature in California if a group wants to use professional signature circulators (Rosenthal, 1988, p. 22). As expensive as this is, the media consulting, production, and purchasing services are even more costly, amounting to as much as half a million dollars for consultants in a single ballot measure campaign (King, 1986a). Consultants often prefer ballot measure elections to candidate contexts because, as one campaign consultant recently said: "Ballot measures don't go sailing to Bimini on the Monkey Business" (Rosenthal, 1988). Not only are initiatives easier to manage than candidates, they are more easily packaged and presented to voters. The strategy is to find "holes [that] can be punched, twists applied. Key arguments can be mined from obscure phrases" (King, 1986a). The decisions about what themes to present, and where and how to present them, bring together all of the elements of the new campaign technology (e.g., computers, electronic media) in an effort to shape public opinion and win the election.

Law is another profession important to the politics of direct legislation. Because the Progressives wanted to insulate these processes from politicians and normal institutional constraints, they removed these processes from the normal checks and balances of legislatures and executives. However, this has resulted in making the courts the policemen of the process. Typically, the litigation over procedural matters begins even before the election and can continue for years if the proposition was approved. Increasingly, courts in several states are striking measures from the ballot on constitutional grounds (Gordon and Magleby, 1988). Much of the judicial activity over this process has centered in California where the courts have not hesitated to declare unconstitutional a successful initiative. In fact, of the ten initiatives approved by California voters between 1960 and 1980, six were struck down in whole or in part by state and federal courts (Magleby, 1984).[4]

VOTING ON BALLOT PROPOSITIONS

Direct legislation is issue voting and therefore quite different from partisan candidate elections in the level of voter involvement, interest and information needed. In candidate elections the voters can and do depend to a substantial extent upon their party identification and the voter's judgment of the candidates' qualities as well as the candidates' name identification (Campbell, 1960). When deciding how to vote on initiatives and referendums, however, party and candidate appeal are important only insofar as parties and politicians take sides on the issue at hand. Without party identification or a candidate's personality or experience as handy economizing devices, voters must actually form their own positions on the issue. In some cases, the issues are either arcane, obscure, or both; and unless there is an advertising blitz it is perhaps not surprising that as many as half of the registered voters report not having seen or heard of a proposition when questioned in a final survey only a few days before the election.

Moreover, on election day as many as one out of four voters "drop off" by failing to vote on one or more ballot questions; and, on initiatives, about 10% drop off (Magleby, 1984, pp. 83–95). It is also not surprising that voters are much more likely in partisan candidate elections to decide their votes early in the campaign than in ballot proposition elections. In the 1982 Michigan public utility propositions, where several million dollars were spent in advertising, more than 40% of those polled did not decide how they would vote until election day or a few days before. Over one-fourth of all voters decided their vote on the 1976 California nuclear power initiative the last weekend before election day; and 19% of Utah voters indicated in a statewide exit poll that they decided their vote on Proposition I, a legislatively proposed tax measure, on election day. This compared to 7% of the same sample who decided their U.S. Senate vote on election day.[5]

Voting intentions are much less stable on ballot propositions than in candidate races. It is often the case that as the proposition campaign proceeds and voters hear both sides of the argument the numbers of unde-cided voters increase rather than decrease, where the opposite is the case in candidate races. Mervin Field, the respected California pollster, has said that "voters seldom have clearly defined opinions about ballot mea-sures" (Baker, 1977, pp. 13–14).

While direct legislation is issue voting, it is important to underscore that all voters may not perceive the question before them in the same way. A proposition on the regulation of public utilities may be perceived by some voters to be a referendum on jobs and energy; a proposition lim-iting smoking to certain designated areas may be understood as a refer-endum on excessive government regulation. The actual wording of the proposition and its short summary on the ballot are typically written by the Secretary of State or Attorney General in such a way that only those with an advanced education are likely to read and understand them (Magleby, 1984, pp. 118–19). Thus many voters will not actually read Amendment #4 but instead may only recall how it has been character-ized to them in television and radio advertising and by the news media. Gary Lawrence, a California pollster with extensive initiative campaign experience, said: "we are going to try to figure out the best possible in-formation to give the people to swing them and the other side is going to be doing the same thing. That's as close as you get to a debate in the ini-tiative process" (King, 1986, p. 10).

In a number of states opinion reversals were up to three times as likely to occur in proposition campaigns as in candidate races, with nearly half of the proposition campaigns ending in opinion reversals. The typical pattern of opinion reversal is from a "yes" to a "no" vote as the campaign proceeds (Magleby, 1988). There are some issues upon which voters exhibit what I have called "standing opinions." On these is-sues the aggregate of voters' opinions change very little throughout the campaign. For instance, on death penalty initiatives there is little fluctua-tion over time in voting intentions because people have strongly held views. But as noted "standing opinion" issues arise less frequently than issues where opinions are more fluid. It is in this latter category of issues that the campaign is crucial in defining and simplifying the choice for voters.

This issue definition and simplification process has, to a significant extent, been mastered by the initiative industry, especially on the "no" side. Fears, concerns, and in some cases, confusion about the conse-quences of the measure are raised in the early advertising campaign. The opposition plays on the tendency to preserve the status quo. The issue is characterized as unnecessary, unpredictable or dangerous. In the last stages of the campaign the message is often that everybody who is anybody is opposed to this measure, and you should be too. When these themes are combined with the reality that the "no" side is often able to significantly outspend the "yes" and that "no" money is more effective than "yes" money (Magleby, 1986, p. 18), it is not surprising that the observed pattern of "yes" to "no" voting shifts occur over time.[6]

IMPACT OF THE PROCESS

Direct legislation and direct democracy give tremendous power to the persons who can determine the issues placed before the voters at the next election. It has in some instances served as a potent check upon special interests, a reluctant legislature, or both. But more often those who use the process either can afford the costs of the initiative industry or rely upon highly motivated volunteers to meet the signature threshold. Interestingly, the initiative issue agenda only rarely reflects the concerns voters list as the most important problems facing government. One way to broaden the initiative agenda would be to lower the signature threshold and permit more propositions to qualify for the ballot. But in several states the likely increase in initiative and referendum activity would almost certainly either exceed the attention span or try the patience of even the most committed voters.[7] Lowering the signature threshold has not been seriously considered in any states in the recent past.

Although direct legislation is technically available to all voters, the rates of participation, knowledge and ability to translate general issue positions into intended votes on propositions are distinctively lower for less educated, poorer, and minority voters (Magleby, 1984). Even on issues of direct relevance, these voters are less able to participate effectively. The extent to which the processes of direct legislation can be seen as an expression of public sentiment on issues is questionable. The hurdle of complex ballot proposition wording appears to limit the participation of many voters (Magleby, 1984, p. 121).

The initiative can do more than exclude minorities from effective participation; it can be dangerous to their rights. The most famous example is the 1964 California initiative approved by voters overturning an open housing law previously enacted by the California legislature (Wolfinger and Greenstein, 1968). The problem remains in the 1980s as voters have decided measures targeted at various minority groups such as establishing English as the official language of the state, or quarantining AIDS victims.

Proponents of enlarging direct democracy, past and present, often assert that one reason turnout is low is that voters do not have meaningful choices. These direct democracy advocates suggest that one remedy to that situation would be to involve voters more directly in decision making about public policy via the initiative and popular referendum. While there is some evidence to support the notion that in a particular election a ballot measure might increase turnout, there is no evidence of any systematic increase in turnout as a result of adopting the initiative or having initiatives on the ballot (Magleby, 1984; Everson, 1981).

In states where the initiative has grown in frequency it has had a profound impact on candidate elections as well. Often the initiative has been diversionary, diverting voters' attention away from candidate choices for governor, U.S. Senator, and other offices to such issues as hand gun control, toxic wastes, clean indoor air, and homosexual teachers. These issues have made it increasingly difficult for candidates to establish their own issue agendas. It is not uncommon for candidates to sponsor or become closely identified with measures which will appear on the ballot at the same time. In this sense the initiative has become much more than a remedy for legislative inaction or abuses; it has become a driving force in the political and electoral process. There is no better example than California's tax reform Proposition 13 of the initiative's ability to serve as a corrective measure. But the more typical pattern is for an issue to emerge on the ballot from the periphery of the issue agenda; then, if it affects important and well-funded interests, the campaign becomes a battleground over whose version of the proposition is correct. Often the result of this process is voter rejection of the proposition and may lead to less attention paid to the other choices on the ballot, most notably the choices between candidates.

Direct legislation has moved to center stage in several American states and local governments. It is technologically possible to expand the scope of direct legislation further to include more frequent referendums on matters of public policy which could be debated on television with an immediate telephone or electronic vote (Arterton, 1987). This sort of tele-democracy has been experimented with in Ohio and Hawaii (Shirley, 1979; Becker and Slaton, 1980). Others have argued that the use of initiative, popular referendum, and recall at the state level ought to be available at the national level as well. Congressman Jack Kemp (R-N.Y.) is an advocate of this change:

> There are stronger democratic processes in the United States than in almost anywhere else in the world, but I think we have learned in the last decade that we could have used more....The time is right, I think, for the United States to take the lead in a fresh global wave of democratization that demonstrates the efficiency of government forms that rest on the wisdom of ordinary citizens. The most fundamental change we could

make, I think, is to provide for a national initiative, through an amendment to the Constitution (1979, pp. 159-62).

The initiative has had a significant impact on public policy and election campaigns.

For political scientists direct legislation is a theoretically rich area for research because it is so varied in its agenda and yet the research completed to date suggests patterns of opinion formation and opinion change across issues. These processes raise several questions: How involved should voters be in proposing legislation and voting on it? Who votes and doesn't vote on ballot measures and why? How do voters behave with this enlarged responsibility? What explains the voting calculus on ballot issues? What role do campaigns play? What impact do election laws have on citizens using devices like these? To what extent does the process influence political elites and institutions? What difference does the process make for public policy and the political system? Initiatives and referendums have the additional benefits of occurring frequently in many places, permitting political scientists to build the research base while working close to home, perhaps doing the research with their own students.

Direct legislation, and direct democracy more generally, significantly enlarge the role of voters. These devices raise anew the old debate of direct vs. representative democracy. Until recently, missing from this debate has been much study of the voter-legislator as well as the implication of electoral structures on the process. The initiative and referendum can and should be a laboratory in which to test several of these issues and inform this important debate.

NOTES

1. Choosing the party's nominees via direct primary was also a progressive era reform which made voters decision makers in a much more direct way. The direct primary experienced its resurgence earlier in the 1970s.

2. Oregon was actually the first state to vote on an initiative in 1902.

3. Initiatives can also establish the means by which they can be amended as in the case of California's Proposition 13 which required only a simple majority to pass but established the requirement for an extraordinary majority to raise the property tax limits contained in the amendment. Provisions like this are often tested in the courts and frequently found unconstitutional (Gordon and Magleby, 1988).

4. The California Supreme Court in the 1970s twice struck down death penalty initiatives, an issue which surfaced in the judicial retention elections of Chief Justice Rose Bird and three associate justices.

5. This pattern of greater voter uncertainty is true throughout the entire campaign. In the 1982 Michigan election, Market Opinion Research found in late September that 11% were undecided in the race for U.S. Senate [Riegle (D) vs. Ruppe (R)], and 14% were undecided in the Governor's race [Blanchard (D) vs. Headlee (R), and Tish (I)], while 78% were undecided in their vote on Measure D (an initiative requiring hearings for utility rate increases), and more than 90% were undecided about Measures G and H (an initiative establishing an elected public utility commission and the legislative alternative to Measure D). This same pattern persisted throughout the campaign (Magleby, 1988).

6. Of ballot measures placed on the ballot by the legislature, voter approval is significantly higher than for initiatives—with more than 60% of legislative propositions approved by voters but under 40% for initiatives (Magleby, 1984, p. 73).

7. It is not uncommon in some states to have as many as 20 ballot propositions on the general election ballot, and in states like California, which permit voting on propositions in the primary election, the number for each election has grown in past years. . . .

REFERENCES

Arterton, F. Chris. 1987. *Teledemocracy: Can Technology Protect Democracy?* Newbury Park, Calif.: Sage Publications.

Baker, Gordon E. 1977. American Conceptions of Direct vis-à-vis Representative Governance. *Claremont Journal of Public Affairs* 4:5–18.

Becker, Ted, and Christa Slaton. 1980. Hawaii Televote: Measuring Public Opinion on Complex Policy Issues. Presented at the annual meeting of the American Political Science Association, Washington, D.C.

Cronin, Thomas E. 1981. The Recall Device—Reconsidered. Presented at the annual meeting of the American Political Science Association, New York City.

Campbell, Angus, Philip E. Converse, Warren E. Miller, and Donald E. Stokes. 1960. *The American Voter.* New York: John Wiley & Sons.

Everson, David. 1981. The Effects of Initiatives on Voter Turnout: A Comparative State Analysis. *Western Political Quarterly* 29:415–25.

Gordon, James D., and David B. Magleby. 1988. Preemptive Judicial Review of Initiatives. Paper presented at the annual meeting of the American Political Science Association, Washington, D.C.

Kemp, Jack. 1979. *An American Renaissance. A Strategy for the 1980s.* New York: Berkeley Books.

King, Peter H. November 9, 1986. Consultants Are King in a Media Age. *Los Angeles Times.*

————. November 10, 1986. Strategists' Goal: Get inside the Public Mind. *Los Angeles Times.*

Magleby, David B. 1984. *Direct Legislation: Voting on Ballot Propositions in the United States.* Baltimore: Johns Hopkins University Press.

_____ . 1985. Ballot Access for Initiatives and Popular Referendums: The Importance of Petition Circulation and Signature Validation Procedures. *Journal of Law & Politics* 2:287–311.

_____ . 1986. Campaign Spending in Ballot Proposition and Candidate Elections: A Preliminary Assessment. Presented at the annual meeting of the American Political Science Association, Washington, D.C.

_____ . 1988. Opinion Formation and Opinion Change in Ballot Proposition Campaigns. In Michael Margolis and Gary Mauser, eds., *Manipulating Public Opinion*. Chicago: Dorsey Press.

National Center for Initiative Review. 1983. *Initiative Provisions by State*. Englewood, Colo.

Price, Charles M. 1975. The Initiative: A Comparative State Analysis and Reassessment of a Western Phenomenon, *Western Political Quarterly* 28:243–62.

Ranney, Austin. 1978. The United States of America. In Austin Ranney and David Butler, eds. *Referendums*. Washington, D.C.: American Enterprise Institute, 67–86.

Rosenthal, Andrew. May 15, 1988. Quest for Ideal Campaign: No Tears, No Monkey Business, No Candidate. *New York Times*.

Shirley, Don. July 17, 1979. Criticism for the Columbus Poll. *Washington Post*.

Wolfinger, Raymond E. and Fred I. Greenstein. 1968. The Repeal of Fair Housing in California: An Analysis of Referendum Voting. *American Political Science Review* 62:753–70.

Zisk, Betty. 1987. *Money, Media and the Grassroots: State Ballot Issues and the Electoral Process*. Newbury Park, Calif.: Sage Publications.

CHAPTER IV

STRUCTURE IN THE POLITICS OF STATE AND LOCAL GOVERNMENTS

INTRODUCTION

State governments are characterized by a separation of powers just as is the federal government. Each of the fifty states has executive, legislative, and judicial branches. Each branch is separately elected or appointed by voters or officials. Each has the capacity to check the others. Each has more or less power depending upon the authority granted in a state's constitution. However, many local governments (counties, cities, towns) are not characterized by a clear separation of powers as are the federal and state governments.

Some executive branches are highly centralized. The governor or the mayor is elected on a short executive ballot and possesses enormous appointment and removal power. The governor or the mayor also has the power to initiate the budget, possesses strong veto, and sometimes even item veto, powers. And, importantly, the governor or the mayor often has the power to reorganize the executive branch in line with his or her agenda priorities. Each of these attributes is said to contribute to an accountable, responsible, and responsive executive branch which can make efficient, economical, and effective public policies.

Some executive branches of state and local governments are very decentralized. The governor or the mayor is simply one of several executive branch officials elected on a long executive ballot. Many executive appointments are made by other elected officials. Concomitantly, the removal power of the governor or the mayor is also restricted: the governor or mayor may not remove those whom he or she has not appointed. The veto and reorganization powers granted to a governor or mayor may also be restricted.

Recently government officials at the state and local levels have sought to make their governments more effective through reorganization of their executive branches. Herbert Kaufman has observed that three political values have directed reorganization movements in the United States: executive representation, neutral competence, and executive leadership.[1] James L. Garnett, in his article, "Organizing and Reorganizing State and Local Government," reprinted in this chapter as Reading 7, spells out the general trends of all executive branch reorganizations at the state and local levels.

Also reprinted in this chapter as Reading 8 is "Politics and Power in the Sunbelt: Mayor Morial of New Orleans" by Huey L. Perry and Alfred Stokes. Examining the impact an African-American mayor had in providing increased economic well-being to the city's black population, they found that Mayor Morial's presence did make a difference in African-

American access to public jobs. They conclude that the "structure" of the population is critical in terms of who gets what, when, and how.

NOTE

1. Herbert Kaufman, "Emerging Conflicts in the Doctrines of Public Administration," *American Political Science Review* 50 (December 1956), pp. 1057-73.

ORGANIZING AND REORGANIZING STATE AND LOCAL GOVERNMENT

James L. Garnett

James L. Garnett begins his article by referring the reader to Herbert Kaufman's explanation of the alternative values traditionally sought by those who would organize and/or reorganize state and local governments. The three key values, according to Kaufman, are *representativeness* (belief in the electoral principle for legislative and executive officials), *neutral competence* (belief in the performance of government work according to objective standards and without regard to party or personal loyalties), and *executive leadership* (belief in giving the executive the means for overall direction of the administrative machinery).

Subsequently, Garnett outlines the forms of state and local government structure and points out the directions in which these governments have recently been organized and/or reorganized. He reports that although reorganizations at the state level have typically been in the direction of executive leadership, in recent years concern with fiscal and economic uncertainty has put state structural issues on the back burner.

The author also notes that the trend in county and municipal reorganization has been toward executive leadership, although at a slower pace since the economic slowdown beginning in the mid-1970s. He concludes that the greater complexity in governmental work and responsibilities at the state and local levels has resulted in an emphasis on single-executive forms and a deemphasis on plural-executive forms.

I. THE SEARCH FOR STRUCTURE

A. Relevance of Organizational Structure

Few issues in American state and local government have generated as much controversy and effort as have issues surrounding *structure*. Issues debated at length include the following: Does a strong governor system enable more effective state government than a weak governor system? Which structure is superior for municipal governments: strong mayor-council plan, weak mayor-council model, council-manager plan, or commission form? What are the potentials and risks for counties moving from the plural executive model to a single executive? Charles Hyneman showed how intensely government officials, scholars, and reformers have debated over structure when he wrote: "most of the rationalizers of state reorganization. . .appear to proceed blithely on the assumpion that God looks after fools, drunkards, and the liberties of the people" (Hyneman, 1939:73). These controversies over state and local structure were often battlegrounds for political and administrative theory (Hyneman, 1939; Waldo, 1948; Gottlieb, 1976; Garnett, 1980) and the testing grounds for structural reforms later adopted by the federal government (Graves, 1949:140; Garnett, 1980:18, 19).

Aside from people's fondness for crusades and controversy, why has so much attention been paid to structural-organizational issues? One reason is that structure affects the pattern of influence and indeed often reflects who has the upper hand. A multimembered county board with both legislative and administrative powers invites a "you scratch my back and I'll scratch yours attitude" (Adrian, 1976:165). Another reason for a preoccupation with structure stems from its effect on government performance. Despite the many attempts to prove the relevance or irrelevance of structure for government effectiveness, the picture is still unclear.[1]

Few would doubt that structure affects performance, but it is difficult to demonstrate how and to what degree this influence takes place. But, the quest to explore this relationship continues.

This chapter first addresses the emphases reflected in government organization and reorganization, then turns to look at the major struc-

Source: James L. Garnett, "Organizing and Reorganizing State and Local Government," in *State and Local Government Administration*, edited by Jack Rabin and Don Dodd (New York: Marcel Dekker, Inc., 1985), pp. 3–32. Reprinted courtesy of Marcel Dekker, Inc.

tures used in state, county, municipal, town, and special district governments and also at the trends in reorganizing those governments.

B. Emphases in Government Organization

State and local government organization and reorganization is a difficult subject to cover. The types of governments involved vary in size, legal status, and political culture. The structural forms differ even among governments of the same type. The motives for reorganizing and the tactics employed also vary considerably.

Because of the scope and complexity of the task, it helps to have a conceptual framework for explaining the patterns of state and local government organization. Herbert Kaufman's classic thesis on public administration doctrine provides such a framework (Kaufman, 1956).

In Kaufman's formulation, state and local (and national) administrative institutions:

> have been organized and operated in pursuit successively of three values
> ...representativeness, neutral competency and executive leadership.
> Each of these values has been dominant (but not to the total suppression
> of the others) in different periods of our history; the shift from one to another generally appears to have occurred as a consequence of the difficulties encountered in the period preceding the change (Kaufman,
> 1956:1057).

These stages in state and local administrative development and some characteristics of each stage are shown in Table 1.

1. REPRESENTATIVENESS

The first emphasis on the part of the state and local governments after independence was toward representativeness in government. This value had its roots in the colonial period and was, in effect, a reaction to the executive dominance exerted by royal or proprietary governors. Kaufman maintained that frequently during this period elected legislatures were seen as champions of the colonists in competition with governors appointed by the King of England or by a branch of directors of a chartered company (Kaufman, 1963:35).

After the Revolution, legislative bodies held the upper hand in most state and local governments and the executives were reduced to mere figureheads. For example, governors were elected by the legislatures in eleven instances, chosen for one-year terms in most cases, and for the most part had negligible powers of appointment and removal, no veto, no supervisory authority, no role in the budgetary process, no legislative

TABLE 1 Emphasis in State and Local Executive Organization: Three Stages of Administrative Development[a]

Characteristics	Representativeness (1787–Civil War)	Neutral competence (Civil War–WWI)	Executive leadership (WWI–Present)
Length of executive's tenure	Executive's tenure short—mostly one-year term	Term of executive increased to two years	Four-year terms with succession allowable
Executive's power of appointment (over administrative officials)	Executive's power negligible—direct election of administrative officers	Appointment power primarily with executive, but appointee tenure staggered and often longer than executive; often protected from removal	Executive has appointment and removal powers over department head
Degree of agency autonomy from executive	No supervisory authority over agencies by governor	Strong legal and administrative autonomy on part of agencies	Reduce autonomy of agencies; consolidate into larger functional departments under executive's leadership
Executive's role in budget	No role in budgetary process	Limited role in budget process	Executive budget
Personnel selection (nonagency heads)	Legislature chooses personnel	Merit apparatus chooses personnel (came to many jurisdictions late)	Opening up merit system to allow more appointees by executive
Executive's involvement in the decision-making process	Virtually all decisions made by legislative enactment	Greater involvement by executive in decision-making but still limited	Strong involvement by executive in decision-making process
Executive's veto power	No veto	Veto	Item veto
Length of ballot	Long ballot	Shorter ballot	Short ballot
Executive's responsibility for administrative action	Low	Moderate	High
Overall power position	Legislative supremacy	Legislative/bureaucratic/executive stalemate	Executive supremacy

[a]Kaufman does not indicate what the governor's budget role was during the phase emphasizing "neutral competence." It could be assumed that the governor's role was primarily greater than that during the representativeness phase and less than that during the predominantly "executive leadership" stage.

Source: From Kaufman (1956, 1963).

function worth noting, no investigatory powers, and practically no staff aid.

Supremacy of the elected legislative body was one reflection of the emphasis placed on representativeness during this period. An almost unquestioning belief in the electoral principal constituted the other element of the "core value" of representativeness. Kaufman describes how faith in the electoral principle was carried to excess:

> The first half of the Nineteenth Century saw the number of elective offices sharply increased, especially after the Jacksonian Revolution burst upon the country. The ballot grew in length until almost every public official from President down to dogcatcher came to power via the electoral route (1956:1059).

Carried to this extreme, it became evident about the time of the Civil War that legislative supremacy, the long ballot, and the spoils system did not increase representativeness in state or local government, but indeed had the opposite effect. Voter confusion and resulting apathy plus lack of cohesion provided the opportunity for political machines to achieve power. Whereas these machines did provide some cohesion, corruption often resulted and decision-making was hardly representative.

2. NEUTRAL COMPETENCE

Unbridled representativeness had proven to be dysfunctional, and reforms were sought to remedy the excess that had resulted. The direction these reforms generally took was toward neutral competence. In Kaufman's terms this core value involved "the ability to do the work of government expertly, and to do it according to explicit, objective standards rather than to personal or party or other obligations and loyalties. The slogan of the neutral competence school became, 'Take administration out of politics' " (Kaufman, 1956:1060).

The mechanisms for achieving neutral competence were using independent commissions and boards to conduct state and local government business and installing and expanding the merit system. Bipartisan and staggered appointment to these boards and commissions was intended to make these bodies more resistant to partisan or corrupt influence, but these measures also had the effect of limiting the chief executive's control over these agencies.

Much of state and local administration at this point could be characterized by fragmentation, proliferation, lack of overall direction, virtual capture of many "islands of decision-making" by special interests. Just as excessive stress on representativeness resulted in problems that proponents of that doctrine had not anticipated, so too did inordinate reliance upon neutral competence lead to overcompensation and dysfunction in state and local government.

3. EXECUTIVE LEADERSHIP

Kaufman contended the "centrifugal drives of the representativeness and neutral competence institutions...found no important counterforce in the legislature or in the courts" (1956:1063). The executive (governor, county executive, mayor or city manager) was thus turned to as a means of giving overall direction to drifting administrative machinery. The formula for achieving executive leadership was essentially that proposed by the administrative orthodoxists—consolidating a large number of agencies into a smaller number of departments organized along functional lines while being legally and politically responsible to the executive. Other elements included augmenting the executive's control through executive budget, shorter ballot, increased veto power, and additional staff assistance.

This framework adds perspective to the more detailed discussion that follows.

II. STATE GOVERNMENT ORGANIZATION AND REORGANIZATION

A. FORMS OF STATE ORGANIZATION

State government structures are usually classified as weak governor systems or strong governor systems. *Weak governor* systems carry over the colonial suspicion of strong executive rule and emphasize representativeness and neutral competence. Further, these systems are characterized by a long ballot (a number of executive branch officials elected besides the governor), weak power of governor to appoint department heads, a large number of state agencies, heavy reliance on boards and commissions to handle administrative work, and relatively weaker gubernatorial bugetary and other powers.

Strong governor systems emphasize Kaufman's core value of executive leadership reflecting strong appointive and removal powers, fewer, more consolidated administrative agencies, and more power centralized in the governor's hands. According to Charles Adrian, Alaska, California, Idaho, Kentucky, New York, Ohio, Pennsylvania, Rhode Island, Virginia, and Washington use strong governor systems (Adrian, 1976:169). Keep in mind, though, that these classifications refer to *formal organization structure*. A governor in a weak governor system may have tremendous informal power because of strong political party discipline, patronage power, force of personality, or some other reason. Likewise, a governor in a strong governor state may lack the experience, expertise, or backing necessary to take advantage of his considerable formal powers.

B. Reorganizing State Government: Types and Trends

A typology developed by George Bell is useful for tracking structural patterns in state reorganization. According to Bell (1973, 1976) there have been three principal types of state reorganization—traditional, cabinet, and secretary-coordinator. The *traditional* type most closely embodies the core value of neutral competence. This is because most state executive branches reflected the dominance of neutral competence when the modern reorganization movement began around 1910. The traditional reorganization is the least drastic, leaving more of the premovement status quo than the other types. A larger number of state agencies, higher proportion of boards and commissions, lower gubernatorial appointment power, and diffused managerial control are characteristic of the traditional reorganization. This type also contains more representativeness since more elected administrators besides the governor are usually found in this structure. (See Table 2 for definitions of the primarily structural dimensions of these three types.)

The *cabinet* type embraces more of the elements of Kaufman's executive leadership value. This includes stronger gubernatorial appointment power, less diffused managerial control, and a lower proportion of agencies run by plural executives.

The *secretary-coordinator* type also is oriented toward the value of executive leadership. This interposes a supercoordinator department-secretary between the governor and the heads of operating departments in an umbrella, superagency structure. It goes further toward the ideal of executive leadership than does the cabinet form, except for the higher degree of management authority retained by the component operating agencies.

Table 3 shows overall patterns in adoption and structure of state executive reorganization from 1910 to 1981. Of the 154 state executive branch reorganizations attempted during this period, 39 (25%) resulted in no adoption at all, and 115 (75%) resulted in adoption of at least some proposals. Based on these results, it would appear that there were favorable odds (about 3:1) of at least some reorganization provisions being adopted. These odds have shifted over time, increasing from the 42 and 57% adoption rates in the 1910s and 1920s to the 90% + rate in the 1960s and 1970s.

Part of the explanation for the more receptive climate for adopting

TABLE 2 Types of State Reorganization

Dimension 1: number of agencies after reorganization
Traditional: (high) ≥ 17
Cabinet: (medium) 9–16
Secretary-coordinator: (low) 1–8

Dimension 2: degree of functional consolidation
Traditional: (low consolidation) over 50% of all consolidation is into single-function agencies, narrowly defined (e.g., water supply, highways)
Cabinet: (moderate consolidation) over 50% of all consolidation is into single-function agencies, broadly defined (e.g., environmental protection, transportation)
Secretary-coordinator: (high consolidation) over 50% of all consolidation is into very large multiple-function or broad single-function agencies (e.g., human resources, natural resources)

Dimension 3: proportion of postreorganization department heads appointed by governor
Traditional: (low) $<50\%$
Cabinet: (moderate) 50%–66%
Secretary-coordinator: (high) $\geq 67\%$

Dimension 4: proportion of postreorganization agencies with plural executives (e.g., boards or commissions)
Traditional: (high) $\geq 25\%$
Cabinet: (moderate) 10%–24%
Secretary-coordinator: (low) $\leq 9\%$

Dimension 5: degree of management authority retained by transplanted agencies
Traditional: (high) most (50%) of the reorganization transplants involve transplant of agencies into other units, with the transplanted agencies primarily retaining their statutory authority, structural identity, and control over management support services (e.g., budgeting, purchasing)
Cabinet: (low) most (50%) of the reorganization transplants involve transplants into other units, with the transplanted agencies primarily relinquishing statutory authority, structural identity, and control over management support services
Secretary-coordinator: (moderately high) most (50%) of reorganization transplants involve the transplant of agencies into superagencies, with the transplanted agencies primarily retaining their structural identity and much of their statutory authority while relinquishing some control over management support services (e.g., submitting to budget review by the superagency)

Source: From Garnett (1980).

TABLE 3   State Executive Branch Reorganization: Adoptions, Failures, and
Types, 1910–1981

	Reorganization[a]		Types[b]		
Years	Adoptions	Failures to adopt	Traditional	Secretary-coordinator	Cabinet
1910–1919	5 (42%)	7 (58%)	4 (40%)	1 (10%)	5 (50%)
1920–1929	21 (57%)	16 (43%)	10 (42%)	0	14 (58%)
1930–1939	25 (76%)	8 (24%)	15 (63%)	0	9 (37%)
1940–1949	12 (75%)	4 (25%)	5 (71%)	0	2 (29%)
1950–1959	8 (89%)	1 (11%)	3 (60%)	0	2 (40%)
1960–1969	24 (92%)	2 (8%)	11 (65%)	3 (18%)	3 (18%)
1970–1979	20 (95%)	1 (5%)	8 (47%)	2 (12%)	7 (41%)
1980–1981	0	0	0	0	0
Totals	115 (75%)	39 (25%)	56 (54%)	6 (6%)	42 (40%)

[a]Adoptions includes those reorganization attempts where at least some restructuring
is adopted. Failures includes those attempts where no reorganization was adopted.
[b]Types are defined in Table 2. Not every reorganization could be typed because of
missing data.
Source: From Garnett (1980); Bell (1973, 1976); and Beyle (1982).

executive branch reorganizations is a greater perceived need for modernizing state governmental machinery. The increased demands and problems facing state governments in the post–World War II era have created
pressures for states to revamp their administrative apparatus to cope. In
the words of Mosher:

> Herein lies a basis rationale, and often the underlying reason, for admin-
> istrative reorganization: to bring up-to-date, or to permit the bringing up-
> to-date, of those aspects of organizational operation and relationships
> that have suffered from "lag"—i.e., that have failed to modify themselves
> through incremental changes sufficiently to keep up with the changing
> context within which they operate (1967:494).

Many executive branch reorganizations in the 1960s and 1970s accompanied an expanded, more active role for states in delivering services
to residents and in relating to federal and local governments.

But these administrative adjustments were not always consistent
with executive leadership values. The less reform-oriented traditional reorganization has been applied more frequently overall (56 times, 54%)
than the more reform-minded secretary-coordinator (6 times, 6%) and

cabinet (42 times, 40%) models. In fact, application of the more rigorous cabinet type patterned after the federal executive branch model has been applied more than might have been expected in light of the greater political and legal efforts necessary for thoroughgoing reform.

Because early reformers like A. E. Buck and Luther Gulick advocated more sweeping reform, and because state machinery then needed more drastic overhaul, states attempted a higher proportion of cabinet reorganizations in the 1910s and 1920s than in later decades. The secretary-coordinator type is a relatively recent phenomenon even though Iowa attempted, but failed to adopt, this type in 1915. California (1961 and 1968), Massachusetts (1969), Virginia (1972), and Kentucky (1972–1973) adopted the secretary-coordinator type patterned after the Department of Health, Education, and Welfare (HEW) model in which many related agencies are clustered in a large umbrella department. But a more recent trend has been away from having so many functions consolidated in so few departments. Such superagencies are usually expensive because extra layers of administration are needed to coordinate many programs and subagencies.

Not only have some types of reorganization been used less in recent years, but states have also relied less on executive branch reorganization itself as a tool for change and reform. After a spurt of executive branch overhauls in the 1960s and early 1970s, no major reorganizations have occurred since 1977 when New Mexico, Connecticut, and West Virginia adopted broad-scale reorganizations. Several reasons exist for this diminished activity in state executive branch reorganization.[2]

1. Most governors and state administrators think structural overhaul is unnecessary in their state and have therefore not pushed for more structural change. According to Eric Herzik, no governors called for overall reorganization in their 1981 "state of the State" addresses compared with fifteen governors announcing reorganization plans in their 1973 addresses (Herzik, 1981). In addition, Deil S. Wright and Ted F. Hebert surveyed 1400 top state agency administrators in 1978 as part of their State Administrators Project (Advisory Commission on Intergovernmental Relations, 1980). They found that 62% of all respondents thought their state did not need major reorganizing. In only five states did a vast majority of respondents think major restructuring needed. Since all but three states—North Dakota, Texas, and South Carolina—have had at least one major executive branch reorganization, the need to bring state governmental machinery up to date is perhaps less keenly felt. And even in these states, incremental restructuring has taken place. As of 1983, South Carolina is strongly considering comprehensive reorganization.

2. That reorganizing that has occurred recently has been more incre-

mental, involving only a few agencies or functions at a time. Consistent with the trend away from comprehensive, all-eggs-in-one-basket tactics, recent reorganizations have been more focused and less sweeping. A study of reorganizations from 1900 to 1975 found that incremental tactics tended to fare better with legislatures and voters than did more ambitious tactics (Garnett, 1979, 1980). This did vary over time and by region, but incremental tactics were typically less risky politically. Examples of states recently undertaking agency-by-agency functional reorganization are: Arkansas, 1980 (energy); Illinois, 1981 (energy and natural resources); Indiana, 1980 (transportation-highways); Kentucky, 1980 (education, energy, and transportation); Louisiana, 1980 (higher education); Minnesota, 1980 (public utilities); Mississippi, 1980 (planning, housing finance, motor vehicles); Montana, 1981 (commerce); North Dakota, 1981 (higher education and corrections); Rhode Island, 1981 (education); Tennessee, 1981 (transportation); Utah, 1981 (energy and natural resources); Washington, 1981 (corrections); and Wisconsin, 1981 (local affairs and development) (Beyle, 1982).

3. Governors and other state officials have been preoccupied with other concerns, primarily with budget crises and the shape of the newest "new federalism." Recent financial crises brought on by inflation, rising costs, flagging tax revenues, and diminished federal aid have tended to take priority over structural reform. Even some of the reorganizing that has occurred has been of the cost-cutting variety. For example, Tennessee's 1981 reshaping of its Department of Transportation was an economy move (Beyle, 1982). In keeping with the recent economic climate, more emphasis has emerged in economy and productivity reforms than in structural change as such. Economy efforts concentrate on improving procedure and management systems and operations, moves more directly related to saving money. For example, in 1980, Kentucky's Governor John Y. Brown, Jr., established an Executive Management Commission "to introduce business practices into the operation of State Government." A team of state employees and business executives loaned to assist state government reviewed twenty agencies aiming to introduce economy and efficiency reforms. Louisiana's Governor David C. Treen started a similar joint economy drive in 1981. New Jersey, the state that started the reorganization movement in 1915, in 1982 dropped the idea of a general reorganization study. Instead, New Jersey's new Office of Management and Budget will spearhead a study to uncover and eliminate waste, duplication of effort, fraud, and abuse. Indeed, such economy and efficiency drives not only replace structural reorganization, they often accompany or follow it as was the case in Kentucky. For example, Colorado in the late 1960s and Oregon in the early 1970s followed struc-

tural reorganization with economy and efficiency campaigns designed to upgrade management practices.

Does all this mean broad-scale executive branch reorganization has gone the way of the saber tooth, that Professor Hyneman's warning is finally being taken seriously? Probably not. State reorganizing has typically occurred in cycles. States not only perceive the need to reorganize based on internal conditions, they also take cues from other states. It is likely then, that changing state responsibilities and changing relationships with federal and local governments will prompt executive branch reorganization in some states. These reorganizations (and similar conditions in other states) will trigger reorganization elsewhere.

Fiscal austerity and political and economic uncertainty now take priority over state structural issues. But whether this austerity and uncertainty vanish or become more pronounced, reorganization may well follow to adjust to changing conditions and changing state roles.

III. LOCAL GOVERNMENT ORGANIZATION AND REORGANIZATION

A. Types of Local Government

Unlike state governments that are recognized by the U.S. Constitution as full-fledged partners in the federal system, local governments have traditionally been creatures of their state with only the structure and powers their state chooses to allow them. States as architects of local government organization either specify the type of structure local governments may use (e.g., some states require all their counties to use the commission form which is described later) or give their local governments a choice of structures. Greater choice, either through state constitutional provision, statute, or grant of home rule powers to local governments, has been the recent trend.

Diversity in size, political climate, and administrative functions makes it difficult to classify local governments. But the classification shown in Table 4 has become generally accepted.

Table 4 shows that school districts and other special (water, sanitation, housing, fire protection, and so on) districts still comprise the majority of local governments, even though the number of school districts has declined significantly. Yet the number of counties, municipalities, and townships has remained fairly stable in the last two decades. This section focuses primarily on these general-purpose local governments and special districts, discussing each in turn.

TABLE 4 Number of Units of Local Government by Type, 1962–1982

	1962	1967	1972	1977	1982	1962–1982 ±	1962–1982 Change (%)
Counties	3,043	3,049	3,044	3,042	3,041	−2	−0.06%
Municipalities	18,000	18,048	18,517	18,862	19,076	+1076	+6.0%
Townships	17,142	17,105	16,991	16,822	16,734	−408	−2.4%
School districts	34,678	21,782	15,781	15,174	14,851	−19,827	−57.2%
Special districts	18,323	21,264	23,885	25,962	28,588	+10,265	+56.0%
Total	91,186	81,248	78,218	79,864	82,290	−8896	−9.8%

Source: U.S. Bureau of the Census (1983 and 1979), Table A.

1. COUNTY GOVERNMENT ORGANIZATION

Counties, derived from the English "shires" of Anglo-Saxon government, are among the oldest and most widespread forms of local government in the United States. Counties occur in every state except Connecticut, Rhode Island, and parts of Alaska, Montana, and South Dakota. Despite widespread use, patterns of county government vary widely among states and even within states. The major forms of county government include the *commission* plan, featuring a plural executive, and the *council-administrator* and *council-elected executive* forms featuring a single executive.

Commission Form. The most traditional and widely used form of county government is the *commission* form. More than 2398 (79%) out of 3040 counties (county-type governments) use the commission form (National Association of Counties, International City Management, 1978). The commission plan remains the only form permitted in Idaho, Iowa, Massachusetts, Oklahoma, Texas, Vermont, West Virginia, and Wyoming (Duncombe, 1977). Under the commission form an elected board of from 2 to over 100 has legislative powers, such as passing ordinances, adopting budgets, and also administrative powers, such as supervising some or all departments and appointing some administrative employees. A hallmark of the commission form is that "county commissioners share administrative responsibility with a number of independently elected 'row' officers who frequently include: a county clerk, auditor and recorder, assessor, treasurer, prosecuting attorney, sheriff and coroner" (Duncombe, 1977:41). This form embodies Kaufman's principle of representativeness with its emphasis on the long ballot, but it also has facets of the neutral competence value as evidenced by the many administrative boards.

In practice, many variations of the commission plan exist. The most common and important variations include:

1. Strong chairman. In many counties the chairman of the board, because of seniority, expertise, or willingness, makes daily administrative decisions. Other commissioners rubberstamp those decisions or delegate decisions to the chairman who functions in some ways like a county administrator.
2. Coequal commissioners. Where no strong chairman of the county board or commission exists, commissioners share leadership and duties, reaching decisions by consensus or vote. As with other commission forms, commissioners have many administrative as well as legislative duties.

3. Supervisor form. The *supervisor* plan is a special case of the commission form characterized by larger county boards ranging from about 20 to 117 members. Traditionally these boards had town or township supervisors sitting ex officio on the county board. The number of townships determined the number of seats on the board. The U.S. Supreme Court, in its landmark reapportionment case, *Baker v. Carr* (1962), reinforced by later decisions, challenged the unrepresentativeness of many supervisor plans. As a result, Wisconsin and Michigan shifted to other forms of the commission plan in the 1960s, and New York, the primary proponent of the supervisor plan, altered the means of selecting supervisors.

4. Strong supporting official. Another variation of the commission plan features a strong elected administrative official, typically a county clerk, who performs much of the administration function in addition to supervising elections, keeping records, and carrying out the other duties of his or her own office. This may particularly be the case when the clerk is full time and the commissioners part time and when there is a heritage of leadership from the clerk's office.

5. Strong appointed officer or assistant. This differs from the preceding variation in that the strong administrative official assisting the commission is appointed rather than elected. An appointed county clerk, administrative assistant, or other official assists the council in preparing the budget and advises commissioners on managerial matters (Duncombe, 1977).

6. Elected judge as commission chairman. In some states, such as Alabama, Tennessee, and Texas, an elected county judge serves as chairman of the county commission. These judges perform administrative duties in addition to their judicial responsibilities and in some cases have the power of an elected county executive.

Council-Admininistrator Forms. As with the commission form, a number of variations of the council-administrator plan exist. But two primary types are the *council-manager* and *council-administrator.*

1. Council-manager plan. This form features a professional manager appointed by the county legislative body—the county commission or board—and serving at the board's pleasure. County managers typically prepare the county budget, appoint most or all department heads, advise the board on administrative matters, and make daily decisions on programs and policies. The county board or commission under this plan performs the legislative role—adopting ordinances, approving taxes, and overseeing administrative operations. Iredell

County, North Carolina first adopted the council-manager plan in 1927. Dade County, Florida (population 1.2 million) is the largest user of this form.

2. Council-administrator plan. The council-administrator closely resembles the council-manager form, differing primarily in the powers held by the administrator. County administrators typically hold most of the budget and advisory powers county managers employ, but usually lack the power to appoint and supervise department directors. The council-administrator form predominates in California. Los Angeles County is the largest user of this form of county government. Of the three primary forms, the council-administrator/council-manager most emphasizes Kaufman's value of neutral competence, but includes some aspects of executive leadership.

Council-Elected Executive Form. The *council-elected executive* organization approximates the relationship between legislature and governor, and between council and mayor. The board or commission carries out the legislative functions, and the county executive is elected to preside over the administrative branch.

County executives typically have power to prepare the budget, recommend legislation, and appoint, supervise, and dismiss all or most department heads. But unlike the county managers, elected county executives usually have power to veto bills passed by the county board, although this veto can be overridden by a two-thirds majority (higher in some counties). Another difference lies in the number of independently elected county administrative officials. Council-executive counties typically have fewer elected administrative officers besides the county executive than do commission plan counties. Of the three basic county structures, the council-executive plan emphasize Kaufman's executive leadership value. Westchester and Nassau counties in New York in the 1930s were the first counties to adopt the council-elected executive form, now used by some other populous counties, such as Maryland's Montgomery, Prince Georges, and Baltimore Counties. In fact, Baltimore County's executive appoints a professional administrator to help supervise agencies, thus freeing the executive for more political and community relations functions.

2. COUNTY REORGANIZATION

The trend in county reorganization is toward *executive leadership*—centralizing more control in the hands of an elected or appointed executive. The use of council-executive structures has increased from 8 counties in 1950 to 142 counties and city-counties in 1977. The single-executive forms have been particularly employed by larger counties, as Table 5 shows.

Data from the *County Year Book 1978* show counties with administrators (administrators, managers, or executives) comprise only 21% of all counties, but 62% of all counties of 100,000 population or more.

Another trend has been toward expanding the services counties provide. Since counties, like other local governments, are creatures of state government, county services have traditionally reflected this role as local units of the state. These traditional functions are still provided: property tax collection (95.6% of all counties) and assessment (92.5%); election administration (96.8%); police protection via county sheriff's office (93.1%); road maintenance (87%); and recording of documents (97.2%). But added to these traditional ones are other services modernization and urbanization have forced or stimulated counties to adopt. Examples include: maternal and child health (74%); communicable disease control (79%); fire protection (54.5%); recreational services (45.3%); airports (42.4%); public assistance (45.6%); family social services (64.7%); and manpower work training (59.7%) (Lawrence and DeGrove, 1976). This expanded role (*local service provider*) supplements the county's traditional role (*unit of state government*) and has accompanied the trend toward executive leadership.

The push for county administrative reform has been limited, however. As the Advisory Commission on Intergovernmental Relations points out:

> While counties have been granted local home rule in 28 states, by 1980 only 75 counties had adopted home rule charters, of which 21 adoptions had occurred since 1972. On the structural front, moreover, over three-fourths of the counties still used the plural executive or board form of government including in 1978, 32 of the 137 counties with populations over 250,000 (ACIR, 1982:240).

As with state executive branch reform, county reorganization continues, but at a slower pace.

3. MUNICIPAL GOVERNMENT ORGANIZATION

The *1982 Census of Governments* defines a municipality as a political subdivision that meets several criteria. (a) Municipal *incorporation* has been established to provide (b) *general* local governments for (c) *a specific population concentration* in a (d) *defined area*. A municipality can be called a *city, village, borough* (except in Alaska, where boroughs are like counties), or *town* (except in New England states, Minnesota, New York, and Wisconsin). In these states, "town" relates to an area subdivision that may be in-

TABLE 5 Forms of County Government by Population Size

Classification	All counties	Counties over 2500	Counties over 5000	Counties over 10,000	Counties over 25,000	Counties over 50,000	Counties over 100,000	Counties over 250,000	Counties over 500,000	Counties 1,000,000 and over
Total, all counties	3040	2944	2751	2255	1274	679	343	137	63	19
Form of government										
Without administrator	2398	2306	2118	1673	838	371	150	43	16	4
With administrator	642	638	633	582	436	308	193	94	47	15

Source: National Association of Counties and International City Management Association (1978).

corporated and be a general government, but that is a geographic area unrelated to a population concentration.

For most citizens, a municipality is the government that most closely affects them. Of all local governments, municipalities in 1977 spent the most for direct services in police, fire protection, parks and recreation, housing, parking, libraries, and highways (ACIR, 1982).

Municipal governments take three basic forms: *Mayor-council, commission,* and *council-manager.* These forms parallel their counterparts at the county level, and also have variations.

Mayor-Council Form. The mayor-council form is used by 54% of all municipalities, 61% of those over 250,000 population, and 100% over 1 million population (International City Management Association, 1981).

Three major variations of the mayor-council form exist: weak mayor-council, strong mayor-council, and strong mayor-council with chief administrative officer.

1. Weak mayor-council. This form predominated in the early and mid-nineteenth century when cities and other municipalities were primarily small, rural and suspicious of strong executive control. Also consistent with the representativeness values of this era, mayors were supplemented with many other elected administrative officials: auditors, assessors, clerks, treasurers, and administrative boards and committees. Some weak mayors had veto power over council actions, but little or no power to develop a budget or coordinate the work of administrative agencies.

Weak mayor-council systems today are likely to have smaller councils than in years past, use nonpartisan elections, and allow the mayor to develop the budget as well as initiate and veto legislation. Weak mayor-council systems exist today primarily in smaller cities and villages, but some large cities, mostly in the South, have weak mayor forms. Chicago, technically, has a weak mayor system. But, as with weak governor systems, *formal* powers, or their lack, are only part of the picture. The late Mayor Richard J. Daley's ability to control administrative machinery via party and personal power has become legend. But [recent mayors have had] to manage a large, complicated, heterogeneous city using limited formal powers.

2. Strong mayor-council. The strong mayor form, like its strong governor and county executive counterparts, is an attempt to overcome the centripetal force of numerous elected officials, boards, and agencies pulling in different directions. The strong mayor form embodies Kaufman's executive leadership value—centralization of authority and responsibility in one office. The municipal reform movement beginning in the 1880s strongly promoted the strong mayor-council plan.

Today this form shows variations among municipalities. Typically, it features the veto and budget preparation powers of the weak mayor form, but gives the mayor few or no other elected administrative officials with whom to compete, fewer boards and commissions, and stronger mayoral appointive and budget administrative powers.

3. Strong mayor-council with chief executive officer. Emphasis on strengthening mayors to cure the ills of overrepresentativeness and independent bureaucratic fiefdoms left some problems unresolved. As with elected county executives and governors, mayors sometimes have greater interest and ability in campaigning, dealing with councils, and relating to community and interest groups than in overseeing administrative and service delivery operations. One remedy many cities use adds a chief administrative officer (CAO) to relieve the mayor of many managerial functions. Variously called "City Administrator," "Deputy Mayor of Operations," or some other title, these CAOs typically serve at the mayor's pleasure and oversee city administration. In some cities CAOs appoint major department heads subject to the mayor's approval. Cities that use the strong mayor-council with CAO system include Washington, D.C., New York City, Los Angeles, Philadelphia, Boston, and New Orleans.

Commission Plan. Like the county commission form of government, the municipal commission plan combines legislative and administrative powers within one body. Collectively, city commissioners serve as the legislature; individually, they administer city departments or functions. The mayor is usually one of the commissioners and serves a largely ceremonial role. But unlike the county commission form which predominates, city or village commissions are used by only 6% of all municipal governments and by only 2% of municipalities over 250,000 population.

After a brief period of popularity following its 1903 inception in Galveston, Texas, the municipal commission form has steadily declined in use since 1917. Today, primarily smaller cities use it. North and South Dakota cities show the highest use of the commission plan. Of the large commission cities, such as Portland, Oregon, and Tulsa, Oklahoma, a chief administrative officer is often used to manage the city (Press and Verburg, 1979). This reduces the problems of diffused authority and lack of coordination almost inherent with the commission form.

Council-Manager Plan. Just as the birth of the commission form was dramatic—civic leaders of Galveston banded together to run the city after a flood had killed or injured one-sixth of the population—the council-manager plan was born more of tedium. "In 1908, the city council members of Staunton, Virginia, became frustrated with the welter of 'administrivia' of city government that tends to crop up under any weak

117

executive model. They decided to hire a professional manager—the council could decide policy, the city manager would execute it" (Henry, 1980:156).

The council-manager form, like the strong mayor-council system, spread widely through efforts of municipal reformers in the Short Ballot Organization, the National Municipal League, in universities, and even in the United States Chamber of Commerce (Stillman, 1974:5–53). Business support for the council-manager plan is understandable in light of the plan's emphasis on "businesslike" efficiency. Under the basic plan, voters (stockholders) select council members (directors) who appoint a manager (chief executive) to oversee administrative operations.

The separation of powers strongly contrasts with the commission plan where commissions hold both legislative and administrative powers. In theory, city councils concentrate on making policy through legislation and allow the manager to administer that policy by preparing and executing the budget and appointing and supervising department heads. In practice, councils often delve into administrative details and city managers frequently initiate policy. Variations of the council-manager model itself also abound. For example, some plans include an elected mayor to serve with the council-appointed manager. The mayor's role in such hybrid forms varies from ceremonial figurehead to political leader, depending on the charter, the local political culture, and the mayor's relationship with the manager. Methods for selecting council members also vary. Some elections are partisan, most nonpartisan. Some council members are elected at large; some represent wards. Some cities have both ward and at-large representatives on the council.

Use of council-manager systems is greater in suburbs than in central cities, greater in the South and West than in the North and East, stronger in white-collar communities than in blue-collar ones, and higher in small and medium-sized cities than in larger ones. But some large cities like Dallas, Kansas City, Phoenix, and San Diego use this form. Of all municipalities, 36% use the council-manager form compared with 28% above 250,000 population and only 16% above 500,000. All cities above a 1 million population have mayor-council systems. But as reported earlier, some of those cities also have appointed administrators.

4. MUNICIPAL REORGANIZATION

The overall trend in the last 50 years has been toward the strong executive structures—the strong mayor form and council-manager plan. This trend includes an increase in the number of administrative agencies. Although precise data are unavailable, the overall number of agencies has likely risen to accommodate many new municipal functions, such as energy conservation, disaster preparedness, airports, and economic development. Accompanying the addition of new agencies to manage new functions has been a trend toward consolidating more functions into fewer, larger agencies of the former Department of Health, Education, and Welfare (HEW) mold. But some municipalities have joined several states in backing away from so much consolidation. New York City, for example, has dismantled several of its superagencies (e.g., Human Resources Administration and Housing Development Administration) because they were costly and tended to overdo "layering," screening directors of operating agencies from the mayor.

City-county consolidation, another approach to municipal reorganization, has been tried and, with exceptions, has had limited impact on reforming municipal government. Marando (1974:17–51), Zimmerman (1980), and the Advisory Commission on Intergovernmental Relations (1982:395–405) have thoroughly documented the political, legal, and economic obstacles to city-county consolidation and its limited use.

At the same time centralization has been the overall trend in municipal reorganization, some decentralization to community districts or service delivery districts within cities has also been undertaken (Shalala and Merget, 1974:153–177).

5. TOWNSHIP ORGANIZATION

"Township" according to the Census of Governments refers to "16,734 organized governments in 20 states. This category includes governmental units officially designated as towns in the six New England states, New York and Wisconsin and some 'plantations' in Maine and 'locations' in New Hampshire, as well as governments called townships in other areas" (Bureau of the Census, 1983). Townships differ from municipalities in that townships serve inhabitants of areas defined without regard to population concentrations. This reflects their roots as geographic subdivisions of counties. Another difference is that townships, unlike the other types of local government, are found in only twenty northeastern and north central states, rather than all or almost all fifty states.

Townships differ widely in role and powers. Town and township governments administer a wide variety of services, including fire and police protection; rescue services; road and bridge repair and maintenance; social services for the poor, elderly, and youth; and parks and recreation facilities. According to the U.S. Bureau of the Census, the most frequently reported township-owned and operated services are libraries, sewage disposal and treatment, landfills, and water supply.

Township structures vary as do their powers. The three principal township forms of governance are the town meeting, the representative town meeting, and council-administrator form.

Town Meeting Form. The town meeting, the closest American form to pure democracy, originated in New England and still sees use there and elsewhere. An annual or semiannual meeting where citizens directly discuss their concerns and vote on local policy is characteristic of this form. Budgets are prepared, ordinances passed, contracts approved, and other major business transacted in open meetings where eligible voters participate. Special meetings can be called by voter petition but most governing takes place in general, scheduled meetings.

Representative Town Meeting. The direct town meeting comes from an earlier, simpler era. Today, larger, urban townships and even many rural townships are too populous and too complex to be governed directly by citizens. In these instances, voters elect representatives called selectmen or councilmen, who serve on town boards or councils and act on the voter's behalf. Nonelected citizens may attend meetings but not vote. In some states, resident citizens are permitted to vote on a limited number of issues; some vestiges of the direct democratic form remain. Between meetings, township government is delegated to the board of usually three to seven members.

Council-Administrator Form. This form parallels the municipal council-manager plan and county council-administrator form. Part-time townships councils unable to handle day-to-day administrative routine have increasingly hired a professional administrator who serves at the council's pleasure. This trend has been particularly at work in New England and other strong township states where demands on townships are stronger. Township administrators function like city managers or county administrators, although typically without such broad responsibility.

6. REORGANIZING TOWNSHIPS

As just noted, a trend toward council-administrator structures exists. About half the township states use Administrators/CAOs to manage township affairs (Dvorin and Misner, 1970:139). This trend is consistent with Kaufman's executive leadership value and, to a lesser extent, neutral competency's emphasis on professional, apolitical administration. Despite this trend, township structures, especially in rural township states, tend to reflect the continued dominance of representativeness.

A more drastic form of township reorganization involves abolishing the township altogether. Five hundred and nine fewer townships existed in 1982 than in 1942. Most of this decline occurred in the Midwest where rural townships predominate. In fact, all rural township states lost townships between 1972 and 1977 except Indiana, where there was no change, and Illinois, which gained four (ACIR, 1982:248–252). Counties and sometimes municipalities have had to assume the load of abolished townships.

On the other hand, townships have increased in some areas, and the populations they serve have increased. Since 1977, township governments with at least 10,000 population increased by sixty-six and gained 2 million people. Similarly, townships with populations of 1000–10,000 gained in number and population between 1977 and 1982.

Townships, like other forms of local government, reflect tremendous diversity. No single level of powers, services, or structures holds for all townships. They vary because of geography, custom, law, politics, and the particular needs of the areas and people they serve.

7. SPECIAL DISTRICT ORGANIZATION

Special districts are limited-purpose units created to perform one or at most several functions. Special districts comprise the most numerous and fastest-growing (a 56% increase from 1962–1982) form of local government, as shown in Table 4. These figures likely understate the real number of special districts due to problems with *Census of Governments* definitions (Walsh, 1978:353–356).

Their narrowness of purpose distinguishes special districts from general-purpose local governments—counties, municipalities, and townships. School districts have traditionally been included in a separate category, although they really constitute a particular case of special district. Most, but not all, public authorities are considered special districts.

All states and the District of Columbia have local special districts. Yet, 64% of all special districts in 1982 were found in thirteen states— Illinois, 2602; California, 2506; Pennsylvania, 2050; Texas, 1681; Kansas, 1370; Missouri, 1195; Nebraska, 1157; Washington, 1130; Colorado, 1030; New York, 923; Oklahoma, 916; Indiana, 897; and Oregon, 825 (*Census of Governments*, 1982:xi). Three of the states relying on special districts most heavily (Illinois, Nebraska, and New York) lost districts between 1977 and 1982. But large increases in other states (especially Oklahoma, California, Texas, Missouri, Kansas, Montana, and North Dakota) offset these declines.

As Table 6 shows, 90.9% of all special districts perform a single function, although this percentage has dropped since 1972. Multiple-function districts, which usually perform no more than several services,

TABLE 6 Special Districts by Function: 1972, 1977, and 1982

By function	1972		1977		1982		Change 1972–1982	
	(No.)	(%)	(No.)	(%)	(No.)	(%)	(No.)	(%)
All special districts, total	23,885	100.0	25,962	100.0	28,588	100.0	+4703	+19.7
Single-function districts, total	22,981	96.2	24,242	93.3	25,991	90.9	+3010	+13.1
Cemeteries	1494	6.2	1615	6.2	1577	5.5	+83	+5.5
Education (school building districts)	1085	4.5	1020	3.9	960	3.4	−125	−11.5
Fire protection	3872	16.2	4187	16.1	4560	16.0	+688	+17.7
Highways	698	2.9	652	2.5	598	2.1	−100	−14.3
Health	257	1.1	350	1.3	451	1.6	+194	+75.5
Hospitals	657	2.7	715	2.8	775	2.7	+118	+18.0
Housing and community development	2271	9.5	2408	9.3	3296	11.5	+1025	+45.1
Libraries	498	2.1	586	2.3	638	2.2	+140	+28.1
Natural resources	6639	27.8	6595	25.4	6232	21.8	−407	−6.1
Parks and recreation	750	3.1	829	3.2	924	3.2	+174	+23.2
Sewerage	1411	5.9	1610	6.2	1631	5.7	+220	+15.6
Water supply	2333	9.8	2480	9.5	2637	9.2	+304	+13.0
Other[a]	1016	4.3	1195	4.6	1712	5.9	+696	+68.5
Multiple-function districts,[b] total	904	3.8	1720	6.6	2597	9.1	+1693	+187.2

[a]Includes parking garages and lots; water transport and terminals; airports; transit districts; and gas and electric utilities.
[b]Primarily districts combining sewerage and water supply, and a lesser number combining natural resources and water supply.
Source: U.S. Bureau of the Census, *Census of Governments*, 1972, 1977, 1982 (1973, 1978, 1983), Table 15 (1972), Table 12 (1977),
Table G (1982); Advisory Commission on Intergovernmental Relations (1982), Table 154.

are increasing faster than those performing single functions, but still comprise 9.1% of all special districts.

Table 6 also reflects the wide range of uses special districts serve. Between 1972 and 1982 special-district use increased in all functions except highways, school building, and natural resources, although natural resources and fire protection special districts continue to be the most widely used form. Housing and community development districts (up 45%) and health districts (up 75%) have proliferated since 1972.

Special district boundaries typically do not coincide with those of general-purpose governments. Only one-fourth of all special districts have boundaries that conform to those of counties, townships, or municipalities. And even though most special districts fall entirely within one county, about 9% of all districts extend into two or more counties (Bureau of the Census, 1983).

Critics claim the proliferation of special districts and their failure to coincide with general governments or with each other cause fragmentation and competition among governments. Another common criticism is that special districts, because they typically have their own revenue source and often investors to satisfy, are less accountable to voters (see Smith, 1964; Walsh, 1978).

For all the criticism surrounding special districts, many reasons exist for their widespread usage. First, despite complaints about special district infringement, general-purpose governments' managerial inability or political unwillingness to assume new functions has sometimes created need for special districts. Boundary restrictions have meant local governments are sometimes too small or bounded in the wrong places to handle functions, such as environmental control or water supply, where economic spillovers or economies of scale pertain. Second, fee-for-service financing, the cornerstone of most special districts, tends to be more flexible and more politically expedient than levying taxes. In fact, in this era of public sector retrenchment, general-purpose governments too are utilizing user fees more heavily. Special districts are also a means for circumventing spending restrictions on general-purpose governments. Third, federal government mandates and incentives have triggered some special districts. Districts or authorities for soil conservation, flood control, and housing are prime examples.

Most special districts and especially larger public authorities model their organization after private corporations (see Figure 1).

Most special districts have a part-time board of directors or commissioners charged with making policy. As with business, these directors usually take their policy cues from the full-time staff. But unlike business, special district directors are typically appointed by officials of those

FIGURE 1   Typical Organization of a Special-District Public Authority
(Adapted from Walsh [1978], Chart 3.1)

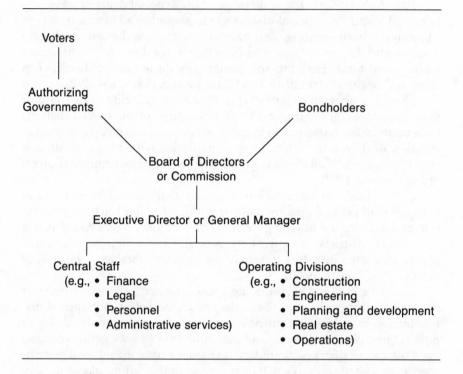

governments sponsoring the district or authority (e.g., governors, mayors, city councils, county executives) rather than bondholders. Directors are typically appointed for staggered terms, many overlapping those of appointing officials. This insulates directors from some, but not all, political pressures in an attempt to emphasize neutral competence. Directors or commissioners normally reach internal consensus on policy, presenting consensus decisions at open meetings.

Operating control is typically centralized in the hands of a general manager or executive director who holds most budget, appointment, and supervisory powers of city managers/CAOs, with greater autonomy than most city or county managers enjoy. Executive directors oversee central staff and operating units like those shown in Figure 1.

8. SPECIAL-DISTRICT REORGANIZATION

One form of special-district reorganization involves changing the method for selecting directors. Most directors are now appointed because they represent special economic or social interests in the district's service area. Another method is to appoint public officials who serve by virtue of their office as transportation commissioner or housing administrator, for example. Most districts have directors of the first type. Many combine private citizens and public officials on the board. To help make special districts more responsive to the public interest, constitutions or laws increasingly specify the inclusion of public representatives on the boards. Another trend is to select directors via direct election by voters. Direct election is more common in the Midwest and Far West, with special districts having taxing powers making them more like general-purpose governments (Walsh, 1978:188).

At the administrative level, reorganization often involves decentralizing powers and functions to staff and operating units closer to actual decisions and incorporating business methods. The Port Authority of New York and New Jersey has undergone several reorganizations of this type and serves as a model for many other special districts.

Special districts typically have greater flexibility to reorganize and to manage internal affairs. But modern structures and methods have yet to reach many special districts, especially the smaller ones. In 1976, 93.8% of all special districts had twenty or fewer employees, and 67.6% had no full-time equivalent employees (ACIR, 1982:253). Small districts may well be the grounds for future reorganization.

IV. OBSERVATIONS ON ORGANIZING AND REORGANIZING

Some general observations are in order. First, the general trend for state, county, township, municipal, and special-district organization has been toward executive leadership—greater centralization of power and consolidation of functions under a chief executive. The greater complexity and faster pace of our technocratic society have emphasized single-executive forms and deemphasized slower plural-executive forms. But this trend has not been universal. Some state and local governments have experienced decades of administrative consolidation, finding that executive leadership, as with earlier emphasis on representativeness and neutral competence, is no cure-all for government problems. This partly explains the slowdown in reorganization emphasizing far-reaching administrative centralization. Other governments with little executive leadership may continue to reorganize along those lines.

Second, any discussion of state and local structure leads to an inescapable conclusion: structures and practices are incredibly diverse, making generalizations risky at best. For example, generalizations about the capacity of states, the efficacy of townships, or the professionalism of special districts would appear foolhardy. Administrative and organizational reality is so varied.

Third, a trend exists for states to give their own agencies and their local government creations greater organizational and managerial flexibility (ACIR, 1982:415). This trend is healthy because it allows governments to better design their organization according to task, environment, clientele, and other factors (Garnett, 1981).

NOTES

1. The quest for the effect of structure on state government performance includes Jacobson, 1929; Dye, 1966; Sharkansky and Hofferbert, 1969; Jacob and Lipsky, 1968; Fenton and Chamberlayne, 1969; Garnett, 1980; and Meier, 1980. For studies exploring the impact of structure on local government policy and operations see Lineberry and Fowler, 1967; Cole, 1971; Levy, Meltsner, and Wildavsky, 1974; Ostrom, 1976; Bahl and Burkhead, 1977; and Jones, 1980.

2. This discussion appeared previously in Garnett, 1982.

REFERENCES

Adrian, C. R. (1976). *State and Local Governments*, 4th ed. McGraw-Hill, New York.

Advisory Commission on Intergovernmental Relations (1980). *State Administrators' Opinions on Administrative Change, Federal Aid, Federal Relationships.* U.S. Government Printing Office, Washington, D.C.

Advisory Commission on Intergovernmental Relations (1982). *State and Local Roles in the Federal System.* U.S. Government Printing Office, Washington, D.C.

Bahl, R. and Burkhead, J. (1977). Productivity and the measurement of public output. In Levin, C. L., ed., *Managing Human Resources.* Sage Publications, Newbury Park, Calif., pp. 253-270.

Bell, G. (1973). State administrative organization activities, 1970-1971. In *The Book of the States, 1972-73.* The Council of State Governments, Lexington, Ky.

Bell, G. (1976). State administrative organization activities, 1974-1975. In *The Book of the States, 1976-77.* The Council of State Governments, Lexington, Ky.

Beyle, T. L. (1982). The governors and the executive branch, 1980–81. In *The Book of the States, 1982–1983*. The Council of State Governments, Lexington, Ky., pp. 141–150.

Cole, R. L. (1971). The urban policy process: A note on structural and regional influences. *Social Science Quarterly* (December): 646–655.

Duncombe, H. S. (1977). *Modern County Government*. National Association of Counties, Washington, D.C.

Dvorin, E. P. and Misner, A. J. (1970). *Governments within the States*. Addison-Wesley, Reading, Mass.

Dye, T. R. (1966). *Politics, Economics and the Public: Policy Outcomes in the American States*. Rand McNally, Chicago.

Fenton, J. H. and Chamberlayne, D. W. (1969). The literature dealing with the relationships between political processes, socio-economic conditions and public policies in the American states: A bibliographic essay. *Polity 1:* 388–404.

Garnett, J. L. (1979). Strategies for governors who want to reorganize. *State Government 52* (Summer 1979):135–143.

Garnett, J. L. (1980). *Reorganizing State Government: The Executive Branch*. Westview Press, Boulder, Colo.

Garnett, J. L. (1981). Implications of state government organizing for targeting resources to urban areas. *The Urban Interest* 3(Special Issue):97–108.

Garnett, J. L. (1982). State organizations decline. *Public Administration Times* (September 15): 3 and 10.

Gottlieb, A. (1976). State executive reorganization: A study of hallucination, supposition and hypothesis. Ph.D. dissertation, The George Washington University, Washington, D.C.

Graves, W. B. (1949). *Reorganization of the Executive Branch of the United States: A Compilation of Basic Information and Significant Documents*. Library of Congress, Washington, D.C.

Henry, N. (1980). *Governing at the Grassroots: State and Local Politics*. Prentice-Hall, Englewood Cliffs, N.J.

Herzik, E. (1981). Governors and issues: A typology of concerns. Paper presented at the Annual Meeting of the Southern Political Science Association.

Hyneman, C. S. (1939). Administrative reorganization: An adventure into science and theology. *The Journal of Politics* 1:62–75.

International City Management Association (1981). *Municipal Yearbook, 1981*. International City Management Association, Washington, D.C.

Jacob, H. and Lipsky, M. (1968). Outputs, structure and power: An assessment of changes in the study of state and local politics. *The Journal of Politics* 30:510–538.

Jacobson, J. M. (1929). Evaluating state administrative structure: The fallacy of the statistical approach. *American Political Science Review* 22 (November):928–935.

Jones, B. D. (1980). *Service Delivery in the City: Citizen Demand and Bureaucratic Rules.* Longman, New York.

Kaufman, H. (1956). Emerging conflicts in the doctrines of public administration. *American Political Science Review 50* (December):1057–1073.

Kaufman, H. (1963). *Politics and Policies in State and Local Governments.* Prentice-Hall, Englewood Cliffs, N.J.

Lawrence, C. B. and DeGrove, J. M. (1976). County government services. In *The County Yearbook 1976.* National Association of Counties, International City Management Association, Washington, D.C.

Levy, F., Meltsner, A., and Wildavsky, A. (1974). *Urban Outcomes.* University of California Press, Berkeley, Calif.

Lineberry, R. L. and Fowler, E. P. (1967). Reformism and public policies in American cities. *American Political Science Review* (September):701–716.

Marando, V. L. (1974). An overview of the political feasibility of local government reorganization. In Murphy, T. P. and Warren, C. R., eds. *Organizing Public Services in Metropolitan America,* Lexington Books, Lexington, Mass., pp. 17–51.

Meier, K. J. (1980). Executive reorganization of government: Impact on employment and expenditures. *American Journal of Political Science 24* (August):396–411.

Mosher, F. C., ed. (1967). *Governmental Reorganization: Cases and Commentary.* Bobbs-Merrill, Indianapolis.

National Association of Counties and International City Management Association (1978). *The County Yearbook 1978.* National Association of Counties and International City Management Association, Washington, D.C.

Ostrom, E. (1976). *The Delivery of Urban Services: Outcomes of Change.* Sage Publications, Newbury Park, Calif.

Press, C. and Verburg, K. (1979). *State and Community Governments in the Federal System.* Wiley, New York.

Shalala, D. E. and Merget, A. E. (1974). Decentralization plans. In Murphy, T. P. and Warren, C. R., ed., *Organizing Public Services in Metropolitan America.* Lexington Books, Lexington, Mass.

Stillman, R. J. (1974). *The Rise of the City Manager.* University of New Mexico Press, Albuquerque, N.M.

U.S. Bureau of the Census (1979). *1977 Census of Governments, vol. 1 Governmental Organization.* Government Printing Office, Washington, D.C.

U.S. Bureau of the Census (1983). *1982 Census of Governments, vol. 1 Governmental Organization.* Government Printing Office, Washington, D.C.

Waldo, D. (1948). *The Administrative State: A Study of the Political Theory of American Public Administration.* The Ronald Press Company, New York.

Walsh, Annmarie E. (1978). *The Public's Business,* MIT Press, Cambridge, Mass.

Zimmerman, J. F. (1980). United States. In Rowat, D.C., ed., *International Handbook on Local Government Reorganization.* Greenwood Press, Westport, Conn.

POLITICS AND POWER IN THE SUNBELT: MAYOR MORIAL OF NEW ORLEANS

Huey L. Perry and Alfred Stokes

Huey L. Perry and Alfred Stokes studied Ernest Morial's eight years as the first African-American mayor of New Orleans to examine the important questions of whether increased black participation in the political process and Mayor Morial's presence increased economic and social benefits to black citizenry.

New Orleans had a white majority population until the late 1970s. However, the "structure" of the population in New Orleans had begun to change as early as 1960 when many white residents moved to suburban communities. By 1980 black residents in New Orleans constituted 55 percent of the city's population.

Importantly, the structure of New Orleans had changed in other ways: manufacturing, transportation, and utilities jobs had all declined. By 1981 the leading remaining sources of employment were wholesale and retail trade, shipping, services (many of these jobs associated with tourism), and government. The decline in jobs exacerbated the negative economic condition of the city's black residents, a substantial number of whom have incomes below the poverty line, which results in New Orleans's rank as the third poorest large city in America.

Two important characteristics of New Orleans stand out: first, it has a rigid social structure dominated by a small number of wealthy white New Orleanians. This elite group is closed not only to the general public but to wealthy newcomers as well. Second, New Orleans has a strong mayor-council form of city government. Considerable power belongs to the mayor because of his appointment and budget authority. Yet the power of a small wealthy elite can present strong opposition to a mayor committed to making economic and social change. The mayor's power to make change is especially circumscribed where jobs are declining and economic resources are meager, as they are in New Orleans.

In the face, then, of the realities of the economic and social structures of New Orleans, what difference did it make economically and socially that the population structure had changed in favor of blacks and that, as a result, an African-American sat, as mayor, atop the local political structure? Perry and Stokes sought the answers to this question in the categories of municipal employment, executive appointments, and municipal contracts. They found that over the first seven years of Mayor Morial's tenure, the black proportion of municipal employment grew by 13 percent. Thus the economic benefits of an African-American in the mayor's office were clear. The social benefits accrued from black employees carrying out their municipal work force responsibilities and in the process gaining an increased measure of personal esteem and social respect.

The election of an African-American mayor also resulted in increased executive level employment for black citizenry. Mayor Morial appointed a black ally to the position of chief administrative officer of the city. Through his chief administrative officer Mayor Morial appointed African-Americans to head seven of the departments, including finance and police. This meant that blacks held 58.3 percent of the executive appointment positions under Mayor Morial as opposed to 41.7 percent under his predecessor. Here, also, Perry and Stokes argue that black citizens benefited socially because of Mayor Morial's appointment of a black police chief who could play a large role in ending police brutality and in improving relations between the police department and the black community.

Finally, Perry and Stokes evaluated Mayor Morial's contributions to the black community in terms of municipal contracts. They observe that Morial attempted to help black citizens do two things: (1) obtain an increased share of the labor force on projects administered or financed by the city, and (2) win an increased share of the contracts awarded by the city. Here Perry and Stokes found that Morial was less successful.

Perry and Stokes conclude that black population growth, black political participation, and the election of an African-American mayor in New Orleans have resulted in considerable economic and social benefits, though not nearly so much as might have been expected. This is so, Perry and Stokes say, because of the existence of rival centers of power in the black political community, and the necessity of blacks to share political influence with whites who continue to make up a sizeable segment of the city's population and who control much of the city's private economic resources.

This [article] describes and analyzes political participation in New Orleans in connection with the two elections and mayoral administrations of Ernest "Dutch" Morial, the first black mayor of the city. A thorough description and analysis of the major factors operating in contemporary mayoral politics in New Orleans is provided. The [article] also describes and analyzes the role that blacks have played in the city's politics over the last eight years. Additionally, [we] assess Morial's successes and failures as mayor of New Orleans and the impact that he has had in terms of providing increased social and economic benefits to the city's black population. The extent to which blacks in New Orleans have benefited as a result of increased participation in the political process is also discussed. We conclude...by discussing and analyzing the election of the second black mayor of New Orleans, Sidney Barthelemy.*

DATA AND METHODOLOGY

The primary data collection techniques used were secondary data analysis, documentary analysis, participant observation, and interviewing. The secondary data analysis component consists primarily of voting data. The primary data analytic methodology used is longitudinal data analysis. The [article] analyzes the eight years of Morial's mayoral tenure to determine the impact that the mayor has had in terms of providing increased social and economic benefits to blacks in three categories: *municipal employment*, *executive appointments*, and *municipal contracts*. For municipal employment and executive appointments, the longitudinal analysis also includes a comparative assessment of the benefits received by blacks under Morial as opposed to those received by blacks under Morial's predecessor, Moon Landrieu.

A DEMOGRAPHIC AND ECONOMIC PROFILE OF NEW ORLEANS

New Orleans is the largest city in Louisiana, the third largest city in the south,[1] and the twentieth largest city in the U.S.[2] Its location on the Mississippi River is largely responsible for its role as a major commercial

---

Source: Huey L. Perry and Alfred Stokes, "Politics and Power in the Sunbelt: Mayor Morial of New Orleans," in *The New Black Politics*, 2nd ed., edited by Michael B. Preston, Lenneal J. Henderson, Jr., and Paul L. Puryear (New York: Longman, 1987). Reprinted by permission.

*Since this paper was originally written a new black mayor, Sidney Barthelemy, has been elected mayor of New Orleans. The second part of this article discusses his election to office.

center for over 200 years. The city covers a 363.5-square mile area, of which about 200 square miles is land. The boundaries of the city are co-terminous with Orleans Parish.[3] New Orleans' population in 1985 was 573,527.[4]

Between 1950 and 1960 New Orleans' population increased by 57,130 or 10 percent. The city's population was 570,445 in 1950 and 627,575 in 1960.[5] Since 1960, however, New Orleans, like most major cities in the U.S., has lost population as residents have moved beyond its municipal boundaries into suburban communities. The population of New Orleans in 1970 was 593,467.[6] This means that between 1960 and 1970 the city's population declined by 34,108 or 5.44 percent. Between 1970 and 1980 the city's population continued to decline; the 1980 population was 557,515.[7] This amounts to a decline of 35,952 or 6.06 percent between 1970 and 1980. Thus between 1960 and 1980, New Orleans' population declined by 70,600 or 11.16 percent. However, between 1980 and 1985 the population increased by 16,012 or 2.87 percent.

Between 1970 and 1980, New Orleans changed from a white majority population to a black majority population. In 1970, New Orleans had a white majority population with blacks comprising 45 percent of the city's population.[8] In 1980, the 308,149 blacks in New Orleans comprised 55.27 percent of the city's population. This amounts to a 15.28 percent increase in the city's black population between 1970 and 1980. By contrast, the 236,987 whites comprised 42.51 percent of the city's 1980 population, which amounts to a 26.72 percent decline in the city's white population since 1970.[9]

As can be ascertained from Table 1, New Orleans' primary industries are tourism, oil and gas, wholesale and retail trade, and shipping. In terms of the table's categories, tourism would most likely be included in Services, oil and gas in Transportation and Public Utilities, and shipping also in Transportation and Public Utilities. Manufacturing, once a strong component of the city's economy, has declined substantially since 1960. As Table 1 shows, in 1960, 44,700 persons were employed in manufactur-ing, comprising 15.5 percent of the city's total employment. By 1970, the 53,800 persons employed in manufacturing comprised 14.4 percent of the city's total employment; and by April 1981 the 54,300 persons em-ployed in manufacturing comprised 10.9 percent of the city's total em-ployment. This means that manufacturing, as a percentage of the city's total employment, declined 4.6 percentage points, or by 29.68 percent, between 1960 and 1981. By April 1984, the number of persons employed in manufacturing had decreased to 47,500; by March 1985, to 47,100; and by April 1985, to 46,500.[10] This amounts to a 2.11 percent decrease in the

TABLE 1   New Orleans Employment by Major Industry, 1960 to 1981

Industry	1960		1970		April 1981	
	Number	Percent	Number	Percent	Number	Percent
Mining	7,900	2.7	13,900	3.7	18,400	3.6
Contract construction	17,500	6.1	22,500	6.0	31,000	6.2
Manufacturing	44,700	15.5	53,800	14.4	54,300	10.9
Transportation and public utilities	43,000	15.0	44,700	12.0	52,000	10.4
Wholesale and retail trade	73,800	25.6	90,500	24.2	124,100	24.8
Finance, insurance, real estate	17,900	6.2	22,900	6.1	30,500	6.1
Services	44,500	15.5	68,200	18.3	110,900	22.2
Government	38,400	13.4	57,300	15.3	78,400	15.7
Total	287,800	100.0	373,800	100.0	499,600	100.0

Source: Adapted from Larry Schroeder, Lee Madere, and Jerome Lomba, *Occasional Paper No. 52: Local Government Revenue and Expenditure Forecasting: New Orleans* (Syracuse: Metropolitan Studies Program, The Maxwell School of Citizenship and Public Affairs, Syracuse University, October 1981), p. 5.

number of persons employed in manufacturing between April 1984 and April 1985.

The only other industry which experienced a decline similar in magnitude to manufacturing, between 1960 and 1981, is transportation and public utilities. As Table 1 shows, the 43,000 persons employed in transportation and public utilities in 1960 comprised 15 percent of the city's total employment. In 1970 the 44,700 persons employed in transportation and public utilities constituted 12 percent of the city's total employment; and by April 1981, the 52,000 persons employed in transportation and public utilities comprised 10.4 percent of the city's total employment. Thus, manufacturing, as a percentage of the city's total employment, declined 4.6 percentage points, or by 30.67 percent, between 1960 and 1981. The other industries listed in Table 1, as a percentage of the city's total employment, either grew or decreased slightly between 1960 and 1981.

As the table shows, the three leading sources of employment in New Orleans in 1981 were wholesale and retail trade, services, and government.

Although the various industries listed provide millions of dollars to the city's economy each year, New Orleans continues to have a major poverty problem. A substantial 26.4 percent of the city's residents live below the poverty level, which makes New Orleans the third poorest large city in the United States.[11] The city's economy has experienced only modest growth and almost no diversification since the middle 1960s; and as a result of unemployment, underemployment, and other mal-effects of a longstanding stagnant economy, poverty is pronounced in New Orleans.

According to James R. Bobo the crux of New Orleans' economic problem is not growth but inadequate economic development:

> The local economy has experienced economic stagnation tendencies since the mid and late 1950s, with chronic and severe stagnation since 1966, not because there was an absence of economic growth, but because economic development did not provide adequate employment opportunities for an expanding labor force. . . . Employment opportunities have been inadequate since 1966 . . . consequently, unemployment has increased both absolutely and as a percentage of the labor force since 1966, reaching 9.0 percent in 1975.[12]

Alvin J. Schexnider's list of the economic problems in New Orleans include "low income and poverty, maldistribution of income, unemployment and subemployment, and low educational attainment."[13]

In New Orleans, as is the case in all cities in the U.S., blacks are not doing as well as whites economically. For example, in New Orleans in 1985 the median family income for blacks was $10,516 as compared to $21,544 for whites.[14] This means that the white median family income was more than double that of blacks; or, expressed differently, for every dollar earned by a white family a black family earned 49 cents. The gap between black and white median family income in New Orleans was approximately the same size in 1980 as it was in 1985. In 1980 the median family income for blacks was $7,598 as compared to $14,898 for whites.[15] Thus, white median family income was just slightly less than double black median family income. For every dollar a white family earned in 1980, a black family earned 51 cents. The gap in median family income between blacks and whites in New Orleans in 1980 was greater than in any other major city in the United States.[16]

Although blacks in New Orleans fared poorly relative to whites in terms of income in 1980, by 1985 their relative situation had deteriorated even further. Extending the time frame of the comparison to 1970 visibly improves black median family income relative to white median family income and at the same time shows how much the economic situation of blacks relative to that of whites deteriorated over the 15-year period between 1970 and 1985. In 1970 the median family income for blacks was $4,745 as compared to $7,445 for whites.[17] This means that white median family income was just over one and one-half times that of black median family income. In other words, for every dollar earned by a white family, a black family earned 64 cents. This compares favorably with 51 cents in 1980 and 49 cents in 1985. In terms of black median family income relative to white median family income, blacks in New Orleans in 1985 were in a slightly less favorable posture than they were in 1980 and a significantly less favorable posture than they were in 1970.

NEW ORLEANS' POLITICAL CULTURE AND GOVERNMENTAL STRUCTURE

Most students of politics recognize the importance of understanding the political culture of a locality in order to understand the nuances of how the governmental and political processes work. The political culture of New Orleans is very different from that of most other cities. Thus a knowledge of New Orleans' political culture is especially relevant for understanding the city's governmental and political processes. New Orleans is a cultural mosaic, consisting of a mixture of "French, Spanish, and southern cultures."[18] The cultural mix of New Orleans society gives rise to two important characteristics of the city's political and social culture. One characteristic is that the general pace of life in the city is relaxed. New Orleanians do not appear to be as intense about life, work, and politics as residents of many other large cities. This is especially true of mass citizenry in New Orleans.

Given the easy-going behavioral style of the masses, it seems somewhat incongruous that a second characteristic of New Orleans society is a very rigid social structure. The pinnacle of the city's social sphere is dominated by a small number of wealthy white New Orleanians whose families have been in the city for several generations. The incongruity between the relaxed pace of the masses and the elitism propagated by the leading lights in the social sphere is, ironically, best illustrated during the city's celebrated annual carnival season, otherwise known as Mardi Gras. During the Mardi Gras celebration, while the masses make an art form out of participating in an open, free-wheeling epicurean revelry, the social elites attend elegant balls which "are closed not only to the general public, but also to everyone except those whose families have been...[in New Orleans] since the turn of the century.[19]

The rigid social structure in New Orleans resulted in a slow emergence of an expanded and more diversified civic and political leadership in the city. Charles Y. W. Chai provides insight into the negative effects that the social structure has had on the growth of new civic leadership in the city.

> A young executive who moves to New Orleans with his family may soon become frustrated by a system which prevents him from enjoying many of the luxuries he feels he deserves. As a result, he may refuse to participate in community affairs. . . . [Many such executives] see no reason to work with the "locals" on community problems, since the "locals" refuse to socialize with outsiders.[20]

Schexnider provides additional insight into the impact that New Orleans' rigid social structure has had on the emergence of black elected political leadership in the city. Schexnider asserts that the rigid social structure:

> is endemic to the political culture of New Orleans. It is clearly dysfunctional to the political system in general, though its adverse impact on the life fortunes of black citizens is probably more pronounced. It was not until 1967 that the city sent its first black (Ernest Morial. . .) to the Louisiana House of Representatives. Nonetheless, it was easier to send a black to the state legislature than to the New Orleans City Council, which was finally integrated in the mid-1970s.[21]

Additional support for Chai's and Schexnider's observations can be gleaned from the efforts of women to penetrate the elected political leadership domain in New Orleans. Although women were first elected to the state legislature from New Orleans as late as the mid-1970s, the first two women (one black and one white) on the city council were elected as recently as March 1986.

Just as it is well known that a knowledge of the political culture of a locality is relevant for understanding the subtleties of how the governmental and political processes work, the same applies to a knowledge of the governmental structure. The city operates under a home rule charter which became effective in 1954. Under Louisiana's Home Rule authority, "The Louisiana Constitution prohibits the State Legislature from enacting any law affecting the structure, organization or distribution of the power and function of any local political subdivision which operates under a home rule charter."[22]

New Orleans has a mayor-council form of government. The mayor appoints the chief administrative officer and the budget officer. The chief administrative officer, who provides overall executive supervision and coordination of the day-to-day functions of city government, appoints, subject to the mayor's approval, 11 of the 13 executive department heads. The two other executive department heads, the city attorney and the director of the Civil Service Department, are appointed by the mayor and the Civil Service Commission, respectively.[23] The city council is a seven-member body, with five seats elected by districts and two seats elected at large. In terms of the electoral subdivisions of the city, New Orleans consists of 17 wards and 428 precincts.

New Orleans, given its poor economic conditions and its atomistic political culture, clearly constitutes a formidable environment for a black mayor to provide social and economic benefits to the black community. But the austerity of New Orleans as a case study to assess the social and economic impact of the black mayor on the black population is helpful in the sense that it is desirable to know the capacity of black political participation to produce benefits in cities with varying degrees of social and economic resources and characteristics. In terms of theory building in the study of black politics, it is important to know the capacity of black mayors to produce social and economic benefits for blacks in localities where supportive economic resources and characteristics are meager and in localities where supportive economic resources and characteristics are more plentiful. Studies of this nature are needed to produce a general assessment of the capacity of overall black political participation to produce favorable social and economic change for blacks.

THE ELECTORAL SUPPORT BASE OF MORIAL IN THE 1977 MAYORAL RACE

Morial was a State Appeals Court Judge when he decided to run for mayor in 1977. Prior to his decision Morial had compiled an impressive list of accomplishments, including several "firsts" for a black person. For example, Morial was the first black graduate of the Louisiana State University Law School in 1954. He became Louisiana's first U.S. Attorney in 1965. Similarly, in 1967 he became the first black since Reconstruction to be elected to the Louisiana Legislature. Morial also subsequently became the first black to serve on the Juvenile Court in New Orleans. In 1974 he also became the first black elected to the Louisiana State Appeals Court.[24]

At the time of Morial's decision to run for mayor, there was not a strong tradition of assertive black political participation in New Orleans, especially with regard to running for public office. Morial had unsuccessfully run for an at-large seat on the city council seat in 1969. Also, Morial decided to run for office only one year after the first black, Reverend A. L. Davis, Jr., had been selected by city council members to fill a

vacancy on the council in 1976. Two other factors which seemingly mini-
mized Morial's chances of winning his first mayoral election were that
registered white voters outnumbered black voters by 58 percent to 42
percent[25] and "that the major black organizations supported white candidates in the primary."[26] Moreover, Morial "was a long-time foe of those
blacks who headed the major political organizations in New Orleans."[27]

In the primary election Morial received the largest number of votes
among the 11-candidate field, but not the majority of votes necessary to
avoid a runoff. Joseph V. DiRosa, the conservative white city councilman
who defeated Morial in the 1969 council race, barely edged out a second
place finish over liberal State Senator Nat Kiefer. Toni Morrison, son of
former New Orleans Mayor deLesseps Morrison from 1946 to 1961 (before the two-term limit was instituted), finished fourth. None of the
other seven candidates was close to the number of votes that Morrison
received.[28]

In terms of the racial distribution of the votes cast in the primary,
Morial received 58 percent of the black vote and 5 percent of the white
vote.[29] DiRosa received 39 percent of the white vote and four percent of
the black vote. Thus both Morial and DiRosa received a similarly small
proportion of other race support. The two other major candidates, Kiefer
and Morrison, received remarkably similar proportions of racially mixed
support. Kiefer received 18 percent of the black vote and 28 percent of
the white vote; whereas Morrison received 16 percent of the black vote
and 25 percent of the white vote. Thus Morial and DiRosa entered into a
runoff.

Also in the 1977 primary New Orleans voters elected State Senator
Sidney Barthelemy as their first black at-large city councilman.[30] Black
turnout for the primary was 66 percent as compared to 74 percent for
whites. Thus black turnout in the primary was eight percentage points
less than that of whites.

Morial's strategy for the primary election was to appeal to black voters in the hope that he would receive a larger enough black vote to put
him in the runoff and at the same time take enough black votes away
from Kiefer and Morrison to prevent them from entering into the runoff.
Kiefer and Morrison were both liberal and would have provided a
stronger opposition to Morial in the runoff than the Conservative
DiRosa. Morial's strategy, undoubtedly aided by the three white candidates' division of the white vote into three sizable chunks, worked to
perfection.[31] Thus Morial finished first in the primary election because he
received a majority of the black vote and a small portion of the white vote
while his three major white opponents divided the white vote.

TABLE 2 Registration and Voting Data for the Two Predominantly Black
Wards and the Five Racially Mixed-Majority Black Wards Carried
by Morial in the 1977 Mayoral Runoff Election

Ward	Voter registration		Votes received	
	Black	White	Morial	DiRosa
(Predominantly black)				
Second Ward	3,289	507	2,304	448
Eleventh Ward	6,028	2,917	4,999	1,803
(Racially mixed-majority black)				
First Ward	1,270	659	903	413
Seventh Ward[a]	16,830	12,764	13,809	8,900
Ninth Ward	29,157	27,405	23,290	19,316
Tenth Ward	3,485	2,091	2,580	1,308
Twelfth Ward	5,645	4,008	5,021	2,297

[a]Data from one precinct are not included in the vote totals for this ward.
Source: Compiled from registration and voting data published in the (New Orleans)
Times Picayune, November 14, 1977.

Morial's runoff election strategy was different from his primary election strategy. Fully cognizant that he could not be elected by black voters
alone, Morial made a strong appeal to white voters in the runoff campaign. This strategy also worked to perfection as Morial won the runoff
election by 95 percent of the black vote and 19 percent of the white vote.[32]
Morial received 89,823 votes to DiRosa's 84,352,[33] thus defeating him by
5,471 votes. In percentage terms, Morial received 51.57 percent of the
votes to DiRosa's 48.43 percent.

Three factors were critical to Morial's victory. Unquestionably one
factor was the tremendous support he received from black voters. Morial's impressive performance among black voters is illustrated in Table 2.
As the table shows, Morial won the two heavily majority black wards
and the five racially mixed-majority black wards by overwhelming margins.[34] Although Morial received only nominal support from the major
black political organizations,[35] black voters gave him near unanimous
support.

A second key ingredient to Morial's victory is the increased interest
that blacks manifested in the electoral process following his entry into
the runoff. This increased interest was manifested in two ways: one, a

TABLE 3 Registration and Voting for the Racially Mixed-Majority White Wards Carried by Morial in the 1977 New Orleans Mayoral Runoff Election

	Voter registration		Votes received	
Ward	Black	White	Morial	DiRosa
Fifth Ward	3,183	5,528	3,190	3,099
Sixth Ward	1,988	2,229	1,773	1,282
Thirteenth Ward	3,451	4,800	3,864	2,567
Sixteenth Ward	1,830	3,447	2,318	1,619
Seventh Ward	6,846	7,279	6,506	4,642

Source: Compiled from registration and voting data published in the (New Orleans) *Times Picayune*, November 14, 1977.

greater increase of black voter registration following the primary; and two, a black turnout rate on election day nearly equal to that of whites. With regard to the former, black voter registration increased by 5 percent during the months between the primary election and the runoff election while white voter registration increased by 3.5 percent.

In terms of the nearly equal rates of turnout between blacks and whites, the black turnout rate was 76 percent as compared to the 78 percent turnout rate for whites. It is unusual in American politics for black voter turnout to be nearly equal to that of whites and the fact that it was indicates an increased interest in the electoral process generated by the prospect of a black having a real chance to win the most important office in city government. This mobilization of the black electorate resulted in blacks increasing their voter turnout rate by 10 percentages points or 15 percent between the primary election and the runoff election (66 percent versus 76 percent, respectively), while whites increased their turnout rate by four percentage points or five percent (74 percent versus 78 percent, respectively).

The third and final key to Morial's victory was the fact that he received almost 20 percent of the white vote. Twenty percent is the upper end of the range of support from white voters that most successful black candidates running for public office in biracial political jurisdictions can hope to receive (10 percent is the lower end of the range). Thus Morial's ability to win 19 percent of the white vote was clearly an impressive accomplishment. Table 3 provides an indication of how well Morial did

TABLE 4 Registration and Voting Data for the Five Predominantly White
Wards Carried by DiRosa in the 1977 New Orleans Mayoral Runoff
Election

Ward	Voter registration		Votes received	
	Black	White	Morial	DiRosa
Third Ward	1,232	5,000	1,397	3,389
Fourth Ward	1,525	12,904	2,168	9,099
Eighth Ward[a]	4,093	11,379	3,456	7,469
Fourteenth Ward	1,478	13,210	4,346	6,436
Fifteenth Ward	6,217	14,684	6,646	8,500

[a]Voting data from three precincts missing.

Source: Compiled from registration and voting data published in the (New Orleans)
Times Picayune, November 14, 1977.

among white voters. As the table shows, Morial won all of the five racially mixed-majority [white] wards in the city.

The strength of Morial's showing in the racially mixed-majority
white wards is best illustrated in the vote totals from the Sixteenth Ward.
Although white registered voters outnumber black registered voters in
the Sixteenth Ward by almost a two-to-one ratio, Morial won the ward by
almost 700 votes. Since there were 1,830 black registered voters in the
ward and Morial received 2,318 votes, this means that Morial received
substantial support from the white voters in the ward. The white voters
who supported Morial were generally middle and upper income whites.

Morial won 12 of the city's 17 wards, which consisted of the predominantly black wards, the five racially mixed-majority black wards, and
the five racially mixed-majority white wards. The remaining five wards
won by DiRosa, as Table 4 shows, were all predominantly white wards.
Although DiRosa won these wards convincingly, he did not win some of
them by large enough margins to significantly cut into Morial's lead from
the other wards. The Fourteenth Ward well illustrates this point. In the
Fourteenth Ward white voter registration exceeds black voter registration
by a nine-to-one ratio (13,210 to 1,478, respectively), yet DiRosa won the
ward by just under 2,100 votes (6,436 to 4,346, respectively). DiRosa's
less than spectacular performance in the predominantly white wards
combined with his losing the racially mixed-majority white wards and
not doing better in the racially mixed-majority black wards are the three
principal reasons why DiRosa lost the runoff election.

In sum, Morial won a convincing victory over DiRosa to become the first black mayor in New Orleans' history. Morial's successful electoral support base consisted of a highly mobilized black vote and a sizable minority portion of the white vote, comprised mostly of middle and upper income whites. Morial's strategy to attract a strong black vote in the primary and, in so doing, prevent all but the weakest of his major opponents from entering the runoff worked to perfection. Similarly, his runoff election strategy to attract a significant minority portion of the white vote while holding onto the black vote worked out according to plan. By all accounts Morial's road to the mayor's office was paved by an ingenious strategy that was brilliantly executed.

MORIAL'S 1982 REELECTION SUPPORT BASE

Morial ran for reelection in 1982. In that year, 54 percent of the white voting age population and 46 percent of the black voting age population were registered to vote. Morial's principal opponents were Ronald Faucheaux, a progressive, business-oriented white and State Senator William Jefferson, a liberal black. A runoff election between Morial and Faucheaux was necessary as Morial led the field by receiving 47 percent of the votes cast, followed by Faucheaux who received 45 percent and Jefferson who received 7 percent.[36] Unlike his first mayoral election Morial received a much higher proportion of the black vote—90 percent. Moreover, with a few exceptions, the major black political organizations in the city endorsed his candidacy[37] as compared with no endorsement from those organizations in his 1977 primary election. The overall voter turnout in the primary was 67 percent, with blacks turning out at 64 percent and whites at 69 percent. Thus white voter turnout exceeded black voter turnout by five percentage points.

Faucheaux received practically all his support from whites. His white supporters consisted of some upper income whites, some whites associated with the business community, and the majority of low income whites. While Faucheaux was supported by a few prominent black individuals like then-State Senator Henry Braden, he received virtually no support from the major black political organizations. Faucheaux's showing among black voters in the primary election was very poor, as he received only 1 percent of the black vote. While Jefferson received racially mixed support, he received more support from whites than he received from blacks.[38] A solid portion of Jefferson's white support came from his white constituency in his senatorial district.

The 1982 runoff election provided a greater challenge to Morial's electability than did the 1977 runoff election. This was due to the circum-

TABLE 5 Registration and Voting Data for the Three Predominantly Black Wards and the Five Racially Mixed-Majority Black Wards Carried by Morial in the 1982 Mayoral Runoff Election

Ward	Voter registration		Votes received[a]	
	Black	White	Morial	Faucheaux
(Predominantly black)				
First Ward[b]	1,511	500	1,024	416
Second Ward	3,310	557	2,763	309
Eleventh Ward	6,110	3,891	5,217	1,815
(Racially mixed-majority black)				
Seventh Ward	18,349	12,321	15,948	8,401
Ninth Ward	35,172	27,606	30,004	21,657
Tenth Ward	3,467	2,161	2,909	1,191
Eleventh Ward	6,110	3,891	5,217	1,815
Twelfth Ward	6,140	3,873	5,553	2,191

[a]The double column figures listed do not include absentee votes.
[b]Note that this ward was a racially mixed-majority black ward in 1977.
Source: Compiled from a tally of official returns recorded by the New Orleans City Council.

stances regarding the field of candidates and Morial's crafty manipulation of those circumstances, which resulted in Morial facing the weakest of his major opponents in the 1977 runoff. Unlike the Conservative DiRosa, who provided Morial a relatively easy basis for mobilizing black voters and luring a significant minority portion of the white vote, the liberal Faucheaux, who appealed to the same type of white voter most likely to vote for Morial, constituted a much more formidable runoff opponent.

In the runoff election the overall turnout rate was 75 percent, which was eight percentage points higher than the 67 percent turnout in the primary. Of the 189,298 votes cast in the runoff Morial received 100,725 votes, or 53 percent, while Faucheaux received 88,573 votes, or 47 percent. Morial won 10 of the city's 17 wards. Morial received 99 percent of the black vote and 14 percent of the white vote, while Faucheaux received 86 percent of the white vote and 1 percent of the black vote. As Table 5 shows, Morial dominated Faucheaux in the three predominantly black wards and won strongly in the five racially mixed-majority black wards. In the predominantly black Second Ward, for example, Morial

TABLE 6 Registration and Voting Data in the Six Racially Mixed-Majority White Wards for the 1982 Mayoral Runoff Election

Ward	Voter registration		Votes received[a]	
	Black	White	Morial	Faucheaux
Fifth Ward	3,502	5,559	3,216	3,271
Sixth Ward	2,083	2,386	1,108	1,988
Eighth Ward[b]	5,358	10,367	4,888	7,687
Thirteenth Ward	3,452	4,982	3,609	2,823
Sixteenth Ward	1,726	3,379	2,075	1,835
Seventeenth Ward	7,117	7,123	6,664	4,841

[a]The double column figures listed do not include absentee votes.
[b]Note that this ward was a predominantly white ward in 1977.
Source: Compiled from a tally of official returns recorded by the New Orleans City Council.

TABLE 7 Registration and Voting Data for the Four Predominantly White Wards for the 1982 Mayoral Runoff Election

Ward	Voter registration		Votes received[a]	
	Black	White	Morial	Faucheaux
Third Ward	1,626	5,142	1,650	2,934
Fourth Ward	1,667	12,919	2,384	8,795
Fourteenth Ward	1,387	13,487	3,209	7,717
Fifteenth Ward	6,749	14,750	6,846	9,739

[a]The double column figures listed do not include absentee votes.
Source: Compiled from a tally of official returns recorded by the New Orleans City Council.

beat Faucheaux by almost a nine-to-one ratio, receiving 2,763 votes to Faucheaux's 309.

Morial received 5 percentage points less of the white vote than he did in the 1977 runoff (19 percent versus 14 percent). This amounts to a 26.32 reduction in white support, which was in great part attributable to the fact that Faucheaux had some appeal to the upper income white voters who supported Morial in 1977. As a result Morial did not win all the racially mixed-majority white wards in the 1982 runoff as he did in the 1977 runoff (see Table 6). In fact Faucheaux won half of the wards in this category. Specifically, he won the Fifth, Sixth, and Eighth Wards. Although Faucheaux barely won the Fifth Ward, he won the Sixth Ward by almost 900 votes and the Eighth Ward by almost 3,000 votes. Thus it was crucial to Morial's victory that he receive a slightly higher percentage of the black vote than he did in the 1977 runoff (99 percent versus 95 percent) to compensate for the reduced white support.

As expected, Faucheaux, like DiRosa in the 1977 runoff, registered strong wins in the predominantly white wards (see Table 7). Faucheaux's impressive strength in these four wards is best illustrated by the vote totals for the Fourth Ward. Faucheaux won the Fourth Ward by better than a three and a half-to-one ratio. His 8,795 votes in that ward exceeded Morial's 2,384 by more than 6,400 votes. Thus Faucheaux won 7 wards and Morial won 10 wards. Faucheaux's performance in this regard was 2 wards more than the 5 wards DiRosa won in 1977 and Morial's performance was 2 wards less than the 12 wards he won in 1977.

Seventy-five percent of blacks turned out to vote in the runoff as compared to 64 percent in the primary. This amounts to an increase of 11 percentage points or 17.19 percent. White voter turnout was 74 percent in the runoff as compared to 69 percent in the primary, which amounts to an increase of 5 percentage points or 7.25 percent. Thus there was a 6 percentage point or nearly 10 percent difference in favor of blacks in terms of the increase in turnout between blacks and whites from the primary to the runoff. Most significantly, blacks were so mobilized for this election that their turnout rate exceeded that of whites—by 1 percent, 75 percent to 74 percent, respectively. There was also a 9 percentage point increase in the proportion of the black vote Morial received in the runoff as compared to the primary—99 percent versus 90 percent, respectively.

The 1982 election results reveal Morial's considerable electoral strength. Despite the fact that both Jefferson and Faucheaux were viable candidates, Morial received the highest proportion of the votes in the primary. While Jefferson and Faucheaux were able to attract enough black and upper income white voters to prevent Morial from being re-elected in the primary, they were unable to attract enough of those votes to deny Morial a first place finish in the primary. That Morial won the runoff election against Faucheaux, who was a more formidable candidate than DiRosa was in the 1977 runoff, was clearly an important indication of his considerable electoral strength.

Although Morial won reelection convincingly, it is significant that his white support dropped considerably from the 1977 race. Rather than Morial's appeal among white voters increasing over his four years in office, it declined considerably. Although it was basically the same electoral support base responsible for his election in 1977 that reelected Morial in 1982, the difference was that the 1982 support base had a larger black and a smaller white presence than the 1977 support base.

MORIAL'S ELECTION VICTORIES AND GENERAL TRENDS IN AMERICAN POLITICS AND BLACK POLITICAL PARTICIPATION

There are several factors about Morial's electoral victories that are squarely consistent with general trends in American politics and black political participation. One such factor is that Morial was twice elected to the mayor's office on the basis of a large, unified black vote and a significant minority portion of the white vote. This kind of coalition typically elects most blacks to public office in the U.S., with the portion of white voters necessary for victory usually falling in the 10 to 20 percent range. A closely related second factor at work in Morial's victories, which is common to black electoral victories in general, is that the 10 to 20 percent of the white vote that most successful black candidates need to win elections in biracial electorates almost invariably come from middle and upper income whites. Morial's white votes in both the 1977 and 1982 elections decidedly came from the more affluent areas of the city.

A third factor evident in Morial's victories, which is fairly typical of races in which there is a viable black candidate, is an increase in black voter turnout as compared to previous elections. Moreover, it is not unusual in such elections for the black voter turnout to approximately equal white voter turnout. This occurred in both the 1977 and the 1982 New Orleans mayoral runoff elections. In the 1977 election 76 percent of the registered blacks voted as compared to 78 percent of the registered whites. In the 1982 election the comparable figures were 75 percent and 74 percent. These observations are significant because blacks generally turn out less than whites and they show how the presence of a viable black candidate can mobilize blacks to turn out to vote at rates significantly higher than normal, and usually without an equally significant counter mobilization among whites.

A fourth way in which Morial's electoral victories are consistent with general trends in American politics is that the votes were quietly cast along racial lines. In the 1977 runoff election Morial received nearly all of the black vote (95 percent) and DiRosa received the great majority of the white vote (81 percent). The comparable 1982 runoff election figures for Morial and Faucheaux are 99 percent and 86 percent, respectively. Despite this pattern of voting along racial lines, race was not made an issue in the campaign, at least not by the candidates, and there was no manifestation of racial bitterness.[39] This is generally the case in most elections involving racially mixed candidacies throughout the United States. In the great majority of elections in the United States with racially mixed candidacies, blacks quietly vote for black candidates and whites quietly vote for white candidates. Racial preference is extremely evident in patterns of American politics, but generally it is not accompanied by racial bitterness.

MAYOR MORIAL'S SUCCESSES AND FAILURES

Having assessed the factors behind Morial's success in winning the mayor's office in 1977 and being reelected in 1982, we now turn attention to an examination of his successes and failures over his eight-year mayoral tenure. This section . . . devotes special attention to an assessment of Morial's impact in terms of providing increased social and economic benefits to blacks in New Orleans.

Morial's mayoral performance has been uneven. There have been both successes and failures and the latter seem to outnumber if not outweigh in significance the former. In his first term Morial used his and the city's ties to President Jimmy Carter's administration to get substantial amounts of federal monies to help the city. Morial's influence with the Carter administration was based on his campaigning very strongly for the election of Carter and the fact that Carter's Secretary of Housing and Urban Development, Moon Landrieu, was Morial's predecessor in the mayor's office. The fact that Morial was able to use his influence with the Carter administration to obtain strong financial aid for the city is a significant accomplishment. Mayors generally seek to cultivate friendly ties with presidential administrations in an effort to gain an advantage for their city in the distribution of financial aid to cities by the federal government.

Morial has experienced his greatest failures in his effort to get the city to take the initiative in resolving its own fiscal problems. In 1978 Morial proposed six revenue measures to the city council as a means of strengthening the city's fiscal resources. These proposed measures consisted of a road use tax of $50 on all cars registered in the city, an employee privilege tax of 50 cents per day to be levied on all employees who work in New Orleans (or an earnings tax as it was better known by), an increase in the sanitation tax from $1 to $3, a special flat real property tax of $100 per home, an insurance tax of 2 percent on gross premium, and a real property improvement tax of 1 percent. With the exception of the sanitation tax increase, the proposals were rejected by the city council.

In 1980, despite substantial public opposition, the city council approved two of the measures it rejected in 1978: a road use tax of $50 on all cars registered in the city and a flat real property tax of $100 per home in the city. These measures were the two most regressive of the original proposals. Also on November 4, 1980 the electorate narrowly passed a half-cent sales tax increase raising the city's tax to 7 percent. This measure had been proposed by the mayor and supported by the city council, with the expectation that, if passed, the council would repeal the road-use tax and flat property tax. Subsequent to the passage of the sales tax increase, the council repealed the two taxes.

On May 15, 1982 the city's electorate approved a second increase in the sales tax. This time the sales tax was increased one cent, which raised the city's tax to 8 percent (and which tied New Orleans with New York for the highest sales tax in the U.S.). This was a temporary increase which was to end in 1983. The purpose of the increase was to provide additional revenue to prevent a substantial reduction in the city's bus services. The black community voted in favor of the measure by a margin of more than six-to-one, while the white community voted against it by a margin of more than two-to-one. The sales tax increase won by a narrow margin of less than 2,000 votes, 39,150 votes for and 37,210 votes against.[40] This was a significant victory for Morial and a benefit for the black community because blacks rely more on bus services than whites. However, this was not a complete victory for Morial because he preferred that the increase in sales tax would have been permanent, but the city council rejected that part of Morial's proposal, thus preventing it from becoming a part of the referendum that went before the voters for approval or rejection.

Another failure of Morial occurred in 1982 when, after having convinced the state legislature to endorse a referendum eliminating the city's homestead exemption, the city electorate and the state electorate rejected the referendum. Additionally, in 1983 Morial proposed to the city council that it enact an earnings tax without the proposal being submitted to the voters for approval. The council rejected Morial's proposal. Also in 1983, with the mayor adopting a publicly neutral position, the electorate approved a city council proposal to extend the one cent sales tax for two years in order to help the city with its continuing fiscal problem. In January 1984, the state legislature increased the sales tax one cent, which raised New Orleans sales tax to nine cents, making it the highest sales tax of all cities in the United States.

Having tried unsuccessfully to get the city council to pass an earnings tax twice (in 1978 and 1983), Morial proposed, and the city council adopted, a 1984 referendum for a one percent earnings tax. The referendum, held on November 6, the presidential election day, was rejected by

TABLE 8   Registration and Voting Data for the Three Predominantly Black
Wards and the Six Racially Mixed-Majority Black Wards for the
November 6, 1984 Earnings Tax Referendum

	Voter registration		Votes received	
Ward	Black	White	For	Against
(Predominantly black)				
First Ward	1,613	789	666	525
Second Ward	4,390	619	1,412	638
Eleventh Ward	5,912	3,185	2,929	2,421
(Racially mixed-majority black)				
Sixth Ward	2,379	2,361	1,456	1,369
Seventh Ward	21,223	11,840	10,517	9,537
Ninth Ward	44,185	27,683	22,372	22,516
Tenth Ward	3,668	1,878	1,880	1,220
Twelfth Ward	7,049	4,048	2,485	2,785
Seventeenth Ward	8,640	7,841	4,469	5,156

Source: Compiled from a tally of official returns recorded by the New Orleans City
Council.

the city's electorate. As shown in Table 8, the voters in the predominantly black wards voted in favor of the measure. However, in the six racially mixed-majority black wards the measure won in four wards, but
was defeated in two wards, including the Ninth Ward, the largest ward
in the city. Although Morial had won all of the wards in this category in
his 1977 and 1982 runoff elections, he could not duplicate that feat for the
earnings tax measure. Moreover, the wards in which the measure passed
(including the predominantly black wards) did not vote in favor of it by
[anything] close to the margins that Morial won over his runoff opponents in 1977 and 1982.

The pattern of the vote in the racially mixed-majority white wards
and the predominantly white wards was uniformly against the earnings
tax, as Table 9 shows. In the five racially mixed-majority white wards the
measure was overwhelmingly defeated in all but the Thirteenth Ward,
where the measure was only narrowly defeated. The Fifteenth Ward best
illustrates the strength of the opposition to the earnings tax measure. In
the Fifteenth Ward, the measure was defeated by almost a two-to-one ratio, 10,857 against to 5,568 for. In the predominantly white wards the
strength of the opposition is best illustrated in the Fourth Ward, where

TABLE 9 Registration and Voting Data for the Five Racially Mixed-Majority White Wards and the Three Predominantly White for the November 6, 1984 Earnings Tax Referendum

Ward	Voter registration		Votes received	
	Black	White	For	Against
(Racially mixed-majority white)				
Fifth Ward	3,938	5,581	2,431	3,231
Eighth Ward	6,828	9,687	4,265	6,690
Thirteenth Ward	3,808	4,978	2,639	2,946
Fifteenth Ward	9,539	17,814	5,568	10,857
Sixteenth Ward	2,056	4,043	1,628	1,957
(Predominantly white)				
Third Ward	1,886	4,230	1,319	2,299
Fourth Ward	1,965	12,872	2,770	7,318
Fourteenth Ward	1,661	13,748	3,675	6,899

Source: Compiled from a tally of official returns recorded by the New Orleans City Council.

the measure was defeated by better than a two and a half-to-one ratio, 7,318 against to 2,770 for.

Most blacks who voted on the earnings tax referendum overwhelmingly voted in favor of it, whereas most whites who voted on the referendum overwhelmingly voted against it. In 48 black precincts 73.96 percent of the voters voted in favor of the measure as compared with 26.04 percent against. In 72 white precincts 74.25 percent voted against the measure as compared to 25.75 in favor.[41] Thus the proportion of the black population voting for and against the earnings tax was just about inversely equal to the proportion of the white population voting for and against the measure. The reason why the measure lost is explained in terms of the racial differential in the percent of those registered who voted. In the white precincts 71.08 percent of the people registered voted on the measure, as compared to 48.31 percent of the people registered in the black precincts.[42] In other words, black turnout was about one-third less than white turnout; that is the reason why the earnings tax referendum was defeated.

The failure of the earnings tax referendum exacerbated the city's fiscal problem. The one-cent increase in the sales tax's extention ended in

TABLE 10 Registration[a] and Voting Data for the Three Predominantly Black Wards and the Six Racially Mixed-Majority Wards for the October 19, 1985 Third Term Charter Change Referendum

Ward	Voter registration		Votes received[b]	
	Black	White	For	Against
(Predominantly black)				
First Ward	1,686	803	589	468
Second Ward	4,518	613	1,714	465
Eleventh Ward	6,905	3,201	3,037	2,139
(Racially mixed-majority black)				
Sixth Ward	2,400	2,388	1,026	1,346
Seventh Ward	21,456	11,693	8,679	9,144
Ninth Ward	45,173	27,503	18,262	15,094
Tenth Ward	3,709	1,919	7,631	1,204
Twelfth Ward	7,087	4,050	3,095	2,647
Seventeenth Ward	7,869	6,759	3,764	4,950

[a]The voter registration data are for August 1985.
[b]The double column figures do not include absentee votes.
Source: Compiled from a tally of official returns recorded by the New Orleans City Council.

1985. The revenue for the city from the World's Fair did not materialize as the fair was a colossal financial disaster. In addition, the federal government under President Ronald Reagan has reduced federal financial assistance to cities. When Morial began his first term in May 1978, 57 percent of the city's annual operating budget of $214 million came from the federal government and state government. By 1982, the portion of the city's budget coming from the federal government and the state government had been reduced to 30 percent.[43] Morial has made repeated efforts to solve the city's fiscal problems, but these efforts by and large have not been successful. The city's fiscal situation has continued to deteriorate.

The last major failure of Morial examined. . . is one which involved his personal political future. On October 19, 1985 a referendum was held on Morial's proposal to change the city's charter to allow a mayor to run for a third term. Morial actively campaigned for this proposal. It was rejected by the electorate. As Table 10 shows the three predominantly black wards voted in favor of the referendum. However, in the six racially

TABLE 11 Registration[a] and Voting Data for the Five Racially Mixed-Majority White Wards and the Three Predominantly White Wards for the October 19, 1985 Third Term Charter Change Referendum

Ward	Voter registration		Votes received[b]	
	Black	White	For	Against
(Racially mixed-majority white)				
Fifth Ward	3,936	5,551	1,613	3,159
Eighth Ward	6,995	9,525	3,042	6,592
Thirteenth Ward	3,846	4,933	1,808	3,089
Fifteenth Ward	8,574	16,206	3,165	10,094
Sixteenth Ward	1,791	3,171	914	2,088
(Predominantly white)				
Third Ward	1,949	4,114	772	2,269
Fourth Ward	2,055	12,825	1,087	7,642
Fourteenth Ward	1,691	13,583	1,222	7,587

[a]The voter registration data are for August 1985.
[b]The double column figures listed do not include absentee votes.
Source: Compiled from a tally of official returns recorded by the New Orleans City Council.

mixed-majority black wards, the measure was defeated in two of the wards, the Sixth Ward and the Seventh Ward.

The third term charter change referendum was resoundingly rejected in the five racially mixed-majority white wards and the three predominantly white wards, as Table 11 shows. In the racially mixed-majority white wards, the measure was defeated by nearly a two-to-one ratio or higher in all but the Thirteenth Ward, where it lost by more than 1,200 votes. In the predominantly white wards, the measure lost almost three-to-one in the Third Ward, more than six-to-one in the Fourteenth Ward, and seven-to-one in the Fourth Ward.

The pattern of the vote on the third term charter change referendum was remarkably similar to the vote on the earnings tax referendum. While a majority of blacks voted for both measures, a significant minority of blacks voted against them. Whites voted against these measures approximately to the same extent that blacks voted for them. In both referenda the measures were defeated in two of the six racially mixed-majority black wards, wards that Morial won easily in 1977 and 1982 runoff elections. The key to both defeats was the significant difference in black voter turnout versus white voter turnout. In both cases black turnout was significantly less than white turnout. Thus it would be inaccurate to blame the loss of these referenda measures on white opposition, given the percentage of whites voting in favor of them exceeded the percentage of the white vote that Morial received in both the 1977 and 1982 runoff elections. These measures lost, quite simply, because blacks did not turn out to vote in large enough numbers and did not vote for these measures by large enough margins. The electoral coalition of blacks and upper income whites that twice elected Morial could have passed the referenda measures had blacks voted the way they did in the 1977 and 1982 runoff elections.

THE SOCIAL AND ECONOMIC IMPACT OF BLACK POLITICAL PARTICIPATION IN NEW ORLEANS

One increasingly studied component of black politics involves the extent to which blacks benefit from increased participation in the political process. Previous studies examining this topic assume that since most blacks in the United States are located on the periphery of social and economic advantages, black elected officials are interested in trying to use public authority to confer social and economic benefits upon their fellow black citizens. This assumption is intuitively appealing. In the case of Morial, however, there is first-hand evidence of his expectation that public authority can be used to extract benefits for disadvantaged citizens. Upon his decision to run for the mayor's office while he was a Louisiana State Appeals Court Judge, Morial said: "I enjoy being a judge, but if I can bring a better quality to life to all citizens, and especially to the underclass in our society, then I will be happy."[44] Thus, Morial sought the mayor's office with the hope that he could use the resources of the mayor's office to provide benefits that would enhance the quality of life of the city's disadvantaged citizens.

Morial's position on the use of public authority to help improve the quality of life of disadvantaged citizens provides an additional justification for examining his performance in providing social and economic benefits to blacks. Not only does the fact of increasing scholarly attention to an examination of the social and economic impact of black political participation make this line of scholarly inquiry an important undertaking, but Morial's position on this issue enhances the importance and justification of this line of scholarly inquiry. This section of the paper assesses the impact of Morial's mayoral tenure in terms of the public sector benefits received by blacks in three categories: *municipal employment, executive appointments,* and *municipal contracts.*

MUNICIPAL EMPLOYMENT

One increasingly studied component of the research examining the social and economic impact of black political participation is an examination of the extent to which black mayors can increase the representation of blacks on the municipal work force. Peter Eisinger finds that while black mayors exert a slight effect on increasing black municipal employment, a majority black population exerts the single largest influence on increasing black municipal employment.[45] Both variables are present in New Orleans and the evidence suggests that blacks have experienced an increase in municipal employment consistent to Eisinger's findings. When Morial assumed the mayor's office in 1977, blacks comprised a significant 40 percent of the municipal work force. Currently, blacks comprise approximately 53 percent.

A 13 percent increase in the black proportion of the municipal work force over a seven-year period is a significant accomplishment. It is also clearly a significant social and economic benefit that blacks have derived from participation in the political process. The 13 percent increase in the black proportion of the municipal work force is primarily an economic benefit to blacks in New Orleans in that more blacks have been able to obtain employment. Between 1970 and 1985, the percentage of black middle class families increased from 10 to 31 percent. This period overlaps the mayoral administrations of Morial and Moon Landrieu, the most liberal mayors in the city's history. The 13 percent increase is also in part a social benefit in the sense that as blacks participate more in the municipal work force, as whites have always done, and carry out the responsibilities of their job as part of a racially mixed work force tending to the governmental needs of a racially mixed public, they will gain an increased measure of social esteem and well-being.

A point related to the discussion of the 13 percentage point increase in the black proportion of the New Orleans work force is the fact that blacks had obtained a significantly high percentage of the city's work force—40 percent—prior to the election of Morial. The major share of the progress that blacks made in reaching the 40 percent level of the municipal work force was made under the eight-year mayoral tenure of Landrieu. Landrieu, a liberal, had been twice elected with a growing black vote playing a key role in his victories.[46] In return for their support, Landrieu successfully worked to increase the number of blacks on the city's work force.

EXECUTIVE APPOINTMENTS

Executive positions in New Orleans include the city's chief administrative officer, department heads, and top mayoral assistants. The importance of blacks penetrating the executive level of city government is at least of threefold significance. One, executive positions provide additional job opportunities for blacks at a fairly high level of financial compensation and prestige. Two, executive appointees are generally policymakers and thus blacks who are appointed to these positions usually get to influence the formulation and/or administration of public policy. This of course provides the opportunity for black municipal executives to influence the policy process in ways favorable to the interests of blacks if they should so desire. Third, because of the above two factors, blacks who hold executive positions in city government are important sources of symbolic or group pride to the black community. Blacks may feel a sense of racial pride and enhanced social esteem from having members of their race hold high-level positions in government.

Similar to municipal employment, blacks in New Orleans made their greatest initial progress in penetrating the executive level of city government during Landrieu's mayoralty. As part of his push to integrate the city's work force at all levels, Landrieu appointed Terrence Duvernay the city's first black chief administrative officer[47] in addition to appointing blacks to five of the 12 department head positions in city government. This meant that blacks headed 41.7 percent of the departments in city government, which included finance, recreation, welfare, property management, and model cities. It is significant that a black headed the city's finance department, given that municipal finance had been especially resistant to black penetration. In addition to the department head appointments, Landrieu also appointed a significant number of blacks to important administrative positions just below the department head level. These positions included the director of policy planning, manpower director, and the mayor's executive assistant. The most visible of all these appointments was clearly the appointment of Duvernay as the city's first black chief administrative officer.

Under Morial, blacks obtained an even higher proportion of department head appointments as he appointed blacks to seven of the 12 department head positions. This meant that blacks held 58.3 percent of the department head positions under Morial as compared to 41.7 percent under Landrieu. In addition to the chief administrative officer and the five departments which were headed by blacks under Landrieu, Morial appointed the city's first black police chief and sanitation department head. The former was clearly Morial's most visible executive appointment, and one which was clearly welcomed by the black community. Morial's appointment of Warren Woodfork as the city's first black police chief, in addition to providing symbolic benefit to blacks, provided the opportunity for substantive benefits to blacks in terms of improved relations with blacks and the police department. The relationship between the black community and the police department in New Orleans has historically been a stormy one with blacks being subjected to a high incidence of police brutality.[48] To the extent that the black police chief succeeds in addressing the problem of police brutality, his appointment provides additional substantive benefits to blacks.

MUNICIPAL CONTRACTS

The final area in which this [article] examines the mayoral impact of Morial on the black community is municipal contracts. Until recently municipal contracts have virtually been ignored in studies focusing on the impact of the black political participation. It is surprising that this has been the case because the awarding of municipal contracts to private companies to perform services and provide goods needed by city governments is a very important means of providing economic benefits through the use of public authority. Ethnic public officials made full use of this practice in the early twentieth century by awarding city contracts to businesses run by fellow ethnic group members. While the urban politics literature tends to emphasize the ethnic political machines' use of awarding municipal contracts to help businesses owned by fellow ethnics, the white Anglo-Saxon Protestants who controlled urban governments prior to ethnic dominance operated on basically the same model, that is, most of the municipal contracts during their governance were awarded to businesses run by fellow white Anglo-Saxon Protestants.

Morial has attempted to use municipal contracting to provide blacks social and economic benefits in two ways: (1) to help them obtain an increased share of the labor force participation on public works and construction projects financed and/or administered by the city and (2) to help black businesses obtain an increased share of contracts awarded by the city. In terms of the former, Morial issued Executive Order No. 83–02 on October 7, 1983, which, among other affirmative action provisions, mandated a 25 percent minority labor force participation rate (based on the total number of work hours on a craft by craft basis) in all city financed and/or administered public works and construction projects.[49] The executive order was later revised to apply to projects in excess of $25,000.[50] The original order was scheduled to go into effect no later than

December 22, 1983, but its implementation did not begin until October 1, 1985.

Morial's initial effort to increase the number of black businesses receiving contracts took the form of Executive Order No. 84–01, which was issued on January 24, 1984. This ordinance specified a goal of 20 percent minority subcontracting participation on projects in excess of $100,000.[51] The order applies only to the companies the prime contractors hire, not to the prime contractors themselves. The 20 percent goal of the policy was later dropped and replaced with the goal that the city sought to provide minority businesses "the maximum feasible opportunity to compete for contracts."[52] The original order was scheduled to go into effect no later than April 1, 1984, but its implementation did not begin until October 1, 1985.

Morial's municipal contracting program for minorities suffers from some shortcomings. The shortcoming of Morial's policy for increasing minority participation in municipal contracting can be seen by comparing New Orleans with some other large municipalities. According to Susan Feeney, New Orleans' minority business program lags far behind those in Atlanta, Philadelphia, San Francisco, Chicago, and Washington, both in terms of the size of the commitment and the actual accomplishment.[53] Table 12 shows the unfavorable comparison of New Orleans with those cities. Of the seven cities, New Orleans ranks last in terms of minority business participation goals and last in terms of the longevity of the program's implementation. It is not possible to rank the city in terms of proportion of city business actually awarded minority businesses because the city does not have the data necessary for that determination.

A major weakness of the Morial mayoralty is the inability to expeditiously enforce an effective minority labor force participation program and a minority business participation program to ensure that blacks would benefit from municipal contracts, both as individual labor force members and as owners of businesses. Equally as significant as this deficiency is the fact that there is no mechanism in place for monitoring compliance with Morial's order instituting these policies. Thus, there is no basis for evaluating the impact of these policies.

THE POST-MORIAL ERA IN NEW ORLEANS POLITICS?

Although Morial's mayoralty was not spectacularly successful from a programmatic perspective, there should be no doubt that Morial was the dominant political figure in New Orleans for the last eight years. In an uncanny manner, he remains so, despite the fact that he was defeated in

TABLE 12 Minority Business Participation Programs in New Orleans and Other Selected Cities, 1985

City	Minority business participation goal	Rank	Proportion of city business actually awarded to minority businesses	Rank	Date of implementation of program	Rank
Atlanta	35% of all city business for minorities	1	31%	2	1974 at 25%	1
Chicago	25% of all city business for minorities	3	17%	4	March, 1984	5
New Orleans	20% of subcontracting for construction projects over $100,000	5[a]	Not available	Unable to rank	October, 1985	7
Philadelphia	15% of all city business	4	17%	4	Mid-1983	4
San Francisco	30% of all city business	2	20%	3	August, 1984	6
Seattle	15% of all city business	4	15%	5	1980	3
Washington	35% of all city business for minorities	1	38%	1	1976 at 25%	2

[a]An assumption is made in this ranking that, in actual dollars, 20 percent of subcontracting participation for construction projects over $100,000 in New Orleans is less than 15 percent of all city business in Philadelphia and Seattle.
Source: Adopted from Susan Feeny, "City Minority Business Program Sputters," (New Orleans) Times Picayune, June 30, 1985.

his effort to convince the New Orleans' electorate to vote for the charter change referendum that would have allowed him to run for a third term, and despite the fact that he suffered some political embarrassments in the 1986 city elections. One such embarrassment was an unusual outcome to a peculiar city council race in District D.

After the third term charter change referendum was defeated, Morial decided to run for a seat on the city council from District D against an incumbent, Lambert Boissiere, who frequently opposed Morial's policy proposals. Morial's decision was considered by many to be degrading given that Morial was the city's first black mayor, at that time president of the U.S. Conference of Mayors, and considered by many as a strong candidate for Congress one day. Morial's decision was also considered to be petty and vindictive, and was seen as a form of political retribution directed not only toward Boissiere, but principally toward Boissiere's council ally Sidney Barthelemy, who was one of the two at-large members of the city council, the leading candidate to replace Morial as mayor, and Morial's chief opponent on the council during his eight-year mayoral tenure. Morial, surprisingly, finished second to Boissiere among a field of seven candidates. Undoubtedly embarrassed by his showing in a district that had consistently supported him in his mayoral elections, Morial withdrew from the runoff election.

Morial's aborted council race was not the only embarrassment that the 1986 city elections would dish out to Morial. Another major embarrassment was the outcome of the mayoral election. Prior to his decision to run for the council from District D, Morial unexpectedly endorsed State Senator William Jefferson for mayor, who was trailing Barthelemy in the polls by a considerable margin. Morial's endorsement of Jefferson was surprising because he reportedly harbored strong feelings against Jefferson for his decision to run for mayor against Morial in 1982, a decision which may have caused Morial the necessity of waging an expensive runoff campaign against Ronald Faucheaux. Although Morial's endorsement of Jefferson helped him to beat out Barthelemy for a first place finish in the primary among a field of three major candidates (the other major candidate was Sam LeBlanc, "an attorney, former state representative, and a Morial appointee to the city transit authority"[54]), Barthelemy defeated Jefferson in the runoff by an overwhelming margin, 93,049 to 67,698, respectively.[55] Barthelemy won 57.89 percent of the vote to Jefferson's 42.11 percent.

Table 13 shows the basis of Barthelemy's victory over Jefferson. Jefferson won the three predominantly black wards. His biggest victory in these wards was in the Second Ward, which he won by better than a two-to-one ratio. Barthelemy and Jefferson split the six racially mixed-

TABLE 13 Registration and Voting Data for All Wards for the 1986 New Orleans Mayoral Election

	Voter registration		Votes received	
Ward	Black	White	Barthelemy	Jefferson
(Predominantly black)				
First Ward	1,686	803	571	661
Second Ward	4,518	613	795	1,878
Eleventh Ward	6,905	3,201	2,334	3,580
(Racially mixed-majority black)				
Sixth Ward	2,400	2,388	1,605	1,068
Seventh Ward	21,456	11,693	11,989	8,503
Ninth Ward	45,173	27,503	23,062	22,623
Tenth Ward	3,709	1,919	1,368	1,998
Twelfth Ward	7,087	4,050	2,833	3,824
Seventeenth Ward	7,869	6,759	5,407	4,515
(Racially mixed-majority white)				
Fifth Ward	3,936	5,551	3,475	1,925
Eighth Ward	6,995	9,525	7,203	3,256
Thirteenth Ward	3,846	4,933	3,047	2,266
Fifteenth Ward	8,574	16,206	9,292	5,561
Sixteenth Ward	1,791	3,171	2,016	1,214
(Predominantly white)				
Third Ward	1,949	4,114	2,407	935
Fourth Ward	2,005	12,825	7,468	1,510
Fourteenth Ward	1,691	13,583	7,277	2,137

Source: "Unofficial Precinct Returns," (New Orleans) *The Times-Picayune/The States-Item*, March 3, 1986, sec. A, p. 19.

majority black wards, with Barthelemy winning the Sixth, Seventh, and Seventeenth Wards and Jefferson winning the Ninth (by less than 500 votes), Tenth, and Twelfth Wards. The remaining wards—the racially mixed-majority white wards and the predominantly white wards—were all won by Barthelemy by overwhelming margins. In the racially mixed-majority white Eighth Ward, for example, Barthelemy defeated Jefferson by better than a two-to-one margin. In the predominantly white Fourth Ward Barthelemy defeated Jefferson by almost a five-to-one ratio.

Barthelemy won the election because he won a significant minority of the black vote and the overwhelming majority of the white vote. The results of this election suggest that the white vote played the same role that the black vote used to play in the 1960s and 1970s when it was the minority component of the electorate. Just as the black vote then used to determine the winner between two white candidates by voting for the one they thought would be more representative of their interests, whites in the 1986 election cast the pivotal votes in Barthelemy's election. What this portends for the future is that in mayoral runoff contests involving two black candidates whites are going to play a critical role.

The final embarrassment that Morial received in the 1986 city election is that two of the three city council candidates that he endorsed lost to opponents endorsed by Barthelemy. This was a major embarrassment for Morial who just four years earlier successfully engineered the defeat of three opponents on the council by running three candidates against them. The eight-year political rivalry between Morial and Barthelemy had, for the next four years, apparently come to an end with Barthelemy emerging as the clear winner. This development has an important implication both for governance in the city and for the social and economic benefits that blacks may receive from the political process. The New Orleans city council now has a fully elected black majority.[56] and the relationship between Barthelemy and the council, unlike the stormy relationship between Morial and the council, should be very positive. With black politics operating from a single center of power in New Orleans, the mayor's office, rather than two centers of power—the mayor's office and the city council, as it did under Morial—municipal governance in New Orleans should be improved and blacks should benefit more than they did previously. Of course the rivalry could resume if Morial runs for the mayor's office in 1990, as many think he will. If he runs and wins, 1986 will not be the beginning of the post-Morial era; rather it will be the beginning of the four-year interlude in the Morial era.

SUMMARY AND CONCLUSIONS

Black political participation in New Orleans, like black political participation in cities throughout the South, increased substantially over the last 25 years. Black political power is clearly a reality in New Orleans. The increasing black vote in the middle 1960s allowed blacks to play a pivotal role in the election and reelection of Moon Landrieu, the city's most liberal white mayor. Subsequent increases in the black vote and black political development in the city led to the election of Ernest Morial as the first black mayor. Additionally, subsequent developments in black politics in

New Orleans has recently led to the beginning of a second generation of black mayoral governance in the city.

Blacks in New Orleans, like blacks elsewhere, have sought to use the political process to achieve some social and economic benefits. By and large, blacks in New Orleans have succeeded in this regard. For example, blacks now constitute a much larger share of the city's work force and the executive level of the municipal bureaucracy than they did in the 1960s. Under Landrieu the black proportion of the municipal work force reached 40 percent and approximately 41.7 percent of all department heads were black. These gains were increased under Morial. Under Morial, the proportion of the municipal work force comprised by blacks reached 53 percent and 58.3 percent of the department heads were black.

Morial's mayoral performance was uneven. From a symbolic perspective, Morial was very successful. From the standpoint of substantive policy accomplishments, Morial was much less successful. In terms of symbolism, the Morial mayoralty has been good for the city and especially for blacks. Morial is very popular among blacks. In the city where poverty is rampant among blacks, it has been a source of pride among blacks to have a black serve in the highest position in city government. Morial is also popular among many upper-income whites. In his two runoff elections he received approximately 20 to 14 percent of the white vote, respectively, which is on the high-end and middle portion of the range, respectively, that a successful black candidate can usually expect to receive from whites. His earnings tax referendum received almost 25 percent from white voters. In all three cases these white voters were middle and upper income whites.

Morial, like many mayors, has had significant difficulties in translating popular appeal into policy successes. He has not done well in getting his policy objectives enacted into public policy. For example, he has experienced repeated failures in his efforts to enhance the city's dismal revenue situation. Several of the fiscal measures that were adopted were not to his liking. Also, the implementation of Morial's minority labor force participation and minority business participation programs was delayed several months. Moreover, the minority business participation program is clearly inferior to that which exists in some other major cities.

Some of the policy successes for blacks in New Orleans came more from blacks on the city council than from Morial. One prominent example in this regard was the one-cent increase in the sales tax which provided the revenue needed to keep the city's bus service from being reduced. The one-cent increase was initially passed for one year, but subsequently extended for two additional years. On both actions blacks on the city council played a vital role, whereas Morial was opposed to the first action and neutral on the second. He rested his argument on the position that these were stopgap measures and the city's dire fiscal problems required more permanent solutions. These measures, Morial objections notwithstanding, were clearly beneficial to the black community since blacks are more dependent on public transportation than whites.

Blacks in New Orleans have considerable political power. It was in huge part that power which elected and reelected Morial as the city's first black mayor. That blacks constitute 51 percent of the city's voters places them in a good position to shape the city's future in a manner favorable to their interests. The 1986 mayoral election results make it clear that blacks will have to share political influence with whites. Whites will now determine the winner of mayoral elections involving two black candidates.

Although blacks in New Orleans have exercised considerable political power over the last eight years, the social and economic impact of that exercise of power on the black community has not been as significant as it could have been. It certainly has not been as significant as the impact of black politics in some other major cities. A principal factor accounting for the less than spectacular success of black politics, in terms of providing increased social and economic benefits for blacks, seems to be that black politics in New Orleans is not consensual, either at the leadership or the mass level. Rather, black politics in New Orleans for the last eight years has had two principal centers of power consisting of Morial in the mayor's office and Barthelemy on the city council. These rival centers of power in the structure of black politics in the city has considerably limited the allocation of public sector resources to the black community.

The challenge that Barthelemy and other black leaders in New Orleans will face is to sustain blacks interests in the political processes at a high level. That will not be easy. As black political participation becomes routinized, emotional and symbolic appeals as a strategy for fueling high levels of black political participation will be less successful. The ability to deliver additional tangible benefits will be more salient for maintaining high levels of black political participation. It will also be much more difficult to realize. The difficulty of the task should be helped by the signs that black politics in New Orleans will operate on a more consensual basis than it has done in the past. If that does not happen, the ironic end result of the enormous political success that blacks have realized in New Orleans over the last 25 years will be that whites will become the institutionalized pivotal center of power in the city's politics. Such an outcome would probably even further limit the capacity of the political process in New Orleans to provide social and economic benefits for blacks.

NOTES

1. Monte Piliawsky, "The Impact of Black Mayors on the Black Community: The Case of New Orleans' Ernest Morial," *The Review of Black Political Economy* (Spring 1985), 6.

2. Bette Woody, *Managing Crisis Cities: The New Black Leadership and the Politics of Resource Allocation* (Westport, Conn.: Greenwood Press), 38.

3. (In Louisiana, parishes are the equivalent of counties.) Larry Schroeder, Lee Madere, and Jerome Lomba, *Occasional Paper No. 52: Local Government Revenue and Expenditure Forecasting: New Orleans* (Syracuse: Metropolitan Studies Program, The Maxwell School of Citizenship and Public Affairs, Syracuse University, October 1981).

4. Silas Lee et al., "Ten Years After (Pro Bono Publico?): The Economic Status of Blacks and Whites in New Orleans—1985," (unpublished report, 1985).

5. Schroeder, Madere, and Lomba, *Local Government Revenue and Expenditure Forecasting*, 2.

6. Ibid.

7. United States Bureau of the Census, *1980 Census of Population and Housing; Supplementary Report: Advance Estimates of Social, Economic, and Housing Characteristics; Part 20, Louisiana Parishes and Selected Places*, PHC80–52–20, (Washington, D.C.: United States Government Printing Office, issued January 1983), 20–4.

8. United States Department of Commerce, Bureau of the Census, *Statistical Abstract of the United States*, 24.

9. Data Analysis Unit, Office of Analysis and Planning, and System and Programming Group, Finance Department, *1980 Census: New Orleans Census Tracts*, City of New Orleans, Ernest N. Morial, Mayor, 1982.

10. (The April 1985 figures are preliminary.) United States Department of Labor, Bureau of Labor Statistics, *Employment and Earnings*, vol. 32, no. 6 (Washington, D.C.: United States Government Printing Office, June 1985) 82–83.

11. Piliawsky, "The Impact of Black Mayors," 6.

12. James R. Bobo, *The New Orleans Economy: Pro Bono Publico?* (New Orleans: College of Business Administration, University of New Orleans, 1975), 1–2.

13. Alvin J. Schexnider, "Political Mobilization in the South: The Election of a Black Mayor in New Orleans," in *The New Black Politics: The Search for Political Power*, ed. Michael B. Preston, Lenneal J. Henderson, Jr., and Paul Puryear (New York: Longman, 1982), p. 223.

14. Lee et al., "The Economic Status of Blacks and Whites," 2.

15. Piliawsky, "The Impact of Black Mayors," 6.

16. Ibid.

17. Lee et al., "The Economic Status of Blacks and Whites," 2.

18. Schexnider, "Political Mobilization in the South," 222.

19. Charles Y. W. Chai, "Who Rules New Orleans: A Study of Community Power Structure," *Louisiana Business Survey* 2 (October 1971) 10.

20. Ibid.

21. Schexnider, "Political Mobilization in the South," 225.

22. City of New Orleans, *Prospectus, Audubon Park Commission on Improvement Bonds Series 1979*, 1979, 9.

23. Schroeder, Madere, and Lomba, *Local Government Revenue and Expenditure Forecasting*, 4.

24. Piliawsky, "The Impact of Black Mayors," 8; and Jeffrey M. Elliott, *Black Voices in American Politics* (San Diego: Harcourt Brace Jovanovich, Publishers, 1986), 341.

25. Schexnider, "Political Mobilization in the South," 227.

26. Ibid., 228.

27. Ibid.

28. "Black Judge Enters Runoff for Mayor of New Orleans," *The New York Times*.

29. All of the electoral data used from this point on in the discussion of the 1977 mayoral election, unless otherwise indicated, were taken from Allen Rosenzweig and John Wildgen, "A Statistical Analysis of the 1977 Mayor's Race in New Orleans," *Louisiana Business Survey* 9 (April 1978), 4–8.

30. "Black Judge Enters Runoff," *The New York Times*.

31. For a fuller discussion of Morial's primary strategy, see Rosenzweig and Wildgen, "A Statistical Analysis of the 1977 Mayor's Race," 8.

32. Ibid., 5.

33. James H. Gillis, "Black Nearly Solid for Morial," (New Orleans) *Times Picayune*, Nov. 14, 1977, sec. 1; and Walter Isaacson, "DiRosa Contests Election; Ouster of Morial Sought," (New Orleans) *States-Item*, Nov. 14, 1977, final edition.

34. In this [article], a predominantly black ward is operationalized as a ward in which black registration exceeds white registration by at least a two-to-one ratio. A predominantly white ward is operationalized as a ward in which white voter registration exceeds black voter registration by at least a two-to-one ratio.

35. Schexnider, "Political Mobilization in the South," 228.

36. All of the electoral data used in this section, unless otherwise indicated, were taken or computed from a tally of official returns recorded by the New Orleans City Council.

37. Garry Boulard, "Power Brokers," *New Orleans*, October 1985, 53.

38. Piliawsky, "The Impact of Black Mayors," 20. Also, Piliawsky, "The Limits of Power: Dutch Morial Mayor of New Orleans," *Southern Exposure* 12 (February 1984), 75.

39. Morial reports that while the other candidates did not make race an issue, the media did. For his assessment of this point, see Jeffrey M. Elliot, *Black Voices in American Politics* (1986), 344.

40. James H. Gillis, "Blacks Voted for Sales Tax," (New Orleans) *Times Picayune*, June 11, 1982, sec. 1, p. 13.

41. An analysis by the (New Orleans) *Times Picayune* operationalizes black and white precincts as precincts in which fewer than 10 voters are members of the opposite race. See James H. Gillis, "The Black and White Voting Split," (New Orleans) *Times Picayune*, Nov. 7, 1984.

42. Ibid.

43. (New Orleans) *Times Picayune,* Oct. 16, 1982, 15, cited in Piliawsky, "The Impact of Black Mayors," 9–10.

44. Alex Poinsett, "Mayor Ernest N. Morial Finds: Running New Orleans Is No Mardi Gras," *Ebony,* December 1978, 34.

45. Peter K. Eisinger, "Black Employment in Municipal Jobs: The Impact of Black Political Power," *American Political Science Review* 76 (June 1982), 391.

46. Schexnider, "Political Mobilization in the South," 226.

47. Poinsett, "Running New Orleans," 38.

48. For a brief discussion of the issue of police brutality in New Orleans, see Piliawsky, "The Impact of Black Mayors," 16–17.

49. Executive Order No. 83–02, Mayor's Office New Orleans, Louisiana, Oct. 7, 1983.

50. Policy Memorandum No. 209, Chief Administrative Office, New Orleans, Louisiana, July 11, 1985.

51. Executive Order No. 84–01, Mayor's Office, New Orleans, Louisiana, Jan. 24, 1984.

52. Policy Memorandum No. 183 (Revised), Chief Administrative Office, New Orleans, Louisiana, April 10, 1984.

53. Susan Feeney, "City Minority Business Program Sputters," (New Orleans) *Times Picayune,* June 30, 1985.

54. Ibid.

55. "Unofficial Precinct Return," (New Orleans) *The Times Picayune/The State-Item,* March 3, 1986, sec. A, p. 19.

56. The city council became majority black in 1985 when Ulysses Williams was selected by council members to fill a seat on the council vacated by the resignation of Wayne Bobvovich.

CHAPTER V

GOVERNORS AND PUBLIC POLICY

INTRODUCTION

Nicholas Henry writes that "governors are moving up in the pecking order of American politics."[1] Other political scientists add that "in most states the governor has gained authority and formal power in recent years, and this has improved policy and managerial leadership performances."[2] And finally, others point out that "in the eyes of many Americans, governors are responsible for everything that happens in their states during their terms of office..."[3] and "often [are] the most important influence on state policy."[4]

Most governors have not always enjoyed the position of influence and power they occupy today. With few exceptions, governors have been "weak" executives for a variety of historical, state constitutional, and political reasons. Larry Sabato, in a selection from his book *Goodbye to Good-Time Charlie*, reprinted in this chapter as Reading 9, traces the rise in gubernatorial power from the early day U.S. governors to the present. The "new" governors, he argues, are no longer "good-time Charlies."

David R. Berman writes that the governor has emerged as the most significant force in state legislative policy-making.[5] The governor formulates legislative proposals and seeks to secure the passage of these proposals in the state legislature. Perhaps the most important policy recommendation the governor makes to the legislature is the state budget. This is so because the budget allows the governor the greatest opportunity to make an impact on state programs and policies.

The governor exercises great influence over budget legislation because in many states his or her veto power includes the *item veto*. The item veto is a state constitutional provision that permits governors to veto individual items in an appropriations bill while signing the remainder of the bill into law. Thus the governor is in a strong position to persuade the legislature to adopt his or her budget and, by extension, his or her programmatic goals. The uses of the item veto are discussed by Glenn Abney and Thomas P. Lauth in their article, "The Line-Item Veto in the States: An Instrument for Fiscal Restraint or an Instrument for Partisanship?" reprinted in this chapter as Reading 10.

NOTES

1. Nicholas Henry, *Governing at the Grassroots: State and Local Politics,* 3rd ed. (Englewood Cliffs, N.J.: Prentice-Hall, 1987), p. 162.
2. James MacGregor Burns, J. W. Peltason, and Thomas E. Cronin, *State and Local Politics: Government by the People,* 5th ed. (Englewood Cliffs, N.J.: Prentice-Hall, 1987), p. 118.

3. Thomas R. Dye, *Politics in States and Communities*, 4th ed. (Englewood Cliffs, N.J.: Prentice-Hall, 1981), p. 160.

4. David R. Berman, *State and Local Politics*, 4th ed. (Boston: Allyn & Bacon, 1984), p. 119.

5. Ibid., p. 120.

THE GOVERNOR IN AMERICAN HISTORY: AN OFFICE TRANSFORMED

Larry Sabato

Larry Sabato writes that "governors as a class have outgrown the term 'good-time Charlie.' " The new governors are well-educated, politically skilled, and forward-looking leaders; they are now armed with considerable constitutional and statutory powers that are adequate for the modern-day subnational executive challenges they face.

The early governors—those who came to office during the revolutionary period (1774–87)—were uniformly limited in their powers and functions. First, each state constitution provided for an executive council whose approval was needed for most executive actions including the pardoning power. Second, while the revolutionary governor had considerable appointment power, special majorities in the legislature were required for confirmation. Third, except for two states, the governor had no veto over legislative enactments and thus had very little direction over state policy. Virtually the only role wherein the governor's power was plenary was that of commander-in-chief of the state militia.

The ratification of the U.S. Constitution in 1787–88 by all states except North Carolina and Rhode Island established the U.S. presidency as a model for stronger executive leadership. As a result, many of the states, over time, rethought their constitutions and revised them in such a way as to grant the governor additional executive authority.

The impetus for additional growth in gubernatorial power occurred during the expansive presidency of Andrew Jackson (1829–37). Gubernatorial terms of office were lengthened and appointive powers were increased. However, Jacksonian democracy was a mixed blessing for the status of the governor. For example, Jackson's advocacy of more elective power in the hands of the people led to the adoption of the *long ballot* by most state legislatures. The long ballot meant that many more executive offices would be filled by popular election rather than gubernatorial or legislative appointment. The result was a "plural" elective executive in which the governor was simply one of several elected officials in the executive branch of state government.

Subsequently, additional factors kept the governorship to a minor role in state government. For example, the adoption of the federal income tax amendment in 1913 permitted the national government to monopolize revenue sources and thus centralize a good deal of power in Washington. Accordingly, citizens began to look to Washington, D.C., rather than their state capitals for the resolution of many important political problems. The Washington government's advantage over the states was accelerated by the events of the Great Depression, which required massive resources for the economic and social problems of the people of the states.

Not until the early 1970s did a reversal of fortunes come for the leadership potential of state governors. By then, constitutional reform had added immensely to the governor's appointment, veto, and reorganization powers, thus giving him or her considerable clout over public policy questions. Moreover, the advent of national administrations from 1968 to the present, including the Carter administration, began fiscal cutbacks at the federal level; this resulted in a need for state leadership which could deal with the states' massive social problems with greatly reduced federal grants-in-aid.

The enormous budget and trade deficits faced by the federal government in the 1980s and 1990s has pushed even more responsibility down to the states to solve their respective economic and social problems. Armed with new constitutional and statutory power on the one hand and a demand from the citizenry on the other to meet pressing public needs, the contemporary governor has a full agenda indeed.

What kinds of persons are elected to head the governments of the 50 states? Are they best described as midgets or giants? Have the changes that have occurred in governors over the last two decades been. . . significant?. . . The analysis herein indicates that governors and their settings have been transformed.

Many of the governors who served earlier in this century have been described as "flowery old courthouse politicians," "machine dupes," "political pipsqueaks," and "good-time Charlies." This does not fairly describe *all* past governors by any means; some governors of the early 1900s could rival in competence any of today's number. Still, it is reasonably clear to American political observers that a greater percentage of the

Source: Larry Sabato, "The Governor in American History: An Office Transformed," in *Goodbye to Good-Time Charlie: The American Governorship Transformed,* 2nd Edition (Washington, D.C.: CQ Press, 1983), pp. 1–12. Reprinted with permission.

nation's governors are capable, creative, forward-looking, and experienced. As Gov. Reubin Askew of Florida, himself one of the impressive new breed, commented:

> I would be hard-pressed to tell you of any governor in the country right now who I did not believe was capable. . . .I have known of some in the past. But I know every governor personally. . .and it's one of the things that intrigues me—how the country has produced a lot of good men and women as governors today.

Former Gov. William Scranton of Pennsylvania gave higher marks to more recent governors than to his contemporaries. He said, "They [the new governors] have a harder job, more to do, and I think they do better at it."

In other words, governors as a class have outgrown the term "good-time Charlie." Once the darlings of the society pages, governors today are more concerned about the substantive work of the office than about its ceremonial aspects. Once parochial officers whose concerns rarely extended beyond the boundaries of their home states and whose responsibilities frequently were slight, governors have gained major new powers that have increased their influence in national as well as state councils. Once maligned foes of the national and local governments, governors have become skilled negotiators and, importantly, often crucial coordinators at both of those levels. Once ill prepared to govern and less prepared to lead, governors have welcomed into their ranks a new breed of vigorous, incisive, and thoroughly trained leaders. The implications of all these changes for the federal system, its constituent parts, and the nation as a whole are not insignificant.

THE HISTORICAL PROGRESSION

The title "governor" is one of the few constants throughout American political history.[1] Even so, the name is the only aspect of the office that has been immune to basic change. Governors in the 1980s, for example, may be more powerful than they were two decades ago, but they cannot compare in strength with most of the colonial governors. As an agent of the crown, the colonial governor served at the king's pleasure (except in Rhode Island and Connecticut where much weaker governors were popularly elected) and exercised broad powers in his behalf.[2] These powers included command of all armed forces, the supervision of law enforcement missions, the appointment of judges and other officials, the convening and dissolution of the legislative body, a veto of legislative acts, and the granting of pardons and reprieves.[3]

As political scientist Leslie Lipson has pointed out, the official powers of colonial governors can give an exaggerated impression of their actual influence, because public sentiment mattered considerably in how the laws were enforced. The colonial governors had little patronage at their disposal, and they did not appoint port and customs officials (thus permitting the colonists to outmaneuver them in the execution of laws such as the Navigation Acts).

Still, the colonial governors were powerful and visible enough to be the focal point of the antiroyalist protests leading to the Revolution. It is not surprising, then, that when the newly independent Americans set out to design their state governments, the distrust of colonial executive power led to a weakened governor and a domineering legislature. The broad veto and legislative dissolution powers were among the first to be removed from the governor's repertoire. The governor was seen to be merely the agent who would carry out the legislature's will in a system with strict separation of legislative and executive departments. As a futher limitation on executive authority, the governor was given a short, fixed term of office.

The governorship was considerably encumbered, as men such as Benjamin Franklin and Thomas Paine argued it should be. At the same time, the efforts of Constitution framers like John Adams kept the office from being rendered totally impotent in all of the states.[4] The governor was weakest in the states (Pennsylvania, Vermont, Georgia, New Hampshire, and, for a time, Massachusetts) that adopted plural executive offices, in which the governor was just the presiding officer of an executive council and in some cases also was appointed by the legislature. Only in New York under the "Jay Constitution" and later in Massachusetts under its "Adams Constitution" did a strengthened governor with extensive veto and appointment powers emerge.

All but three of the original state constitutions limited the governor's term to one year. John Adams' dictum prevailed: "Where annual elections end, there slavery begins." From Pennsylvania southward, all states had severe restrictions on re-eligibility—Georgia, for example, permitted its governor no more than a one-year term in any three-year period—and appointment by the legislature also was the rule. North of Pennsylvania, however, the governor was not bound so tightly. While still a weak office in most cases, the governorship in northern states was elective, with legislative selection only when no candidate garnered a majority of the votes. There were no restrictions on re-eligibility in these states, and long tenure (as well as the potential for increased influence that accompanied it) often resulted. George Clinton, for example, was governor of New York for six successive three-year terms (1777–1795), and William Livingston held the governorship in New Jersey for 14 consecutive one-year terms (1776–1790).

The powers and functions assigned to governors in the early state constitutions were almost uniformly limited, though more wide-ranging than might be supposed at first. Every state had some type of "executive council" that variously advised, limited, or overruled the governor. (Only two such councils survive today, in the New England states of Massachusetts and New Hampshire.) While the governors usually had a considerable number of appointments to make, legislative confirmation of their choices was a prerequisite.

Most legislative powers, by contrast, had no executive check. No longer could governors dissolve the assembly and, except in Massachusetts and New York, there was no provision for a veto. Still, the governor usually could call special legislative sessions and in a few states actually participate in the legislature's proceedings. Judicial powers given to the governors were no more extensive than their legislative authority. Except for appointing judges, governors were virtually powerless in the judicial field. Even the pardoning power, a traditional executive prerogative, was qualified by special prohibitions and the need for the council's consent.

In sum there were many checks and few balances in the governorships designed by the early state constitutional conventions. One North Carolina delegate returning home from his convention was asked how much power the governor had gotten. "Just enough to sign the receipt for his salary," was his reply.[5] Only the governor's military position was a strong one, with all states designating him as commander-in-chief.

In most states the governors clearly were subordinated to the legislature. James Madison called the governors "in general little more than cyphers" when compared with the "omnipotent" legislatures.[6] Nevertheless, even the mistrustful constitutional fathers gave the governors modest powers—a significant admission that discretionary executive authority was necessary to some degree. That the degree granted was not great enough became apparent during the years between the end of the Revolutionary War and the beginning of the Constitutional Convention in 1787. One scholar, in condemning the results of Virginia's executive limitations, described the situation that existed in almost all the newborn states:

> The executive apparatus which emerged from the [1776 Virginia Constitutional] Convention was weak in constitutional stature, confused in lines of authority, and wholly and irresponsibly subservient to the legislative will.[7]

The governorship in this sorry position might be likened, in at least one respect, to the vice presidency of the United States as it has existed for much of the country's history. The early enfeebled governorship sometimes served as a harmless repository for ambitious and frequently capable politicians who were out of favor with "establishment" forces—a kind of "kicking upstairs" that also gave the United States some of its vice presidents. Patrick Henry of Virginia, for one, was elected governor in 1776 by this process. As political scientist Rowland Egger sized it up, the Virginia governorship was

> ...designed to provide institutional care, under properly septic [*sic*] conditions, for politicians at the margin of the oligarchy whose popularity could not be altogether ignored.[8]

The restricted Virginia model, however, can give a slightly distorted picture of the early governor, as Joseph Kallenbach has warned. Limited though they were, the designs of the first states served as a resource lode from which a strong presidency later was extracted.

> Taking all the state constitutions into account, essentially all the major elements that were later combined in the creation of a strong national chief executive were found in one or more state plans.[9]

The New York and Massachusetts constitutions, in particular, provided models for the 1787 Constitutional Convention. Those states without strong governors served, in a sense, as negative models because they advertised the results of executive enfeeblement. Finally, most of the men who held the office of governor just after the Revolutionary War were distinguished and capable persons. Their temperaments and administrations provided considerable reassurance to a public very wary of executives.

FROM JACKSON TO PROGRESSIVISM

The governorship, in turn, benefited gradually from presidential example. During the robust presidency of Jackson the governor's term was lengthened, usually to four years, and in many states appointive, veto, and pardoning powers were initiated or broadened. Well-publicized instances of legislative corruption and incompetence lent impetus to the movement for a strengthened governorship. Adding to the governor's basic legitimacy and representativeness was the universal institution of an elected governorship and the expansion of the suffrage.

Jacksonian democracy, however, was hardly a panacea for the governor's ills. Rather, the seeds of executive disaster were sown in this period with the adoption of the "long ballot." More and more public offices were filled by popular election, and an often ill-informed electorate chose the occupants of offices that a governor should, by all administrative logic, have been able to fill by appointment. This loss of administrative control caused a corresponding loss of coordinated action. Governors frequently were hamstrung by the executive departments they were supposed to rule. The plural elective executive was democracy's excess, and governors as well as their peoples were to suffer the consequences for many decades. (Indeed, state governments still are paying a considerable price for long ballots, which persist in spite of all the evidence of their undesirability.)

The situation reached its nadir in the 1880s and 1890s as urban residents demanded an increase in state services. Old and new agencies grew like Topsy at the behest of the legislatures. In New York, for example, there were only 10 state agencies in 1800. By 1900 the number had mushroomed to 81, and by 1925 the state bureaucracy claimed 170 constituent parts.

The governors were unable to exert control over this multitude of new agencies. Instead they were the dominions of special boards and commissions (normally appointed by the legislatures at least in part) or other elected executive officials. So paltry had the governor's authority become that by 1888 James Bryce could write: "Little remains to the Governor except his veto.... State office carries little either of dignity or of power."[10] Nevertheless he hastened to add: "A State Governor...is not yet a nonentity."

The wisdom of Bryce's proviso can be seen in the actions of many governors in the Progressive era. Gubernatorial leadership was a major factor in the success of Progressive legislation in many states. State executives such as Robert LaFollette of Wisconsin, Hiram Johnson of California, Theodore Roosevelt of New York, and Woodrow Wilson of New Jersey channeled into successful reform programs the public's revulsion at revelations of corruption and squalor.

The governorship, never really strong since colonial days, became more prestigious as a result of the battles many of its occupants fought with industry and party bosses. The reform impulse meant added influence for the governors, if only temporarily. Gov. Woodrow Wilson claimed: "The whole country...is clamoring for leadership, and a new role, which to many persons seems little less than unconstitutional, is thrust upon our executives."[11]

Despite the increased prestige, though, the governorship was not empowered to break the heavy chains that bound it to a minor role in government. Governors had neither the basic constitutional and statutory authority nor the control over their own branch of government that would have been necessary for them to loom larger. Even Wilson admitted that he would not be able to accomplish his plans fully because of the development " . . . not systematically but by patchwork and mere accretion [of] the multiplication of boards and commissions."[12] At base, governors did not have authority to match their responsibility. As the states' acknowledged political leaders, they were the focus of public attention and were expected to solve perceived problems, but a myriad of institutional handicaps kept them from fulfilling either the public's or their own expectations for performance. The disappointment and disillusionment resulting from the governor's failure caused a demanding public to look elsewhere for action.

THE GOVERNORSHIP'S MODERN DECLINE

Several developments on the national level in this century also served to relegate states and their governors to a position of secondary importance both in fact and in the public's eyes.[13] The Sixteenth Amendment to the Constitution, ratified in 1913, handed the federal government a vitally important tool: the income tax. Its utilization of this tax instrument, and the effective monopolization of revenue sources that accompanied it, gave Washington "the most powerful advantage of all" in the long run. The centralization involved in preparing for and fighting in World War I also shifted attention to the national level.

The Great Depression was an even more crucial milestone for the states, which had neither the resources nor in many cases the will to combat the era's massive social problems. First, of course, the Depression's causes were national and international in scope, and any single state was helpless to effect an overall solution. Moreover, the inefficient and illogical machinery of state government was wholly unprepared to administer even piecemeal remedies. The times called for decisive action, which the governors and the states were unable to provide. The citizenry turned instead to Washington, and President Franklin D. Roosevelt captured the nation's imagination and ministered attentively to the hopes of the country. Terry Sanford of North Carolina, a governor-turned-academic, observed:

> From the viewpoint of the efficacy of state government, the states lost their confidence, and the people their faith in the states; the news media became cynical, the political scientists became neglectful, and the critics became harsh.[14]

State governments did not cease functioning after the 1930s nor did they remain unchanged. Most observers believe that state administration became increasingly complex. Coleman Ransone asserts that "...the functions of the states increased markedly" even during the period of their greatest eclipse, from the New Deal forward.[15] However, the gap in authority, responsibility, and citizen confidence between national and state governments widened considerably; as the federal government modernized and expanded at a rapid rate, the distance between the performances on national and state levels became more apparent.

The critics, as Sanford noted, did indeed become harsh. In 1949 journalist Robert S. Allen issued a severe indictment of the states:

> State government is the tawdriest, most incompetent, and most stultifying unit of the nation's political structure. In state government are to be found in their most extreme and vicious forms all the worst evils of misrule in the country....Further, imbedded between the municipalities at the bottom and the federal system on top, state government is the wellspring of many of the principal poisons that plague both.[16]

Allen's criticism was well-grounded and documented by the states themselves. A litany of evils is conjured up by state government researchers. Corruption existed in a thousand forms. Ignorance of social needs and the consequent crippling of cities was widespread. Outright incompetence was the standard in some states. Violation of basic constitutional rights was not unheard of. Malapportionment and unjust representation in the legislatures frustrated the popular will. Special interests, vested economic powers, and political machines dominated one or more branches of state governments.

The situation seemed to change little, for in the mid-1960s Terry Sanford still could catalogue a list of state ills not unlike those of Robert Allen:

> The states are indecisive.
>
> The states are antiquated.
>
> The states are timid and ineffective.
>
> The states are not willing to face their problems.
>
> The states are not responsive.
>
> The states are not interested in cities.
>
> These half-dozen charges are true about all of the states some of the time and some of the states all of the time.[17]

Governors contributed to and were victimized by this state of affairs. Allen had exempted some enlightened governors from blame because they were "...sadly thwarted and frustrated by the stifling inadequacies and imbecilities of state government," but enlightened governors were "pathetically few in number."[18]

Harold J. Laski believed that state governments were so hopeless that the governors elected to head them were either "second rate politicians" satisfying a generalized ambition for public office or future national political stars whose careers in state politics were "no more than a stage in an ascent."[19] Laski insisted that " . . . The significance of the governor is set in the framework of his federal ambitions rather than of his purposes in the state." In the 1940s and 1950s some academics and government officials predicted, and governors feared, that the federal system would dissolve, thereby leaving the states as mere administrative regions of the national government. Governors, it was thought, would fade further into the obscurity they so richly deserved.

A REVERSAL OF FORTUNES

The converse of these predictions comes closer to the truth. Instead of obscurity, governors have achieved wide public recognition. By 1972 pollster Louis Harris was able to report that "Governors are easily the best known political figures in the country" with the sole exception of the president. Almost nine out of ten people could correctly identify their governors, while only about six out of ten could accurately name at least one U.S. senator from their state.[20] It has not hurt the image of governors, either, that in 1976 and 1980 former governors were elected to the presidency of the United States.

The enhancement of the governors and their dominions, the states, is the product of many forces. . . . Yet even a glance at the annual governors' messages to the state legislatures indicates the change in the tone and quality of governors in the last three decades. In 1951 the "state of the state" proposals were dominated by civil defense, highway construction, and "efficiency" measures necessary to cut "waste" in state government. Governors advocated "tax relief" instead of services. Scores of social and urban needs were scarcely mentioned, if at all. The programs that were advocated by progressive governors were noteworthy precisely because they were so exceptional.

By the 1980s the agenda conceived by the governors was a crowded one. Even in times of economic difficulty, an exceedingly wide range of social, health, and education programs, with devotion to urban needs in particular, was evident. Innovations in all major policy areas now abound in the states, and the federal government has found itself outstripped in several fields.[21] A succession of presidents has recognized the states' new capacities, and Washington has begun to transfer significant programs back to the states—programs that strain the states fiscally but also present new opportunities and confer increased responsibilities and powers. . . . The states, once the "fallen arches" of the federal system, have become the system's "arch supports."[22]

This change has not gone undetected. Academics hailed the states' attempt to shake off their cobwebs and noted that simultaneously ". . . governors have moved from low-visibility and low-activity to positions of more positive executive leadersihp within the states and the nation."[23] The public also seemed to sit up, take notice, and nod approval. The Gallup Poll in October 1981 found that "an almost complete reversal" of the public's view of state versus national government had taken place since the New Deal.[24] Where Americans in 1936 had preferred by 56–44 percent that power be concentrated in the federal government rather than in the states, the public in 1981 favored state governments over Washington by a wide margin (64–36 percent). By even larger proportions Americans saw state governments as more understanding than the federal government of the real needs of the people, as able to administer social programs more efficiently than Washington, and as far less wasteful in the use of the tax dollar. Other surveys have reported similar findings in recent years. . . . [25]

NOTES

1. Only New Hampshire and Georgia ever designated the executive head differently—by calling him "president"—and this was for only a brief time after the Revolutionary War. Since 1792 the states universally have used the title "governor."

2. Joseph E. Kallenbach, *The American Chief Executive: The Presidency and the Governorship* (New York: Harper & Row, 1966), 3–5. See also Evarts B. Greene, *The Provincial Governor in the English Colonies of North America*, vol. 7, Harvard Historical Studies (New York: Longmans, Green, 1898).

3. Bennett M. Rich, *State Constitutions: The Governor*, State Constitutional Studies Project, series 11, no. 3 (New York: National Municipal League, 1960), 1–2; and Leslie Lipson, *The American Governor: From Figurehead to Leader* (Chicago: University of Chicago Press, 1949), 9–11.

4. W. F. Dodd, "The First State Constitutional Conventions, 1776–1783," *American Political Science Review* 2 (November 1908):1545–1561.

5. Lipson, *The American Governor*, 14.

6. As quoted by Louis Lambert, "The Executive Article," in *Major Problems in Constitutional Revision*, ed. Brooke Graves (Chicago: Public Administration Service, 1960), 185.

7. Rowland Egger, "The Governor of Virginia, 1776 and 1976," *University of Virginia Newsletter* 52 (August 1976):41.

8. Ibid., 42.

9. Kallenbach, *The American Chief Executive,* 25; see also pp. 30–67.

10. James Bryce, *The American Commonwealth,* vol. II (London: Macmillan, 1888), 149.

11. Address before the Commercial Club of Portland, Ore., May 18, 1911, as quoted in "The New Role of the Governor," John M. Matthews, *American Political Science Review* 6 (May 1912):224.

12. "First Annual Message of Woodrow Wilson, Governor of New Jersey, to the Legislature of New Jersey, January 9, 1912," *N.J. Legislative Documents* 1 (1911):4.

13. A more thorough discussion of these factors can be found in Terry Sanford, *Storm over the States* (New York: McGraw-Hill, 1967), 20–24.

14. Ibid., 21.

15. Correspondence with the author, November 11, 1976.

16. Robert S. Allen, ed., *Our Sovereign State* (New York: Vanguard Press, 1949), vii.

17. Sanford, *Storm over the States,* 1.

18. Allen, *Our Sovereign State,* xi.

19. Harold J. Laski, *The American Democracy: A Commentary and an Interpretation* (London: Allen and Unwin, 1949), 146.

20. As quoted in *The State of the States* (Washington, D.C.: National Governors' Conference, 1974), 5. Many other surveys since 1972 have produced similar results.

21. See, for example, *State Government News* 24 (December 1981):10–16; and *Governors' Policy Initiatives: Meeting the Challenges of the 1980s* (Washington, D.C.: National Governors' Association, 1980).

22. See *In Brief: State and Local Roles in the Federal System* (Washington, D.C.: Advisory Commission on Intergovernmental Relations, 1981), 3–10.

23. J. Oliver Williams, "Changing Perspectives on the American Governor," in *The American Governor in Behavioral Perspective,* ed. Williams and Thad L. Beyle, (New York: Harper & Row, 1972), 1.

24. The Gallup Poll was a random-sample, in-person survey of 1,540 adults conducted September 18–21, 1981, and released October 18, 1981.

25. See, for example, the series of surveys on federalism cited in *Opinion Outlook,* October 5, 1981, 1–3. Also see Parris N. Glendening, "The Public's Perception of State Government and Governors," *State Government* 53 (Summer 1980):115–120.

THE LINE-ITEM VETO IN THE STATES: AN INSTRUMENT FOR FISCAL RESTRAINT OR AN INSTRUMENT FOR PARTISANSHIP?

Glenn Abney and Thomas P. Lauth

Forty-two of fifty state governors, according to Glenn Abney and Thomas P. Lauth, have the line-item veto power. They also note that the rationale for the item veto has been its purported capacity to promote legislative efficiency by particularly discouraging pork barrel appropriations. A major question for them, then, is: "Is this the only gubernatorial use for the line-item veto?" Abney and Lauth sought the answer to this question by means of a mail survey of state legislative budget officers. Their main concern was whether governors use the line-item veto as an instrument of fiscal restraint to prevent pork barrel appropriations by the legislature or as an instrument to promote executive and partisan interests—and thus enhance the political power of the governor.

The data gathered indicate that legislatures against which the item veto is used are not more fiscally irresponsible than other legislatures. Moreover, vetoes are not cast more often in states with legislatures having a tendency to engage in pork barrel appropriations. In addition, just as the line-item veto is not used as an instrument to block pork barrel, it is also not used against legislatures tending to increase executive spending recommendations. Accordingly, Abney and Lauth conclude that there is no linkage between the use of the item veto and fiscal restraint. They believe that this finding results mainly from the ability of some legislatures to avoid a gubernatorial line-item veto by writing appropriations bills that make a governor's veto difficult without damaging his or her own fiscal goals. In short, the line-item veto is not found to produce fiscal restraint.

Abney and Lauth do find a linkage between partisanship and the governors' use of the line-item veto. The line-item veto is *more likely* to be more used where there is divided government, that is, where the governor and the legislature belong to different parties, or where the government is truncated, that is, where the governor belongs to one party and has a majority of his or her party in only one of the two houses of the legislature. On the other hand, the item veto is *less frequently* used where party government exists, that is, where the control of both the executive and legislative branches is in the hands of one party.

In sum, Abney and Lauth report that the line-item veto is often used as a partisan instrument whereby the governor increases his or her own political power rather than as an instrument for fiscal prudence and efficiency. Nevertheless, anytime the governor uses the item veto, a state's budget is reduced. This is not the same as efficiency, but it certainly does equate to a measure of fiscal restraint.

INTRODUCTION

Ronald Reagan has proposed that the president be given the power to line-item veto appropriation bills in order to reduce the deficit and to discourage wasteful spending.[1] Throughout his administration, President Reagan has been thwarted by Congress in his attempt to eliminate certain established programs from the federal budget. He has also had to accept appropriation bills containing both items he desired and pork barrel items desired by members of Congress.[2] If President Reagan possessed the item veto, then his power vis-à-vis Congress would have been enhanced in these cases.[3]

Although this reform is discussed in the literature,[4] little empirical or comparative evidence is available as to whether the line-item veto actually works to curtail spending and promote efficiency in government. It is usually argued that the line-item veto, through its use or the threat of its use, mitigates logrolling and pork barrel appropriations and makes government more fiscally responsible. However, a chief executive could also use the line-item veto as an instrument to promote partisan and/or executive interests. Such usage would be most likely to occur where the chief executive confronts a legislature wholly or partially under the control of an opposition party. Although such use of the veto would reduce expenditures, fiscal restraint would be only a symbolic goal.

Source: Glenn Abney and Thomas P. Lauth, "The Line-Item Veto in the States: An Instrument for Fiscal Restraint or an Instrument for Partisanship?" *Public Administration Review* 45 (May/June 1985), pp. 372–77. Reprinted by permission.

This article examines the line-item veto in state governments to determine whether it is used as an instrument for fiscal restraint or an instrument of partisanship. The line-item veto is available to 42 (or 43 depending upon interpretation[5]) of the 50 state governors. Although an investigation of the veto power in state government is a legitimate and valuable end in itself, research findings from the state level may also inform discussions about incorporating this power into the national Constitution. State budgeting is, of course, different from national budgeting in that state budgets are often required by constitutional provision to be balanced. Nevertheless, similarities between the two levels of government regarding budgeting are more common than differences. Both levels of government are subjected to conflicting pressures for the expansion of services and the alleviation of tax burdens. Further, proponents of the item veto for the president frequently cite as evidence in support of their cause the fact that the item veto is possessed by governors.

The virtues and limitations of the line-item veto have been debated for over half a century in the literature.[6] A principal virtue of the item veto is its reputation as a tool for legislative efficiency. It is said to provide the chief executive with the opportunity to discourage pork barrel activities, logrolling, and extravagance in appropriation bills because it protects the integrity of the gubernatorial veto. In appropriation bills, legislatures may include expenditures which are unacceptable to the governor along with those desired by the executive. The value of the governor's veto power is weakened unless he or she is able to eliminate objectionable items without having to veto the entire appropriation measure.

The limitations of the item veto, however, are not insignificant. First, it is said to reduce the responsibility of legislative bodies.[7] Legislatures may include a host of "pork barrel" provisions expecting the governor to veto many of them. Thus, the veto power, and the line-item veto in particular, may be an invitation to legislative irresponsibility. In this way the item veto might actually promote inefficiency by discouraging legislative discipline. As one governor is reported to have commented: "Avoid threatening to veto a bill. You just relieve the legislature of responsibility for sound legislation."[8]

A second set of limitations focuses on the impact of the executive on the legislative process.[9] The item veto may enhance the influence of the executive over the legislature so as to violate the principle of separation of powers. This concern was expressed by President William H. Taft when he wrote: "While for some purposes, it would be useful for the Executive to have the power of partial veto, if we could always be sure of its wise and conscientious exercise, I am not entirely sure that it would be a safe provision. It would greatly enlarge the influence of the President, already large enough from patronage and party loyalty and other causes."[10] For Taft the concern was not just the increased influence of the executive, but also how the executive might use that power. If it were used to reward loyal legislators and to promote partisan causes, then the item veto would threaten the separation of powers principle. Even if the executive should not use it to reward and punish individual legislators, the item veto would enhance the legislative powers of the governor and thereby provide the executive with a dominant role in the appropriation process.[11]

Despite the extensive discussions in the literature on the pros and cons of the line-item veto, little empirical evidence exists upon which to base an assessment of how this instrument of executive power has actually been used. We have attempted to inform the item veto debate by asking participants in the state budgetary process about their perceptions of how the item veto is actually used in state budgeting. Our data come from a 1982 mail survey of state legislative budget officers. In those states which do not have a legislative budget office, the chief staff member of the house appropriations committee served as the respondent. Responses were received from 45 of the 50 states. Although our respondent population of 45 state officials is relatively small, it does represent 90 percent of the relevant experts.

USE OF THE ITEM VETO

The use of the line-item veto varies greatly among the states. Respondents were asked to indicate how many times in the three years prior to the survey their respective governors had used it. Thirteen of the respondents indicated that the governor had not used the item veto during that period; however, eight of those respondents were from states where the governor does not have item veto power. Another seven respondents reported that the veto had been used only once. At the other extreme, seven respondents reported use of the veto 100 or more times during the three years prior to the survey. Fourteen respondents reported frequencies which were scattered between these extremes. Four respondents failed to provide information about the frequency of item vetoing in their states. Of those respondents from states with the line-item veto who reported frequency (n = 33), 20 indicated that the veto was used less than three times per year and 13 reported use of three or more times per year.

When governors use the veto, their actions are not usually overridden by votes of the legislatures. Of the respondents (n = 28) who reported the veto having been used in their states in the past three years, 20 reported no overrides. However, in one state (Alaska) with a Republican governor and an assembly with a Democratic majority in both houses, 75 of 100 vetoes were reported to have been overridden in the past three years. This state is a very unique case.

The lack of successful overrides of line-item vetoes can be explained in part by requirements of extraordinary majorities. Furthermore, the ability of legislatures to write appropriation bills so as to make even line-item vetoes difficult for the governor may reduce the need for overrides. Sixteen of the 37 respondents from states having the item veto reported that legislatures write appropriations acts so as to limit the item veto opportunities of the governor.

Just as the effectiveness of the general veto has been thwarted by legislative manipulation, so also has the purpose of the item veto been at least partially undermined. Legislatures can combine items desired by governors with those opposed by them into one item. In most states, governors cannot reduce an item, they must either accept or reject it. Furthermore, in general, governors can veto the item of appropriation but they cannot change the legislative intent as expressed through substantive language.[12] The Virginia Supreme Court has held: " 'An item in an appropriation bill is an indivisible sum of money dedicated to a stated purpose. It is something different from a provision or condition, and where conditions are attached, they must be observed....' "[13] In a Missouri case the state supreme court held that the governor's veto power does not include authority to eliminate words indicating the purpose of the appropriation.[14] Unable to veto the legislature's intent or conditions, governors may find vetoing particular items difficult.

FISCAL RESTRAINT AND THE ITEM VETO

Do governors use the item veto against legislative bodies engaged in fiscal irresponsibility?[15] If governors use the item veto to promote fiscal restraint, then governors theoretically should use it against spendthrift legislative bodies. Opponents of the item veto suggest that such use discourages fiscal restraint by legislatures and thereby encourages irresponsibility.[16] The opposition to the item veto suggests that it may shift final responsibility for legislation from the legislature to the chief executive, causing lack of discipline by legislatures and increasing the powers of governors.[17] Whether the use of the item veto actually encourages fiscal restraint or causes fiscal responsibility may be in dispute, but the conclusion that the use of the veto and fiscal irresponsibility are found together does not appear to be in dispute. However, our data do not support this conclusion. Legislatures against which the item veto is used are not more fiscally irresponsible than are other legislatures.

We have used three measures of fiscal restraint or responsibility to determine the linkage between use of the item veto and degree of legislative discipline. The first measure was the propensity of the legislature to make decisions on the basis of benefits for the districts of legislators. Such behavior is often referred to as pork barrel and is generally considered wasteful and inefficient. To measure such propensity, we asked the respondents to indicate if "addition of items benefitting constituents or districts of individual legislators tends to characterize legislative changes in the executive budget each year." Fifty-six percent of all respondents indicated agreement with this statement. Where legislatures have this characteristic, governors might be expected to use their veto power to restrain the legislature. Our data do not necessarily support this proposition. Nine of the 17 respondents (53 percent) with governors who used the item veto less than three times per year characterized their state legislatures as adding pork barrel benefits to the executive budget compared to eight of 13 respondents (62 percent) from states where the veto was used three or more times. While governors are slightly more likely to use the veto in states with a pork barrel legislature, this tendency is too slight to attach importance to it. A similar result is obtained when examining a second measure of pork barrel. Respondents were asked to identify what kinds of information the legislature is most interested in during its consideration of the budget. The significance of an "agency's program for the districts of legislators" was cited by 10 of the 20 respondents from states where governors cast less than three vetoes per year and by seven of the 12 respondents from states where governors cast three or more vetoes per year. While we have chosen three vetoes as a cutting line for discussion purposes, other divisions of the data provide a similar conclusion; vetoes tend not to be cast more often in states having legislatures with a tendency to use pork barrel.

A second measure of legislative restraint used to assess the linkage between veto use and legislative responsibility was the propensity of the legislature to increase the budget recommendations of the governor. Nineteen of 41 respondents characterized the legislature as tending to add to the governor's proposed expenditure levels compared to 14 of 41 who said that the legislature tends to decrease the overall expenditure amounts. If the veto is used to promote restraint by governors, presumably it would be used against legislatures tending to increase executive recommendations.

Just as the line-item veto is not used as an instrument to block pork barrel, it is similarly not used to maintain the expenditure levels of the executive budget. Forty-two percent of the respondents (15 of 36) from states having the line-item veto characterized legislative changes in the executive budget each year as being an "overall increase in proposed expenditures." Seven of the 17 respondents (41 percent) from states where less than three vetoes per year were cast characterized legislative behavior in this manner compared to six of the 13 (46 percent) from states with three or more vetoes per year. Again, different divisions of the respondents by number of vetoes cast does not affect the conclusion.

A third measure of legislative restraint used to assess the linkage between use of the item veto and legislative responsibility was the respondents' perception of the consideration of an agency's efficiency in legislative decisions about the agency's budget. Presumably, governors who use the item veto to promote efficiency would use it more frequently against the less "efficiency minded" legislatures. Thirteen of 20 (65 percent) respondents from states where governors have the item veto and where the chief executive has used the veto less than three times each year indicated that such information was important to the legislature, compared to nine of the 12 respondents from states where the veto was used at least three times annually in the three years prior to the survey. Although the difference between the two groups is in the predicted direction of supporting a linkage between concern for efficiency and use of the veto, it is too small to conclude that the use of the veto is strongly related to executive concern for fiscal restraint.

Perhaps the absence of a linkage between the use of the veto and fiscal restraint results from the ability of some legislatures to avoid the veto by writing appropriation bills so as to make such gubernatorial action difficult. As noted earlier, 16 of the 37 respondents from states where the governor possesses the item veto reported that their legislatures write the appropriation act so as to limit the veto opportunities of the governor. If legislatures in these states are successful, the item veto would tend not to be used even though the legislatures might be fiscally irresponsible. Thus, the failure of our data to establish a linkage between the use of the veto and fiscal irresponsibility on the part of the legislature may result from successful legislative undermining of the veto. In fact, where legislatures are perceived by respondents as writing appropriation acts so as to limit veto opportunities of governors, governors are less likely to use the line-item veto. Ten of 15 respondents from states where the governor has used the item veto no more than one time in the last three years reported such a legislative strategy compared to six of 17 respondents from states where governors have used the veto more often.

Even though this legislative activity is linked to reduced use of the item veto, it does not appear related to fiscal irresponsibility on the part of legislatures. Indeed, legislatures engaged in so writing appropriation bills are apparently more fiscally disciplined than other legislatures. Fifteen of the 16 respondents from states where the legislatures are perceived to write restrictive appropriation acts reported that their legislatures seek information about the efficiency of an agency in considering its budget compared to eight of the 20 respondents from other legislatures. Only six of the 16 respondents from the former states characterized legislative changes in the executive budget as adding benefits for districts and constituents compared with 13 of the 20 respondents from the latter states. Respondents (8 of 16) from the former states were also more likely to characterize legislatures as acting to reduce executive budgets than were respondents (5 of 20) from the latter. In essence, legislatures which write appropriation acts so as to limit gubernatorial vetoes are fiscally more restrained than other legislatures. The absence of a linkage between the use of the item veto and fiscal irresponsibility does not seem to result from legislatures' taking the veto away from the governors.

While the line-item veto may not be used to encourage fiscal discipline, does evidence show that its presence may encourage fiscal restraint? Specifically, do states with governors who lack this power have less restrained legislatures than do other states? Our data suggest that the two types of states are not necessarily different in regard to fiscal restraints. While legislatures in states where the governor possesses the item veto are more likely to reduce the expenditure requests of governors, they are in fact more prone to use pork barrel and less likely to use information on efficiency. In essence, the presence of the veto does not seem to produce fiscal restraint.

In fact, on the basis of these data it could be argued that the presence of the veto discourages legislative discipline.

PARTISANSHIP AND THE VETO

Previous research on the relationship between partisanship and gubernatorial use of the general veto found that governors of states where the opposition party controls the legislative branch veto a higher proportion of bills than their counterparts from states where the same party controls both branches of government.[18] A linkage between partisanship and use of the item veto also exists. Republican governors might be expected to use the veto more than Democratic governors. In the past, Republicans have decried the spending policies of Democrats. The line-item veto would theoretically offer Republican governors an opportunity to make a symbolic if not tangible point. As can be seen in Table 1, Republican governors are more likely to use the line-item veto than are Democratic gov-

TABLE 1 Number of Item Vetoes Cast in Each State[a] by Party of Governor

		Number of item vetoes in each state in three years prior to the survey		
Party of governor	None	One or less per year	Between one and three times per year	Three or more times per year
Democratic	5	4	2	6
Republican	0	4	5	7

[a]This table excludes respondents from states lacking the item veto power and from states where the party of the governor changed in the three-year period prior to survey.

ernors. According to our respondents, eight of the 17 (47 percent) Democratic governors used it more than one time annually compared to 12 of the 16 (75 percent) Republican governors.

The line-item veto is also more likely to be used where the governor of one party faces a legislature wholly or partially controlled by the opposition party. This statement appears true for Democrats as well as Republicans. However, the latter are more likely to confront this situation than are Democratic governors in the states. Consider the seven Republican governors in the cell of highest veto use in Table 1. Five of the seven governors confronted legislatures in which the number of Democrats outnumbered Republicans. In fact, five of the seven confronted legislatures with both houses under Democratic control. On the other hand, three of the four Republican governors who cast one or fewer vetoes per year faced legislatures in which Republicans outnumbered Democrats. Only one of the four (a Southern governor) faced a legislature with both houses controlled by Democrats.

The same point can be made about Democratic governors. Of the six governors in Table 1 who cast three or more vetoes annually, two faced legislatures where both houses were controlled by Republicans, and one faced a legislature with divided control. Two of the other three governors faced legislatures where Republicans were within six votes (three seats) of the Democrats in one house. The sixth Democratic governor of this group was from a Southern state with a legislature known for its professionalism, independence and a relatively large (for a Southern state) Republican contingent (33 percent of the legislature). The five Democratic governors in the table who had not cast a veto were from states where

TABLE 2   Number of Item Vetoes Cast in Each State[a] by Division between Governor and Legislature in Party Identification

Party affiliations of governor and legislature	Number of item vetoes cast in the states in the three years prior to the survey			
	None	One or less per year	Between one and three times per year	Three or more times per year
Governor of same party as majority in both houses of legislature	5	4	2	3
Governor of different party as majority in one or both houses of legislature	0	6	3	10

[a]This table excludes respondents from states lacking the item veto power and from states where the party of the governor changed in the three-year period prior to survey.

Democrats solidly controlled both houses. For the five states combined, Democrats held 594 seats to 120 seats for the Republicans. Three of the states in this group are Southern.

The relationship between the party of the governor, the partisan nature of the legislature, and the use of the veto is further demonstrated in Table 2. Where control of both executive and legislative branches is in the province of the same party, the veto is used much less frequently than in states with divided control. At least, two (California and Florida) of the three states in the cell (three or more vetoes with control of both branches by one party) that contradicts this point have legislatures known for their professionalism and independence.[19] Partisanship and the use of the veto are intricately related. This finding is consistent with research on use of gubernatorial vetoes in the states.[20] Furthermore, it is neither a Republican nor Democratic instrument, it is used by both. In that Republican governors tend to face legislatures under the influence of the other party more often than Democratic governors face Republican legislatures, the line-item veto does tend to take on a Republican flavor.

When Republican governors use the veto, they may be more concerned about fiscal restraint than Democratic governors. At least, the characterizations of legislative behavior offered by respondents suggest such a difference between Democratic and Republican legislatures. The latter appear to be more concerned about fiscal conservatism. Consider

TABLE 3 Legislatures Characterized as Using Pork[a] by Partisan Nature

Partisan nature of legislature	Legislature does not tend to use pork[a]	Legislature does tend to use pork[a]
Both houses have Democratic majorities	10 (7)[b]	15 (7)[b]
One house has Democratic majority and one house has Republican majority	3	1
Both houses have Republican majorities	8	5

[a]The respondents characterized legislative changes in the executive budget each year as benefitting constituents or districts of individual legislators.

[b]Numbers in parentheses exclude the Southern states which were members of the Confederacy.

the matter of pork barrel legislation. The data in Table 3 suggest that states with Democratic legislatures are more prone to use pork. However, many of the states where pork is present are Southern. Controlling for the Southern states results in a great deal of similarity between states with Democratic and Republican legislatures. The propensity of Southern state legislatures for pork may result from the absence of party discipline in these legislatures and/or the close linkage between state and local governments in the South. In any event, controlling for Southern states, the difference between Republican and Democratic legislatures diminishes in regard to pork. Yet, there is evidence of a greater sense of fiscal restraint on the part of Republican legislatures.

Republican legislatures are more likely to place greater value on information regarding efficiency when they consider the budget requests of agencies. Ten of 12 legislatures (83 percent) with Republican majorities in both houses value such information according to our respondents, compared to 17 of 26 (65 percent) legislatures with both houses controlled by the Democrats. Also, Democratic legislatures tend to increase executive budgets while Republican legislatures are more likely to decrease executive budgets. The respondents characterized only two of 10 Republican legislatures as tending to increase executive budgets compared to a similar description by 13 of 23 (57 percent) respondents of Democratic legislatures. In regard to decreasing executive budgets seven of 12 respondents from states with Republican legislatures so characterized the behavior of their assemblies compared to only five of 23 (22 percent) respondents from states with both houses of the legislature controlled by Democrats. This information suggests that Republican legislatures and presumably Republican governors are fiscally more conservative. When Republican governors use the item veto, it is more likely to serve as an instrument of fiscal restraint.

CONCLUSION

Is the line-item veto used as an instrument for fiscal restraint or an instrument for partisanship? Often, it is a partisan instrument that may have the result of promoting fiscal restraint. Of course, any time the item veto is used, a state's budget is reduced. However, reductions are not the same as efficiency. Indeed, reductions can be inefficient. Furthermore, efficiency is a relative term. What may seem an extravagance for one person may be seen as a necessity by another. It is easier to portray the item veto as an instrument of the executive increasing his or her legislative powers rather than as an instrument for efficiency.

Does the item veto encourage fiscal responsibility? The line-item veto has been around in most states for a considerable time. Legislatures in states with it do not seem more fiscally responsible than legislatures in other states. Of course, our data are not longitudinal, and we cannot measure change following the introduction of the veto. However, given its partisan use, the item veto probably has had minimal effect on making legislatures or state government fiscally more restrained.

Because the president does not have the line-item veto, we can only speculate about how it might be used if established in the future. However, based upon state experiences with the item veto we anticipate it would enhance the president's ability to deal with the Congress on matters of a partisan nature, but it is not likely to have much impact on such fiscal matters as the size of the deficit.

NOTES

1. Richard E. Cohen, "Congress Plays Election-Year Politics with Line-Item Veto Proposal," *National Journal*, vol. 16 (February 11, 1984), pp. 274–276.

2. "Reagan's Deficit-Cutting Bid May Spotlight Line-Item Veto," *Congressional Quarterly*, vol. 42 (January 21, 1984), pp. 114–115.

3. Though the item veto may have enhanced the president's power in these cases, figures from the Congressional Budget Office suggest that the utility of the

item veto as an instrument to reduce the federal deficit is limited. The CBO has noted that a large percentage (54 percent) of the federal budget would be exempt from the item veto. Included in this exemption would be such nondiscretionary items as entitlements and interest on the federal debt. If defense expenditures are added to these nondiscretionary items, only 18 percent of the budget contains domestic items that would be subject to the item veto. *Ibid.*

4. Russell M. Ross and Fred Schwengel, "An Item Veto for the President," *Presidential Studies Quarterly*, vol. 12 (Winter 1982), pp. 66–79.

5. In Maryland the governor may only item veto supplemental appropriation bills and capital construction bills. In several other states, limitations are placed on the use of the item veto. Council of State Governments, *The Book of the States 1982–1983* (Lexington, Ky.: Council of State Governments, 1982), pp. 212–213.

6. V. L. Wilkinson, "The Item Veto in the American Constitutional System," *Georgetown Law Journal*, vol. 15 (November 1980), pp. 106–133; Roger H. Wells, "The Item Veto and State Budget Reform," *American Political Science Review*, vol. 18 (November 1924), pp. 782–791.

7. For an example of such behavior in Pennsylvania, see Wells, *op. cit.*, p. 784.

8. Thad L. Beyle and Robert Hueffner, "Quips and Quotes from Old Governors to New," *Public Administration Review*, vol. 43 (May/June 1983), pp. 268–269.

9. Wells, *op. cit.*, pp. 784–786; Timothy P. Burke, "The Partial Veto Power: Legislation by the Governor," *Washington Law Review*, vol. 49 (1974), pp. 603–615.

10. William H. Taft, *Our Chief Magistrate and His Powers* (New York: Columbia University Press, 1916), p. 27.

11. Wilkinson, *loc. cit.*

12. For a discussion of the state of Washington as an exception to this point, see Burke, *loc. cit.* For a discussion of Wisconsin as another exception to the point, see "The Use of the Partial Veto in Wisconsin," *Information Bulletin 75-1b-6* (Madison: Legislative Reference Bureau, State of Wisconsin, September 1975), pp. 1–6.

13. Ada E. Beckman, "The Item Veto Power of the Executive," *Temple Law Quarterly*, vol. 31 (Fall 1957), pp. 27–34.

14. J. M. Vaughn, "Constitutional Law—The Governor's Item Veto Power," *Missouri Law Review*, vol. 39 (Winter 1974), pp. 105–110.

15. Previous studies have raised questions about the efficiency of the item veto as a means of fiscal restraint. In 1950 Frank Prescott, referring to his study and that of Wells in 1924, said, "The doubts pertaining to its efficacy as an instrument of budgetary control which were cast upon this device by Professor Wells some twenty-five years ago appear to have been well founded in light of the new evidence." Frank W. Prescott, "The Executive Veto in American States," *Western Political Quarterly*, vol. 3 (March 1950), pp. 112; Wells, *loc. cit.*

16. Wilkinson, *op. cit.*, p. 122; Beyle and Hueffner, *loc. cit.*

17. Wilkinson, *op. cit.*, pp. 122–123; "Item Veto," *State Policy Reports* (November 1983), pp. 22–23.

18. Charles W. Wiggins, "Executive Vetoes and Legislative Overrides in the American States," *The Journal of Politics,* vol. 42 (November 1980), pp. 1110–1117.

19. Alan Rosenthal, *Legislative Life: People, Process and Performance in the States* (New York: Harper & Row, 1981); Citizens Conference on State Legislatures, *The Sometimes Governments* (Kansas City, Mo.: Citizens Conference on State Legislatures, 1971).

20. Wiggins, *op. cit.,* p. 115.

CHAPTER VI

STATE LEGISLATURES IN THE POLITICAL PROCESS

INTRODUCTION

While policy initiation is primarily the function of the governor and indirectly that of the bureaucracy and interest groups,[1] it is the duty of the legislature to make the laws. In this regard, David Saffell writes that no self-respecting legislature should be content to simply deal with a governor's program or routinely approve members' bills.[2] Rather, the legislature has a responsibility to carefully weigh a wide variety of proposals reaching it and when necessary provide alternatives of its own.[3]

Because of malapportionment or gerrymandering, legislatures have not been until recently truly representative of the states' polity. Thus they were unable to reflect the will of the majority in making the laws. Moreover, short legislative sessions, inadequate legislative staffs, and low pay for legislators all contributed to a legislature which did not enjoy the fullest respect, trust, and support of the citizenry.

In recent years the state legislative capacity to participate in the governance process has been enhanced immensely. William T. Pound, in his article "Reinventing the Legislature," which is reprinted in this chapter as Reading 11, indicates why, as he puts it, "the legislature has been reinvented."

Legislators do more than make laws. They perform vital services to their constituents in their legislative districts. Citizens often have complaints about their contacts with state administrative agencies.[4] A state representative will seek to resolve constituent complaints and thereby gain loyal supporters.

Legislators perform additional constituency services which include helping with requests for job consideration at nonstate agencies, providing letters of reference to colleges and universities, inquiring into the well-being of a relative in a state mental or penal institution, and explaining their vote on various pieces of legislation. Alan Rosenthal, in his article "The Consequences of Constituency Service," which is reprinted in this chapter as Reading 12, examines such casework by state legislators.

NOTES

1. See Thomas R. Dye, *Politics in States and Communities,* 4th ed. (Englewood Cliffs, N. J.: Prentice-Hall, 1981), p. 158.

2. See David C. Saffell, *State and Local Government: Politics and Public Policies* (New York: Random House, 1987), p. 108.

3. Ibid.

4. John J. Harrigan, *Politics and Policy in States and Communities,* 3rd ed. (Glenview, Ill.: ScottForesman, 1988), p. 212.

Reading 11

REINVENTING THE LEGISLATURE

William T. Pound

State legislatures have in recent years vastly increased their capacity to govern, according to William T. Pound's view. Much of the improved capacity of legislatures is due to *Baker* v. *Carr* (1962), which resulted in subsequent federal and state court decisions mandating equality of population in all representational districts as well as to the emergence and growth, especially since 1969, of specialized legislative staffing especially for budgetary purposes. Other factors include the removal of limits on the length of legislative sessions; the removal of limits on legislative salaries, and the removal of many limits on matters legislatures can consider.

The federal mandate that all representational districts should enjoy equality of representation meant that no longer would a minority in the legislature be able to thwart the will of the majority. The speed with which legislators could move on perceived problems was greatly enhanced by the practice of one-person one-vote, especially in legislatures where a small number of representatives from rural areas could block the decisions of a large number of representatives from urban areas.

The emergence and growth of budgetary staff, in particular, provided state legislatures with a very strong independent budget analysis and development capacity. Prior to the hiring of budgetary staff, state legislatures could do little more than simply ratify the executive budget.

Constitutional and/or statutory provisions limiting legislative sessions have been removed in most states. Many states which previously could meet only biennially now meet annually and have many members who consider themselves full-time legislators. This change has given legislators an opportunity to cope with problems facing the state on a daily basis and an opportunity to exercise regular and ongoing oversight of the executive branch.

State legislators, in most states, are no longer bound by their constitutions to salaries out of kilter with economic realities. Constitutional restrictions on salary increases have been removed and replaced by statutes which usually provide for a pay commission to make binding or advisory recommendations regarding actual compensation and vouchered and unvouchered expenses. State legislators who are adequately paid and able to meet their family obligations can better afford the time necessary for legislative activity and constituent services.

Legislators can now respond almost immediately to changing social and economic conditions. They need not wait to convene themselves at some fixed time long after events have passed them by. Moreover, the length of the legislative session gives legislators greater opportunity to override gubernatorial vetoes. They have done this with greater frequency than in those years before the extended sessions.

Legislatures now engage in new functions that earlier legislatures could not undertake. Mechanisms have been put in place to review (and perhaps veto) administrative rules; program evaluation offices have been established to consider the effectiveness and efficiency of legislative authorized programs; and district offices for constituent services have been established, especially in large states.

Pound concludes that most state legislatures have established themselves as powerful entities fully capable of performing their legislative and constituent functions. However, the growing power and independence of state legislatures have resulted in regular constitutional confrontations between legislatures and executives over legislative assertions of authority.

Each one is unique, yet they are all strikingly similar. Each has diverse responsibilities, yet they all share common problems. State legislatures— "the first branch of government"—are the most revitalized, changed and challenged governmental institutions in America and today they have a vastly increased capacity to govern.

Interested citizens, legislative staff, lobbyists and even lawmakers themselves may take the resources and capabilities that have fostered this change for granted, but state legislatures in 1986 have progressed more than any other governmental institution over the past 20 years. As recently as the 1950s, a national study referred to state legislatures as "19th-century institutions." But by the early 1980s, futurist John Naisbitt called state and local governments "the most important political entities in America." Legislatures had been transformed in a number of ways to make them equal partners in state government.

Source: Reprinted with permission from *State Legislatures,* vol. 12 (July 1986), pp. 16 and 18–20. Copyright © 1986 by National Conference of State Legislatures.

The reapportionment revolution of the mid-1960s was the catalyst for the modernization of state legislatures. State and federal courts handed down the one-man, one-vote rule, requiring equality of population in all representational districts. But the impetus for change had already begun.

The beginnings of the modern legislature can be traced back to 1901 when Wisconsin established the first permanent legislative staff by creating the legislative reference bureau. Prior to that, administrative functions in the legislatures were limited to the clerk and secretary, two positions derived from English parliamentary tradition. During the middle third of this century, a majority of states established legislative councils (the first council was established in Kansas in 1933) to allow the legislature to function during interim periods and give it some permanent research and legal capability—independent of the executive branch or outside resources.

After World War II, specialized legislative staffing began to emerge, particularly in the fiscal area. California and Texas were among the first legislatures to establish a strong, independent budget development and analysis capability. Previously, legislatures merely ratified executive budgets—still the case in some states—or depended entirely on the executive branch for budget analysis.

Modernizing the state legislature, however, involved not only the growth of staff capacity, but the removal of many limits on sessions and salaries, and on matters legislatures could consider. As recently as 1941 only four legislatures held annual sessions. That number grew to 19 by 1962, to 35 in 1972 and to 43 today. Only Arkansas, Kentucky, Montana, Nevada, North Dakota, Oregon and Texas retain biennial sessions.

Adequate pay for legislators was an important element in legislative modernization. Constitutional restrictions on legislators' salaries were removed. Today only nine states establish legislator salaries in their constitutions. In the remainder, statutes control, often with some type of compensation commission to make binding or advisory recommendations. Those states retaining salary limitations tend to provide the lowest levels of legislator compensation. Current salaries range from $100 per year in New Hampshire to $46,800 in Alaska. The average legislative salary in 1986 was slightly above $17,000. In fact, though, this figure understates actual legislative compensation due to the widespread payment of vouchered and unvouchered expenses to legislators and additional compensation paid to leaders (and sometimes committee chairmen) in 42 states.

The removal of restrictions on sessions has been accompanied by a continuing discussion as to how much time legislatures should spend in session and what is the most effective use of legislative time. Should the legislator's role be considered "full time" or "part time"? Can a legislature operate with fairly limited sessions and still maintain an active policy and oversight role through effective use of the interim?

The argument about limited sessions is often couched in terms of preserving the "citizen" nature of state legislatures as opposed to developing "professional" or full-time legislatures on the congressional model. There is no question that the amount of time spent in session and the level of compensation affect the composition of the membership of legislative bodies. Many argue that it is desirable that the predominant occupation of members of legislatures not be that of legislator, but that legislative bodies represent a broad spectrum of vocations. However, the growing demands on state legislatures and the greater legislative role in initiating policies, budgeting and overseeing programs have increased the pressure on legislative time.

There is no limit placed on the length of sessions in 12 states. Of 32 states that constitutionally limit legislative sessions, two limit only the second year and the remaining six states have statutory or indirect limitations based on cutoffs in salaries or per diem expense payments.

During the 1960s and 1970s, limits on legislative sessions were eliminated or relaxed. Recent years have brought a mixed response to the question of session length. Alaska adopted a 120-day limit in 1984, replacing its previously unlimited sessions. Colorado adopted a second-year session limit of 140 days in 1982, and Washington set session limitations when it went from biennial to annual sessions in 1981. Utah lengthened its sessions by 10 days per biennium in 1984 when it changed from a 60-day first year/20-day second year system to 45 days per session. New Hampshire adopted annual sessions effective in 1985. Several legislatures, notably Arizona and Iowa, have limited their sessions by legislative rule or statute. Movements to adopt more restrictive session limits surface periodically, particularly in the states having the longest sessions.

Whether a legislature is full time in nature can generally be measured by time spent in session, level of compensation and occupational self-definition of the members. The legislatures of California, Illinois, Massachusetts, Michigan, New Jersey, New York, Ohio, Pennsylvania and Wisconsin have lengthy sessions, relatively high legislator salaries and many members whose primary occupation is that of legislator. None of these states have constitutionally imposed session limitations, though both California and Wisconsin adopt a systematic schedule of committee and flow activity, as well as recess periods, at the beginning of each biennium. Many of the legislatures that have longer sessions meet only two or three days per week, while in other states with more restricted sessions, five- and six-day workweeks are common. Several of the medium-size states actually spend as many days in session as do the full-time legislatures. Full-time legislators are likely to spend considerable time in district offices and place a high priority on service to constituents. More than two-thirds of the legislatures were in session more than 100 legislative days each biennium during the 1980s.

Legislators who define their occupation as "legislator" are increasing in number. A recent survey of state lawmakers conducted by NCSL found that more than half the legislators in New York and Pennsylvania define their occupation as "legislator." This study also indicated that the number of "business owners" who are legislators in the larger states is much smaller than in the states with more limited sessions. Lawyer legislators exist in greatest numbers in the South, but their numbers are decreasing. In a number of states persons engaged in "education" outnumber as legislators those coming from any other professional background. Persons engaged in "agriculture" are still found in every legislature, but serve in greatest number in the rural Midwestern and mountain states. Women and minority representation continues to increase each biennium: There are now more than 1,100 women and nearly 400 minority members among the country's 7,461 state legislators.

Women and minority legislators are gradually moving into leadership positions. There are currently two black speakers (California and Pennsylvania) and a female speaker and senate president (Oregon and New Hampshire).

A continuing preoccupation of legislatures is the management of time during sessions. Most legislatures have adopted some type of committee and floor scheduling systems, and deadlines for bill filing and legislative action. The practice of prefiling bills and allowing the carry-over of bills to the second session has become more prevalent in legislatures in the past 20 years. Forty-four states allow prefiling today; fewer than 10 used this procedure 20 years ago. In the mid-1960s, only nine states had bill carry-over provisions; in 1986, 25 legislatures carry over bills to the second session. Limitations on bill introductions are gaining favor in a few states. These limitations often do not apply to prefiled bills and thus allow a fast session start and the scheduling of an even flow of legislation.

Other factors contributing to the modernization of state legislatures include stronger committee systems and procedures, and a greater emphasis on interim committee activities. While committee strength varies from state to state, committees in most legislatures have been reduced in number, have greater substantive expertise than in past years and are more influential in the shaping of legislation. In many legislative bodies today, most bills are killed in committee, not on the floor. Money committees have become increasingly powerful, corresponding with the assertion of legislative budget authority.

Legislatures have also become more active during the interim period between sessions. Florida and Washington use committee weeks or weekends to get interim work done while minimizing time demands on legislators. They concentrate all interim committee meetings within a three- or four-day period each month.

The effectiveness of interim committees varies widely. A growing trend is to use standing committees during the interim. In states with strong interim or legislative council traditions, interim committee bills often have a high rate of passage. Even where no direct legislation results from interim work the interim may have a substantial educational effect on subsequent legislative action.

Other results of the reduction in constitutional restrictions and the changing operating environment of state legislatures are seen in the ability of 29 legislatures to call themselves into special session and the increased frequency with which special sessions have been held. An emerging practice in some states without constitutionally limited sessions is to recess subject to the call of the leadership rather than to adjourn *sine die*. This practice allows the legislature to act at any time and react immediately to changing situations rather than reposing interim authority entirely in the executive branch.

Legislatures also override gubernatorial vetoes with greater frequency than in past years. In part this is due to the development in some states of veto sessions that provide the legislature greater opportunity to consider the governor's action on bills. But in a number of states it is primarily due to increased independence in the legislative branch and to split partisan control of the branches of government. There are states, such as New York, where until recent years, more than a century passed without a veto override.

These changes have been accompanied by continual expansion of legislative capacity through staffing, facilities and information resources. The permanent staff of state legislatures totals more than 16,000 employees, with another 9,000 temporary or session staff. Nearly all this staff growth has occurred since 1969, with the development of specialized staff in areas such as fiscal, legal services, auditing and program evaluations, administrative rule review, computer services and committee staff. There has been a similar growth, particularly in the past decade, of personal staff for legislators and of caucus staff.

Legislative staff was at one time largely organized in central agencies, under leadership direction. Recent years have seen the decentralization and specialization of legislative staff. Louisiana and Oklahoma have most recently moved to separate House and Senate staffs from a centralized structure. Individual members now employ staff in many legislatures and committee staff is used extensively in California, Florida, Pennsylvania and New York.

Staff decentralization may be an irreversible trend, but both Illinois and Nebraska have recognized management problems with a fragmented staff situation and moved to assert more centralized leadership control.

Legislative facilities have been improved in nearly every state. At the beginning of the legislative reform movement, few states provided more to legislators than their desk on the floor. Committee rooms were non-existent or inadequate. Legislatures have gradually moved other governmental offices out of capitol buildings, increasing the space available to the legislature and providing the opportunity to construct offices for legislators and modern committee and staff facilities.

In a like manner, the information resources available to legislatures have expanded steadily. Increased staff resources have meant greater independent information and support for state legislatures. As recently as the 1950s, the majority of legislatures were primarily dependent on the executive for information and support services. Computers are having a significant impact on the legislative process. Modern word processing and information systems facilitate electoral tasks and communication with constituents. Such systems also can develop models of the possible implications of legislation and track appropriations and can contribute to more effective legislative oversight. Computers have made legislative bill processing and record keeping much faster and allow both legislators and the public to have more information about bills and bill status.

Legislatures have undertaken many new functions. They have become aggressive in the oversight of programs, though legislative oversight is sometimes performed badly and inadequately linked to the ongoing legislative process. Some legislatures have created some mechanism for the review and/or veto of administrative rules. Program evaluation units have been established in many legislatures. Constituent services, district offices and public information efforts have been developed by a number of legislatures, particularly in the larger states.

Changes in state legislatures have not occurred at the same pace in all states. In states that are dominated by one political party, such as Kentucky, Louisiana and Tennessee, the catalyst for development of legislative independence and expansion of the legislative role has often been the capture of the executive branch by the other party. The last few years have seen a consolidation of earlier legislative reforms and their gradual spread throughout the states. Legislatures are again paying more attention to their own procedures and staff structure, as evidenced by the number of studies of rules, staffing and operations during the mid-1980s.

One result of legislative independence has been constitutional confrontation between legislature and executive, often over legislative assertions of authority. Considerable variation exists in the role and power of the legislature in budgeting but, in general, legislatures are playing a much more assertive role in fiscal policy. The legislature dominates the budget process in states such as Colorado, New Mexico, and Texas and is at least an equal partner in others.

State legislatures are dynamic, ever-changing institutions. The environment in which they function is changing as the relations and responsibilities of our various governmental levels change. With the responsibility for most domestic programs becoming centered in the states, there is increased lobbying pressure on state legislatures and the cost of legislative election campaigns is rapidly rising. The number of registered lobbyists in many states has more than doubled in the past 10 years. And the costs of state legislative election campaigns have risen to the hundreds of thousands of dollars in the larger states, with proportionate increases in the smaller states. These pressures no doubt will result in continued changes in state legislatures.

The role of the state legislator has not necessarily become easier, despite the increased resources available. Programmatic, budget and constituent demands will continue to grow. As John Bragg, a veteran Tennessee legislator, commented, "Have you noticed that all those funny stories we told about the legislature happened more than 10 years ago? Things are more serious and difficult now. Then it was all fun and frivolity; either you were with the governor or against him, and that was all you had to know."

THE CONSEQUENCES OF CONSTITUENCY SERVICE

Alan Rosenthal

Alan Rosenthal asserts that the most significant "public" for legislators are the people who live in their districts, and that a large part of the legislator's job is representing and providing service to these constituents. Generally, *constituency service* means communicating with constituents, which includes visiting and talking at community meetings, establishing district offices, writing letters, and sending pamphlets. Specifically, constituency service means providing assistance to persons in one's district who have some problem which presumably can be resolved by a government agency or by a private sector agency with which the legislator may have some influence.

While some legislators still conduct their constituency service activities with limited office space and staff resources, one of the strongest present tendencies among state legislatures is that of providing members with personal staffing and district offices to permit fulfillment of the constituency role. However, constituency service has certain effects on both the legislator and the legislature.

First, it takes up much of the legislator's time, thus precluding other activities such as legislative caucuses, committee meetings, and floor sessions.

Second, legislators may and often do find the constituency role more rewarding than the legislative role, which can be very frustrating since one's legislative proposals will often not get out of committee.

Third, constituency service redounds to the electoral benefit of the legislator. Constituents as voters tend to vote for those who have helped them. Moreover, the district offices and staff play an important part of the *perennial campaign*—the continuous search for votes and reelection. In short, constituent service and reelection politics become inextricably interwoven.

Fourth, constituency service is presumed by some observers to buy legislator freedom on policy matters—a legislator who enjoys great voter support based on service to his or her constituency often can take a position contrary to that of the district. Thus a large constituency service "practice" permits a legislator to behave as a *trustee* as opposed to a *delegate* of the district in policy matters.

Fifth, the concern with the constituency service role is changing the composition of the legislatures. Legislatures are moving from a body of part-timers to a body of full-timers simply to have adequate time to do the constituency function well. Importantly, the constituency function is promoting fragmentation in the legislature. This happens because the closer legislators are tied to their districts, the more difficult it is for them to consider statewide problems.

Sixth, there is no evidence that a relationship exists between constituent service and public support for state government. Rather, the data show that despite the fact that incumbents are favorably regarded, there is less than overwhelming public support for state legislatures.

Professor Rosenthal concludes that the overall results of increasing constituency service are positive. Incumbent legislators benefit; constituents benefit. However, the popularity of legislatures, per se, has benefited very little from the constituent services the legislators perform. Rosenthal suggests that in the future legislators will have to work as much to strengthen their institution as they do to strengthen their individual positions.

More significant than any other public, in the eyes of legislators, are the people who live in their district—their constituents. A large part of a legislator's job has to do with representing his or her constituency and providing service to constituents. Service to this district is the name of the game, according to people in the business. It is the bread and butter of every elected office holder.

Few legislators today would omit mention of constituent service as one of their duties. For example, when asked recently to assess the importance of various legislative functions, 77 percent of the members of the Connecticut General Assembly rated constituent service as "very important" (with another 16 percent rating it as "somewhat important"). Along with making policy, appropriating funds, and exercising oversight, servicing constituents is one of the legislature's principal functions.

Source: Alan Rosenthal, "The Consequences of Constituency Service," *Journal of State Government* 59, (Spring 1986), pp. 25–30. Copyright © by The Council of State Governments. Reprinted with permission.

THE NATURE OF CONSTITUENCY SERVICE

What is meant by constituency service varies from state to state and from member to member. At a general level, service entails communicating with constituents—listening, explaining, and helping. It may involve writing letters, sending pamphlets, distributing newsletters, making visits, giving talks, and running district offices. At a specific level, service involves providing assistance to people who have run into some problem in their dealings with government: a matter of welfare, workmen's compensation, college admission, zoning, a contract, employment, or just where to go in order to get information. At that level it is generally referred to as casework.

Malcom Jewell of the University of Kentucky in his book, *Representation in State Legislatures* (1982), examines the range of legislative service activities. Focusing on nine states, he concludes that service is of high priority in California, Massachusetts, Ohio, and Texas; of medium priority in Indiana, Kentucky, and Tennessee; and of low priority in Colorado and North Carolina. According to Jewell, legislators who are most service oriented are found in states where constituency service norms are strong and where greater staff resources are available. They tend to be experienced members with career ambitions.

In some states legislators still conduct their constituency service activities much as their predecessors did before them. They attend various meetings throughout the district and hold office hours once a month or so in a local town hall. They do not have personal staff to help them, but they still respond diligently to the requests that come their way. They are only part-time legislators, and they are also only part-time ombudsman. The individual and institutional resources devoted to the service function in these states continue to be limited, but the function is performed nonetheless.

The trend, however, is in the development of the constituent service function, particularly casework, after the fashion of Congress. Indeed, one of the strongest tendencies among state legislatures today is that of providing members with personal staffing and district offices, which are used to reach out to constituents. As with many other elements of legislative modernization, these features were instituted first by California about 20 years ago. Since then 18 state Senates and 11 state Houses have undertaken to provide personal aides for members, and 10 legislatures have devised district office programs of one sort or another.[1]

Support varies in amount from place to place and from Senate to House, with allowances, furnishings, and supplies calculated differently depending on the particular state. At one end of the continuum, California members receive a lump sum for both capitol and district office expenses, including personnel, averaging $182,000 per Assembly member and and $388,000 per Senate member. In addition, they are supplied with office equipment, telephones, postage, and funds for newsletters. In New York, staff allowances depend upon a member's leadership position, seniority, and affiliation with the majority or minority party. Senators have between one and six staff members, and $10,000 for district office rent and utilities. Assembly members are allocated a basic staff allowance of $22,000 per year and are furnished district offices, telephones, office equipment, supplies, and postage. At the other end of the continuum, Connecticut members are not provided with district offices per se, but are allocated $3,500 a year which usually is used to cover such expenses. Maryland members also receive modest amounts for offices and staff.

New Jersey offers as good an example as any of how legislators use offices and staffs for constituent service. Take William Schuber, one of New Jersey's Assemblymen, a Republican from a suburban county. Schuber is prodigious when it comes to constituent service. He puts in hour after hour, hopping from club meeting to parade to picnic, trying to get known and drumming up business for his district office. He mails copies of relevant legislation introduced in Trenton to fire departments, zoning boards, and local councils. He delivers copies of the state legislative manual to libraries, appears on local cable TV shows, and works to get his news releases to his district's weekly papers. His staff of six part-time people comb newspapers for announcements of weddings, births, promotions, and obituaries, so Schuber can follow up with appropriate letters to constituents.[2] Or take Matthew Feldman, a veteran Democratic senator from the same county as Schuber. In his district Feldman has one full-time secretary, one full-time office manager, and one part-time caseworker. His office reportedly generates 50,000 pieces of mail a year and handles 1,000 constituent cases.[3]

INDIVIDUAL AND INSTITUTIONAL EFFECTS

Although it is not possible to measure the change in constituent service activity this past decade, there can be little doubt that practically everywhere such activity has increased. Indeed, if the 1970s witnessed the development of committee and caucus staff in state legislatures, the 1980s is witnessing the development of personal staffing, with an emphasis on constituency service activity. Given the likelihood of this trend's continuation into the future, it is worthwhile to look at the effects of constituency service—both on the legislator as an individual and on the legislature as an institution.

First, constituency service takes up a large part of the time and energy legislators spend on their overall job. One might think that members devote relatively little of their own time to such tasks, leaving it to their personal staff. That is not the case, however. Even in Congress, with its abundant staffing, it is estimated that the average member spends 40 to 45 percent of his time on service activities. In fact, members spend, on the average, almost two out of five days back in their districts where, among other things, they tend faithfully to their constituents.[4] At the state level, time commitments vary tremendously. One study, conducted in 1977–78, reported that Minnesota and Kentucky legislators spent their time as is shown below[5]:

Percentage of legislator time spent on constituent service

Time spent	Minnesota	Kentucky
Less than 25%	32	24
25 to 49%	64	38
50% or more	4	38
	100%	100%

The mean amount of time spent on the function was 25 percent in Minnesota, and 40 percent in Kentucky. The commitments were quite different, but substantial in both places.

If we define service to include just about any form of contact, as most legislators do, the range from 25 to 40 percent of one's time, depending upon the state, seems not too far from the mark. Take Wisconsin (which does not provide district offices) as an example at the lower end of the range. A 1983 questionnaire, distributed by the legislature's Compensation Study Committee, found that members spent about 48 hours a week on legislative business, with about 12 hours, or 25 percent, given over to constituent contact and services. Or take Florida (which does provide district offices) as an example at the high end of the range. As of 1979 it was estimated that an active senator could be expected to spend 200 days a year on legislative work, with 96 days, or 48 percent, of total time on district office and constituent work.

There are limits on the amount of time legislators have at their disposal. If time and energy are channeled into constituent service, then they are not available for other activities. This means that legislators will have to spend less on floor sessions, committee meetings, and caucuses—activities that relate to other legislative functions. If they are part-time legislators, they will have to spend less on their outside occupations. Or they will have to squeeze the extra amounts out of that which is normally allocated to family life and recreation. Whatever the case or combination, more time on constituency service means less spent elsewhere.

Second, constituency service provides legislators gratification they cannot otherwise achieve. Although some legislators undoubtedly regard service as a chore, most recognize the function as an essential one in a representative democracy. It is something that they, as elected representatives of the people, have an obligation to do, and thus take pride in doing it. Moreover legislators, as a breed, like helping people. While some do prefer to focus on law-related pursuits and analytical endeavors, many others are "people persons." They are concerned about individual people, like dealing with them person-to-person, and are inclined to enjoy constituency service.

A few years ago, an examination of what New Jersey legislators particularly liked and disliked about their jobs revealed that about half of the members and former members liked having contact with people and making a difference in their lives. The results obtained from intervening with a state agency, or in some other way, on behalf of a constituent are a source of considerable satisfaction to a legislator. This is particularly true when something concrete is achieved in a constituent's favor. The legislative process itself can be frustrating, and extremely so for minority, freshman, and chronically impatient members. One's bills frequently go nowhere. Clear, identifiable victories can be rare. No wonder, then, that a successful intervention with bureaucrats in the state capitol can be a rewarding experience for an otherwise embattled legislator.

Third, and by no means least, constituency service helps an incumbent win re-election. There is a belief among a number of people that a congressman can get re-elected by what he does for folks back home. Few doubt that at least some electoral benefit is derived by congressmen from their constituency service activities. Granting that service at the congressional level helps, the question is, "How much?"

According to Richard F. Fenno, Jr., "Our best present estimate is that incumbency, or extra constituent service, adds an average of five percent to a House member's electoral total."[6] We do not know what the electoral payoffs are at the state legislative level. But it would appear that many legislators—even those in what might be regarded as relatively safe districts—feel insecure electorally. For that reason, among others, they are strongly motivated to provide constituents as voters with service.

Although the ostensible purpose of district offices and staff is not the re-election of incumbents, it is difficult to ignore the political potency of many of these operations. They are integral parts of what has been called "the campaign that never ends." Take the case of New Jersey.[7] The tendency of legislators here is to divvy up the $30,000 allotted for personal staff among more, rather than fewer, aides, retaining a goodly number of people on the payroll rather than only a few. Out of a total of 730 aides (excluding hourly employees) working for senators and assemblymen, only eight receive $20,000 or more in salary, while 396 receive $2,500 or less. The result is a distribution of aides among district offices as shown below:

District office staff in New Jersey

Number of aides per district office	*Number of district offices*	
	Senate	*Assembly*
One or two	8	7
Three to five	17	27
Six to ten	11	38
Eleven to fifteen	4	5
	40	77

It would appear that a number of New Jersey's aides are employed largely for political, i.e., re-election purposes.

Or take New York. Here a member of the legislature made use of his staff in a successful race for Congress. The U.S. Attorney, the Brooklyn District Attorney, and the Justice Department all became involved in this case. The member pointed out in his defense that the New York Legislature drew no distinction between the use and abuse of hired staff; and the *New York Times* editorialized (August 26, 1985) as follows:

> A legislator's staff cannot and should not be hermetically sealed from campaign-related work. What's needed are guidelines from Albany.

But the *Times* also reasoned that what else could a legislator do but use staff for constituents and campaigns since, "A penny-wise legislature has historically refused to finance adequate staffs for its members."

The demarcation between constituent service on the one hand and re-election politics on the other is a fuzzy one. Not only is good service good politics, but much of the self-promotion and publicizing that legislators would place in the service category is political indeed. Furthermore, as the New York case indicates, and the New Jersey personnel figures suggest, district aides and other staff are readily convertible into electoral resources. The more of them, the merrier. And there is little doubt that, along with other factors, constituency service gives incumbents a real edge. It helps explain why anywhere from one-fifth to three-fifths of them, depending on the particular state, are not even challenged when they come up for re-election.

Fourth, constituency service has effects on the legislative process, in terms of both policy making and oversight. The dominant view is that effective service buys legislators freedom on policy matters. By trying to help, by appearing to help, and by actually helping people, representatives build up support that can be transferred to the policy arena. Thus they may be able to get out in front on an issue, or take a position contrary to views held by many of their constituents, and still not risk repudiation at the polls.

But the strength of legislators' district orientations and service responsiveness also may help to shape the way they behave in other domains. Accordingly, the more responsive they are to their constituents on requests for service, the more they will try to discern and represent constituency views on substantive issues too. If one adopts this line of reasoning, then instead of buying freedom, legislators simply become more parochial and tied to district apron strings across the board.

Casework, as one aspect of constituency service, can be considered a form of legislative oversight. Thus service may bear on the effectiveness of state programs and the performance of state agencies. One study explored this subject, finding substantial differences between Kentucky and Minnesota in the performance of casework and its conversion into oversight. Much of the casework amounted to asking for special favors and exceptions, but some of it led to administrators correcting themselves, to further examination of practices, or to the introduction of legislation to remedy a deficiency caused by a particular problem.[8]

For the most part, however, casework is an extremely particularistic approach to oversight. Ordinarily, it is not advisable to generalize from one case to an entire agency or program. Nor does a particular problem encountered by a constituent—even one's own constituent—necessarily justify a change in administrative behavior or modification of a statewide program. But on occasion this happens; a single case has more general consequences.

The fact is that constituent cases are treated as individual occurrences. Information is not cumulative across all the state's districts or over some period of time. Therefore, it is not possible to figure out whether a problem is part of a pattern, requiring a change in policy or practice. If legislatures made collective use of casework data, it could be integrated with other oversight information. Currently, however, administrators respond to individual cases raised by individual legislators, and not to findings arrived at by the legislature as a whole.

Fifth, individual constituency service affects the legislature as an institution. Although these institutional effects are subtle, over time the consequences may be considerable. Along with an electoral preoccupation, the concern with the constituency service function promises to change the composition of legislatures. The trend is toward full-time members, career politicians. Where legislative salaries make it at all possible, more members are serving on as essentially full-time basis. One assemblyman from New York, for example, in a discussion of professional and citizen legislators, said that it just was not possible in New York to be a part-timer anymore. "When I'm in the district, people bombard me constantly with requests for one thing or another," he explained. "There's no way to say, 'Leave me alone, I'm just part-time.' "

The more resources legislators put into districts, the more demands they generate. It is difficult for elective politicians to resist local demands, and the tendency undoubtedly will be to spend more time at the job. In about one-third of the states, the transformation has already taken place. Legislatures have changed from being composed primarily of citizen members, attached to their districts both by residence and by outside occupation, to being composed primarily of full-timers, attached to their districts by residence also, but by service activity rather than by any private calling. Among the distinguishing characteristics of the contemporary professional legislature are district offices and personal staff.

Not only are legislatures becoming professional, they are also becoming fragmented. Constituency service reflects and promotes that fragmentation, along with single-member districts, the proliferation and intensification of interest groups, and electoral uncertainty. The closer legislators are tied to their district, the more difficult it may be for them to consider statewide interests or institutional concerns.

Sixth, and perhaps as significant in the long run as anything else, are the effects that constituency service has on public confidence in government. In this era of large, complex, and bureaucratic government, it is critical that people have someone with whom they can communicate on a personal, one-to-one basis. With an attentive representative, or even with the attention of a representative's staff, constituents have an opportunity to express themselves. As Frank Smallwood, a former member of the Vermont Senate, puts it, "People can get things off their chest. What people want to know is that someone is listening to them and is ready to come to their assistance."[9] Whether citizens have lost their confidence in government or have become alienated from government, a system of diligent representation can have ameliorative results. As Jewell writes, "If citizens discover that legislators are effective in making the bureaucracy more responsive, they may be expected to become more supportive of state government."[10]

The relationship between constituent service and public support for state government is a plausible one. The evidence supports the contention that service strengthens constituent support for the representative. But there is no evidence that support for the representative carries over to support for the legislature in which the representative services. At the congressional level, polls show that while people like their congressmen they do not particularly like Congress.[11] At the state level, data suggest less than overwhelming support for state legislatures, despite the fact that incumbents are favorably regarded. It would be ironic, indeed, if the increasing popularity of the individual legislator and the unpopularity of the legislature as an institution were related phenomena. Are members buying their support at the expense of the institution of which they are a part? Even if they are not, there is little evidence that they are seriously trying to promote the legislature and the legislative process beyond their own interests, and perhaps those of their party.

CONCLUSION

Where the professionalization of legislatures is advanced and electoral considerations are powerful, constituency service tends to be a major operation. Where professionalization has not gone as far and electoral considerations are more muted, constituency service is a less prominent feature of the terrain. But the trend toward increased attention to the constituency service function by state legislatures is likely to persist.

The results overall are positive. Incumbents surely benefit, and constituents benefit as well. There is also the possibility that, because of direct contact with their representatives, citizens will develop more supportive attitudes toward government in general, and legislatures in particular. Thus far, however, the legislature as an institution has reaped few benefits from the constituent services its members assiduously perform.

This condition can and should be changed. But that will happen only if legislators, in rendering constituency service, take into account the needs of the institution as well as their own needs. They will have to work in the future to strengthen their institution, just as they work today to strengthen their individual positions.

NOTES

1. The following information on district offices and staff in several states has been collected by the National Conference of State Legislatures.

2. John Shure, *Record*, August 23, 1982.

3. *Star-Ledger*, January 6, 1985.

4. Richard F. Fenno, Jr., *Home Style: House Members in Their Districts* (Boston: Little, Brown, 1978), p. 32.

5. Richard C. Elling, "The Utility of State Legislative Casework as a Means of Oversight," *Legislative Studies Quarterly*, v. 4 (August 1979), p. 357.

6. Fenno, p. 109. See also Robert S. Erikson, "The Advantage of Incumbency in Congressional Elections," *Polity*, v. 3 (Spring 1971), pp. 395–405.

7. Data on New Jersey are provided by the Office of Legislative Services.

8. Elling, pp. 353–379.

9. Frank Smallwood, *Free and Independent* (Brattleboro, Vermont: Stephen Green Press, 1976), pp. 172–173.

10. Malcolm E. Jewell, *Representation in State Legislatures* (Lexington, Kentucky: University Press of Kentucky, 1982), p. 163.

11. One reason is that the criteria for evaluating Congress and those used in evaluating congressmen are very different. Congress is assessed on the basis of its policy performance, while the assessments of representatives tend to be based upon constituency service and the personal attributes of incumbents. Glenn R. Parker and Roger H. Davidson, "Why Do Americans Love Their Congressmen So Much More Than Their Congress?" *Legislative Studies Quarterly*, v. 4 (February 1979), pp. 56–57.

CHAPTER VII

COURTS IN THE AMERICAN STATES

INTRODUCTION

The third branch of state government is the state judiciary. Today it is widely recognized that the courts participate in the state policy-making process. Certainly, any decision rendered by a state court promotes one interest over another. While the policy role of state courts is most visible in matters involving state or federal constitutional law, the decisions of the state courts in other matters may have far-reaching consequences for state behavior.

Consider, for example, the 1990 decision of a trial court judge in Philadelphia to order striking Temple University professors back to work under the provisions of Pennsylvania Public Law 195. The judge could have easily determined that the "health and welfare" of the community was not at stake and permitted the strike to continue to the detriment of a major quasi-public institution of higher education in Philadelphia. As it was, the university was able to cut its losses, and the striking teachers returned to their classrooms with only a modicum of their demands met. In short, state courts make public policy in the process of resolving a conflict.[1]

The typical hierarchical structure of the state court system includes several levels. At the lowest level are the trial courts of limited jurisdiction where relatively minor criminal or civil cases are heard. Juvenile, family, orphans, probate, and traffic courts are among the courts at the lowest trial level.

Slightly above the courts of limited jurisdiction are the trial courts of general jurisdiction. These courts hear major disputes such as murder, robbery, rape, and arson. At the next level are the intermediate appellate courts where decisions of the trial courts are appealed. Finally, each state has a court of last resort usually called a supreme court. Here final appeals to lower court decisions are made unless a federal question is involved and appeal is made to the federal appellate courts.

States vary considerably in the amount of money they spend on court systems. In millions of dollars New York, California, Illinois, Massachusetts, North Carolina, and Pennsylvania spend the most, while states such as Idaho, Montana, Nevada, North Dakota, Oklahoma, Vermont, and Wyoming spend the least. Looked at in per capita expenditures, however, Washington, D.C., and Alaska spend the highest amounts, while Indiana, Oklahoma, Ohio, and Texas spend much lower amounts.[2]

The court reform movement that began in the 1970s and is continuing seeks to reorganize the state courts into a more unified court system—one that consolidates and centralizes the various courts into a single hierarchical administrative unit. Consolidation would reduce the number of separate courts as well as eliminate the problem of overlapping jurisdictions. Centralization would place all judges under the general supervision of the chief justice of the state supreme court.

Under a unified court system there would exist a single, much strengthened state supreme court. The appellate and trial courts would fall hierarchically below and be subordinate to the supreme court. Accordingly, the state supreme court could ensure that laws are interpreted and applied consistently and evenhandedly throughout the state. Moreover, under the American Bar Association's model state judicial article, personnel management and record keeping, budgeting, and rule making would come under the authority of the state supreme court.[3]

Three important questions for state court reformers have been (1) how to select judges, (2) how to discipline and remove judges if improper judicial conduct has occurred, and (3) how to end the tenure of judges under normal circumstances. The result has been a movement toward the use of the Missouri Plan in the selection of judges, the creation of organizations in many states with the capacity to discipline or remove judges, and the enactment of a mandatory retirement age to end tenure normally. Henry R. Glick, in his article "The Politics of Court Reform: In a Nutshell," reprinted in this chapter as Reading 13, reports on the latest accomplishments of the court reformers.

State courts had long been considered "sticks-in-the-mud" for ignoring important civil rights and civil liberties questions. Indeed, during the 1950s, 1960s, and early 1970s, the U.S. Supreme Court overturned state school segregation laws, forced state legislatures to reapportion themselves to meet "one-person, one-vote" guidelines, broadened the rights of the accused, expanded voting rights, and legalized abortion. However, in recent years the U.S. Supreme Court has become more conservative in its opinions and, as it has done so, several state courts have determined not only to buy into the minimum civil rights and civil liberties standards set by the U.S. Supreme Court but to exceed them. Thus since the 1980s, at least, many state courts have begun to expand their jurisdiction into areas once left solely to the U.S. Supreme Court. Elder Witt reports on this phenomenon in this chapter in his article, Reading 14, "State Supreme Courts: Tilting the Balance toward Change."

NOTES

1. See Thomas R. Dye, *Politics in States and Communities*, 7th ed. (Englewood Cliffs, N.J.: Prentice-Hall, 1991), p. 216.

2. These data are drawn from Richard D. Bingham and David Hedge, *State*

and Local Government in a Changing Society, 2nd ed. (New York: McGraw-Hill, 1991), p. 179.

   3. On this point see Ann O'M. Bowman and Richard C. Kearney, *State and Local Government* (Boston: Houghton Mifflin, 1990), p. 284, and John G. Grumm and Russell D. Murphy, *Governing States and Communities: Organizing for Popular Rule* (Englewood Cliffs, N.J.: Prentice-Hall, 1991), p. 200.

Reading 13

THE POLITICS OF COURT REFORM: IN A NUTSHELL

Henry R. Glick

In the opinion of Henry R. Glick, state court reform is proceeding rather quickly in the United States. This is manifested in the increasing number of official and private reform organizations, the increase in the number of professional administrators hired by state and federal governments, and the rise in government funds spent on judicial administration. The major goals of the reformers are (1) to replace localism, independence, and wide variation in court organization with centralized judical management, (2) to streamline state court organization, and (3) to provide nonpartisan court staffing, funding, and procedure.

Court reform is not politically neutral. First, reform of the state judicial process would transfer power from the trial and appellate courts to the state supreme court. Second, reform would create a judiciary selected according to professional legal standards rather than by popular or partisan methods. Third, merit selection is frequently viewed as giving conservative lawyers the opportunity to dominate the state judiciary.

How would the reformers accomplish their goals? According to Glick, they favor the following actions:

1. State courts would be consolidated so as to end overlapping jurisdictions.
2. Management of the courts would be centralized under the state supreme court in order to bring about uniform procedure.
3. Judicial rule making would be centralized under the state supreme court to permit the supreme court to make rules governing judicial procedure as well as rules regarding admission to the practice of law.
4. Court budget decisions would be centralized under direction of the state supreme court in order to bolster its authority vis-à-vis the governor and local courts.

5. Full state funding of the courts would be established in order to limit local governments' control of court operations.
6. Merit selection of judges would be promoted in order to achieve objective decision making.
7. Finally, special state commissions would be set up with authority to hold hearings and recommend disciplinary action by the state supreme court against unethical judges or disabled judges who refuse to retire voluntarily.

As Glick points out, a good deal of court reform has already occurred. Many states have eliminated overlapping jurisdictions. And many state supreme courts now have the power to make uniform statewide rules for judicial procedure and for the practice of law. Some state supreme courts even have the power to temporarily transfer judges to help reduce backlogs at the trial court level. Disciplinary commissions have been created which have the capacity to remove or retire judges from office. However, to date, these commissions had disciplined very few judges.

The way in which judges are selected remains the most controversial of the proposed court reforms. More than half of the states, however, now use merit procedures to select state judges. This means that screening commissions which restrict governors to choosing judges from a limited list of individuals are gradually replacing elections and "unrestricted" gubernatorial appointment as the means of selecting state court judges.

Professor Glick concludes that because of considerable conflict over court reform, compromise is the typical outcome. Neither side gets all it wants. Moreover, neither supporters nor opponents of court reform have been able to provide research or evidence to back up their political positions. Where evaluation research has been conducted, the evidence shows no support for the belief that court reform has produced significant changes in court behavior or for the theory that an elevation in the formal training and experience of judges has occurred as a result of merit selection. This is so because the operation of trial courts is actually much more complex than court reformers realize. Delay in the completion of a case is not necessarily due to a crush of judicial business but to lawyers drawing out litigation through repeated bargaining and continuances. Glick argues that if court reform is to be successful, future social science research will need to develop recommendations based on the actual workings of the courts, especially of trial courts.

Court reform has become a growth industry in the United States (Wheeler 1979:134). The number of official and private reform organizations is increasing, the number of professional administrators hired by state and federal governments is up, and government funds spent on judicial administration is rising. There is no doubt that court reform has caught on and is here to stay.

Historically, state judicial organization and management have been very decentralized, with much judicial independence and local control of the courts. Terms like "state judicial systems" convey an artificial picture of order and unity. Instead, state courts usually are loose networks of semiautonomous trial and appellate courts. Individual judges and court clerks have been free to manage "their" courts as they see fit without much interference or direction from state supreme courts or court administrators. Close interaction between judges and clerks and other local political officials regarding court staffing, budgets and capital improvements has been common.

Court reformers intend to change all this. They would replace localism, independence and wide variation in court organization with centralized judicial management, streamlined state court organization and non-partisan (ideally apolitical) court staffing, funding and procedure (Berkson and Carbon, 1978; Tesitor and Sinks, 1980).

Like *law* and *justice*, court reform has strong and positive political appeal. Although its image is inviting and seemingly universal, court reform requires particular values and policies which effect political careers, and the goals of various elites. Court reform, therefore, is not politically neutral, but promotes a certain model of the judicial process. Most reforms advance state centralization and hierarchical judicial control through state supreme courts and increase the role of legal rather than popular political elites in managing and directing the courts.

ELEMENTS OF STATE COURT REFORM

Programs to reform the courts include seven major goals summarized below:

Consolidation and Simplification of State Court Organization. Reformers hope to combine many state courts to end overlapping jurisdiction and confusion concerning which courts are to be used for different types of cases. According to reformers, each state should have a supreme court,

Source: Henry R. Glick, "The Politics of Court Reform: In a Nutshell," *Policy Studies Journal* 10 (June 1982), pp. 680–89. Reprinted by permission.

possibly an intermediate court of appeals, one type of trial court with broad or general jurisdiction, and one or two types of specialized trial courts of limited or specialized jurisdiction.

Centralized Management of the Courts. Reformers believe that state supreme courts should have the final authority in the operations of state courts and should provide leadership in judicial administration. Unsupervised and widely varied local management practices should be scrapped in favor of uniform procedures. State court administrators will monitor the courts, collect information on case flow and should develop innovations which create efficient and economical courts. Local judges and court administrators are expected to respond to state leadership.

Centralized Judicial Rule-making. Reform calls for placing authority in state supreme courts to make all rules regarding judicial procedure and evidence and to govern admission to the practice of law. In many states, this power has rested with state legislatures. Reformers believe that the third branch ought to have authority to manage its own internal affairs.

Centralized Judicial Budgeting. In most states, courts have had very limited budgeting authority. Court budgets often are part of the executive budget and governors may veto judicial requests. Centralized budgeting is expected to bolster supreme court authority by limiting the financial independence of local courts and transferring political power from the governor and local officials to the centralized judiciary.

Full State Funding for the Courts. Most state court systems obtain their funds from a variety of sources, including some state money, funds from local government as well as court fines and fees. A hodge podge of funding sources is seen by reformers as contributing to decentralization and local independence. State-level funding is expected to reduce local variation in financial support, limit the control of local governments over court operations and upgrade the importance of courts for state officials.

Merit Selection of Judges. Reformers often believe that effective judicial administration can come only when judges are selected according to professional legal standards of education, experience, temperament, etc. So long as judges are chosen by popular or partisan methods, the courts will not become professional or unified organizations. Merit selection also is considered necessary for developing truly non-partisan and objective judicial decision-making and proper personal conduct.

Judicial Discipline and Removal. Reformers also believe that judicial systems ought to have an effective method for reprimanding or possibly removing judges who behave unethically or become disabled and will not retire voluntarily. Years ago, the only method to deal with corrupt or disabled judges was through cumbersome legislative impeachment which always required removal from office, a step that usually was much too drastic for the misstep or problem involved. Judicial reform calls for the creation of special state commissions with a staff and budget and powers to receive and investigate complaints, hold hearings and make recommendations to the proper authority (usually the state supreme court) for disciplinary action. Grounds for discipline or removal are general and should include: willful misconduct, failure to perform duties and habitual intemperance.

TRENDS IN COURT REFORM

Court reform has produced a number of changes in state courts during the 1970's. Probably the most significant has been *streamlining and consolidating the courts.* In place of a long chain of trial courts of general and limited jurisdiction, many with names and functions drawn from old England, about 20 states have created one or two courts which combine the jurisdiction of earlier courts. Many county courts, for example, now deal simultaneously with traffic cases, juvenile crime, small claims, divorce, probate, and other matters (Council of State Governments, 1978).

Two other management areas where state court reform has produced changes include the power of state supreme courts to temporarily *transfer judges* to help reduce trial court backlogs and to make *uniform statewide rules* for law practice and judicial procedure. Supreme courts have been given more authority in these areas mainly because the control is "in house" with few political implications for other elites and institutions in state politics. But even in these least controversial areas of judicial administration, the power of courts is not absolute or without political checks. In one-quarter of the states, supreme courts still have no power to transfer judges and almost half of the states still provide for a legislative veto of judicial rule-making.

A more controversial change is the use of *merit procedures (Missouri Plan) to select state judges.* Every year more states drop election or gubernatorial appointment in favor of screening commissions which restrict governors to choosing judges from a limited list of individuals. Lawyers and judges are guaranteed seats on these commissions, and are expected to apply legal rather than partisan standards in selecting nominees. Ten years ago, less than a dozen states used merit selection, but today about half of the states use the plan for recruiting at least some judges. More states are expected to adopt merit selection and to use it to choose more judges (American Judicature Society, 1979).

As of 1980, all but one of the states had created a state *disciplinary commission*. Although all of these commissions have similar powers and duties, there is much variation in staffing, budgets and activities of these agencies. Only 13 state commissions have a full-time director while 26 others have a part-time administrator or the agency is supervised by the state court administrator. In the remaining 11 states, a secretary is the only regular employee. About a dozen commissions have budgets over $100,000 and handle several hundred complaints annually. All other commissions have smaller budgets and deal with fewer complaints. Most conduct commissions discipline very few judges. Of nearly 3800 complaints filed in 1979 in all states, only four judges were removed from office. Another 47 retired before or after charges were filed and about 350 received a warning or other admonition. With the exception of California, South Carolina and Texas, the states dismissed the vast majority of charges (Tesitor and Sinks, 1980:50–53). It appears from these figures that judicial conduct commissions are symbolic in most states.

Except for these changes, local judicial independence, decentralization and local governmental control of state courts still is common. In half of the states, supreme courts have no authority to supervise the management practices of the local courts. They do not review budgeting and spending, purchasing for new equipment, case management procedures, nor can they establish statewide court personnel and employment standards. One-quarter of the states have authorized the supreme court to prepare a unified budget for all state courts, but many of these continue to require indirect submission to the legislature through the executive branch. State funding also is scant. In only ten states does eighty percent or more of court funding come from state sources. In over thirty states, state governments provide less than forty percent of court funds, with the remainder coming from local government and court fines and fees. The powers of state court administrators also tend to be weak; they usually have no authority to require compliance with state management practices and can only gather information about court operations and make recommendations for new procedures.

POLITICAL CONFLICT AND COURT REFORM

Court reform is supported and opposed by many different groups and elites in state politics. Although court reform issues pale in political significance when compared to other state issues such as major spending and tax bills, they are crucial for judges, lawyers, court employees, local political parties and many of their allied interest groups.

Reform typically is supported by high-status lawyers, leaders of state bar associations and a variety of middle class, government reform and civic organizations (Watson and Downing, 1969; Glick and Vines, 1973). Leagues of Women Voters, Associations of University Women, Chambers of Commerce, Kiwanis, Rotary, Boards of Realtors, and others generally cooperate with bar leaders in working for court reforms which represent their views of organizational efficiency. They often believe that, like prospering business, courts should produce the greatest number of uniform products (decided cases) at the least possible cost. Combined with beliefs that the rule of law should determine judicial decision-making and personal conduct, the "non-partisan business efficiency model" of the courts has widespread appeal.

Court reform also involves conflicting partisan and social attitudes. Many reformers, especially high status business lawyers and bar leaders, are Republicans who oppose the Democratic Party which dominates many cities. The influence of local Democrats on judicial recruitment, court financing, and charges of bias in decision-making leads reformers to sponsor what they argue are non-partisan substitutes for local partisan control of the courts. Urban Democrats and their supporting interest groups, however, usually counter charge that non-partisan reforms really are smokescreens for substituting Republican influence for the rightful role of local voting majorities in local government, including the courts. Merit selection, for example, frequently is viewed as giving conservative lawyers an opportunity to dominate the judiciary (Glick, 1978).

Although bar leaders are most visible, court reform is not unanimously supported by lawyers. Many urban and small town lawyers who work solo or in small partnerships usually handle a large volume and variety of cases, frequently file suits, motions, etc. and plan to go to trial. Lawyers who regularly use the trial courts frequently object to basic changes in court organization and procedure because it interferes with their routines. Accustomed to using the courts and familiar with court employees, they do not welcome having to learn new rules, procedures and organization. They also frequently object to plans to consolidate courts or change their jurisdiction because they prefer having alternative courts and judges available to them.

Many judges and other court employees also object to court reform because it may require them to learn new jobs, re-learn different areas of law and perfect new procedures. They also usually value their independence and see themselves as professionals who should not be supervised by others.

Compromises among supporters and opponents are the typical outcomes in the politics of court reform. Generally, court reforms are adopted most easily when they require little change in court organization and procedure, affect few job holders and do not substantially decrease legislative and executive power (Sweet, 1978; Cook, 1970). Many different kinds of compromises have occurred. For example, instead of winning merit selection for all state judges, reformers frequently are forced to accept changes in the selection of smaller groups of appellate or supreme court judges. Later, however, when merit selection has become accepted, reformers frequently try to obtain an extension to other courts. Sometimes entire reforms such as merit selection are sacrificed in order to win approval of court consolidation, procedural changes or other items. Still other political compromises exempt certain cities from court reform and legislative support for court reform is traded among representatives for votes on other political issues.

AN EVALUATION AND THE FUTURE OF THE COURT REFORM

Reformers assert that justice will be improved by making changes in the courts while defenders of the *status quo* praise the sanctity of tradition and local control. But neither side provides any dispassionate research or other evidence to support their political positions. However, social scientists are beginning to conduct objective research on the impact of court reform and to make comparisons between the old and new ways of conducting judicial business. Research has been done which contrasts court behavior before and after various reforms have been adopted and comparisons have been made between courts which have and have not adopted reforms. Studies over time and experiments in individual courts also have tested the net effect of changes in court operations.

Most of the evidence gathered so far shows that court reform generally fails to produce important improvements or significant changes in court behavior. Most of the assertions made by reformers also reveal a lack of understanding of how courts work and the complexity of local justice. Faced with this growing volume of research, reformers sometimes respond that so many compromises are necessary to achieve *any* reform that a "pure" model of court reform does not exist and cannot be fairly tested. The negative evidence, though, is mounting and the "wait and see" policy is not very convincing.

Some of the strongest evidence concerns the impact of merit selection. Reformers argue that the caliber of judges and judicial conduct will be improved and that decision-making will become more objective since judges will no longer be influenced by partisan politics. Many also believe that states which use merit selection will be more likely to adopt other court reforms since merit selected judges will be more supportive of professional court management. The evidence against these claims is overwhelming. There is no support for the belief that the backgrounds of judges, including formal training and experience, are affected by merit selection or that decision-making and judicial conduct have been altered. Moreover, merit selection has no demonstrated impact whatsoever on the tendency of the states to adopt other administrative reforms (Canon, 1972; Berg *et al.*, 1975; Glick, 1981).

Delay in courts is a major issue in judicial management. Many procedural changes concerning how cases are assigned to judges (calendaring techniques) and the use of pre-trial and pre-appeal conferences have been proposed to boost efficiency. State judicial administrators also spend enormous amounts of time and money gathering statistics on trial court caseloads and reform organizations such as the National Center for State Courts repeatedly publish newsletter accounts for the latest experiment or technique used for fighting clogged dockets. The prevailing assumption is that court workload is directly related to the time required to dispose of cases and that adding or transferring judges alleviates crowding since the fewer the number of cases a judge has to handle, the more work courts can produce.

Comparative research on large numbers of courts and studies of individual courts over time reveal that there is no connection between the amount of work to be done and the time it takes to do it, and that more judges do not necessarily decide more cases. Moreover, various new procedures do not necessarily speed up the process (Levin, 1975; Feeley, 1978; Church, 1976 and 1978; Goldman, 1978; Nimmer, 1974). A basic difficulty in most innovations and experiments is that court organizations are much more complex networks of informal social relationships than court reformers realize. Accustomed to thinking in terms of formal rules and law, they usually assume that new regulations will solve what they believe is a straightforward mechanical problem. Their reforms cannot accomplish much, though, since they do not take into account the way trial courts actually operate and the strategies used by lawyers in litigation (Gallas, 1976; Saari, 1976). Reformers seem to assume, for example, that lawyers are eager and prepared to go to trial but that if they were required to negotiate, cases could be settled more quickly. Many factual studies show, however, that as many as ninety percent of all cases are settled through informal negotiation or are abandoned by the litigants. Cases that go to trial or appeal also involve pre-hearing discussion and bargaining. Delay often is caused, not by the crush of judicial business, but by judges who permit lawyers to draw out litigation through repeated continuances and who generally tolerate a "motion practice." Centralized court systems or adding more judges is not likely to affect this behavior.

Social science research is not likely to deter court reformers, however. Fueled by a law-business ideology which glorifies the importance of formal rules and law and hierarchical professional administration, the politics of court reform can be expected to continue much as before. New careers in centralized state judicial systems also are promoted through the reform model of judicial administration. Consequently, research showing that reforms generally fail to achieve their goals is not likely to be welcomed.

In order for reform to have an impact beyond building new bureaucracies of state judicial managers, it needs to use social science research and to develop recommendations for change which take the actual workings of court into account. Producing change initially requires understanding the basic attitudes and values of lawyers and judges toward the practice of law and the role of courts. Perhaps reformers then can find ways to change these views to produce benefits for more of the people who use the courts. This certainly is not an easy task, but current reform is not likely to make much of a dent on the operations of American courts.

NOTE

My observations about the state courts are derived from the data on individual states contained in Appendix A in Berkson and Carbon (1978).

REFERENCES

American Judicature Society (1979). "Judicial Selection and Retention in the United States: A State-by-State Compilation," January, 1979.

Berg, Larry, *et al.* (1975). "The Consequences of Judicial Reform: A Comparative Analysis of the California and Iowa Appellate Systems." 28 *Western Political Quarterly* 263.

Berkson, Larry, and Susan Carbon (1978). *Court Unification: History, Politics and Implementation.* (Washington, D.C.: National Institute of Law Enforcement and Criminal Justice, Law Enforcement Assistance Administration, U.S. Department of Justice).

Canon, Bradley C. (1972). "The Impact of Formal Selection Processes on the Characteristics of Judges—Reconsidered." 6 *Law and Society Review* 579.

Church, Jr., Thomas (1978). *Justice Delayed.* (Williamsburg, Va.: National Center for State Courts).

———— (1976). "Plea Bargaining, Concessions and the Courts: Analysis of a Quasi-Experiment." 10 *Law and Society Review* 377.

Cook, Beverly Blair (1970). "The Politics of Piecemeal Reform of Kansas Courts." 53 *Judicature.*

Council of State Governments (1978). *State Court Systems,* rev. ed. (Lexington, Ky.: Council of State Governments.)

Feeley, Malcolm (1978). "The Effects of Heavy Caseloads," in S. Goldman and A. Sarat (eds.), *American Court Systems.* (San Francisco, Calif.: W.H. Freeman and Co.).

Gallas, Geoff (1976). "The Conventional Wisdom of State Court Administration: A Critical Assessment and an Alternative Approach." 2 *Justice System Journal* 35.

Glick, Henry R. (1981). "Innovation in State Judicial Administration: Effects on Court Management and Organization." 9 *American Politics Quarterly* 49.

_____ (1978). "The Promise and Performance of the Missouri Plan: Judicial Selection in the Fifty States." 32 *University of Miami Law Review* 509.

Glick, Henry R., and Kenneth N. Vines (1973). *State Court Systems.* (Englewood Cliffs, N.J.: Prentice-Hall).

Goldman, Jerry (1978). "The Civil Appeals Management Plan: An Experiment in Appellate Procedural Reform." 78 *Columbia Law Review* 1209.

Levin, Martin A. (1975). "Delay in Five Criminal Courts." 4 *Journal of Legal Studies* 83.

Nimmer, Raymond T. (1974). "Judicial Reform: Informal Processes and Competing Effects," in H. Jacob (ed.), *The Potential for Reform of Criminal Justice.* (Beverly Hills, Calif.: Sage Publications).

Saari, David J. (1976). "Modern Court Management: Trends in Court Organization Concepts—1976." 2 *Justice Systems Journal* 35.

Sweet, Linda F. (1978). "Anatomy of a 'Court Reform.' " 62 *Judicature* 37.

Tesitor, Irene A., and Dwight B. Sinks (1980). *Judicial Conduct Organizations.* (Chicago: American Judicature Society).

Watson, Richard A., and Rondal G. Downing (1969). *The Politics of the Bench and the Bar.* (New York: John Wiley & Sons).

Wheeler, Russell (1979). "Judicial Reform: Basic Issues and References." 8 *Policy Studies Journal* 134.

Reading 14

STATE SUPREME COURTS: TILTING THE BALANCE TOWARD CHANGE

Elder Witt

It is Elder Witt's opinion that state courts are proving to be willing participants in the revitalization of state governments by becoming partners in the policy process. State courts are giving new meaning to the values of state constitutions by going beyond the question "Is it legal?" to "Does it meet the public purpose requirements of the state's constitution?"

Several recent court decisions illustrate the deepening involvement of state courts in state policymaking. In Michigan, for example, the supreme court permitted cities to engage in *tax increment financing* (the use of property taxes to cover redevelopment costs, i.e., to benefit private interests). The Michigan high court rationalized its decision by stating that "the creation of jobs and the promotion of economic growth in the state are essential governmental functions and constitute essential public purposes."

Other state supreme courts have made economic development decisions akin to that made in Michigan. For example, the Florida Supreme Court upheld the issuance of tax-exempt bonds to finance the construction of a motel near Disney World of Orlando, while Maryland's supreme court upheld the power of the state stadium authority to issue bonds to fund a stadium. State supreme courts also have been involved in other policy matters. In New Jersey the state supreme court entered the debate over housing the state's poor when it ruled that Mount Laurel and every other municipality in the state had to permit and provide its fair share of housing for low-income persons.

Witt observes that state supreme courts are running ahead of the U.S. Supreme Court in the area of public school financing. Nationally, public school districts depend on property taxes in their respective districts to finance elementary and secondary schools. The result is considerable inequities in financial support for schools between rich and poor districts. In an appeal from a Texas state supreme court decision, the U.S. Supreme Court in 1973 held that the district property tax system of financing public school education did not violate the equal protection clause of the U.S. Constitution. Numerous state courts, including those of New Jersey, California, Connecticut, Wyoming, Arkansas, and West Virginia, have held, however, that financing systems which create inordinate variation in spending per pupil are unconstitutional. As a result, many state legislatures have made policy decisions providing for more equitable funding for poorer school districts.

It is Witt's conclusion that despite growing state court involvement and innovativeness in the states' policy processes, such activity is still very limited. This is so for the following reasons: (1) state legislatures can resist judicial decisions requiring state funding; (2) state constitutions can be amended; and (3) state judges who make decisions at variance with popular will in their state risk retribution at the polls. Nevertheless, state court involvement in the policy process, even in only a few states, contributes to the diversity and pluralism of policy approaches and of judicial thinking in the American political system.

Their robes don't resemble lab coats and their courtrooms don't look like laboratories, but issue by issue, state judges are proving to be willing partners in the ongoing experiment of government.

"When you look to the revitalization of state government, state courts are some of the lead players in that drama," says University of Virginia law Professor A. E. Dick Howard. "The activity of state courts reflects the vitality of state government generally."

As a direct result of rulings by their own supreme courts, Michigan cities are moving to revive their aging downtowns, West Virginia's legislature is rethinking its system of supplementing local school budgets, municipal officials in New Jersey are working to increase the supply of low-income housing, and communities from California to Virginia are exerting more control over how they grow.

Judges are not legislators or executives; they cannot reach out for issues, but must wait for them to arrive at the courthouse. They depend on the legislature or the executive to enforce their decisions. Notwithstanding such inherent restraints, state courts often go beyond simple interpretation of the meaning of laws and state constitutions to become makers of public policy. "The active participation of state judges in the policy process is much more taken for granted and much less controver-

---

Source: Elder Witt, "State Supreme Courts: Tilting the Balance toward Change," *Governing* (August 1988), pp. 30–38. Reprinted with permission. Copyright 1988, *Governing* magazine.

sial than the involvement of federal judges in the national government," says Oregon Supreme Court Justice Hans A. Linde, one of the foremost exponents of a vigorous state judiciary.

"They've been making policy all along," says Mary Cornelia Aldis Porter, co-author with Rutgers' G. Alan Tarr of a new book, *State Supreme Courts in State and Nation....* "But generally the things they did were considered more or less routine," such as reform of a state's tort system.

What's new are the subjects the courts are addressing and the responses they are demanding. "People sit up and take notice when courts say you've got to do something about the way you pay for education. When they say you've got to allocate resources differently, you've got to raise taxes, that's very different from saying that someone can sue if a coffee urn blows up in his face," says Porter.

Cities, towns and counties are finding out that state judges are good people to have on their side, effective allies in permitting or preventing change. Creative solutions to longstanding problems often provoke legal challenges, Howard points out. "These questions of innovation become state constitutional issues, ending up in the state supreme courts."

The answers they give, says Howard, "really define the quality of life in a community," shaping economic, educational, aesthetic and social opportunities for government and citizens alike. As they pour modern meaning into constitutional phrases such as "public purpose" and "general welfare," they adapt the framework of the past to the needs of today's governments.

State constitutions are the basic texts for state supreme courts. Just as there is no typical state court, there is no average state constitution. Twenty states operate today under their original constitutions, most of them substantially amended. Massachusetts' 1780 constitution, a decade older than the U.S. Constitution and now amended 116 times, is the oldest. Louisiana has had the most state constitutions, a total of 11; Georgia is currently living with its 10th.

Justice Linde is blunt. "The states demystify constitutional law," he has written. "State constitutions have little mystique. Some have all the literary quality of the Yellow Pages." But literary quality aside, state constitutions reflect the values of the people they govern, and as state courts apply them, they give meaning to those values. Virtually all state constitutions make mention of public education, many expressly protect environmental values, and others specifically guarantee personal privacy.

"State constitutions contain much more detail than the federal constitution about how the state government is to operate," says Robert F. Williams of Rutgers University, editor of the Advisory Commission on

Intergovernmental Relations' *Cases and Materials on Understanding State Constitutional Law.* "What happens when you put all this detail in your constitution?" Williams asks. "It invites litigants to involve state courts in these daily questions about how the government operates." Not only is there more to argue about in state courts, but it's easier to get into state courts than federal courts to make those arguments, Williams continues. "The result is popular participation in government by lawsuit."

"Variability is the real hallmark of this area of the law," says Michael E. Libonati, an expert on local government law and a professor at Temple University. "The real title of Williams' book ought to be *Amazing Stories.* There's a lot of intellectual experimentation going on," he continues. "You'll find some bizarre ideas out there, some good, some not so good. But any single state constitutional law case can change your way of looking at the law."

Traditional liberal-conservative labels often don't apply to state court decisions interpreting constitutional choices about government. For example, Williams says, legislators in many states sit on executive-branch boards and agencies, in apparent conflict with strict separation of powers. "Should an environmental protection board have among its members the legislators who in the first instance passed these laws and now are working on executing them? These kinds of questions really cut across liberal-conservative lines when you talk about how government should operate," says Williams. "The question is often more than 'Is it legal?' We need also to ask, 'Is that a good idea?'"

"That's the kind of dialogue about government that's more important than whether you can search a suitcase in a car's trunk for drugs," he adds.

Michigan's experience proves Williams' point. When constitutional questions clouded the hopes of its cities for using an innovative twist on the property tax—known as tax increment financing—to cover some redevelopment costs, the cities, the legislature and the governor turned to the state Supreme Court. They asked for an advisory opinion measuring this new device, already approved by law, to see if it would fit within the state's constitutional framework.

Like many state constitutions, Michigan's requires that any "lending of the state's credit" be for a "public purpose." The question was whether tax increment financing violated this principle by using taxpayers' money to benefit private interests.

Tax increment financing treats an area's tax base like a cake with icing. Its taxable value at the time that redevelopment starts is the cake; the value added by roads, utility lines and other improvements is the icing.

Property tax revenues from the cake are divided among all area taxing authorities; all revenues from the icing go to the governments that funded the infrastructure improvements.

The state Supreme Court approved tax increment financing, agreeing with the legislature that "the creation of jobs and promotion of economic growth in the state are essential governmental functions and constitute essential public purposes."

Attorneys for affected cities agree: It is difficult to overstate the importance of the court's action. St. Clair Shores, an aging suburb, can now transform the marine slum that blights its waterfront into an asset. "The life of the community was at stake," says Norman Hyman, who represented St. Clair Shores before the state's high court.

Also given a go-ahead by the court's ruling is a major new development in downtown Detroit, where more than 400 acres have been cleared for a new Chrysler auto assembly plant near the outdated one it will replace, keeping thousands of jobs and dollars downtown. The decision had "almost a life-and-death effect" on the city, says David Baker Lewis, Detroit's municipal bond counsel. Without clearance to issue tax increment bonds to pay for acquiring the land, demolishing the structures on it and providing necessary utility service, Detroit might have lost the Chrysler plant to a site in suburbia, he says.

For many cities across the country, Hyman says, "tax increment financing has become an urban redevelopment and fiscal recovery weapon of first *and* last resort."

In reaching their decision, Michigan's justices could look at how other state supreme courts had resolved public-purpose challenges to creative financing mechanisms. Their opinion cited decisions by courts in Colorado, Florida, Minnesota, Oklahoma and Pennsylvania. This sort of cross-fertilization among states is often described as "horizontal federalism," in contrast with the "vertical federalism" of the traditional federal-state-local relationship.

Earlier, when Utah's Supreme Court was pondering a challenge to a state law setting up a non-profit public corporation to assist emerging small businesses, it was able to study relevant cases from Arkansas, Florida, Idaho, Illinois, Iowa, Kentucky, Maryland, Tennessee, Washington and Wisconsin.

To facilitate the flow of ideas from state to state, the National Association of Attorneys General has set up a state constitutional law clearinghouse that produces a monthly bulletin on state constitutional law, an annual seminar and an annual report, due out this month. In addition, the American Academy of Political and Social Science recently devoted an entire issue of its journal to the subject. This fall, Williams' book, the first modern casebook on state constitutional law, will be published by the ACIR, which also has commissioned a study of the trend's impact on the relationships among federal, state and local governments.

While state court decisions affecting individual rights have attracted considerable attention from the national media, the less publicized rulings about the powers and duties of government itself are of more importance to state and local officials. On many of these issues, says Temple University's Libonati, state courts enjoy "tremendous doctrinal flexibility. The accordian of public-purpose doctrine is one courts can expand or contract depending on their policy sense," he says.

Contraction can be painful for local government, says the University of Virginia's Howard. "If the state court views public purpose narrowly, it severely limits the kinds of initiatives the state government can take in partnership with the private sector," he says. "If a city wants to go redevelop a blighted area in partnership with a developer, but the state supreme court rules that is not a public purpose, the area may stay blighted."

Most state supreme courts, though, have found their constitution's public-purpose requirement flexible enough to permit these arrangements. Florida's Supreme Court upheld the issuance of tax-exempt bonds to finance construction of a motel near Walt Disney World. Maryland's Supreme Court upheld the power of the state stadium authority to issue bonds to fund the stadium.

Unlike Michigan's Supreme Court, which entered the policy conversation after a solution had already been approved by the legislature and the governor, New Jersey's Supreme Court itself initiated a long and cantankerous debate over the problem of housing the state's poor. Today, 13 years after the debate began, New Jersey is still far from solving the problem. But its state court, for decades the most innovative in the nation, has made certain that the issue remains high on the political agenda. The court "irrevocably changed the name of the political game in New Jersey," says John M. Payne, president of the Alliance for Affordable Housing and professor of law at Rutgers' Newark campus.

Mount Laurel is a New Jersey township a few miles from Philadelphia. Black families sued town officials there who refused to use federal funds to build low-income housing. In 1975, the court ruled that Mount Laurel, and every other municipality in the state, had to provide its fair share of low-income housing. The decision was rooted in a concept of the regional general welfare—the belief that the state constitution requires local government to use its power to benefit the larger community. Tangible results—after three Supreme Court rulings, dozens of legal complaints and a new state law—include 2,000 new, already occupied housing units for poor people and at least 10,000 more under construction.

It didn't happen quickly. As judges do, the New Jersey court at first left it up to Mount Laurel and other affected towns and cities to decide how to meet their responsibility. That didn't work, producing little but litigation. In 1983, the Supreme Court issued a second decision, creating a judicial mechanism to implement the goal of shared obligation for the provision of low-income housing. Three Superior Court judges were designated to oversee compliance. Not surprisingly, these judges, who had the power to revise local zoning ordinances to permit low-income housing, "came to be regarded as housing czars," says Payne.

A move to change the constitution to overturn the Mount Laurel ruling was short-circuited when the legislature passed a law putting implementation back in the hands of an executive agency, the Council for Affordable Housing. "The principal benefit of the process," says Payne, "is only partially the housing that has been constructed. Of more lasting benefit is the conversation that it set off. What the court did was to force upon the legislature consideration of an issue that the legislature did not want to think about and would not have done anything about but for the litigation. The problem was brought into sunlight by litigation."

Other states have invoked the concept upon which the Mount Laurel ruling was based, but reached different conclusions. "The doctrine of the regional general welfare can be used as an affirmative tool or a negative tool," says Robert H. Freilich, professor of law at the University of Missouri-Kansas City School of Law and a recognized authority on land use.

New Jersey's court invoked the regional general welfare as an affirmative tool, to ensure development of sufficient low-income housing. Washington state's Supreme Court has used that concept to permit a city or suburb to challenge a neighboring community's plans for development.

Educating children is a prime function of local government, the fulfillment of a state constitutional guarantee. Supreme courts in 18 states have taken a hard look at the way local public schools are financed—and the 19th high court, in Texas, will get its case soon. At the heart of these cases is the uneven base of support for public schools that is built on local property taxes. Challenged as unconstitutional, this interdistrict inequality has been the problem of state courts since 1973, when the U.S. Supreme Court refused to intervene in a challenge to Texas' school finance system, declaring that this was not a matter for federal courts.

California's Supreme Court had already ordered reform of its educational finance system and equalization of spending to bring it in line with state constitutional guarantees. In the Texas case, the U.S. Supreme Court emphasized that its decision was not to be read as approving the status quo. "The need is apparent for reform in tax systems which may well have relied too long and too heavily on the local property tax," it declared, taking note of California's ruling and of a similar case then pending in New Jersey. Reform, however, was a matter for state legislators, not federal judges, wrote the decision's author, Justice Lewis F. Powell Jr., himself a former member of the Virginia and Richmond boards of education.

Less than two weeks later, the New Jersey Supreme Court ruled that the state's school financing system was denying some of its children their constitutionally guaranteed state right to a public education. Careful to maintain local prerogatives, the court did not order equalization of spending but instead directed the state to shoulder more of the burden of financing elementary and secondary education. The eventual result was the reluctant adoption of a state income tax to fund this aid.

Over the past decade, 16 other state supreme courts from Connecticut to Wyoming have measured their systems of paying for public schools against the promises of their state constitution and the concerns of local government. Eleven have upheld the system. "These courts saw the challenge to local school funding as necessarily having implications for police, fire, roads and other local services. Yet unequal levels of local services and taxation were deemed characteristic of the American system of local government," writes Richard Briffault of Columbia University's law school. Indeed, several courts "expressly vindicated the right of school districts to spend more than the state required or than their neighbors could afford."

But in Arkansas, Connecticut, Washington, West Virginia and Wyoming, state courts ordered reform. As West Virginia and New Jersey attest, such a ruling was just the beginning of a long-running dialogue.

In 1979, West Virginia's Supreme Court of Appeals ruled that its constitutional promise of "a thorough and efficient system of free schools" required basic change in the way those schools were financed. This summer, nine years later, the legislature was wrestling with a sequel to that decision made necessary by a decision of the state Supreme Court earlier this year, which struck down the legislature's plan for supplementing teachers' salaries. The court found that the plan created new inequalities among teaching salaries, penalizing counties that had increased their own taxes in order to raise salaries.

In New Jersey, too, a second-round challenge to the school finance system is working its way back to the Supreme Court, based on the contention that the promise of the court's earlier ruling has not been realized.

And in Texas, where the legislature waited more than a decade after the first case to approve finance reform legislation, the same school district that was home to the Supreme Court case, along with a dozen other property-poor districts, is back in court to challenge the system. But this time, it's making its argument in state court.

Land use is everybody's issue in urbanized America, and local governments seeking to control the shape of growth often find themselves defending their actions in court. As a result, state courts often exert "extraordinary power in deciding what the shape of our countryside will be," says Virginia's Howard.

State courts run the gamut in their rulings on land use, reflecting the differing values and heritage of their populaces. When Vermont's legislature moved to discourage land speculation by taxing short-term gains on land at a much higher rate than long-term gains, the tax was challenged by developers—and upheld by the state Supreme Court. In California, the Supreme Court has not only deferred to government action protective of environmental concerns—it has approved use of the initiative process to challenge government's land-use decisions on specific developments. As a result, the initiative has become the chief instrument of public policy on questions of growth. In the past two years, there have been well over 100 local ballot initiatives of this type.

Through the 1970s, on the other hand, Virginia's Supreme Court was "uncommonly protective of property rights and very tough on county efforts to control growth," Howard explains. When reviewing county efforts to restrict the density of development, the court tended to give more weight to the property owner's right to realize a maximum profit from his land than to the county's right to limit the burden the development would impose on schools, roads and other public services.

But things have changed in the 1980s, says J. Patrick Taves, assistant county attorney for Fairfax County. "What we've seen is a shift in the importance that the Supreme Court of Virginia places on the prerogative of local governing bodies," says Taves. "The court is now telling local governing bodies that it will uphold their actions so long as they are reasonably consistent with the county's comprehensive land-use plan."

That change in attitude tends to discourage extended land-use litigation. When the Fairfax County Board of Supervisors in 1982 downzoned 40,000 acres in the Occoquan Basin—land that drains into the reservoir that provides the county's water supply—to permit only 8,000 homes in the area, not 40,000, 50 lawsuits were filed challenging its action. After two years of litigation, the local trial court upheld the county's action. There was no appeal.

The involvement of state judges in the policy process is a natural consequence of the fact that more than half of them are elected; most of the others are appointed initially but must later stand for election to retain their seats. "As elected representatives, like legislators, they feel less hesitant to offer their policy views than do appointed judges," explains Oregon Justice Linde in "Observations of a State Court Judge," an essay published by the Brookings Institution. . . .

Having to win approval at the polls invariably renders state judges vulnerable to adverse public opinion. A California judge once said that he never forgot there was "a crocodile in our bathtub." The crocodile bit in 1986 when California voters ousted their chief justice, Rose Bird, and two of her colleagues because they disagreed with the court's liberal rulings, particularly its opposition to capital punishment.

(It bears noting that the members of New Jersey's innovative high court do not have to worry about crocodiles. They are appointed and do not stand for election.)

State judges can sometimes have their say on a policy matter, even without a real legal controversy, Linde notes. At least a dozen state supreme courts can issue advisory opinions to legislative and executive agencies, without waiting for a case to arise. The Michigan court's tax increment financing decision was just such a ruling.

Judges should be careful not to invoke their constitutions too often, Linde warns; it's important to keep the policy conversation going. "Try to tell people what they can or cannot do in terms of the ordinary law and only reach a constitutional issue when you have to. To make it a constitutional issue takes it out of the day-to-day policy-making arena," he says.

But state supreme courts rarely have the last word on state law. The people can always claim that prerogative by tossing out the judges, passing a new law or amending the state constitution to correct a judicial misstep.

Constitutional amendments come with particular frequency in states whose citizens can use the initiative process for this purpose. State supreme courts in Massachusetts and California declared the death penalty in violation of the state constitutions. The people of both states then amended their state constitutions to overturn those decisions. After the Florida Supreme Court read its state guarantee against search and seizure as more protective of individual rights than the federal one, Floridians expressed their disagreemeent, amending the constitution to reverse that ruling.

"The realm of state constitutional law is a beehive of activity," says John Kincaid, executive director of the ACIR. "Together, the present constitutions of the 50 states have been amended more than 5,300 times."

That sort of exchange of views between court and citizens, says Virginia's Howard, "is part of the ferment." The conversation it continues is particularly valuable because it "has no counterpart at the federal level. It can involve the state legislature, the governor, the state courts, the localities and the people."

"It's what law is all about," says Temple University's Libonati, "and it really is what politics ought to be about, listening to the other side of the story."

CHAPTER VIII

STATE AND LOCAL GOVERNMENT FINANCES

INTRODUCTION

Raising revenues for state and local expenditures includes decisions about what goods and services (such as highways, parks, state colleges, public schools, and public libraries should be provided, how revenue (from wage taxes, sales taxes, property taxes, user fees, etc.) is to be raised for these goods and services, and from which sources (wage earners, property owners, ratepayers, small businesses, corporations, etc.) revenue will be raised.

Historically, states and localities have paid for most of their own goods and services through property taxes, sales and excise taxes, and business license fees. However, because the federal government at present collects between 55 and 65 percent of all revenues, financial power has shifted from state and local governments to the federal government.[1] Ironically, as state and local financial power has declined, the responsibilities of state and local governments have grown and their expenditures have nearly tripled since the mid-1950s.[2] Not surprisingly, much of the increased burden on states and localities, especially on northern industrial states and large urban cities, has been due to a declining physical infrastructure greatly in need of major overhaul or replacement, and a human infrastructure a large part of whose members live below the poverty line. Importantly, also, as the federal government has commanded the largest chunk of available revenues, it has since the 1980s reduced the amount of its grant-in-aid contributions to the states and localities. In "Recent Trends in the Finances of the State and Local Sector," reprinted in this chapter as Reading 15, John T. Carnevale reports the present condition of state and local government finances, how these governments have coped with declining federal aid, and the prospects for the future.

Many students of local government and politics have treated cities as if they were nations with the capacity to do for themselves what nations can do for themselves, arguing that somehow cities can easily make up for shortfalls in federal aid. But others point out that just as states under the American Articles of Confederation were limited in what they could achieve alone, so it is that cities under U.S. state constitutions are limited in what they can accomplish within their borders. The nation-state, because it includes within its borders all of the wealth (and poverty) of the nation and because it monopolizes the printing of money and the raising of revenues, is assigned the responsibility for redistributional activities (health and income maintenance programs, etc.). Paul E. Peterson writes that the demands of some interests in local communities for a politics of redistribution, especially in light of declining federal aid, face certain obstacles which he does not believe can be easily overcome.[3] Those obstacles are the subject of his article, Reading 16, "City Limits: The Politics of Redistribution."

NOTES

1. See Thomas R. Dye, *Politics in States and Communities*, 7th ed. (Englewood Cliffs, N.J.: Prentice-Hall, 1991), pp. 480–81, especially Table 18–1 on page 481.

2. See David C. Saffell, *State and Local Government: Politics and Public Policies*, 3rd ed. (New York: Random House, 1987), p. 191.

3. For a study of one city, however, in which evidence was mustered for a significant measure of redistribution occurring, see Carolyn Teich Adams, *The Politics of Capital Investment: The Case of Philadelphia* (Albany, N.Y.: State University of New York Press, 1988), pp. 154–57.

Reading 15

RECENT TRENDS IN THE FINANCES OF THE STATE AND LOCAL SECTOR

John T. Carnevale

The pattern of federal-state-local fiscal relations has changed, according to John T. Carnevale, from one of increasing centralization wherein the federal government assumes the leading financial role in state and local governments to one of decentralization in which the federal government plays a smaller fiscal role in state and local governments. These trends have been occasioned by a large federal budget deficit facing the nation as well as by the New Federalism policies of the Reagan and Bush administrations.

Despite this new pattern of governmental relationships, Carnevale finds that states and localities did not fare badly between 1980 and 1984. He argues that state and local governments coped with fiscal stress during this period by increasing taxes and reducing expenditures to balance their budgets. Beginning in 1984, however, increasing medical care and public safety expenditures zoomed beyond the capacity of state and local governments to keep pace through their own-source receipts. The result has been a decline in the fiscal health of the states and cities since 1984.

The big change in state and local government receipts has been a function of reduced federal grants. Although federal grant dollars to states and localities increased from 1980 to 1986, the federal percentage of total receipts declined. Important to note, also, is that there were 428 federally funded programs in 1980, but only 340 in 1986.

Carnevale concludes that state and local governments experiencing fiscal stress are no longer able to rely on federal money to finance a large part of their budget needs; they can only increase taxes or reduce expenditures. Yet as Carnevale points out, if the states and localities are going to meet the growing demand for public goods and services which are no longer paid for by the federal government, they will need to increase *both* taxes and expenditures. The latter increase is usually acceptable to the citizenry, but the former raises important election survival questions for elected public officials.

In recent years the pattern of federal-state-local fiscal relations has changed from one of increasing centralization in which the federal government assumed the leading financial role to one of decentralization. This had serious implications for the state and local fiscal condition. When confronted with fiscal stress in the past, the sector would turn to the federal government for financial assistance. Recent trends in federal grants-in-aid demonstrate that the federal government is now resolved to playing a smaller role in the fiscal affairs of state and local governments. This means that any challenges to the sector's fiscal integrity must be met by the sector's own tax and expenditure actions, not those of the federal government.

Recent trends in state and local government receipts and expenditures reveal a sector that has used its own tax and expenditure policies, rather than relying on the federal government to provide aid, especially countercyclical aid as it did just a few years earlier, to achieve balanced budgets in times of fiscal stress. Despite the recessions of the early eighties, the lingering effects of the tax revolt, and the decline in federal aid, the sector has coped with fiscal stress by using its tax and expenditure policies to maintain fiscal balance. In response to the 1981–82 recession, for example, about three quarters of the states enacted some type of tax increase. While many of these tax increases were temporary, they were sufficient to give the sector its biggest surplus ever—reaching $19.8 billion in 1984. While the economic recovery also had a role in creating the surplus, the response of the states is more significant.

Most state and local program expenditures have experienced remarkably similar rates of growth in recent years. There are two exceptions, however. Medical care and public safety related expenditures are increasing faster than other program areas. Medical care expenditures are growing because of the continued high rate of inflation in medical costs. Public safety expenditures are growing because of increasing

Source: John T. Carnevale, "Recent Trends in the Finances of the State and Local Sector," *Public Budgeting and Finance* (Summer 1988): 33–48. Reprinted with permission of Public Financial Publications, Inc.

prison populations resulting from tougher state sentencing policies and court ordered improvements in prison living conditions.

Since 1984, the fiscal health of the sector, as measured by the Bureau of Economic Analysis' (BEA) other funds surplus measure, has declined. This decline was greater for state governments, going from a $6.1 billion surplus in 1984 to a $2.8 billion deficit in 1986. Local governments were also in surplus over the same period, starting with a $13.7 billion surplus in 1984 and ending with a slightly lower one of $10.3 billion in 1986. Evidence shows that changes in federal aid are not a major factor in the changing surplus position of the sector. The key determinant of the decline is the increased use of borrowing to finance the sector's capital program.

The outlook for the state and local sector in the near term depends primarily on general economic trends and the sector's own policy decisions; and secondarily on federal grant policy and the effects of federal tax reform on state and local receipts.

TRENDS IN STATE AND LOCAL GOVERNMENT FINANCE

The state and local sector experienced three distinct patterns of growth in the post–World War II period. The first was a period of rapid growth that lasted to the mid-seventies. During this period, the sector absorbed an increasing share of the economy's resources. State and local government expenditures as a percent of GNP increased from less than eight percent in 1950 to a historical peak of 14.7 percent in 1975—own-source receipts (taxes, fees, and charges) rose from seven percent to twelve percent.

Federal aid played an important role in financing the sector's growth. Between 1950 and 1975, federal aid grew at an annual rate of 13.5 percent, much faster than the 9.5 percent growth in the sector's own-source revenues. The increasing importance of federal aid made state and local governments more dependent on the federal government. In fact, federal aid comprised almost one fourth of the increase in total state and local revenues between 1950 and 1975.

Beginning in the mid-seventies, the growth experienced by the sector came to an abrupt halt. The sector's share of GNP declined from 14.7 percent in 1975 to 12.6 percent by 1984. Two sets of circumstances contributed to the reversal of the growth pattern. One is the tax revolt that began in California in 1978, which restricted the growth of government. The other is the cutback in federal aid also beginning in 1978. In response to growing budget deficits, federal grant outlays measured in constant (1982) dollars peaked at $109.7 billion in 1978 and declined continuously until 1983. Compounding these circumstances is the fiscal stress introduced by the back-to-back recessions of the eighties.

Beginning in 1984, the state and local sector experienced renewed growth, but much more slowly than before. Expenditures increased from 12.6 percent of GNP in 1984 to 13.3 percent by 1986, and tax receipts increased slightly from 8.9 percent to 9.2 percent.

RECENT TRENDS IN REVENUES

The largest component of total state and local government revenues is own-source receipts, which includes taxes, fees, and charges. The second largest source is federal grants-in-aid.

As Table 1 shows, total state and local government revenues increased by $228.8 billion between 1980 and 1986. About two-thirds of this increase occurred at the state level, financed mostly by own-source receipts. In fact, own-source receipts account for about 92 percent of the increase in the sector since 1980, expanding by $210.6 billion. The increase in federal aid of $18.2 billion comprises the remaining eight percent increase in total receipts.

OWN-SOURCE RECEIPTS

About three-quarters of the total own-source receipts of state and local governments are derived from various tax sources. The major tax sources are the individual income tax, sales taxes, and property taxes. Together, these taxes provide over 80 percent of the sector's total tax receipts. State governments are most dependent on sales and individual income taxes whereas local governments rely mostly on property taxes. Less significant tax sources include estate and gift taxes, motor vehicle licenses, severance taxes, and corporate profit tax accruals. Other own-source receipts include fees and charges such as tuition and related education charges, hospital and health charges, rents and royalties, and fines.

In this decade, state and local governments have come to rely heavily on own-source receipts to provide for their revenue requirements, especially during times of fiscal stress, rather than on the federal government, which has demonstrated a strong reluctance to provide assistance. This is why so many states enacted some type of tax increase in response to the 1981–82 recession.[1] As will be shown later, during the 1981–83 period 28 states enacted personal income tax increases and 30 states enacted sales tax increases to compensate for recession induced revenue losses. Many of the states currently experiencing fiscal stress have taken tough actions to alleviate fiscal pressures created by declining revenues.

TABLE 1 State and Local Total Revenues, 1980–1986 ($ billions)

	Calendar year							Dollar change from 1980–86
	1980	1981	1982	1983	1984	1985	1986	
Total	390.0	425.6	449.4	487.7	540.5	579.6	618.8	228.8
Own-source	301.3	337.7	365.5	401.5	446.9	479.9	511.9	210.6
Taxes	231.0	256.6	274.1	300.7	337.3	363.4	385.3	154.3
Other	70.3	81.1	91.4	100.8	109.6	116.5	126.6	56.3
Federal grants	88.7	87.9	83.9	86.2	93.6	99.7	106.9	18.2
State governments								
Total	246.5	268.7	278.8	304.4	340.1	364.0	389.1	142.6
Own-source	182.0	202.7	214.3	236.7	265.7	283.4	301.0	119.0
Federal grants	64.5	66.0	64.5	67.7	74.4	80.6	88.1	23.6
Local governments								
Total	143.4	156.8	170.7	183.2	200.4	215.6	229.7	86.3
Own-source	119.2	135.5	151.3	164.7	181.3	196.5	210.9	91.7
Federal grants	24.2	21.3	19.4	18.5	19.1	19.1	18.8	−5.4

Source: Bureau of Economic Analysis, *Survey of Current Business* (various issues).

What is most remarkable about this behavior is that it constitutes a dramatic turnaround from earlier days of waiting for federal largesse to remedy fiscal stress caused by cyclical changes in the economy.

FEDERAL GRANTS

The most significant change in state and local receipts is the reduced role played by the federal government, primarily in federal grants. Federal grants increased $18.2 billion from $88.7 billion in 1980 to $106.9 billion in 1986. However, as a percent of total receipts, federal grants declined over the entire period. In fact, they peaked in 1978 at 23.4 percent and declined to 17.3 percent in 1986. As Figure 1 shows, the reduced role was accompanied by a dramatic shift in the composition of federal grants. Grants for payments to individuals have increased in the eighties whereas other grants have decreased. Among the larger grants for individuals are medicaid, AFDC, low-income home energy assistance, and food and nutrition services. As a share of total grants, grants to individuals have increased from about 35 percent in 1980 to about 47 percent in

FIGURE 1 Changing Composition of Federal Grants Relative to Total State and Local Expenditures

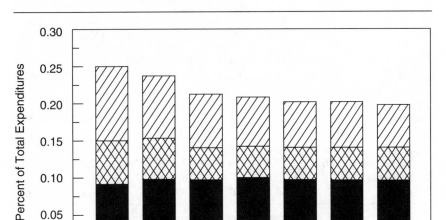

1986. Grants for physical capital are about one fourth of all grants and are used almost entirely to finance transportation and community and economic development projects. Other grants to state and local governments have declined from about 41 percent of total grants in 1980 to about 30 percent in 1986.

According to a recent Office of Management and Budget report, since 1980 the number of federal grant programs to state and local governments changed significantly.[2] There were 340 funded programs in 1986, down considerably from the 428 funded programs in 1980. Most federal grant programs are small. About three-quarters of the total funded grant programs in 1986 had obligations of less than $50 million. The fewest federal grant programs were found in 1982 when there were 297 funded programs. This reflects the effects of the Omnibus Budget Reconciliation Act of 1981, which established nine new block grant programs consolidating 57 categorical grant programs. Overall since 1980,

TABLE 2 State and Local Expenditures by Function, 1980–1985 ($ billions)

	Calendar year						Growth rates 1980–85
	1980	1981	1982	1983	1984	1985	
Total	363.2	391.4	414.3	440.2	475.9	516.5	7.3%
Education	141.6	152.4	163.6	174.2	187.4	203.6	7.5%
Income support & welfare	57.4	63.9	64.9	66.4	72.3	77.6	6.2%
Health and hospitals	34.3	38.9	42.8	45.7	48.1	52.1	8.7%
Transportation	36.0	37.6	39.1	42.4	47.4	52.1	7.7%
Public safety	26.9	30.0	33.8	36.9	40.3	44.9	10.8%
Other	67.0	68.6	70.1	74.6	80.4	86.2	5.2%

Note: Growth rates are estimated at average annual rates.
Source: Bureau of Economic Analysis, *Survey of Current Business* (various issues).

there have been 181 additions and 269 deletions to the number of funded grant programs.

RECENT TRENDS IN EXPENDITURES

State and local government expenditures increased from $363.2 billion in 1980 to $561.9 billion in 1986, about 7.5 percent per year. Table 2 shows that, on a program basis, most individual programs increased at rates not markedly different from overall expenditures. The more notable exceptions were expenditures for public safety and health and hospitals. This occurred for both state and local governments. On average, reflecting their more rapid growth, expenditures for health and hospitals and public safety increased their share of total state and local expenditures by one percentage point. Health and hospital expenditures grew rapidly because of the high rate of inflation in the health care industry over the period. Public safety expenditure growth reflects court-ordered pressures to improve prison living conditions and the need to expand existing prison capacity to accommodate the effects of tougher sentencing practices in many state judicial systems. About two-thirds of the states are under court order to improve prison living conditions. This, coupled with the tougher sentencing guidelines being imposed in many states,

TABLE 3 State and Local Government Expenditures, 1980–1986 ($ billions)

| | Calendar year | | | | | | | Growth rates |
	1980	1981	1982	1983	1984	1985	1986	1980–86
Expenditures	363.2	391.4	414.3	440.2	475.9	516.5	561.9	7.5%
Purchases	322.2	345.9	369.0	391.5	425.3	464.7	503.5	7.7%
Employee compensation	192.2	209.3	226.9	241.7	258.5	278.3	299.9	7.7%
Structures	48.6	46.1	43.7	43.2	47.3	53.6	61.4	4.0%
Other	81.4	90.5	98.4	106.6	119.5	132.8	142.2	9.7%
Transfers to persons	65.7	73.6	79.9	86.5	93.7	101.5	110.1	9.0%
Other	(24.7)	(28.1)	(34.6)	(37.8)	(43.1)	(49.7)	(51.7)	(13.1%)

Note: The category "other" includes mostly net interest earnings and dividends earned on securities. Growth rates are estimated at average annual rates.
Source: Bureau of Economic Analysis, *Survey of Current Business* (various issues).

caused public safety expenditures to grow faster than all other program areas. In fact, expenditures on corrections, a component of public safety expenditures, grew from $6.7 billion in 1980 to $13.9 billion in 1985, increasing by 15.7 percent per year.

STATE AND LOCAL GOVERNMENT PURCHASES

State and local expenditures are comprised essentially of two types: purchases of goods and services, and transfer payments. As shown in Table 3, state and local purchases are for durable and nondurable goods, compensation of employees, purchases of services, and structures. About 90 percent of total state and local government expenditures are purchases, with the largest component of purchases being compensation of employees. By comparison, about one-third of the federal government's expenditures are for purchases.

On the surface, purchases of state governments appear to constitute a smaller share of total expenditures than for local governments. About half of state government expenditures are purchases, much less than the 98 percent share of local governments. The remaining half is comprised of state aid to local governments and transfer payments. State aid is used by local governments for their purchases and could, therefore, be viewed as "indirect" purchases by state governments. If we exclude state aid to local governments from total state government expenditures, we find that state government purchases are closer to 80 percent of state expenditures.

Because a substantial portion of state and local government expenditures are purchases, the pattern of expenditure growth tends to be insensitive to the economic cycle: because state and local purchases buy the services of labor, capital equipment, and structures. Outlays for these categories of purchases are unlikely to be easily manipulated to maintain a balanced budget during a recession. While some categories of purchases may be postponed, e.g., filling potholes, the pattern of expenditure growth suggests state and local governments are unable to substantially reduce expenditure growth in times of fiscal stress because of the difficulties associated with workforce reductions or delaying spending on major contracts.

Only purchases of structures seem to exhibit much sensitivity to the cycle. Since reaching a record low of $43.2 billion in 1983, purchases of structures have increased by 12.7 percent per year, much faster than the growth of total purchases, reaching $61.4 billion in 1986. It seems that the sector can postpone new construction projects (as opposed to delaying let contracts) in response to pressures created by a recession, as it did in the early eighties. However, given that purchases of structures comprise about 10 percent of total purchases, state and local governments total purchases growth, and, hence, total expenditure growth, tends to display little responsiveness to cyclical fluctuations. Thus, during a contraction, without federal compensatory assistance, the pattern of expenditure growth makes any revenue shortfall all the more serious for the state and local sector. This could prompt the sector to take aggressive steps on the revenue side of the budget. As is discussed below, this is exactly what the sector did in response to the back-to-back recessions of the early eighties.

STATE AND LOCAL FISCAL CONDITION

The standard indicator of fiscal condition most often used is the "other funds surplus or deficit," published by the Bureau of Economic Analysis, which is defined as the difference between the gross receipts and gross expenditures, adjusted to exclude social insurance funds. Social insurance funds are excluded because they are not available for operating budget purposes. The other funds surplus or deficit, if used with care, can provide useful information on the sector's fiscal health.

FIGURE 2 State and Local Government Surplus or Deficit

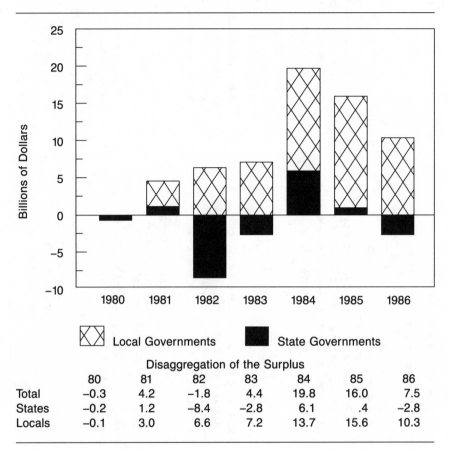

Disaggregation of the Surplus

	80	81	82	83	84	85	86
Total	−0.3	4.2	−1.8	4.4	19.8	16.0	7.5
States	−0.2	1.2	−8.4	−2.8	6.1	.4	−2.8
Locals	−0.1	3.0	6.6	7.2	13.7	15.6	10.3

RECENT TRENDS IN THE SURPLUS

Figure 2 shows that the state and local sector finished 1986 with a surplus of $7.5 billion. The sector finished the fourth quarter of 1986 with a deficit of $0.7 billion, compared to a fourth quarter surplus of $14.7 billion a year before (both at annualized rates).

The surplus has declined from its 1984 all time high of $19.8 billion. However, as Table 4 shows, the decline in the surplus position does not necessarily imply deteriorating fiscal condition. The surplus may change for many reasons unrelated to the general ability of state and local governments to meet their responsibilities. These reasons include changes

TABLE 4 Factors Affecting the State and Local Government Surplus

Factor	State and local receipts	State and local expenditures	Surplus	Possible source of fiscal stress?	Comments
General economic conditions	Sensitive to the cycle: receipts fall during contractions and rise during expansions.	Not sensitive: state and local expenditures tend to fluctuate little over the cycle.	Sensitive to the cycle: sensitivity is due to behavior of state and local receipts.	Yes	Assumes no change in discretionary tax and expenditure policies of state and local governments and no compensatory fiscal actions by the federal government.
State and local capital programs	Proceeds from borrowings are not included in state and local receipts.	Capital expenditures financed by borrowing are included in expenditures.	Sensitive to decisions regarding funding of capital program: surplus will decline when increased capital spending is financed by proceeds from borrowing.	No	If new capital spending is financed from general revenues, the surplus is unchanged.
Federal grant policy	Sensitive to changes in federal grants.	Should decline unless other funding is found.	If grant funded expenditures remain unchanged and alternative sources of revenues are not found, the surplus will decline.	Yes	Changes in federal aid have financed little of the total change in receipts since 1980. Grants have become less important compared to other factors.

in general economic activity, changes in capital financing, and changes in federal grant policy.

Changes in economic activity have a greater impact than any other factor, and this impact is greater on receipts than on expenditures. The elastic nature of the state and local tax base means that revenue growth will slow during a contraction and will increase during an expansion. Expenditures, on the other hand, are relatively stable over the cycle because they are for items such as wages and salaries and structures, all of which are much less sensitive to cyclical changes in the economy. Therefore, it is reasonable to expect the surplus to decline during contractions and to increase during expansions.

Changes in capital financing affect the surplus. Because the proceeds from debt are not counted as receipts even though the capital spending financed by the debt is included in expenditures, any increase in debt-financed capital spending will cause the surplus to decline (the sector ran a continuous deficit from 1955 through 1971 for this very reason).

Federal grant policy changes in the level of federal aid unaccompanied by commensurate changes in state and local spending will cause the surplus to decline.

THE EFFECTS OF BORROWING ON THE SURPLUS

The decline in the state and local surplus that began after the historic peak of $19.8 billion in 1984 reflects anything but deteriorating fiscal health. As Table 5 suggests, the reason for the steady decline to $7.5 billion in 1986 is the substantial borrowing to finance capital expenditures. Beginning in 1982, the volume of new issue long-term tax-exempt bonds virtually exploded. While an increasing share of these new issues was for refunding purposes, it is clear the sector's capital program became increasingly reliant on debt financing.

The decline in the surplus since 1984 is much different than the sector's movement to deficit in 1982. At that time, the sector experienced severe fiscal stress because of the 1980–82 recessions. The sector responded with widespread tax increases to compensate for revenue shortfalls. Most of these tax increases were temporary and designed to carry the sector over the fiscal hump created by the recessions. The current downward trend in the surplus, however, is not indicative of fiscal stress, as was the decline to deficit early in the decade. This decline is essentially due to technical nuances surrounding the measurement of the surplus by the BEA.

TABLE 5 Tax-Exempt Financing, 1980–1986 ($ billions)

	1980	1981	1982	1983	1984	1985	1986
Total new bond issues*	54.5	55.1	84.9	93.3	115.7	221.2	145.4
Private purpose	32.5	30.9	49.6	57.1	74.0	121.6	29.9
Housing issues	14.0	4.8	14.6	17.0	20.5	41.5	7.7
Single-family	10.5	2.8	9.0	11.0	12.8	14.3	5.1
Multi-family	2.2	1.1	5.1	5.3	5.5	25.0	2.2
Other	1.3	0.9	0.5	0.7	2.2	2.2	0.3
Public purpose	22.0	24.2	36.3	36.2	41.7	99.6	115.5
Percent of new issues used for refunding purposes	3%	2%	5%	16%	11%	28%	39%

*The volume of new issues includes only long-term, tax-exempt bonds. Short-term issuances are excluded.

Sources: Special Analyses: Budget of the United States Government, Fiscal Year 1989, Special Analysis F, p. F-60, and unofficial estimates of the Treasury Department, Office of Tax Analysis.

THE EFFECTS OF FEDERAL GRANTS ON THE SURPLUS

Of the factors affecting state and local fiscal condition, federal grants-in-aid play a much less important role in the eighties than ever before. In the seventies, for example, the sector relied on the federal government to compensate for the revenue shortfalls created by the 1974–75 recession. The Anti-Recession Fiscal Assistance and the Local Public Works programs provided billions of dollars to the sector. Interestingly, most of the outlays from these programs occurred well after the trough of the 1974–75 recession and did little to directly alleviate the effects of the recession. As is shown below, knowing the funds were coming was sufficient to postpone tax increases. In fact, of the $254.2 billion increase in the sector's total receipts between 1970 and 1980, federal aid of $64.3 billion financed 25 percent of the increase. Since 1980, federal grants provided only eight percent of the $228.8 billion change in the sector's total revenues. State and local governments have taken up the slack by more intensive use of their own sources.

Changes in federal grants may not affect state and local fiscal condition for many reasons. If grant recipients endorse the reductions (i.e., cut-back on expenditures), the grant reduction has no effect on the surplus. In some cases, the reduction in federal grants may actually help their fiscal condition. The removal of mandates and matching requirements that affect state and local resources may make decision making more efficient.

THE FISCAL IMPACT OF STATE AND GOVERNMENT FISCAL POLICIES ON THE ECONOMY

How state and local governments behave over the cycle brings back to center stage concerns regarding the impact of state and local government fiscal policies on the economy. Ever since the seminal work of Hansen and Perloff on the subject, there has been an intermittent debate on the relevance of their so-called "perversity hypothesis."[3] This hypothesis states that state and local governments reduce expenditures and increase taxes to maintain fiscal balance in a recession, thereby exacerbating the downturn. The opposite behavior during an expansion retards the expansion. Research on the subject in the late fifties and sixties refuted the perversity hypothesis. Apparently, the growth of federal aid cushioned state and local budgets, thereby mitigating the need for such tax and expenditure actions.

The requirement that all states (except Vermont) maintain balanced general fund budgets means that budget officials will take discretionary actions to compensate for negative movements. These actions may involve discretionary tax increases, reductions in expenditures, or petitions to the federal government for financial assistance.

Table 6 summarizes tax actions taken by states over selected periods since 1959. It is clear that tax adoptions and tax increases were critical to the states during the period of rapid growth that began in the fifties and lasted into the mid-seventies. During the period of tax revolt, many states reduced taxes. It was during this period that federal countercyclical aid played, perhaps, its most important role by providing an offset to the reductions in taxes that occurred. The willingness of the federal government to provide such aid made it easier for state governments to respond to the tax revolt.

It is clear that in the eighties, states extensively used tax increases to finance the revenue shortfalls caused by the back-to-back recessions. With the new administration intent on reducing the federal role in the fiscal affairs of state and local governments, state and local budget officials had to pursue their own fiscal policies to keep their

TABLE 6 Number of States Taking Discretionary Tax Actions with
Respect to Sales and Personal Income Taxes during
Selected Periods

Period	Income	Sales	Comments
1959–77			
New tax adoptions	13	12	Period of rapid growth in
Tax increases	75	76	the states and local sector.
Tax decreases	—	—	Federal aid finances about one quarter of the sector's growth.
1978–80			
New tax adoptions	—	—	Tax revolt period. Sector's
Tax increases	2	6	rapid growth ends.
Tax decreases	35	19	Federal countercyclical aid programs buttress state budgets.
1981–83			
New tax adoptions	—	—	Period of recession.
Tax increases	28	30	No countercyclical
Tax decreases	2	1	programs. Sector relies on own sources.
1984–86			
New tax adoptions	—	—	Period of uncertainty.
Tax increases	7	16	Many states allow
Tax decreases	28	7	temporary tax increases enacted earlier to expire.

Sources: ACIR, Significant Features of Fiscal Federalism, 1985–86 Edition, Table 53, page 76, and Significant Feature of Fiscal Federalism, 1987 Edition, Table 49, page 64.

budgets in balance. States responded by increasing sales and personal income taxes to cover revenue shortfalls. Most of these tax increases were temporary and raised sufficient revenues to carry the sector through the recession. It is also clear that these tax increases contributed to the substantial surplus position of the sector in 1984. Since then, most states have recorded tax decreases vis-à-vis the expiration of temporary tax increases. Despite these decreases, the sector experienced substantial surpluses in 1985 and 1986, although the trend is one of decline.

OTHER FACTORS AFFECTING THE SURPLUS

An assessment of fiscal condition should also consider trends in fund balances of state and local governments. Most state and local governments maintain positive fund balances that may be carried over into subsequent years. Furthermore, a number of states maintain contingency funds, or "rainy-day" funds, to compensate budgets during periods of fiscal stress. Currently, 29 states have "rainy-day funds" (up from 20 in 1983) in which the revenue gains from economic growth are set aside to compensate for the financial risk associated with a recession. Rainy-day funds are a relatively new fiscal tool being tested by states. In 1986, the total deposits in such funds were $3.9 billion ($2.8 billion excluding California), an average of $134 million for each of the 29 states.[4] This level of funding seems insufficient to hedge anyone's bets against the down side of a recession.

OUTLOOK FOR THE STATE AND LOCAL SECTOR

A number of factors are at work that will affect the fiscal condition of the state and local sector for the rest of this decade and into the next. The most important is the economy, i.e., growth in GNP, personal income, prices, and interest rates. Other factors include the effects of tax reform on state and local budgets, decisions on capital spending, and to an uncertain extent, federal grant policy.

GENERAL ECONOMIC TRENDS

The most significant factor affecting the sector's fiscal condition is general economic trends. The sensitivity of the revenue side makes state and local budgets at risk during a contraction. A reduction in economic growth during a contraction creates revenue shortfalls that can only be financed by increasing taxes or cutting expenditures, unless the federal government intervenes on the sector's behalf.

The sensitivity of state and local government receipts to the cycle has serious consequences for the surplus position of the sector. Because of the elastic nature of the sector's tax system, during contractions state and local governments tax receipts will change more than proportionately to the change in income. Because expenditures are much less sensitive to the cycle, the surplus position of the sector can quickly deteriorate. Unless there exist sufficient "savings" in rainy-day funds or in other fund balances, state and local officials may have to enact tax increases and expenditure reductions to compensate for budget shortfalls.

EFFECTS OF FEDERAL TAX REFORM

While the Tax Reform Act of 1986 is designed to be revenue neutral at the federal level, it is anything but neutral at the state and local level. The act reduces individual tax rates but broadens the tax base for both individuals and corporations. It also limits federal tax expenditures by repealing the deductibility of sales taxes from the federal income tax and the exemption of interest earned on certain municipal bonds.

By far, the revenue source most affected by tax reform is the individual income tax. Because of the direct linkage of most state and federal tax codes, the base broadening implicit in federal tax reform means more receipts for states so long as they do not adjust their own tax rates.

Forty-three states and the District of Columbia have individual income taxes. Of these, four states do not link their systems to the federal tax code and are unaffected by tax reform. The remaining states and the District of Columbia link their tax codes to the federal tax code in various ways. Thirty states and the District of Columbia link their tax codes to some definition of federal income, either gross income, adjusted gross income, or federal taxable income. This group will find its individual income taxes increasing so long as their tax rates remain unchanged. Four states link their tax codes to the federal tax liability. These states will find their individual tax receipts will decline under tax reform because of the reduction of federal individual income tax liabilities. Five states link their tax codes to specific segments of the federal tax code (i.e., capital gains) and may experience minor increases in their income taxes.[5]

State and local corporate income tax liabilities will also be affected by tax reform. The removal of the investment tax credit will boost corporate tax liabilities. Currently, 45 states have a corporate income tax and 36 of these link their tax codes to federal taxable income. The extent of the corporate income tax fiscal windfall is not known. Not one state plans to return this windfall.[6]

STATE AND LOCAL CAPITAL SPENDING DECISIONS

In recent years, most of the capital spending was for educational and office buildings, water and sewer facilities, and prisons. Highways are financed primarily from federal grants and own-source receipts. All else equal, if the pace of construction continues to be financed by borrowing, the sector's surplus will continue to decline.

The evidence suggests that construction spending will continue to increase in 1987. Constant dollar purchases of structures in the first quarter of 1987 are $57.9 billion, up 18.9 percent above the $48.7 billion registered in the first quarter of 1986.[7]

FEDERAL GRANT POLICY

The 1988 federal budget projects that federal grant-in-aid outlays will decline $4.0 billion from $112.4 billion in FY 1986 to $108.4 billion in FY 1987. Thereafter, the decline ends. Grants increase steadily beginning in 1988 from $116.7 billion to $131.5 billion by 1993. The growth in federal grants is at an average annual rate of growth of 2.4 percent, 0.9 percentage points below the projected rate of inflation. In the balanced budget environment in which all state and local governments (except Vermont) operate, a slow rate of increase in federal aid relative to the overall rate of inflation will force the sector to decide whether to continue these programs using their own sources or drop them. To date, the evidence points to some willingness to fund these programs from own revenue sources.

CONCLUSIONS

The eighties [was] a decade of dramatic change for the state and local government sector. Rather than relying on the federal government to finance its growing expenditures, it has become increasingly self-reliant. Federal aid, once an important revenue source to state and local governments, provides a decreasing share of the revenue needs of the sector.

The trend towards financial self-sufficiency has serious implications for the fiscal condition of the state and local governments. Should the sector experience fiscal stress, it will no longer be able to rely on the federal money machine to finance its revenue shortfalls. Instead, it is left with two basic options: it can increase taxes and it can cut expenditures. Unlike the federal government, it cannot finance the deficit by borrowing in the credit market.

The trend of increasing decentralization could undo changes brought about by the tax revolt. If state and local governments are going to meet the growing demand for public goods and services, especially those goods and services once financed by federal aid, they will need to remove the shackles that the tax and expenditure limitations represent.

The trend of increasing decentralization does not mean that the federal government will eventually be out of the state and local government affairs. There is now a renewed discussion of the federal role in buttressing weak state economies. The recent demise of General Revenue Sharing as well as reductions in other types of federal aid has rekindled the perennial debate about the role of the federal government in assisting the poorer states. It is a well established fact that not all states are equally capable of providing public goods and services to their citizens. This will make the concept and measurement of fiscal capacity of greater concern to federal officials, who will be looking for ways to improve the targeting of existing federal grant programs to the poorest jurisdictions.

NOTES

1. See Advisory Commission on Intergovernmental Relations, *Significant Features of Fiscal Federalism*, 1985–86 (Washington, D.C.: ACIR, 1986), 76.

2. The report is prepared annually by the Budget Review Division of the Office of Management and Budget and is titled, "Number of Funded Federal Grant Programs in the *Catalog of Federal Domestic Assistance* Included in the Budget Concept of Grants to State and Local Governments." The report dated March 1987 covers the period from 1980 to 1986.

3. Alvin H. Hansen and Harvey S. Perloff, *State and Local Finance in the National Economy* (W. W. Norton, 1944).

4. This is based on estimates of rainy-day fund balances reported by the ACIR in its 1985–86 *Significant Features of Fiscal Federalism*.

5. According to a report of the Advisory Commission on Intergovernmental Relations, 28 states and the District of Columbia will have their income tax receipts boosted by amounts ranging from less than one percent (DC and Oregon) to 28 percent (Louisiana). At the other extreme, 15 states would have their individual tax liabilities fall on a range of one percent or less (8 states) to 12 percent (North Dakota). This analysis assumed that state legislatures do not alter their tax laws in response to tax reform.

6. The size of the fiscal windfall from the individual income tax depends on the state response to tax reform. Many states have already revised their tax codes. According to the recent National Conference of State Legislatures paper, "State Budget Actions in 1987" (Legislative Finance Paper #58, 29 July 1987) of the 15 states that have completed work on tax bills in 1987, one state (North Dakota) did not have a tax windfall because its tax code links to the federal individual income tax liability. It took no action with respect to income taxes. Four states (Georgia, Hawaii, New York, and West Virginia) plan to return the windfall. (New York will return more than the windfall because of its own tax reform.) Three states (Maryland, Arkansas, and Virginia) plan to return a portion of the windfall. Seven states (Idaho, Indiana, Kansas, Mississippi, Montana, New Mexico, and Utah) will keep the windfall because of their deteriorating fiscal conditions.

7. Based on information presented in Table 3.8B in the May 1987 U.S. Bureau of the Census *Survey of Current Business* (Washington, D.C.: GPO, May 1987).

Reading 16

CITY LIMITS: THE POLITICS OF REDISTRIBUTION

Paul E. Peterson

According to Paul E. Peterson, "there are sharp limits on the degree of redistribution that can easily occur" in central cities "because redistributive policies are usually at odds with the economic interests of the city . . . ." Thus proponents of such policies will have great difficulty in securing support for them.

Peterson argues, first, that trade unions, which are most likely to support at the national level redistributive policies on behalf of their working-class membership to include educational, housing, medical care, welfare, and other entitlement programs, do not do so at the local level. This is because local unions are very small and usually very homogeneous; as a result, their goals are very narrow and material-oriented. Second, redistributive politics does not get very far at the local level simply because local politicians realize that such policies would push middle- and upper-class residents into adjacent counties. Third, the Democratic Party, which sends representatives to the national government who pursue a redistributive politics, does not push redistributive policies at the local level. Even when local politicians identify with the city's needy, they propose only those redistributive policies that are not very expensive. Any expensive policies proposed by local politicians tend to fall into the category of economic development.

Whenever demands for redistribution are articulated, Peterson claims, local political leaders usually resort to one or more of three strategies: (1) they may delay their response to such demands, thus allowing the demands to dissipate; (2) they may convert a redistributive issue into an allocational one (this means that such government leaders disaggregate the demands or proposals so that they can make some response based on the resources available); or (3) they may convert an economically redistributive issue into a political one (that is, they may convert a demand for redistributive government services into a demand for the redistribution of local power). While officeholders are reluctant to share power, sharing some power with minorities by increasing the number of governmental positions available to them is often an effective way of co-opting the leadership of redistributive movements.

Peterson concludes that a city's capacity to engage in a politics of redistribution is limited by the structural characteristics of local governments which must raise revenues from their own resources—mostly property, wage, and business taxes. These resource bases limit the capacity of local governments to engage in a comprehensive politics of redistribution.

Redistribution is seldom a significant aspect of local government operations, and therefore the issue is largely excluded from the local political agenda. Although in central cities some redistribution occurs in the process of distributing similar services in all parts of the city, and even though wealthier localities can afford a higher level of redistributive services than poorer localities..., even under the most favorable circumstances there are sharp limits on the degree of redistribution that can easily occur. Because redistributive policies are usually at odds with the economic interests of the city, proponents will find difficulty in gathering support for them. Since the policies are manifestly unrealistic economically, even those groups which themselves would in the short run benefit from redistribution lend little support to such proposals. To contribute to a cause so unlikely of success is not worthwhile, whatever the possible benefits.[1] The policies of redistribution thus become what Matthew Crenson has called "unpolitics."[2] It is a policy arena where issue formation occurs only sporadically. When issues do arise, those responsible for protecting the interests of the city devise political strategies that enable the city to avoid implementing substantial redistributions.

REDISTRIBUTIVE POLICIES: DOES BUSINESS KEEP THEM OFF LOCAL AGENDAS?

The absence of a local politics of redistribution has led some analysts to conclude that at the local level a power elite keeps certain issues off political agendas.[3] Threats of economic reprisal and social ostracism are thought to be powerful enough to keep deprived groups from exercising their rights of expression and organization even in liberal democracies.

Source: Paul E. Peterson, "City Limits: The Politics of Redistribution," from *City Limits* (Chicago: The University of Chicago Press, 1981), pp. 167–183. Reprinted by permission.

Although instances of such repression can certainly be identified,[4] it is unlikely that this is the major explanation for the paucity of redistributive issues in local politics. Instead, it is the negative economic consequences of locally sponsored redistribution that shape this policymaking arena. . . .

TRADE UNIONS

Trade unions are potentially the most powerful set of organizations likely to propose redistributive policies in big-city politics. At least since World War II, trade unions have commanded positions of great power in large industrial cities with predominately working-class populations. Even in the United States, where unions are less politicized than in Europe, mayors regularly consult trade union leaders as a routine part of governing the city.[5] Unions have representation on most local boards and commissions; many council and other minor elected officials are dependent upon unions for financing their election campaigns; and municipal unions, with their recently discovered capacity to strike, can cripple a city through industrial actions that can be undertaken quite outside the normal political process. On many issues of importance to the trade union movement, big-city politicians move with speed and alacrity.

Unions also have a strong, demonstrated interest in securing redistributional policies for their working-class constituents. Although much is made of the so-called conservatism of trade union leaders, the welfare state is difficult to conceive apart from union power.[6] Even in the United States, where unionization occurred later and unions have been less militantly socialist than in Europe, trade unions have formed an alliance with the Democratic party and, within that coalition, have campaigned with considerable success on behalf of welfare, housing, health, and educational programs.[7]

Union pursuit of redistributive objectives has been most vigorous at the national level. In big-city politics, union demands have seemed to many observers to be strangely narrow and self-interested. Unions press for city ordinances requiring that union labor be used in the construction and repair of local buildings. They have successfully gained control over entry into skilled labor occupations, thereby allowing members to secure higher wages for specialized services. Unions have been able to win wages and benefits for unionized employees in the public sector that are roughly comparable to those in the private sector. But local unions have done little to legislate high minimum wages for nonunionized labor, nor have unions aggressively campaigned at the local level for larger benefits for welfare recipients, for low-income housing, for extended medical services to the needy, or for welfare programs aimed specifically at the poor.[8] As Banfield and Wilson have said, "Local leaders are generally less ideological than national ones."[9]

In a comprehensive analysis of union politics, both nationally and in three large cities, Greenstone dwells at some length on these national-local differences. Distinguishing between a pluralist interest in allocational politics and a welfare-state orientation toward redistributive issues, Greenstone notes that

> organized labor's electoral participation locally...reflected a pluralist concern for the organizational interests of particular unions. [In Los Angeles] unions supported a conservative incumbent mayor in 1961 and displayed little enthusiasm for a liberal candidate in 1965. Yet, the same unions pursued welfare state goals in partisan election campaigns for state and especially national office on behalf of relatively liberal Democratic party candidates. Similar...differences between union behavior in national and local elections were apparent in Detroit and Chicago. ...More generally, most labor efforts in local politics have remained the preserve of...relatively pluralist nonfactory unions....But as we have seen, a great number of ideological industrial unions have devoted most of their resources to national politics.[10]

One explanation for the peculiar conservatism of local trade unions is their small constituency. McConnell has observed more generally that, if a constituency is small and homogeneous, "the ends it most probably seeks will be narrow, specific, concrete, and usually material in character. If the constituency is large and heterogeneous, its ends will be large, general and sometimes vague."[11] From this perspective, the nonredistributive orientation of unions at the local level is attributable to the smaller, homogeneous constituency of the local labor movement. Greenstone's own interpretation of the national-local differences in union politics takes this form:

> Homogeneous constituencies are much more common in local as opposed to national politics. The federal government is far more diverse in terms of the number of citizens and variety of interests it comprises than are the states and localities....In local politics, with fewer interests to be satisfied than in national politics, the possibilities of making particular arrangements with individual interests...are increased.[12]

A complementary explanation is that broad-scale redistributive policy proposals are inappropriately addressed to local governments. For example, if a city-wide minimum wage is passed, it will drive business outside the city's boundaries. If good-quality, subsidized housing is built with local funds, not only must it be paid for out of local tax dollars, but it might very well attract low-income families from other places. Other redistributive policies have similar consequences. As a result, unions instead concentrate on securing from local governments those particular benefits that can be limited to their own members. Their redistributive impact is sufficiently curtailed that they have few adverse economic consequences.

Unions press for narrow allocational benefits. But they also participate enthusiastically in the politics of development. Plans for the economic expansion of a community are often drawn up with the participation of at least some union leaders. Subsidies for business firms migrating into the community are supported because they will increase employment opportunities. For such statesmanlike contributions to a community's welfare, union leaders win a respected place in a local community's institutionalized bargaining process. In a consensual world of mutual deference and consideration, the particular interests of greatest concern to the movement are protected. Redistributive demands, which create class conflicts in national politics, have little place in local politics. Significantly, the limits on what the city can do often work to the advantage of local union leaders. In an atmosphere of local harmony and good will, unionists win a respected place in the community without sacrificing reasonable worker demands.

WORKING-CLASS PARTY ORGANIZATIONS

Political organizations heavily dependent upon working-class votes are also likely proponents of redistributive policies. Especially in central cities where the working class constitutes an overwhelming majority of the population, these parties may feel compelled to pursue a redistributive approach to urban problems simply to sustain their working-class support. Certainly, these political parties send representatives to the national legislature who align themselves on the redistributive side of most national political issues. Even in the United States the distinction between the Democratic and Republican parties on redistributive issues has been fairly clearly drawn since the New Deal. Moreover, the elements within the Democratic party most supportive of redistributive policies have been those representing urban areas.

At the local level this redistributive orientation is much less apparent. Democrats who in national politics favor a national health insurance program are unwilling to extend the public health services to low-income groups within the city. Democrats who vote for increases in national minimum wages oppose increased wages for local public employees. Democrats who support national financial aid for the education of economically deprived children tolerate the redirection of these funds to middle-class children within the local community. Significantly, systematic studies of state and local public policies in the United States seldom find that partisan political differences have policy consequences.[13] Once socioeconomic factors are taken into account, the balance of power between the political parties has only modest policy consequences. In an extensive review of the literature on the determinants of public policy, Fried finds a "lack of party impact that may be disturbing from the perspective of the 'responsible party governments' model of urban democracy."[14]

The lack of a distinctive partisan impact on local policy outcomes does not prevent local campaigns from being at times addressed to the needs of workers and the poor. Out of either ideological conviction or political necessity, candidates regularly seek to identify themselves with the needy and deprived of the community. But when they do, they usually select policies that do not have negative economic consequences. A variety of strategies are available. Candidates may call for policies that produce economic growth and therefore more employment opportunities for workers. If they call for redistributive policies, such as better housing or improved welfare benefits, they will recommend that the policies be funded with revenues from higher levels of government. Sometimes liberal candidates may propose locally funded programs for the needy, but, however popular, these will be relatively inexpensive programs, such as recreational programs for young adults or low-cost transportation fares for the elderly during off-peak hours.

Even modest plans for redistribution that have little more than symbolic value may not always be supported by local officials. Open-housing legislation in Wisconsin in the late 1960s is a case in point.[15] The proposed legislation prohibited racial discrimination in the housing market. But the legislation had little more than symbolic significance, both because the federal Constitution, as interpreted by the courts, already forbade such discrimination, and because establishing the fact of discrimination in any particular case was particularly difficult. Laws passed at the state and local levels have been both redundant and ineffectual. Yet Henry Maier of Milwaukee, a popular and effective mayor with liberal credentials, was unable to give open-housing policy his full support. He strongly endorsed this symbolically significant civil rights reform when proposed on a statewide basis for all of Wisconsin, but opposed any local ordinance applicable solely to the city of Milwaukee. A local ordinance passed without comparable laws covering surrounding suburban communities would only hasten white flight from the central city, he claimed.

PROTEST GROUPS

Although local redistributive policies are seldom proposed by either trade unions or big-city politicians and very few interest groups propose major schemes for redistribution, a new brand of protest group was spawned in the United States in the 1960s by the civil rights movement and the Vietnam War. These groups were new participants in the local political game, generated by a wave of citizen participation and often subsidized by federal agencies and national foundations which had little sense of economic limits on local policy. Analysis of their agitation is instructive in several ways: (1) the divergence of their demands from the traditional patterns of local politics clarifies just how nonredistributive local issues typically are; (2) the processes by which the local system responded to these demands demonstrate the capacities local systems have for handling vigorously stated redistributive demands; and (3) the decline of these groups in local politics shows the fragility of the politics of redistribution in the local arena.

Michael Lipsky's study of the rent strikes of Harlem in 1964 remains a seminal analysis of the politics of protest, and it is worth examining the ways in which the events he describes reveal the limits of city politics.[16] In the first place, the demands of the New York City rent strikers involved massive redistribution. They demanded nothing less than comprehensive rehousing or rehabilitation of existing housing for the poor minorities of New York. This could be accomplished (a) by insisting that private landlords maintain low-income housing at a standard that met the city's building code; (b) by public assumption of the properties in the hands of private landowners and the allocation of public funds to bring properties up to standard; or (c) by the construction of new, adequate housing for low-income residents. In pursuit of one or a combination of these policies, a collective withholding of rents to landlords was organized until code violations were repaired. To achieve an effective strike, the strike leaders launched a publicity campaign designed to reach the hundreds of thousands of poor living in housing that failed to measure up to the New York City code.

Second, the rent strike was quite successful, given the redistributive objectives that the strikers were pursuing. Jesse Grey, the leader of the protest movement, was able to enlist several hundred participants in his strike—a much larger number of activists than are usually mobilized in local political controversies. He secured the assistance of college students and other volunteers from outside the community, who lent their technical skills to a cause otherwise short on canvassers, typists, and pamphleteers. In addition, newspapers found the subject newsworthy and hence gave the rent strike much more free publicity than would be given activist groups in later years. Moreover, many in City Hall recognized the legitimacy of the rent strikers' complaints. New York was governed by a liberal mayor, Robert Wagner, many of whose advisers and departmental officers were sympathetic to the needs and objectives of the strikers. Grey also benefited from the highly politicized context in which policy was being formulated. The Wagner administration was nearing its conclusion, and many candidates were searching for issues, allies, and liberal credentials for the forthcoming election, in which John Lindsay would emerge as the winner. Since poor minorities numbered in the hundreds of thousands, their demands could hardly be ignored. In short, one can hardly imagine a local political context better suited to a group calling for redistribution.

But even all these politically favorable factors did not yield much substantive fruit. Adequate response to striker demands was simply not within the limits of the government of New York City. For one thing, it could not enforce the building code. At one level this was a function of the shortage of building inspectors and of the organizational routines of the building department, which did not concentrate inspectors in the areas of greatest need. At another level these organizational factors were themselves conditioned by the fact that proper enforcement of the city's building code would have driven most low-income housing in New York into receivership. Maintaining the buildings at code level would have escalated costs for many landlords far beyond any return they received in rent. And since buildings in low-income areas had little, if any, capital value, the landlord could be expected to relinquish control of the property to the city through failure to pay taxes. Many such properties had already become "nationalized" through just such a procedure.

City assumption of slum properties had its own difficulties. To avoid simply replacing one exploiting landlord with another, the city would have to repair and rehabilitate the housing. The costs of rehabilitation could not be covered by the rents low-income residents could afford. And if the city chose to subsidize the housing, the burden to local taxpayers might well become astronomical. An alternative was the destruction of tenement housing and erection of modern low-cost housing in its stead, but this, too, would be fiscally prohibitive, if financed out of local funds. Since federal funds were limited, there was little that could be done to meet the broad-scale demands of the rent strikers.

The task of local political leaders in such circumstances is to manage conflict. The demands of the strikers cannot be rejected out of hand, and their protest cannot be suppressed through punitive action unless the protestors seriously disturb public order. In the early 1960s poor minorities and even liberal-minded middle-class residents of the city were sympathetic to these redistributive demands. Outright suppression might only provoke a wider and more virulent political agitation. On the other hand, the strikers' demands could not be met in any substantively significant manner. To do so would have undermined the economic viability of the city. In these circumstances political symbols are of extraordinary value.

New York City's government employed a wide range of political symbols, all of which were designed to give the appearance of responding to the protest—but which at the same time did not require significant redistribution. Horror cases were given special treatment. These incidents, particularly frightening to the public at large, provided dramatic stories for the news media, and some government response was essential. For example, federal funds were used to establish an emergency heating program for tenants whose buildings were without heat on bitter-cold winter days. A federally funded rat extermination program was created in response to stories of rodents biting small children. On a longer range basis, a city commission was established to investigate the possibility of reorganizing the departments responsible to housing policy. Plans for new federal housing programs in low-income areas were announced with considerable fanfare.

Lipsky's detailed analysis shows that, substantively, little was changed in the housing markets of New York's low-income communities. Any visitor to the city can soon discover that the residential slums of the city remain; if anything, their boundaries only enlarged in the decade and a half following these events. However, the protest movement itself subsided. It proved impossible to maintain enthusiastic involvement in protest action for more than a few months. Almost inevitably, Jesse Grey made tactical errors. Newspaper reporters discovered he had exaggerated the size of the rent strike. Strikers realized that, to be effective, they had to pay rent into a court-designated fund while their dispute with the landlord was being resolved. Without a financial incentive for joining the strike, their continued cooperation proved hard to sustain. In the meantime public attention drifted to other issues. By manipulating political symbols, New York political leaders were able to minimize the impact of a vigorously asserted campaign for redistribution.

MANAGING CONFLICT

On the basis of the research by Lipsky and other students of protest politics, it is possible to specify a range of techniques available to local political leaders whenever demands for redistribution are forcefully articulated. They can be grouped under three general headings: (1) delay substantive response, thereby allowing the demanding group to become discouraged; (2) convert the redistributive issue into an allocational one; and (3) convert an economically redistributive issue into a political one.

The delay strategy is the most convenient and the easiest to implement. In the beginning, public leaders simply ignore demands they do not have the resources to grant. The fact that the demands seem so unreasonable makes the group illegitimate and the motives of leaders suspect. In the expectation that others will see the demands in this same light, public officials simply continue with business as usual. High-level officials refuse to see the group, to concede that the group has any public support, or to allow that any significant problem exists. However, if the group gathers support or is able to gather public attention or manages to disrupt a vital service of the community, the official employs more complex delay tactics. He may at long last grant an interview to the group, which sometimes is sufficient by itself to satisfy complaints. The mere fact that the authorities recognize the legitimacy of a complaint will be enough to dampen it. A certain satisfaction comes from having been able to ventilate a complaint or from having been able to tell an official off. Perhaps at the moment of recognition—in the sanctity of the mayor's office, say—the group itself begins to realize the unreality of its proposals.

If mere political recognition does not dampen protest, the government has other delay techniques available. Establishing a committee or commission to study the problem is probably the tactic most frequently employed. Since the group demands a major change from present policy, it is necessary to consider the matter at length before determining what can be done. Moreover, since the group's own proposals seem so unrealistic, it is evident that the matter must be handed to a group that has experience and expertise in the field.

The outstanding examples of this form of response were the numerous riot commissions established at both national and local levels in the late 1960s.[17] These commissions were set up only after several years of protest by black organizations. They were appointed in an atmosphere of potential violence that threatened the stability of the political regime. Simply ignoring the concerns of the black community was no longer a safe political strategy. Instead, broadly representative ad hoc commissions were established to investigate race-related problems and to come up with comprehensive solutions. The work of these commissions usually took several months to two years to complete, and once completed the commission itself had no power to implement them. But in the meantime, political leaders, without actually implementing economically redistributive policies, could declare that something positive was being done. By the time the commissions reported, pressures for change were no longer so intense and the most redistributive of the recommendations could be set to one side.

Authorities resort to a more sinister version of the delay strategy only *in extremis*. Protesting groups are sometimes able, through *extra*legal tactics, to capture physical resources that authorities consider vital. Inhabitants of houses that need to be torn down in order to make way for a major thoroughfare may sometimes refuse to leave their condemned property. Or environmental action groups may chain themselves to trees. In these circumstances the government needs to make an effort to negotiate—to give the appearance of reasonableness—without sacrificing its ultimate objective. In such cases, the glove of negotiations covers the mailed fist of coercive force. In the most extreme cases of terrorist skyjackings, authorities may make false promises to allow time for coercive action; the isolation of the terrorist group from public opinion allows for outright dissimulation on the part of the authorities. In the case of local protest, authorities try to persuade groups to cooperate without making false promises. On the other hand, the more isolated from public opinion the group becomes, the easier it is to utilize a combination of dissimulation and coercive force.[18]

A second strategy of political leaders is to convert redistributive issues into allocational ones. When groups demand redistributive reforms at the local level, government leaders explore ways of disaggregating the proposals so that from the resources available to them they can make some response. One of the most useful approaches is to meet very specific demands of the group calling for major change, while doing little or nothing about the overall problem. For example, in the rent strike the complaints of the group engaged in the strike were given first priority by city departments. To placate the unrest, efforts were made to satisfy the immediate problems of specific complaining groups, though the elimination of substandard housing throughout the city could hardly be considered.

This technique is valuable, but it can sometimes be counterproductive. If complaining is rewarded too quickly and easily, others will be induced to make similar demands. For example, when groups in two New York communities obtained community development funds from the juvenile delinquency program, their success encouraged the formation of many more like-minded groups in other parts of the city.[19] And when special benefits, such as winter clothing allowances, were given to active members of the Welfare Rights Organization, the concessions only encouraged other welfare recipients to join the organization and make similar demands.[20]

To avoid these kinds of difficulties, government agencies often sponsor experimental programs. Ostensibly, the policy is called an experiment because the government wishes to discover whether the plan will work in one specific context before being applied more generally. In fact, the agency simply does not have the resources to implement the policy throughout its jurisdiction, no matter how well the approach might resolve a given social problem. But by calling the project an experiment, the authority is able to respond to pressures from some particular group without conceding that a far more costly general policy of this sort is at hand. Consequently, the authority does little in the way of experimental design research to determine whether the policy is effective at treating the problem, and few, if any, redistributive experiments are generalized.[21]

An alternative form of this disaggregation strategy involves identification of group leaders and giving them special concessions. If used effectively, this approach need not consist of outright bribery. Instead, group leaders can be employed in relevant public-service positions, given an honored position in policy deliberations, or invited to participate in conferences at distant places. Although these techniques are usually called "cooptation," they can also be understood as providing training in public policy analysis. By being exposed to the problems of formulating adequate responses to redistributive demands, these leaders, without necessarily giving up their objectives, are encouraged to channel their energies into more realistic approaches.

Another useful method of disaggregation is to concentrate on the tip of the iceberg. Addressing the most visible aspect of a problem allows authorities to give the appearance of responsiveness to political pressure without sacrificing the larger interests of the city. The treatment of horror cases in the New York rent strikes is an obvious case in point. The availability of emergency rooms at hospitals is another. Although medical services may not be distributed evenly, in life-and-death situations medical treatment is available to anyone.[22] More generally, local plans for relief of the poor, though hardly adequate welfare assistance programs, have for decades taken the edge off demands for a more equitable distribution of wealth.[23]

Delay and disaggregation are familiar techniques available to authorities faced with demands to which they cannot respond. A third device, less frequently used, is the conversion of a demand for redistributive government services into a demand for the redistribution of local power. Changing the governance structure of a city in response to political protest is usually undertaken only after prolonged disputes. Because officeholders are reluctant to share their positions of power, they change the governing structure only when pressed. But political changes by themselves do not affect the economic productivity upon which the city's long-range welfare depends. Political innovation is thus a final measure that can be used to protect a city from economically redistributive policies.

The community action program of the War on Poverty provides one illustration of government responsiveness to demands from disadvantaged racial minorities for a sharing in political power. The requirement included in the poverty legislation, that community residents should have opportunities for "maximum feasible participation," became the vehicle for widespread involvement by racial minorities in the policymaking processes for a variety of local government programs.[24] Such participation changed allocational policies to some extent; racial minorities received a larger share of government services, and they were particularly favored in the recruitment of new employees to staff these innovative programs. But even though allocational decisions were affected by these changes in political power, local government undertook very few redistributive commitments.[25]

School politics in large cities of the United States offers another instructive example of the way in which political forms can be altered to accommodate protest.[26] As a by-product of the civil rights movement, central-city schools in the late 1960s came under increasing scrutiny by black leaders and neighborhood groups. School boards were subjected to a variety of unrealistic redistributive demands, including demands for racial integration, massive increases in school funding, reallocating of teachers, complete equalization of educational resources, and even compensatory educational policies that would allocate extra resources to schools serving low-income areas. However, school boards in most central cities did not capitulate to the most redistributive of these demands, even where blacks made up a large proportion of the city's voting population. Every strategy for deflecting civil rights demands was brought into play. Protest groups were ignored. When that was no longer possible, study groups and investigatory commissions were asked to write reports, which, when concluded, were either drastically revised by the board or not implemented at all. To make some concessions to political pressures, boards established experimental programs and pilot projects. They gave positions of responsibility within the school system to community leaders. But in some cities none of these strategies proved sufficient, and public officials devised a more dramatic policy alternative, namely, decentralization of school governance to neighborhood boards thoughout the city. In Detroit and New York, the two cities where this change in political organization was most fully executed, it proved successful in reorganizing the basis of political conflict. Instead of demands for massively redistributive policies by a central board, community groups concentrated on improving schools in their area by electing members to local boards. These local boards had limited resources, were dependent on other agencies for financing, and were constrained by policies determined at higher levels of government. Although allocational policies were changed, substantial redistributions in the delivery of educational services remained beyond the economic capacity of the local boards.

CONCLUSIONS

The politics of redistribution at the local level is thus an arena where certain kinds of citizen needs and preferences seldom become demands; an arena where demands, when voiced, do not gain much support; and an arena where redistributive questions, even when posed as major political issues, are treated by a variety of strategies designed to forestall, delay, and preclude their implementation. Some have concluded from these facts that a powerful elite keeps redistributive issues off the agenda of local politics.[27] It is said that this elite is so potent that groups favoring redistribution, fearful of economic sanctions or social ostracism, are dissuaded from making these topics local political issues. But in our view the absence of redistributive political issues is seldom due to the suppressive activities of an organized economic elite.[28]

It has also been claimed that the very structure of local governing institutions discourages local groups from raising redistributive issues, that these institutions are so structured that there is little hope there will ever be a response to redistributive demands. Put in these terms, the claim that the local political system is "biased" is more persuasive. . . .[29] Proposals for economic growth gain access to the local political agenda with greater ease than do proposals calling for social redistribution. Moreover, the consensus that often is formed behind developmental proposals seems to be due to the structural characteristics of local governments, which are called upon to raise revenues out of their own resources and finance capital expansion through transactions in private bond markets. Conversely, these same structural constraints limit the redistributive plans of local governments.

But even though local political systems in the Unites States are biased against redistributive issues, one cannot generalize from this fact to the character of politics in the United States as a whole. What may be difficult to achieve at the local level is open to bargaining in national politics. If redistribution is not an appropriate function of local government, that does not mean that the United States, taken as a whole, has no capacity to redistribute socially valued things. National political systems in a market economy are constrained by international flows of capital and credit, but the constraints are not as severe as they are at the local level. Nations control human migration, they erect tariff walls, and they prohibit the flow of capital outside their boundaries. These and other powers make redistribution a possible focus of national government action. The extent to which it occurs in any national political system is open to investigation. Demands which at the local level may be rejected out of hand or dealt with through symbolic manipulation and tactical maneuvering may in national politics be given due consideration.

NOTES

1. Peterson 1975.
2. Crenson 1971.
3. Bachrach and Baratz 1962.
4. Agger, Goldrich, and Swanson 1964, chapter 11.
5. Banfield and Wilson 1963, chapter 19; Reichley 1959; Greenstone 1969.
6. On Great Britain, see Beer 1969.
7. Greenstone 1969, chapters 2, 11.
8. On national-local differences in housing policy, see Freedman 1969; on poverty, see Greenstone and Peterson 1976, pp. 77–78.
9. Banfield and Wilson 1963, p. 279.
10. Greenstone 1969, pp. 170–71.
11. McConnell 1966, p. 345.
12. Greenstone 1969, p. 170.
13. Dye 1966; Brazer 1969; Lewis-Beck 1977.
14. Fried 1975, p. 345.
15. This instance is taken from Lipsky and Olson 1977, p. 279.
16. Lipsky 1970. The following paragraphs draw freely from this case study, though Lipsky's own interpretation relies on a bargaining framework within which the rent strikers are said to be a relatively powerless group.
17. Lipsky and Olson 1977.
18. One can find illustrations of such strategies in the emerging Marxist literature on local politics. See Castells 1977; Cockburn 1977.
19. Greenstone and Peterson 1976, pp. 41–42.
20. Wilson 1973.
21. Marris and Rein 1967.
22. Crawford 1974.
23. Piven and Cloward 1971.
24. This analysis is taken from Peterson and Greenstone 1977.

25. Greenstone and Peterson 1976, chapter 10.
26. On school politics in the United States, see La Noue and Smith 1973; Rogers 1968; Peterson 1976; Crain 1968.
27. Bachrach and Baratz 1962.
28. Wolfinger 1971.
29. Schattschneider 1960.

REFERENCES

Agger, R.; Goldrich, B.; and Swanson, B. 1964. *The Rulers and the Ruled.* New York: John Wiley.

Bachrach, P., and Baratz, M. S. 1962. "Two Faces of Power." *American Political Science Review* 56:947–52.

Banfield, E. C., and Wilson, J. Q. 1963. *City Politics.* Cambridge, Massachusetts: Harvard University Press.

Beer, S. 1969. *British Politics in the Collectivist Age.* Westminster, Maryland: Random House.

Brazer, S. 1959. *City Expenditures in the United States.* Occasional Papers No. 66. New York: National Bureau of Economic Research.

Castells, M. 1977. *The Urban Question.* London: Edward Arnold.

Cockburn, C. 1977. *The Local State.* London: Pluto Press.

Crain, R. 1968. *The Politics of School Desegregation.* Chicago: Aldine.

Crawford, R. 1974. *The Politics of Hospital Utilization.* Doctoral Dissertation, University of Chicago.

Crenson, M. 1971. *The Un-Politics of Air Pollution.* Baltimore, Maryland: Johns Hopkins University Press.

Dye, T. R. 1966. *Politics, Economics, and the Public: Policy Outcomes in the American States.* Chicago: Rand McNally.

Freedman, L. 1969. *Public Housing: The Politics of Poverty.* New York: Holt, Rinehart, & Winston.

Fried, R. C. 1975. "Comparative Urban Policy and Performance." In *Handbook of Political Science,* Vol. 6, ed. by F. Greenstein and N. Polsby, pp. 305–79. Reading, Massachusetts: Addison-Wesley.

Greenstone, J. D. 1969. *Labor in American Politics.* New York: Alfred A. Knopf.

Greenstone, J. D., and Peterson, P. E. 1976. *Race and Authority in Urban Politics.* Phoenix Edition. Chicago: University of Chicago Press.

LaNoue, G. R., and Smith, B. L. R. 1973. *The Politics of School Decentralization.* Lexington, Massachusetts: Lexington Books.

Lewis-Beck, M. S. 1977. "The Relative Importance of Socioeconomic and Political Variables for Public Policy." *American Political Science Review* 71:559–66.

Lipsky, M. 1970. *Protest in City Politics: Rent Strikes, Housing and the Power of the Poor.* Chicago: Rand McNally.

Lipsky, M., and Olson, D. J. 1977. *Commission Politics: The Processing of Racial Crisis in America.* New Brunswick, New Jersey: Transaction Books.

McConnell, G. 1966. *Private Power and American Democracy.* New York: Alfred A. Knopf.

Marris, P., and Rein, M. 1967. *Dilemmas in Social Reform.* New York: Atherton.

Peterson, P. E. 1975. "Incentive Theory and Group Influence: James Wilson's *Political Organizations* and the End of Group Theory." Paper prepared for the annual meeting of the American Political Science Association.

Peterson, P. E. 1976. *School Politics Chicago Style.* Chicago: University of Chicago Press.

Peterson, P. E., and Greenstone, J. D. 1976. "The Community Action Controversy as a Test of Two Competing Models of the Policy-making Process." In *Theoretical Perspectives on Urban Politics,* ed. by M. Lipsky and W. Hawley, pp. 67–99. Englewood Cliffs, N.J.: Prentice-Hall.

Peterson, P. E., and Greenstone, J. D. 1977. "Racial Change and Citizen Participation: The Mobilization of Low-Income Communities through Community Action." In *A Decade of Federal Antipoverty Programs,* ed. by R. H. Haveman, pp. 241–78. New York: Academic Press.

Piven, F. F., and Cloward, R. 1971. *Regulating the Poor.* New York: Pantheon.

Reichley, J. 1959. *The Art of Government: Reform and Organization Politics in Philadelphia.* New York: Fund for the Republic.

Rogers, D. 1968. *110 Livingston Street.* New York: Random House.

Schattschneider, E. E. 1960. *The Semi-Sovereign People.* New York: Holt, Rinehart & Winston.

Wilson, J. Q. 1973. *Political Organizations.* New York: Basic Books.

Wolfinger, R. E. 1971. "Nondecisions and the Study of Local Politics." *American Political Science Review* 65:1063–80.

283

CHAPTER IX

EDUCATION POLICIES IN STATES AND CITIES

INTRODUCTION

Within any of the fifty states final authority over educational policy rests with the state government. Nevertheless, for much of the nation's public school history, state governments, with the exception of Hawaii, have delegated most of their school authority to local, separate, and independent school districts. However, in recent years, the role of the states in public school education has increased as a result of demands from local governments for larger amounts of financial aid and as a result of a growing demand from a number of quarters—parents, business persons, educational associations, etc.—to improve the quality of public school education in the states of the nation.[1]

A central issue arising in the governance of public school education and one which has commanded the attention of reformers and state leaders in recent years is the fiscal disparity among individual school districts—a situation that contributes to educational inequalities among the districts.[2] Much of the problem of school finance can be traced to the reliance of a local school district on local property taxes. This means simply that school districts which do not have much taxable property cannot finance their schools as well as school districts containing a good deal of wealthy taxable property. As one student of local government put it:

> Frequently, wealthy communities can provide better education for their children at lower tax rates than poor communities can provide at higher tax rates simply because of disparities in the value of taxable property.[3]

As a result of inequalities in per pupil expenditures among school districts in the same state, the charge has been made that students in poor districts were being denied equal protection of the law as guaranteed by the Fourteenth Amendment. The effort to secure such equal protection of the laws was made to the U.S. Supreme Court in *San Antonio Independent School District* v. *Rodriguez* (1973). In this case the U.S. Supreme Court overturned a federal district court ruling which held that the Texas system of school finance violated the equal protection clause of the Fourteenth Amendment because it discriminated against poor school districts.

Many state courts did not agree with the U.S. Supreme Court on the legitimacy of financing public schools via the local property tax.[4] David C. Long, in his article *"Rodriguez: The State Courts Respond,"* reprinted in this chapter as Reading 17, reports on the response of the states since the *Rodriguez* decision.

In light of inequities in school financing between school districts and in the performance of schoolchildren, a number of reformers have proposed *public school choice* or *parental choice* to reflect the fact that parents should have an opportunity to choose among schools for their children. Several states, the outstanding example being Minnesota, as well as a number of school districts have experimented with choice plans.

Most public or parental choice school plans would give parents a voucher to spend each year on primary and secondary schooling for their children at the school of their choosing. Theoretically, a voucher system would encourage competition among schools since no school would be guaranteed students or funds. Each school would have to earn its fair share of the education vouchers to stay in business. Poor schools would be forced to either improve themselves or close.[5]

Bella Rosenberg, in her article "Public School Choice: Can We Find the Right Balance?," reprinted in this chapter as Reading 18, outlines a variety of public school choice plans and suggests that we should experiment with these models in order to find the right balance.

NOTES

1. On these points, see Ann O'M. Bowman and Richard C. Kearney, *State and Local Government* (Boston: Houghton Mifflin, 1990), pp. 432–33 and David R. Berman, *State and Local Politics*, 6th ed. (Dubuque, Ia: Wm. C. Brown, 1991), p. 294.

2. On this point, see Richard H. Leach and Timothy G. O'Rourke, *State and Local Government: The Third Century of Federalism* (Englewood Cliffs, N.J.: Prentice-Hall, 1988), p. 287.

3. Thomas R. Dye, *Politics in States and Communities*, 7th ed. (Englewood Cliffs, N.J.: Prentice-Hall, 1991), p. 422.

4. Parenthetically, Thomas R. Dye writes that perhaps objections to local property tax financing would end if states collected all property taxes statewide and distributed the revenues equally among all communities. See ibid., pp. 423–24.

5. Paradoxically, the research of James S. Coleman et al. has shown that there is no significant relationship between school resources and student performance. Rather, high achievement is correlated with family and socioeconomic background, with a disciplined educational environment, and with teacher-parent agreement or consensus on values and norms to be imposed on the students. See Coleman et al., *High School Achievement* (New York: Basic Books, 1982).

Reading 17

RODRIGUEZ: THE STATE COURTS RESPOND

David C. Long

In this article David C. Long points out that although the U.S. Supreme Court in *San Antonio Independent School District* v. *Rodriguez* (1973) refused to strike down as unconstitutional the school district local property tax for the financing of public schools, many state courts have held state school finance systems unconstitutional because they discriminate against children in low-wealth school districts. Not only have many state courts done what the U.S. Supreme Court failed to do, but many state legislatures have enacted legislation designed to bring the level of educational resources in low-wealth districts on a par with the educational tasks the districts must perform.

On the other hand, a number of state courts and legislatures have used the *Rodriguez* decision to let continue inequalities resulting from differential school district wealth. And with inflation, poor school districts have fallen even further behind the wealthier ones.

The first state court decision to come after *Rodriguez* was *Robinson* v. *Cahill* (1973), in which the New Jersey Supreme Court struck down, as violating the state's constitution, the New Jersey school finance statute requiring the legislature to provide for the maintenance and support of a system of free public schools. This decision relied on the education provisions of the state constitution and not on the equal protection clause of the Fourteenth Amendment.

In 1976 the California Supreme Court reaffirmed its 1971 decision in *Serrano* v. *Priest* (often referred to as *Serrano I*) when it held that California's constitution makes wealth-related inequalities in educational expenditures unconstitutional and rejected the principle of "local control" as justifying discrimination against children in low-wealth school districts. The 1976 decision was designated *Serrano II*.

Since *Rodriguez,* state courts have found statewide school finance systems discriminatory and unconstitutional because such systems base allocation of educational resources among school districts on factors having nothing to do with education. Moreover, educational opportunities have become a function of whether a youngster lives in a high-wealth (high local property tax) or a low-wealth (low property tax) school district.

Long observes that while the major reason for courts' sustaining inequitable financing systems which stem from unequal tax bases has been the preservation of "local control," the state courts have not endorsed as desirable the inequalities emanating from such school financing. In addition, according to Long, school financing reforms in many states have shown that methods do exist for eliminating discriminatory funding while maintaining local control. It is Long's hope that this argument to justify discrimination will soon disappear. Long concludes that the legitimacy of inequitable school financing systems has now been considerably undermined, and that the U.S. Supreme Court's decision in *Rodriguez* should not be considered an immutable precedent.

March 1983 marks the 10th anniversary of the decision by the U.S. Supreme Court in *San Antonio Independent School District* v. *Rodriguez*. That decision was a milestone in the withdrawal by the Burger Court from issues of discrimination and fairness in the allocation of governmental benefits, not only in education but in other areas as well.[1] At the time, many observers believed that, without a Supreme Court mandate to eliminate discrimination in the provision of educational opportunities for children in poor school districts, states would continue to allocate education funds based on the fortuity of school district wealth. One view was that state courts would be unwilling to take on constitutional issues of this magnitude or that state legislatures on their own would make the necessary reforms.

The broad range of school finance litigation and legislation that followed *Rodriguez* suggests that this view was too pessimistic. Across the nation the major state constitutional issue of the decade became whether state courts should strike down inequitable statewide school finance systems under provisions of state constitutions pertaining to education and equal protection. And many state courts—even those without any previous history of grappling with complex constitutional issues—held school finance systems unconstitutional, because they discriminated against children in low-wealth school districts or failed to insure that all children were provided the educational opportunities mandated by state constitutions. Following *Rodriguez*, a number of state legislatures also en-

Source: David C. Long, *"Rodriguez: The State Courts Respond," Phi Delta Kappan* 64 (March 1983), pp. 481–84. © 1983, Phi Delta Kappan, Inc. Reprinted by permission.

acted major reforms to limit the effect of the fiscal capacity of a school district on school spending and to bring the level of educational resources available to all school districts in line with the educational tasks that the districts must perform.[2]

This is the bright side of the aftermath of *Rodriguez*. But there is another side as well. A number of state courts and legislators responded just as the pessimists had predicted. Following the lead of the U.S. Supreme Court, some state appellate courts chose to side-step the discrimination resulting from their school finance systems. And, if they did not always endorse the status quo, they allowed it to continue, unchecked by constitutional restraint. Many state legislatures, lacking a constitutional mandate from the state courts, let the inequalities among school districts continue, while inflation caused the poor districts to fall even further behind their affluent neighbors. Some legislatures provided property tax relief to the voters, called it school finance reform, yet left existing inequalities in educational resources untouched.

In what follows, I summarize briefly this mixture of progress and neglect following *Rodriguez*—particularly the mixed response of state courts.

In its 1971 pre-*Rodriguez* decision, *Serrano* v. *Priest (Serrano I)*, the California Supreme Court was the first to question the constitutionality of inequalities in school district spending, which were caused by disparate taxable wealth. In the months following the California decision, more than 30 cases challenging school finance schemes were filed in other states. One of these cases was *Rodriguez*. It was heard by a three-judge federal district court, which found the Texas school finance system unconstitutional under the equal protection of the 14th Amendment to the U.S. Constitution. When the Supreme Court reversed this decision, holding that the Texas school financing provisions were not unconstitutional under the Constitution, it returned the issue of school finance to the states.

Most state supreme courts—with a few exceptions, such as California and New Jersey—were untested in complex constitutional issues. During the two decades prior to *Rodriguez*, plaintiffs challenging discrimination as unconstitutional had generally ignored state courts in favor of the federal court system, which they perceived to be more receptive. Therefore, most state courts lacked a tradition of creative constitutional adjudication. At the time of the *Rodriguez* decision, state courts were long shots for plaintiffs challenging discrimination in school finance systems.

Plaintiffs did not have long to wait for the first test of the viability of school finance litigation in the state courts. Only one month after *Rodriguez*, the New Jersey Supreme Court, in *Robinson* v. *Cahill*, struck down the state's school finance law for violating the provision of the state constitution that requires the legislature to "provide for the maintenance and support of a thorough and efficient system of free public schools." This was the first case in which a state supreme court relied on the education provisions of a state constitution, rather than on equal protection requirements, to find discriminatory funding of schools unconstitutional. The New Jersey court condemned not only the inequalities resulting from inadequate tax bases, but also those resulting from inadequate tax efforts. In addition, the court held that the state had never spelled out the content of the educational opportunity mandated by the state constitution.

Although the first response by a state court to the retreat of the federal courts from school finance issues came quickly, school finance litigation in state courts unfolded slowly during the three years following *Rodriguez*. During this period plaintiffs did well in state trial courts. Between 1973 and 1976, trial courts in Idaho, California, and Connecticut found school finance systems unconstitutional. However, supreme courts in four western states followed the lead of the U.S. Supreme Court in *Rodriguez* and found that inequalities in state school finance systems resulting from the disparate fiscal capacities of school districts did not violate state constitutions.[3]

Beginning late in 1976, plaintiffs' fortunes in state courts changed dramatically for the better. In general, the cases that reached state supreme courts during this period were tried after *Rodriguez* and profited from the lessons learned from earlier losses. Factual records were generally more extensive. There were more witnesses and documents, and the trials took longer. Plaintiffs meticulously documented how state school finance systems discriminate against children as a result of the fiscal capacity of the school district—a factor that has nothing to do with education. They also documented the ways in which inequalities in financing resulted in unequal educational facilities, staff, course offerings, equipment, and instructional materials.

In late 1976 the California Supreme Court reaffirmed its 1971 decision in *Serrano*.[4] In declining to follow *Rodriguez*, the California Supreme Court asserted the "independent vitality" of the equal protection provisions of the California constitution. The court held that wealth-related inequalities in educational expenditures are unconstitutional under the equal protection provisions of the *state* constitution, unaided by the 14th Amendment. Although the U.S. Supreme Court had found that education was not a fundamental interest under the U.S. Constitution, the California court held that education was constitutionally fundamental in California. This meant that wealth-related inequalities were subjected to strict judicial scrutiny to determine whether they were justified by a compelling state interest. The court rejected the concept of local control as a state interest justifying discrimination against children in low-wealth school districts.

Following *Serrano II,* state supreme courts in Connecticut, Washington, and Wyoming found their school finance systems unconstitutional, and the West Virginia Supreme Court, in sending back a school finance case for trial, expressed serious doubts about the constitutionality of the West Virginia school finance system.

Plaintiffs have not succeeded in all state supreme courts, however. Since 1976, plaintiffs have suffered major losses in supreme courts in Ohio, Colorado, Georgia, and New York.

Although the outcomes of school finance cases in state supreme courts have been mixed, 11 of the 12 courts that have conducted trials dealing with school finance inequities since *Rodriguez* have found state-wide school finance systems discriminatory and unconstitutional. Trial courts have struck down school finance systems in Arkansas, California, Colorado, Connecticut, Georgia, Idaho, Maryland, New York, Ohio, Washington, and West Virginia.[5]

It is particularly striking that the trial judges in these cases have come from extremely diverse backgrounds. Some were from large metropolitan centers, such as Los Angeles, Cincinnati, Denver, and Seattle. Others presided over courts in small towns in rural Arkansas and Georgia. In New York, the trial court was in suburban Long Island. Most of these judges had not previously conducted lengthy trials involving constitutional questions; nor did they spring from a single ideological mold or from a single political party.

What distinguishes these trial judges is simply that they took the time to understand how school finance systems operate. Two conclusions were inescapable: that these systems allocated educational resources among school districts on factors that have nothing to do with education and that educational opportunities are the result of the happenstance of where a child lives.

At bottom, I believe the trial judges were convinced that the school finance systems they reviewed were simply irrational. As a matter of law, education in nearly every state is a function of state, not local, government. In this regard education is unlike sewer, police, or fire departments. In virtually every state, school districts are considered legal agencies of the state, whose function is to assist the state in carrying out its constitutional obligation to provide a free public education to all children. Yet, in carrying out this obligation, the state compels children to attend school districts having vastly different levels of resources. More than any other factor, the irrationality of school finance systems' allocating funds fortuitously appears to explain the nearly unanimous conclusion of those trial judges closest to the facts that these systems are discriminatory and constitutionally untenable.

At trial, school finance issues have been largely factual and concrete. The central issues have been the magnitude of disparities in revenues and expenditures among school districts, the causes of these disparities, and the inequalities in educational opportunities that result from them. In most cases these inequalities have been so clear as to be virtually conceded by state officials.

On appeal, however, the issues have been more abstract. Several recurrent questions have divided state supreme courts. One is whether education is a fundamental interest under the state constitution. This is an important issue with regard to equal protection, because the courts scrutinize more closely the necessity and reasonableness of classifications affecting fundamental state interests. Another question is whether the state's asserted interest in preserving local control justifies treating children in low-wealth school districts differently from those in high-wealth school districts. Courts that have found inequitable school finance systems unconstitutional have rejected the notion that wealth-related spending inequalities promote local control. By contrast, courts that have found school finance systems constitutional have typically pointed to local control as a justification. Still another common concern of the appellate courts has been whether the challenged inequalities violate the education provisions of state constitutions, which frequently require "thorough," "efficient," "general," "uniform," "suitable," or "adequate" systems of free public schools.

Even those appellate courts—including the U.S. Supreme Court—that have refused to find inequitable school finance systems unconstitutional have not endorsed these systems as desirable. Justice Potter Stewart, concurring with the majority in *Rodriguez*, nevertheless concluded that the Texas school finance system was "chaotic and unjust."[6] Justice Lewis Powell, who wrote the majority opinion in *Rodriguez*, also noted that the funding of public education has relied "too long and too heavily on the local property tax" and called for "greater uniformity of opportunity."[7]

State supreme court decisions that have refused to strike down school finance systems have also stopped short of endorsing the inequalities. For example, the Georgia Supreme Court found that the conclusion was unassailable that the state school finance system provided unequal educational opportunities to children in low-wealth school districts; nevertheless, the Georgia constitution afforded no relief. The concurring justice on the Colorado Supreme Court, who cast the deciding vote in *Lujan*, found that the Colorado system "barely meet[s] constitutional standards."[8] The New York Court of Appeals, though it denied the plaintiff's claim, conceded that the New York school finance scheme produces "great and disabling and handicapping disparities in educational opportunities across our State."[9]

Aside from the simple unwillingness of certain state supreme courts to become involved in school finance issues, the major reason offered by these courts for sustaining inequitable financing schemes has been the preservation of "local control." The issue of local control was disputed in *Rodriguez* as well. Justice Powell relied heavily on this justification to sustain the Texas system, while Justice Byron White, in dissent, found no rational relationship between the Texas system and the state's asserted interest in the promotion of local control, because the system effectively denied local control to property-poor districts.[10]

This dispute has continued in state courts. Local control has been such a convenient justification for courts because it is an extremely nebulous concept. Courts that have chosen to rely on this rationale have seldom explained how it justifies prevailing inequalities. This glaring omission ignores the fact that, in most cases, patterns of unequal spending among school districts stem from unequal tax bases and not from significantly different tax rates. Indeed, poor districts typically tax residents at higher rates but obtain less revenue than their wealthy counterparts. The California Supreme Court in *Serrano I* referred to the purported justification of local control as a "cruel illusion" because poor districts "cannot freely choose to tax [themselves] into an excellence which [their] tax rolls cannot provide. Far from being necessary to promote local fiscal choice, the present financing system actually deprives the less wealthy districts of that option."[11]

Serious treatment of the extent to which the states' interest in "local control" justifies inequitable school finance systems would require the courts to consider whether alternative methods of funding could eliminate discrimination without interfering with local control. In *Rodriguez*, Justice Powell could argue that such nondiscriminatory alternative systems were untried. Since that time, however, reforms in many states have demonstrated that methods exist for eliminating discriminatory funding and preserving local control. Indeed, information on nondiscriminatory alternatives is contained in the records of most cases in which state supreme courts have asserted "local control" to justify the constitutionality of inequitable school finance systems.

There is another reason that local control is not a sufficient justification for unequal school financing systems: discriminatory school finance

systems often affirmatively bar school districts from exercising local control. For example, poor districts in Georgia were at the maximum property tax rate that school boards could levy, yet they still remained poor. In
other states, such as Colorado, state statutes cap the annual amount by
which school boards can increase their budgets. These caps lock current
spending inequalities in place. To obtain relief from these caps, school
districts must petition a *state* agency. Furthermore, most states impose
limits on indebtedness that frequently prevent poor districts—but not
wealthy ones—from providing adequate school facilities. Other restraints
on local control also exist. For example, in Arkansas nearly 80% of all incremental state funds received by a district must be used to increase the
salaries of *existing teachers,* even if the number of pupils in the district is
increasing and new teachers are needed.

The local control argument is more an assertion of an abstraction
than a reasoned response to the inequalities of school finance systems.
This very hollowness provides reason to hope that this argument will not
have power to justify such discrimination very much longer.

In the long run, the local control argument is likely to lose its appeal
even for those in charge of local school systems. School boards and edu-
cators, even in many wealthy districts, have grown weary of a "local control" that too often is simply a euphemism for a taxpayers' revolt aimed
at cutting school taxes and funds.[12] As the proportion of voters with children in schools decreases, local referenda on school budgets and levies
are likely to become harder to pass, and debate is likely to stray further
from education. In states that require annual referenda on school district
budgets or tax levies, probably nothing detracts more from the ability of
school boards and administrators to make rational-educational judg-
ments than the need to mount continual referenda campaigns.[13]

Whether plaintiffs have won or lost, they have succeeded in destroy-
ing the legitimacy of school finance systems that treat children differently without regard to any educational criteria. Even courts that have
found school finance systems constitutional have condemned the resulting inequalities. Moreover, the weaknesses of local control as a justification for unequal funding may render these decisions vulnerable to
renewed challenges in the future.

Although the time is not now ripe for a return to the federal courts—
and may not be for some time—*Rodriguez* should not be considered an
immutable precedent, barring relief under the U.S. Constitution forever-
more. The doctrinal underpinnings of *Rodriguez* may already be shifting.
Rodriguez held that education was not a fundamental federal interest;
consequently, the Court applied the rational basis test used to review
classifications in which constitutional interests of no special importance

are involved. Recently, the Supreme Court in *Plyler* v. *Doe* struck down the denial of educational opportunities to illegal aliens.[14] One reason the Court offered for its decision was that education is of greater constitutional importance than other forms of social welfare legislation.[15] Because of this and other factors, the Court applied not the rational basis test but rather the test of whether the discrimination "furthers some substantial goal of the State."[16] *Plyler* may provide a future ground for reexamining certain inequalities resulting from state school finance systems.

To the extent that state courts and state legislatures do not deal with these persistent inequalities, U.S. Supreme Court intervention becomes more likely. However, a number of state courts have thoroughly considered these inequalities and found them unconstitutional. Children subjected to inequitable school finance systems in these states will not have to wait for a more sympathetic High Court to obtain relief.

NOTES

1. *San Antonio Independent School District* v. *Rodriguez*, 411 U.S. 1 (1973).

2. The Education Commission of the States (ECS) has chronicled much of the legislative activity in school finance reform. See, for example, Allan Odden and John Augenblick, *School Finance Reform in the States: 1981* (Denver: ECS, 1981).

3. Arizona, Idaho, Oregon, and Washington *(Northshore School District* v. *Kinnear).*

4. In *Serrano I,* 5 Cal. 3d 584, 487 P. 2d 1241 (1971)., the California Supreme Court sent the case back to a lower state court for trial. In 1974 the trial court held the California financing system unconstitutional after a lengthy trial, and it was this decision that the California Supreme Court affirmed in 1976. This 1976 decision was the California Supreme Court's first opportunity to consider *Serrano I* in light of *Rodriguez. Rodriguez* created uncertainty because *Serrano I* had been based largely on the grounds of federal equal protection, which evaporated with *Rodriguez.*

5. The only state court that did not find an inequitable school finance system unconstitutional after trial was in Oregon.

6. *Rodriguez,* at 59.

7. Ibid., at 58.

8. *Lujan* v. *Colorado State Board of Education* (Justice Erickson specially concurring, Slip Opinion, p. 1).

9. *Board of Education, Levittown Union Free School District* v. *Nyquist,* Slip Opinion, p. 21 (N. Y. Court of Appeals, 1982).

10. *Rodriguez,* at 63–70.

11. *Serrano I,* at 1241, 1260. This finding was reaffirmed in *Serrano II,* 18 Cal. 3d 728, 557 P. 2d 929 (1976)., at 929, 953.

12. The unwillingness of voters to support the public schools was a major

reason why plaintiffs in the Ohio and Washington (*Seattle School District* v. *State of Washington*) school finance cases sought the aid of the courts.

13. The "taxpayers' revolt," now somewhat slowed because of the decline in inflation, has also had another effect that may ultimately be positive for school finance equalization. It has reduced the proportion of school revenues that come from local property taxes and forced the states to increase their shares. As the proportion of state funds increases, opportunities to eliminate discriminatory funding patterns also increase.

14. 50 U.S.L.W. 4650 (15 June 1982).

15. Ibid., at 4655.

16. Ibid., at 4656.

Reading 18

PUBLIC SCHOOL CHOICE: CAN WE FIND THE RIGHT BALANCE?

Bella Rosenberg

There are two major categories of arguments for public school choice. The first Bella Rosenberg calls the *principled argument,* which asserts that our society has a public interest in maintaining a public school system but that there is no concomitant public interest requiring children to attend one public school over another. Accordingly, this argument states parents should be allowed to choose the public school their children will attend. This view also assumes that distinctions of wealth and residence would be reduced or eliminated and equality of opportunity advanced. However, Rosenberg has serious reservations about whether public choice can work until equality in school financing is also achieved.

The second call for public school choice is the *instrumental argument.* This view sees choice as the means to achieve educational diversity, student achievement, and parent satisfaction. This argument assumes that competition promulgated through public school choice would increase educational opportunity and consumer satisfaction the same as in a market economy. But schools cannot easily work like a free market economy. For the most part, gaining or losing students under choice plans would not result in making or losing profit for a school and therefore would not be a stimulus to its improvement. Wealthy districts hardly want to attract students who will raise their costs of education while low-income school districts have no capacity to attract students from wealthy districts.

Before we decide to rush ahead with public choice schools, we should sort out the various models of choice and their respective costs, benefits, and trade-offs. The first and most common model of choice we need to examine is the *interdistrict model,* which allows urban students to attend suburban schools and vice versa. Typically, interdistrict choice plans have been a one-way ticket from the cities to the suburbs. Importantly, the suburban schools which participate in choice plans act just like private schools: to wit, they keep out "undesirable" urban students. So while the urban students who enter the choice programs have usually been successful, left behind are the majority of urban school students with no role model students and parents to push for the betterment of their schools.

Statewide choice is another model of public school choice. Such plans permit students to attend school in any district in the state so long as the nonresident school district is willing, has space, and the transfer does not imperil racial balance. State aid follows the student, thus reducing the financial excuses for districts not to accept nonresident students. However, statewide choice does not really accomplish as much as it implies: the reason is that very few parents are going to send their children to anything but their own school district or to a nearby adjacent school district. On the other hand, statewide choice plans which end up looking like interdistrict plans have the virtue of overcoming the fiscal opposition of suburbanites to nonresidents in their school districts.

Controlled choice programs are another form of choice. Such programs "compel" parents and students to choose a school anywhere in the district or within some zones within a district, subject to the maintenance of racial balance. Accordingly, racial balance is the factor which determines whether students get their first, second, or third choices. On balance, controlled choice plans encourage improvement in school attendance, student achievement, and racial diversity. However, transportation costs are greatly increased.

While competition and choice may promote diversity in our schools, diversity is not the same thing as quality. Nor should competition and choice become ends in themselves. Rosenberg avers that we need to discover how to best educate our children, and that to aid in that effort we should not accept or reject school choice whole. Rather, some models should be tried and from them we may garner examples of how to best improve our schools.

The current American preoccupation with public school choice illustrates yet again that, while there may be nothing new under the sun, there's always something newly hot. Many public school districts and schools have offered some form of choice for many years now. Yet, with the exception of an occasional researcher, no one outside these districts— and frequently even inside these districts—has paid much attention. The

Source: Bella Rosenberg, "Public School Choice: Can We Find the Right Balance?" Reprinted, with permission, from the Summer 1989 issue of AMERICAN EDUCATOR, the quarterly journal of the American Federation of Teachers.

only exception to this general indifference has been desegregation-related public school choice plans. But suddenly within the last year, and quite apart from desegregation goals, about half of the states in the nation have either considered or implemented some form of public school choice, and many local districts are doing the same.

The federal government also has embraced public school choice. Most public school supporters feared that last January's White House Seminar on School Choice would herald the transfer of the tuition-tax-credit-and-vouchers baton from the Reagan to the Bush administration. Instead, public school choice was the rage of the day (quite literally so for school privatization advocates), and President Bush made it one of the main planks of his education platform.

Why the sudden fuss? One rather cynical explanation is that public school choice is merely the prelude to choice that includes private and religious schools. Having lost the privatization battle for now and in light of federal and state fiscal crunches, choice advocates have cooked up the half-loaf of public school choice in order to accustom the public's palate to the idea of public-private choice. Then, when budget woes are alleviated or there is even greater distress with public education, it will be easier to serve up the rest of the choice loaf—tuition tax credits and vouchers.

While such a strategy on the part of privatization advocates is not implausible, the newly found fervor for public school choice can neither be so easily explained nor summarily dismissed—especially since so many among the fervent are also strongly opposed to privatization. Rather, what seems to have inspired this movement is a set of claims so powerful and compelling that no champion of children and public education can fail to be moved: Public school choice, its advocates say, promotes educational diversity and quality, student motivation and achievement, and parental involvement and satisfaction. Public school choice, in this view, may be *the* reform that transcends and negates the need for most other education reforms.

To the extent that these claims can be substantiated, public school choice may indeed have powerful implications for accelerating and achieving education reform. On the other hand, if these claims fail to pass muster, public school choice may end up diverting resources from more promising ideas or, worse, substituting for and thereby derailing education reform.

Where does the evidence point? Unfortunately, in a number of different and frequently contradictory directions. For one, even the arguments over choice fall into diverse categories, and each of them suggests a different course of action. Second, the evidence on choice is thin and is based on relatively few and diverse examples. Third, although people speak of public school choice as if it were a singular policy or phenomenon, it is in fact a rubric for a variety of policies and programs. It may mean intradistrict choice or interdistrict choice. Interdistrict choice, in turn, may mean only contiguous districts or an entire state. It may mean magnet schools or magnet programs operating either in an inter- or intradistrict context. It may mean creating a few magnet schools or programs or a virtually all-magnet system or no magnets at all. And it may mean some combination or permutation of these.

Perhaps the only conclusion one may confidently draw about public school choice at this time is that if it has been the salvation of some, it also has been the damnation of others. As this suggests, working one's way through the evidence does not so much lead to a choice between being for or against public school choice as it does to a series of dilemmas. Dilemmas are discomfiting. But given that the "some" and the "others" are children, teachers, parents, and public schools, this kind of equivocal and vexing research conclusion is not an excuse to read no more, succumb to our biases, and allow only politics to decide. It is, instead, reason to initiate a discussion.

DO WE NEED MORE CHOICE IN PUBLIC EDUCATION?

Since there are many things that people want but don't have or have but could lose, political movements are generally not created around something desirable that is already widely available or safe from threat. The emergence of a public school choice movement would therefore suggest that there is no or very little diversity and choice in public education and that this is a bad thing, or that diversity and choice are under attack. Is this true? No and yes.

We certainly already have a considerable amount of diversity and choice within public schools, especially high schools. As *The Shopping Mall High School* made abundantly clear, most American high schools have adopted just about every fad, fancy, option, or requirement that has been marketed over the past fifteen or twenty years, and students have been free to pick and choose these wares in just about any way they saw fit.

Why take physics if something easier were available and it "counted" as much as physics? Why offer foreign languages when it was hard to find teachers, and students preferred the "Language of Rock"? Why figure out different ways of getting diverse students to be successful in valuable and rigorous subjects when you could help them and yourself to avoid the issue altogether by giving them the choice to substitute ersatz courses with sexy and "relevant" titles? And who was responsible when students emerged from this choice system uneducated? Everyone, and no one at all.

During the past five to eight years, this kind of diversity and choice has been under attack. Virtually every state has raised its high school graduation requirements and more closely prescribed the courses necessary to meet those requirements. As a result, many electives and courses of study that once were acceptable for high school graduation have disappeared. It is therefore true that diversity and choice have been considerably curtailed. But that is because they have been judged to be a major reason for the ignorance of so many of our high school students and for the shortcomings of our public secondary education system—precisely the conditions that choice proponents claim that more diversity and choice will overcome.

There is no reason to think that public school choice proponents want our educational system to be organized like a shopping mall, where all offerings are equally valid, where survival necessitates schools' pandering as much to the worst as to the best in customers, and where students vote with their feet and society pays for the recalls. But if history is any guide, it is not unreasonable to worry that choice will produce that outcome. Indeed, we already know that not every student is far-sighted enough to want or to be able to judge a quality education, not every district or school is above casting aside professional judgment about quality and standards in order to placate its various and diverse constituents, and not every parent is able or willing to discriminate wisely among schools.

The burden of any responsible choice system, then, is to balance individual freedom with social needs, diversity with commonality, style with substance, and parental and student preference with professional judgment about what constitutes a good education. That's easy to say but hard to do. Doing so also presents a paradox: Maximizing the chances that a public school choice system will improve education may mean regulating and delimiting choice.

Public school choice proponents are therefore wrong in arguing that there is no diversity and choice in American public education. That is certainly not the case with secondary education. And they may be naive in thinking that choice always produces diverse examples of exemplary behavior and good outcomes, for the experience of education and other sectors proves otherwise. Nevertheless, their fundamental argument about the lack of diversity and choice in public education is quite right. While there may be a great deal of it *within* schools, there is little of it between schools and between school districts. There are a great many *dif-*

ferences between schools and school districts, largely because of enormous differences in their funding and student-body composition. But apart from that important exception, American schools and school districts vary little in their structure and methods, in the ways in which they have organized teaching and learning.

Given that we have more than sixteen thousand public school districts, many times that number of schools and no national system of education, this degree of standardization is quite astonishing. Most of our school districts admit and discharge students according to the same school calendar and organize their education by semester, usually two and no more than four a school year. The probability that these districts are using one or more of the ten most popular textbook series is very high, and the probability is even higher that their standardized testing system has been purchased from one of the five or six major American testing companies. Now that their curriculums are being realigned to fit these tests, chances are that even their scopes-and-sequences are becoming more similar.

As John Goodlad has pointed out, this similarity also extends to classrooms. Most of them are self-contained, with students sitting in rows facing one teacher at the front. Chalk-and-teacher-talk is still the prime teaching technology, and information processing, drill and practice, and recitation still the predominant mode of organizing learning. Greater variation in the organization of teaching and learning exists in the lower grades; very little in secondary schools, where Carnegie units and forty- or fifty-minute class periods conducted by teacher subject-matter specialists prescribe the routine of the day and week.

Although many of the features of this standardized school system are relatively new, its basic assumptions, structure, and methods have remained relatively intact for more than one hundred years. Reform waves have come and gone, depositing or clearing away the latest educational or social flotsam or jetsam, but the basic characteristics of the system have only become more firmly entrenched, elaborated, and rationalized. Whether this school system has been governed by thirty thousand or sixteen thousand locally elected or appointed boards, been decentralized or centralized, free of regulations or choked by them, the ways and means in which it has educated children has remained fundamentally the same. And little wonder: That is what it has always been asked to do.

Of course, it is not the dispiriting sameness of this school system that is at issue, but its lack of quality and its appalling results. Why does a broad spectrum of Americans who readily understand this nonetheless believe that choice can turn that system and its results around?

THE ARGUMENTS FOR PUBLIC SCHOOL CHOICE

The case for public school choice essentially falls into two categories. The first is based on principle, and the arguments here are on solid grounds but infrequently invoked. The second and more instrumental category contains the arguments about the effects of choice, which are weakly grounded but repeatedly and loudly made.

The principled argument for public school choice asserts that a free and democratic society has a transcendent public interest in maintaining a public school system, but there is no similar public interest in requiring children to go to one public school rather than another. Parents therefore should be allowed to choose which public school their children attend, irrespective of the district or neighborhood they happen to live in.

Opponents of public school choice might attack this argument on bureaucratic and administrative grounds, but they'd be hard pressed to deny the principle. The egalitarian component of this argument is even harder to assail. Public school choice, in this view, would reduce or eliminate the distinctions of wealth and residence in access to quality schooling and thereby equalize educational opportunity. Poor and minority children, especially, would be able to leave poorly funded, failing schools in the impoverished neighborhoods they live in through no fault of their own and attend well-funded, more successful schools in the wealthier neighborhoods that they and their parents can't afford to live in. Public school choice, then, would mean that no child would be trapped in a bad or poor school simply because of the economic or social circumstances of his parents.

The egalitarian argument for public school choice is highly compelling, but it is not without its ironies. For one, the last time public school choice was in the political limelight, during the heyday of desegregation, it was cast as an argument for preserving the right to stay in neighborhood schools and keep nonresidents out.

Second, although the egalitarian argument is now a mainstay among both liberal and conservative proponents of public school choice, neither group has yet addressed in their rhetoric or in their policies how the considerable political, social, practical, and fiscal barriers to creating such a choice system might be overcome. For example, virtually no current interdistrict choice plan requires districts to accept nonresident students; most of them are voluntary and on a space-available basis, and few wealthy districts volunteer and few spaces materialize. In the few instances where suburban districts have been required to accept students from their neighboring cities, they have behaved pretty much like selective private schools.

Of course, this behavior can be stopped—as was recently ordered in Milwaukee's suburbs after a long court battle—or it can be prohibited—as is the case in a number of recent interdistrict choice plans. But so long as public school choice is on a space-available basis, so long as parents from wealthier neighborhoods and schools are permitted to remain in their assigned schools and show no inclination to send their children to poor neighborhoods and schools—and until school finance equalization is also achieved—it is hard to imagine the egalitarian principle of public school choice's being realized in practice. It is also hard to envision these conditions' being met without bumping into the reality that increasing the freedom and choices of some members of society frequently involves curtailing the freedom and choices of others. This is hardly an unprecedented event, but neither is it one without political, social, and economic controversy and pain—and, frequently, some unintended consequences that undermine the very goals such policies have strived to achieve.

It is therefore not surprising that most organizations representing the interests of poor and minority children have either been negative, skeptical, or conspicuously silent about public school choice. For although choice proponents may genuinely believe that this reform will advance the interests of poor and minority children, so far none of the choice proposals or laws has either raised or resolved any of the issues that must be addressed to make others believe in the possibility of this outcome.

The second set of arguments for public school choice is directly concerned with outcomes. Unlike the principled case for choice, in which choice is an end, a good in and of itself, the instrumental case sees choice as the means to attain educational diversity and quality, student achievement, and parent, student, faculty, and community satisfaction.

The way public school choice will achieve these outcomes, this argument goes, is through competition, which is currently lacking in public education. Competition, in turn, is the means or incentive for increasing educational quality and "consumer" satisfaction, just as in a market economy. Deprived of their more-or-less guaranteed student bodies, schools will have to become more responsive to consumer demand (which is presumed to be for educational rigor and quality) in order to attract customers and the public dollars that come with them. Weak schools will have to improve or lose students and resources and perhaps go under, while good schools will be rewarded with more students and resources. Choice, then, would bring the accountability of the market to bear on public schools, and the result would be a large net gain in educational quality and public satisfaction, if not total improvement.

It is worth exploring what this argument tells us about what a growing number of intelligent people think is responsible for the poor performance of our public education system. Our educational woes, they are telling us, are largely due to the fact that our public education system has a virtual monopoly on schooling. Because we have few competitors and a more-or-less guaranteed supply of customers, if our "products" are not turning out right, then there is little to compel us to improve. There are no rewards and few incentives for improving—indeed, there are many disincentives—and there are no negative consequences for failing to improve. This may not explain why and how the personnel within the system behave, a kinder version of this argument goes, but it does describe the public education system. And a system like that is bound to have an astringent effect on the imagination and energy of the individuals within it and on their inclination to search out and try new ways of doing things when the old ways are failing.

A few quibbles notwithstanding, this is not an inaccurate account of public education. The question is: To what extent can the remedy it suggests work? Will choice in public education bring the principles of a competitive market economy to bear on schools? The answer logically depends on the extent to which schools do or can work like a free or even regulated market. And that is very little or not at all.

As American Federation of Teachers president Albert Shanker has pointed out:

> In the private for-profit sector. . .[t]here is a lot of ingenuity because you can make or lose a lot of money. But that's not what happens in school choice plans. A school district that loses students loses at most only the money it takes to educate those students. Many large urban districts have been losing thousands of students over the years and, unlike profit-making businesses, have done little to stem the tide. Nor do they expand the school programs that have waiting lists or do something about the schools that are failing and being abandoned.
>
> Similarly, why would any district want to attract more students if these students bring with them, at most, only the money it will cost to educate them? For the most part, gaining or losing students under choice plans does not result in making profit or losing profit and would therefore not act, as many claim, as a stimulus to improvement.[1]

Individual schools are even less like profit-making businesses than school districts. For one, they have very little control over their own budget. Second, they have decreasing discretion over their own programs. Third, they can't respond if there is increased consumer demand by increasing their space, at least not without the permission of central authorities and voters. And finally, they, too, get just enough and, frequently, not enough money to educate their students. Poor districts and schools are therefore hardly in a position to attract students from high-spending districts and schools, while wealthy districts and schools are unlikely to want to attract students who will raise their costs of education.

Consider the case of Westonka, a small, low- and middle-income community in Minnesota, the first state in the nation to offer statewide public school choice. Seventy percent of Westonka's residents do not have school-age children. The voters recently defeated a property tax increase, which forced the school board to slash $750,000 from its projected $12 million budget. Seven teaching positions were eliminated, as well as funds for teacher salary increases and building maintenance. About 117 of the district's twenty-five hundred students have applied for transfers to other school districts. If they leave, Westonka will lose an additional $350,000 in state funds and be forced to trim its budget and program further.[2] The result is likely to be further deterioration in the quality of education and further loss of students and funds.

Westonka may be pursuing an economically rational course for itself by downsizing and perhaps phasing out its educational system. And according to the laws of the market, this will be good in the end. But while the discipline of the market sorts itself out, Westonka's remaining students are likely to be treated to an inferior or partial education. And certainly Westonka's schools, which have every incentive to attempt to attract nonresident students and the state dollars they would bring, will be unable to compete.

What of the districts and schools that are attracting Westonka's students? Since they are only receiving the state funds attached to Westonka's students, they must make up the additional costs out of their own pockets. How much longer can they do so or for how many more nonresident students? How much longer will they be willing to do so, considering that the parents of nonresident students don't pay taxes in their districts? And what if money were no object, but classroom space ran out? Would district A be able to expand its schools to accommodate the students from districts X, Y, and Z as a successful for-profit business could? Would district A be able to take over the school buildings of another district whose schools were being abandoned, much like a successful business could take over a failing firm?

Or consider the case of intradistrict choice, where the funding issues are less complex. Schools A, B, C are desirable, schools X, Y, Z are not. Many parents want their children out of schools X, Y, Z, but few parents wish to transfer their children out of A, B, C, so there are few places to accommodate the excess demand for the desirable schools. Are parents all told that the playing field will be leveled, that is, that they will not be given first preference for their neighborhood school? This will make happy parents unhappy, give unhappy parents some hope, and, ultimately, result in roughly the same number of happy and unhappy parents. Or will desirable schools A, B, C be expanded by adding portable classroom space? That would mean hiring new teachers—from the excessed teachers from schools X, Y, Z, the unsuccessful schools, or from some other source? And what happens to schools X, Y, Z, the "leftover" schools? How many students have to leave before it is declared a failure and shuts down? And what about the need for space? Can schools A, B, C take over undesirable and depopulating schools X, Y, Z? Can they successfully replicate their program and run more than one school? Do they inherit the principals and faculties of the unsuccessful schools or hire anew? Or does nothing happen except for the development of a long waiting list for the successful schools? In that case, will the "bad" schools continue to compete to hold on to their students, knowing that the good schools don't have and can't get space? How, then, will competition drive out poor quality and promote overall improvement?

None of the problems these questions raise is insurmountable, and none of them constitutes an argument against choice. They do, however, suggest that school systems and schools do not work like free markets. Consequently, choice will not automatically bring the discipline of the market to bear on education, at least not without a host of other changes that choice proponents have not grappled with and society thus far has been disinclined to pursue.

The other major argument for choice also has its roots in economic thought, but it is less dependent on market analogies. This argument says that when an individual is able to choose a product or a service, the result is a greater commitment to that product or service. Similarly, when an individual chooses to be part of an institution or group and that entity chooses to accept the individual, there is greater mutual commitment and satisfaction. In short, choice is better than coercion, not only for moral reasons but because of its more positive results. Irrespective, then, of competition, incentives, and the other accoutrements of a market, choice proponents argue, if families/students could choose their public schools, then there would be greater mutual commitment between families/students and schools and greater satisfaction. Thus far, the evidence tends to support that argument.

The final, and unquestionably the premier, argument for public school choice is that it will improve student achievement and lower dropout and absentee rates. No other argument for public school choice has so captured the public imagination, and no other argument has been so oft repeated. Unfortunately, the evidence supporting this claim is highly suspect.

The evidence choice proponents use comes largely from the experience of magnet schools. By and large, magnet schools do tend to achieve average student test scores that are higher than the district average and dropout and absentee rates that are lower than the district average. This, however, is not surprising because the students in magnets and other schools of choice tend to represent a selected student population. Students at the lowest end of the achievement scale are rarely found in magnets, while students at the upper end of the motivation scale are disproportionately present. (Even if the student is not especially motivated, his parents generally are or else they wouldn't have gone to the trouble of seeking out an alternative to their neighborhood school. Families or students are not, after all, randomly assigned to schools of choice.)

Nor is this the case only with selective magnet schools. Even where magnets have no academic admissions criteria, they tend to tap a selected student population whose motivation is high even if their prior achievement scores do not reflect it. And even when magnets admit a cross-section of the achievement range (high, middle, and low), the resulting student body is still unrepresentative because few neighborhood urban schools today have such an academically mixed student body.

We therefore do not really know if magnet schools are "adding more value" to their students than other schools do because magnet students as a group were generally already above the district or neighborhood school average prior to their coming to the magnet. Indeed, the only way to substantiate the case that choice by itself "adds value" to students is to find or create a control group of students whose characteristics match the magnet students but who do not attend a magnet and then research the outcomes for these two groups. Ideally, too, there would be controls for the different characteristics of the magnet and assigned school, such as different levels of funding. No such work has yet been presented.

Since District 4 in New York City is perhaps the most commonly used reference for the benefits of public school choice, it is worth exploring how the district achieved its results. District 4, in East Harlem, is one of the city's poorest districts and once had the lowest achieving schools in the city. About ten years ago, the district adopted a choice plan and implemented schools-within-schools, mostly, but not exclusively, in its junior high schools. Over the years, choice has also spread to elementary schools. And over the years, District 4's schools have gone from the lowest end of the achievement scale to about midpoint.

Did choice perform a miracle in District 4? There is no question that the district's schools have improved. But District 4 is now also drawing students from throughout the city, and many of those students come from affluent homes. The fact that District 4 can now attract these students is testimony to its efforts. But it is also the case that District 4's improved average test scores may be the result of a new and different student mix.

It is possible that District 4 has kept separate data on the performance of its resident students and that this data indicate that their achievement is higher relative to comparable students in nonchoice schools. Such data would certainly make a very strong case for choice on the basis of student outcomes. If such data are available, I have been unable to find them. Such a result, however, would not be unlikely. There is, for example, evidence that poor children who are low achievers perform better in economically and academically mixed schools than they do in schools attended predominantly by low-achieving poor children. To the extent, then, that choice promotes economic and ability integration, it may indeed improve the achievement of poor and/or low-achieving youngsters. This may occur in an assigned neighborhood school as well as a choice school, but current residential patterns make this level of economic and social integration rare in a neighborhood school.

District 4 has therefore produced a rare phenomenon in poor neighborhoods: a school system that attracts families and students from outside its boundaries. But if choice has been the mechanism for doing so, good schools have been the reason. Put another way, choice did not create the improved schools in District 4. Rather, it was the opportunity and assistance the district gave to the faculties in its schools to rethink and redo policies and practices that weren't working for their students that helped turn the schools around. Unlike the teachers in most of the city's schools, District 4's faculty were treated like knowledgeable professionals. Allowed to work together in a collegial fashion, to concentrate more on the needs of their particular students than on following the directives of a distant bureaucracy, they created new programs and improved traditional ones and broke the mold of perpetual failure. Would choice have made an educational difference in District 4 without the efforts at change the district made prior to and along with introducing choice? It hardly seems possible. To offer a choice of roughly similar and similarly failing schools would have been to offer no choice at all.

Ironically enough, although District 4 and other schools whose faculty have been permitted to depart responsibly from standardized policies and practices have been much admired, they have not been widely emulated. Instead, they remain exceptions at the margins of a system that seems to prefer the habits and routinization of failure to the risks necessary for success. Choice has now been deemed the reason for District 4's and others' success. But if that is the only lesson carried away from their experience, then we should not be surprised if the nation becomes dotted with choice systems that afford some students a geographical change but fail to stimulate an educational cure.

CHOICE PLANS COME IN MANY VARIETIES

The recent hurry to choose up sides for or against public school choice has created the impression that choice is a singular policy or program when it is actually a rubric for a variety of policies and programs. Moreover, the generally sloppy way in which both advocates and opponents of choice have used the evidence has intensified that impression. Regrettably, by citing the results of one choice model to attack or support a very different model, they have managed to talk not only past one another but down to the public. Staking out a position on choice is therefore more than a matter of sorting out principles and arguments. It also involves sorting out the various models of choice and their respective costs, benefits, and tradeoffs.

INTERDISTRICT CHOICE

The most common form of this type of choice plan permits urban students to cross district lines and attend suburban schools and vice versa. Most of these plans were motivated by court-ordered desegregation or the imminence of such an order, and most of them regulate choices on the basis of their racial impact. In practice, this tends to mean that only minority students may leave city schools, and only white students are eligible to leave suburban schools. The participation of suburbs is generally voluntary; the participation of cities is generally not.

The major, and significant, expense of such plans is transportation, with the state and the city generally assuming the burden. Some states fully or partially double-fund for interdistrict choice, while others do not. Double-funding means that both the resident school district that students leave and the nonresident district where they attend school can count the students for state aid. Double-funding cushions urban districts from the impact of declining enrollment and is supposed to help them improve the quality of their schools and thereby attract suburban students. Double-funding is, of course, expensive, and as the competition for scarce resources increases, the inclination to double-fund decreases.

In order to attract white suburban students into the cities, most interdistrict choice plans have involved the creation of city magnet schools. Some such magnet schools have been successfully integrated, others have not. Virtually all of them, however, have received a relatively large amount of state and local funds (as well as federal funds earmarked for this purpose) compared to the funding of neighborhood schools. Magnet school costs in St. Louis, for example, average 42 percent more per student than regular, city elementary schools, 25 percent more than middle schools, and 27 percent more than traditional high schools. In some cases, these funds represent "new" money specially appropriated for the purpose of promoting choice and integration. In other instances, it represents money siphoned from neighborhood schools or at least money that could have been spent to improve neighborhood schools. In just about every case, the superior funding of magnet schools leads to resentment among the staff in neighborhood schools.

Typically, however, interdistrict choice plans have been a one-way street from the cities to the suburbs. For example, Milwaukee County's interdistrict choice plan began in 1976 with eight suburban districts volunteering to assist the city in complying with a federal court order to desegregate. Eleven suburban students entered city schools, and 323 city students transferred to suburban schools. Twelve years and another court battle later, 4,300 city students are attending schools in twenty-three suburban districts, and the city has attracted 1,070 suburban students, about half of whom attend magnet schools.

Interdistrict choice in St. Louis provides another example of a one-way street from the city to the suburbs. Initiated in 1983, St. Louis's plan was designed to attract at least six thousand suburban students into city schools. The main vehicle for realizing this plan was to be twenty-four magnet schools, with more to follow. By 1988, the plan's sights were lowered from six thousand to 1,670 students. In the fall of 1988, only about six hundred suburban students were in city magnet schools, while 11,131 city students were enrolled in suburban schools.

The typical one-way street of interdistrict choice plans has also been a restricted street. That is, while suburban districts have been volunteering to accept urban minority students, they have refused to accept students with discipline problems and special needs and have "creamed off" the most academically (and, sometimes, athletically) talented and motivated youngsters from urban schools. Put another way, many suburban districts, through student record reviews, parent and student interviews, and the like, have been acting just like private schools. Moreover, not only have they been keeping "undesirable" urban students out, they have frequently failed to inform their students of the city school option or refused to let them transfer.

From a number of perspectives, then, most interdistrict choice plans have not worked well. Certainly their high costs have not resulted in benefits that are commensurate with the goals of these plans. Yet if interdistrict choice plans are judged on the standard of helping to rescue individual students, then a measure of success must be conceded to them. For although many of the urban minority students who transferred to suburban schools would probably have succeeded no matter what school they went to by virtue of their motivation or talent, many of them might have succumbed to the uncongenial academic atmosphere now so typical of poor neighborhood schools. Some of these students' parents might have taken them out of the public school system altogether, at great hardship to themselves and to the detriment of support for public education. And without these plans, even fewer white and minority children might have shared a common school experience, a dream of public education.

But the price of rescuing individual students has been high, very high indeed, for the majority of urban schools and youngsters. For the evidence is strong that interdistrict choice plans have also depressed the quality of urban neighborhood schools by "creaming off" their role model students and the parents who are voices for educational excellence and by skimming off many of their most talented teachers and financial resources.

STATEWIDE CHOICE

There are very few statewide choice plans currently in operation. Minnesota's was the first, and its plan is only about a year old. But statewide choice is now the hottest choice model in the nation, and a number of states have followed Minnesota's lead, with more likely to follow.

Statewide choice plans permit students to attend school in any public school district in the state so long as the nonresident school district is willing and has space and the transfer does not upset racial balance. State aid follows the student, which means that the higher the state's share of per-pupil costs, the more equitable a state choice plan is likely to be and the fewer the financial excuses for districts not to accept nonresident students. Many of the architects of statewide choice plans have learned the lessons of interdistrict choice plans and included regulations designed to prevent districts from picking and choosing their students.

Based on current discussions, transportation will be handled in one of a few ways: The state will only pay the costs of transporting poor students out of their resident districts; a district will pay for transporting students to the border of the nonresident district and the host district will take over from there; or families will be responsible for any transportation out of their resident districts.

In many respects, statewide choice is more rhetorical than real, an example of symbolic politics. Very few, if any, parents are going to send their children clear across a state to attend a public school. The claims of statewide choice opponents that the policy will result in massive chaos and defections are therefore greatly exaggerated. Last year, for example, the first year of the full implementation of Minnesota's statewide choice plan, only 440 students availed themselves of the opportunity. (About 5,400 eleventh and twelfth graders used a postsecondary option, which is less than 5 percent of those eligible.) Next school year, Minnesota expects one thousand students to take advantage of open enrollment, which is still under 1 percent of those eligible.

What have been the results of Minnesota's choice plan thus far? Although the evidence is thin, it seems that some students who dropped out or were on the verge of dropping out are completing their studies in schools outside their resident districts. Many high schools have introduced advanced-placement courses in order to retain their students. Schools are generally taking parents' wishes more seriously because they know that their children might be transferred. A number of districts are offering more choices within their borders. And, in a surprise development, about three thousand students have returned from private to public schools.

On the other hand, some districts whose schools were already underfunded, like Westonka, are reeling from the loss of students and state aid, and there is a good likelihood that a number of districts will be forced to consolidate. (Some critics claim that this was the chief purpose of Minnesota's choice policy.) Two of the wealthiest districts in the state have refused to participate. The cities seem to be losing many more students than they are attracting, and the ones they are losing are the student role models. Information on choices is not widely available, and, as is the case with many other choice plans, relatively few poor parents are exercising choice. There is also no evidence that choice has produced an epidemic of experimentation and innovation in districts and schools.

A number of recent developments in Minnesota also suggests that the state is trying to put some lid on diversity and choice. Statewide standardized testing programs and more specific curriculum frameworks are being actively discussed. If these materialize, the result may be a system that has found a balance between diversity and commonality, student/family preference and professional judgment, and individual desires and social needs. But the result could also be more standardized practices and test-driven schools—and a choice system in which schools are all pretty much alike, save in the important respects of wealth and student-body composition.

A final note: Since statewide choice plans will likely involve only neighboring districts, they are really like the interdistrict choice model writ large but without the exclusive city-to-suburb, suburb-to-city focus. It is unfair to attack statewide choice initiatives on the basis of the sins of past interdistrict choice programs, as many people do. It is, however, prudent to apply the lessons learned from those programs and monitor statewide choice very carefully lest we rescue a minority of students while damning the majority.

INTRADISTRICT CHOICE PLANS

Loosely defined, intradistrict choice refers to any option available to students within a given public school district. This may range from something as common as offering students a choice of curriculum (e.g., academic, vocational, general) and electives within a high school—the most common form of choice in America—to a districtwide open enrollment policy that, theoretically at least, allows students to attend any school in the district.

Current discussions of intradistrict choice generally refer to more proactive and reform-conscious versions of choice than the ones above. Chief among these newer options are magnet schools and controlled-choice plans. Unlike most earlier choice policies, these options generally involve an effort to promote diversity, that is, to create distinctive schools to choose from.

OPEN ENROLLMENT

Open enrollment permits students in a district to enroll in any school in that district, on a space-available basis and usually subject to racial balance guidelines.

Open enrollment is a fairly common policy in urban school districts, but it tends to be a well-kept secret from parents. Those parents who do know about this option tend to be economically better off and/or better educated and generally savvier about making systems and institutions work for them. The fact that many open enrollment plans do not include transportation further limits their accessibility, particularly for poor parents. Therefore, although open enrollment in such districts is theoretically open to all so long as the choice does not promote segregation, it is known and used only by few. (It also is a popular device for recruiting and transferring athletes into certain schools.)

Another reason open enrollment leads to few transfers is that, with a few exceptions, schools within a district are relatively standardized and most parents prefer the convenience of their neighborhood school. In fact, open enrollment by itself is neither concerned with nor does it result in greater programmatic diversity among schools. In this sense, it is not so much an educational or social policy as a sort of individual "safety valve" for those who are disgruntled with and might leave the public school system. Typically, then, the choices being made have less to do with educational programs or processes (except insofar as individuals have informally heard of something special going on in a school) than they do with educational inputs, particularly with student-body composition and the financial and other resources of a school.

For these reasons, open enrollment, *per se,* is not a major piece of the dialogue on education reform and public school choice these days. Open enrollment coupled with magnet or alternative schools is, however, a different story.

MAGNET SCHOOLS/PROGRAMS

Next to statewide choice, magnets are currently the most talked about variety of choice. They also represent the most firmly entrenched example of choice and the one for which we have the most empirical evidence. Since the previous discussion focused on magnets created as part of an interdistrict choice plan, only intradistrict magnets will be considered here.

Magnets have their roots in competitive high schools (though these were never called magnets) that admit students throughout a city on the basis of an examination. New York City's examination high schools are perhaps the oldest and best known of this genre.

The use of the term "magnet" is more recent, however. What we now mostly think of as magnet schools are the result of desegregation efforts in which one or more secondary schools were given some special focus and extra resources in order to attract whites into predominantly minority schools. (Sometimes it was the other way around, but rarely.) Magnets initiated for desegregation were largely boosted by federal funds available for this purpose. Desegregation continues to be a major, but no longer exclusive, purpose of magnets.

Magnets are organized around an academic specialty or two (mathematics, performing arts, humanities) or teaching philosophy (traditional, open education, Montessori) or, sometimes, theme (technology, sports, the environment). They may either encompass a whole school or a program within a school and are most commonly found at the secondary level; elementary school magnets, however, are becoming increasingly popular. Magnets are generally open to all the children within a district on the basis of open enrollment and are usually subject to racial balance guidelines.

Unlike neighborhood or assigned schools, magnets accept students on the basis of an application, which may range from little more than a sign-up sheet to an academic screening mechanism. Some magnet schools have highly selective admissions standards, others have modest or no requirements. Some are on a first-come, first-served basis, while some hold lotteries if the demand exceeds the supply of spaces, and others encourage excess demand in order to shape a representative student body. And some magnets operate rather disingenuously by purporting to accept an academically representative sample of the district's students but in fact skimming off the students in the highest end of the middle- and low-achievement bands.

As the earlier discussion suggested, upon closer inspection it turns out that even the least academically selective magnets are in fact selective because it has generally been the case that choice is disproportionately exercised by motivated and well-informed students/parents. (The most vivid and graphic representation of this are scenes of parents camping outside a magnet school, sometimes for more than one day and night, to sign up their children. There are probably many more parents who would go to this trouble, but are unable to take time off from a job or leave other children unattended.) There are therefore few if any magnet schools that are representative of the student body of a district; all the students are there by virtue of self-selection, which in education and other areas is a very powerful selection mechanism.

This does not necessarily pose problems—or, rather, dilemmas—if a district supports a substantial number of magnets and makes information about their availability widely and easily available. Unfortunately, that is not the case in most districts—hence, the camping-out scenes. Indeed, the fewer the magnets available in a district, the fewer the actual choices available to parents/students, despite the ostensible existence of an intradistrict choice policy; the fewer the choices available, the more those choices are available to and exercised only by the more privileged or motivated members of the community; and the more the choices are exercised by the stronger members of the community, the more the students in magnets represent a select rather than a representative student population.

With this caveat in mind, the evidence to date about well-designed magnet schools suggests that the arguments being made by their proponents are substantially correct. Choosing and being chosen do lead to greater mutual commitment and satisfaction among students, parents, and teachers alike. Student absenteeism and dropout rates and teacher absenteeism and turnover tend to be lower, and parental involvement and student achievement higher. But unfortunately—as noted earlier about interdistrict magnets—many of the factors that account for the success of these magnets—such as student self-selection and higher funding levels—have also had a devastating effect on the quality of neighborhood schools.

Although a policy debate about intradistrict choice can ill afford to ignore this dilemma, it need not be paralyzed by it. There is an alternative to improving the educational opportunities of the few at the expense of the many, on the one hand, and foregoing magnet schools altogether, on the other. And that is to make every school in a district or every school at a particular level of education a school of choice. This is not the same thing as open enrollment—merely allowing parents and students to choose which school in the district they wish to attend. Rather, it represents an effort to "reform" each school or level of schooling in a district by giving them all the opportunity and means to create a distinctive program and then offering a choice among them.

There are, in fact, a few systems that have done so, largely as part of a desegregation effort. In the course of going to an extensive magnet system, however, they discovered some educational as well as social benefits. Consequently, this variety of choice, generally known as "controlled choice," is now receiving increasing attention as a means to promote reform.

CONTROLLED CHOICE

This system of choice (also known as districtwide choice) in effect "compels" every student/parent to choose a school either anywhere in the district or within some zones within a district. In some school systems, typically small or modestly sized ones, such choice may extend from elementary to secondary schooling. In other, larger school systems, the policy may be confined to middle or secondary schools. All the schools at that level then become schools with a distinctive focus or philosophy.

The most common restriction districts have put on such choice systems is that the choices not be allowed to upset racial balance—hence the term "controlled choice"—which means that racial balance is a factor in whether students get their first, second, or third choice. Sibling attendance is also frequently taken into account, so that families may remain together. The only other admissions criterion seems to be student or parent interest; applying to a school seems to be a relatively simple matter of indicating interest and filling out a form.

The most notable and successful examples of controlled-choice districts are Cambridge, Massachusetts; Montclair, New Jersey; and District 4 in New York City. Both Cambridge and Montclair are relatively small districts and offer choice from the elementary through the secondary levels; District 4 is a mixed intra- and interdistrict choice model, since it accepts students from other school districts in the city, and the choices it "compels" are for the junior high school level. Each of these districts considers all the schools within the scope of its choice plans to be distinctive magnets, including neighborhood schools that operate in a "traditional" fashion.

On balance, the evidence about well-designed controlled-choice plans indicates that they result in a modest but encouraging improvement in district and school racial balance and in student attendance and achievement (probably because schools with high concentrations of poor and low-achieving students become more integrated by social class and ability levels). Increases in teacher morale and parental involvement are also reported, and a few controlled-choice districts have attracted private school students back to the public school system.

On the other hand, controlled-choice plans increase district costs, especially the more successful plans. Transportation seems to be the biggest budget item, which is probably one of the reasons such plans tend to be found only in small cities or in one district within a large city. Large cities that are now contemplating such a plan for the entire school system seem to be heading in the direction of dividing the city into zones and making choices available only within those zones, thereby creating a number of intradistrict choice plans within a city.

Another cost of controlled choice—and one that some districts skimp on—is information. The availability of choice and the types of choices available must be publicized. Frequently, there also must be an aggressive outreach campaign to encourage parents to exercise choice and avoid increasing social and economic segregation among schools. As this suggests, most parents, and poor parents in particular, tend to prefer the convenience and familiarity of their local neighborhood school and may not have the wherewithal to search out the school that may work best for their particular children. Given that most parents will choose their neighborhood schools, a choice plan that concentrates only on designing a few specialty schools rather than improving all schools is a plan headed for failure.

What, then, seems to distinguish successful controlled-choice plans from nominal and less successful ones? First, every or virtually every school within the district is given the opportunity and resources to become distinctive and successful. Sometimes the district may provide school faculties with a menu of themes to choose from, which the district, in turn, may have derived from a survey of parents, teachers, principals and, sometimes, students throughout the district. Sometimes the decision is exclusively school based. In all cases, the decision and plans are worked out by the school faculty working toegether.

Second, there is a common set of goals throughout the district and sometimes even a common set of curriculum guidelines, but individual schools have discretion over the particulars of content and how to achieve the common district goals.

Third, parents have equal access to reliable information about the choices being offered and what they mean, and there is an especial effort to ensure that poor parents are well informed. Then, parents and/or students apply to the schools, listing their top choices, and the district endeavors to honor those choices, subject to desegregation and other criteria that may be locally appropriate. Although few districts pay attention to this criterion, schools of choice that admit a student body that is representative by achievement as well as by race have shown some striking success.

Fourth, the district administration and teachers union work out procedures to enable teachers to choose the type of school program/ philosophy in which they wish to practice, while ensuring that no school is deprived of critical faculty.

Fifth, the district provides transportation, preferably for all but at the least for poor students. And, finally, the schools work hard at ensuring that parental involvement does not end with choosing a school.

There is another criterion of successful controlled choice that is not revealed by the research but by common sense. When schools have a prior bad reputation and are physically in disrepair, unsafe, and starved of resources, many parents will leave them at the first opportunity. Even if these schools go through an educational renaissance, it is hard to convince parents that they have changed, especially if they continue to look like dumps. They will be just about everybody's last choice. They nonetheless will be filled because space in more desirable schools will be limited. Repairing crumbling schools or making them safe may not be as new or sexy an idea as public school choice, but it is very much a part of what it will take to make choice real.

Last, but far from least, is the issue of space availability. Controlled-choice, as well as other choice plans, strives to give parents one of their first three choices of schools, subject to racial-balance guidelines. Since most parents prefer their neighborhood school—and, clearly, most parents who have moved to a particular part of town primarily for the quality of its schools will prefer those neighborhood schools—it is virtually impossible to honor parents' first preferences *and* achieve greater racial balance. Some choice systems deal with this problem by "grandfathering" children into their present school if that is the first choice of their parents. There is fairness in that approach but also a contradiction of the notion of choice. (It certainly violates the free-market assumptions underlying choice.) Undoubtedly, it will make parents who are presently satisfied with their neighborhood school happy. And just as certainly, it will limit the opportunities of parents who wish to transfer their children out of less desirable schools.

And what of school systems that do not "grandfather," that attempt to create a level playing field? They, too, attempt to honor parents' top choices but do not guarantee continued access to the neighborhood school. This, too, is a fair approach, especially if a district is trying to improve racial balance. Yet, just like "grandfathering," it also contradicts the notion of choice and is bound to make some parents unhappy and perhaps even drive them from the public school system.

It is not altogether surprising that there has been little or no discussion of such contradictions and tradeoffs, for no research evidence can resolve controversial issues that are squarely in the realm of values and politics. But it is not inappropriate to call for a little more honesty in the choice debate: It is a rare case when increasing the choices of some does not constrain the choices of others.

HOW MUCH CHOICE DO PARENTS WANT?

Since choice implies involvement, no matter how minimal, it would be a mistake to view the public school choice movement apart from the issue of parental involvement in education. Concerns about parental involvement are, of course, not new. They were in large part responsible for the school decentralization movement of the 1960s, such as the one in New York City, and are implicated in the recent and more radical decentralization reforms in Chicago, where every school will elect a board on which parents must be the majority. The goal of increasing parental involvement is also motivating many of the calls for school-based management.

But if public school choice is another manifestation of the drive for parental involvement, it is also a less political one. This seems a curious observation in light of the intense politics surrounding public school choice. But whereas decentralization and school-based management are concerned with governance, with giving parents, as a group, more authority over their local schools or school, choice is more concerned with fulfilling individual preferences and giving parents more control over their particular child's education. In Albert Hirschman's terms, public school choice celebrates individual exit over collective voice; it's the difference between switching or staying to fight for change for oneself and others. And in this sense, the public school choice movement is very much a sign of our times: the increasing disillusion with politics and with our ability to change our institutions, the fragmentation of civic and cultural life, and the retreat from society into self. It certainly seems to be the case that public school choice represents a feeling that parents can't trust schools or school systems to make the right educational decisions for their children and that therefore parents would be better off if they made those decisions for themselves.

The popular passion for public school choice thus seems entirely understandable; if you believe that the system is unresponsive, that it cannot or refuses to be salvaged, then you concentrate on saving yourself and those closest to you. Yet this also suggests that the extent and depth of the demand for public school choice, per se, has been oversold. To be sure, there are plenty of polls and surveys to substantiate the popular demand for choice. It is also true that virtually every poll or survey that asks the public whether it would rather have a choice of product or service X, Y, Z, or no choice finds that the answer is "choice." That is not surprising and it is healthy, a sign of our individualism and our democratic habits.

But when a respondent is probed and told the costs and benefits and other terms of the choice, or when actual behavior is studied, the results come out differently. Suddenly, choice is not the concern; it is instead quality, costs, familiarity, convenience, the tradeoffs among them, and the like. The mere prospect of choice or of acquiring product X may no longer seem so desirable; product Y may not be perfect, but it now appears preferable.

Indeed, if we look at the rather superficial surveys on school choice alongside other polls on education and against actual behavior, we find that, first and foremost, parents want a quality education for their children in safe, local neighborhood schools. Judging from their behavior, they also seem to want the right to pull their child out of an uncongenial or unsuccessful classroom—the kind of "little divorce" that the public school bureaucracy now makes so difficult (and which choice, the threat of leaving the school altogether, may make easier). As for teachers—and no one is much talking about teacher choice—choice for them means the ability to fulfill the desire to practice in schools where good practice is possible and to get out of schools and districts where it is not. Is the is-

sue, then, choice? Only collaterally so. The basic issue is quality education and the conditions that make it possible.

Unfortunately, there is still disagreement over what quality education is. More troubling, we still don't know a great deal about what
works in education, for whom, and when. Choice proponents seem to
believe this, too, and use it as an argument for why parents need to
choose the schools that work best for their kids. But another argument
may be that public school choice is an admission of our ignorance, for if
schools knew what worked, for whom, and when, then wouldn't they be
doing it? Wouldn't we then accuse the schools that weren't doing it of
malpractice and find a way to make them practice what works? And then
wouldn't there be no educationally compelling reason for choice?

Competition and choice may indeed promote some much-needed
diversity in our schools. But diversity is not the same thing as quality,
and there may be as many diverse examples of bad or mediocre schools
as successful ones. It seems, then, that the zeal for diversity ought to be
marshalled to a search for commonality, for the ways and means that enable students to learn. This does not preclude diversity any more than an
architect's obligation to build a structure that stands and resists stress
precludes using a variety of design and decorative styles. But it does suggest that if diversity and choice become ends in and of themselves rather
than another systematic means to discover how best to educate our children, then like an architect's dazzling but flawed structure, our school
system will continue to crumble.

After five intensive years of education reform, all too many of our
children are still not learning, and quality education is still beyond our
grasp. For public school choice proponents, that is a *prima facie* case for
choice. For public school choice opponents, that is cause to focus only on
the lack of ideal conditions for choice and on what could go wrong. In
this regard, the argument goes to the public school choice proponents.
There is no evidence that the more-of-the-same-old-things-but-better approach to education reform that has characterized the past five to eight
years is working. By concentrating only on the risks of change and insisting that we wait for a more perfect world before we act, public school
choice opponents are sure to help perpetuate the status quo. That is unacceptable.

There is a third and more agnostic point of view, and that is that public school choice—at least some models of it—may indeed be an engine to
improve our schools, but it is not the whole vehicle and it doesn't drive
by itself. If choice is coupled with the restructuring of our schools, with a
systematic search for new ways of organizing learning and teaching,
then there is reason to think that it will deepen and accelerate education

reform. But if choice is used as a cheap substitute for this more fundamental pursuit, then the prospects for turning around our public school system and dramatically improving the education of our children will be more remote than ever. Public school choice will then certainly be the prelude to privatization, as some choice opponents have charged. But not because of some political conspiracy; it will be because we preferred a quick-fix fantasy over the reality of hard work. The choice is ours to make.

NOTES

1. "Where We Stand," *The New York Times,* Feb. 12, 1989, Section IV, p. 7.
2. "Public Schools Go to Market, Giving Parents More Choices," Barbara Vobejda, *Washington Post,* Jan. 2, 1989, p. A1.

CHAPTER X

ECONOMIC DEVELOPMENT POLICIES IN THE STATES AND CITIES

INTRODUCTION

Ann O'M. Bowman and Richard C. Kearney make the following statement: "Although there is no single definition of economic development, it traditionally has meant increases in per capita income and community investment." Consequently, "cities and states with higher per capita incomes and higher levels of capital investment are considered more economically developed than their counterparts, and this translates into ample employment opportunities and an adequate tax base."[1] We add that economic development also refers to state and local activities to build state and local economies with federal, state, and local cash or in-kind support for specific projects and activities.[2]

Economic growth and development have been among the major agenda items of nearly every state and major city in America since the beginning of the nation.[3] However, economic development for states and localities became one of the highest priorities as a result of the following events: the New York City fiscal crisis of the 1970s; the downturn in the economy resulting from the OPEC-generated oil embargo in those same years; competition from foreign products and the reduction in U.S. industrial and manufacturing jobs; and severe shocks emanating from the 1981–82 recession.

The deteriorating state and local economies caused many to believe that a larger measure of government intervention was needed to promote economic development. Accordingly, both the national and subnational levels of government initiated a number of programs designed to stimulate economic development in the most distressed areas of the country. The fundamental goal of this effort has been to save and increase jobs, to lower unemployment, and to bolster tax revenues without increasing tax rates.[4]

Economic development means that states and localities are, in effect, in the market for jobs for their citizenry. To secure these jobs, states and localities must go after business and manufacturing firms and woo them to their respective jurisdictions. In every state and locality there are *controllables* (tax policies, the floating of industrial revenue bonds, the granting of public lands for private purposes, etc.) which states and localities may utilize to attract firms. On the other hand, there are *uncontrollables* (availability of energy, location in the transportation matrix, quality of labor available, etc.) which are fairly static and not easy to change. These factors also influence locational decisions of firms.

Barry M. Rubin and C. Kurt Zorn, in their article "Sensible State and Local Economic Development," which is reprinted in this chapter as Reading 19, discuss whether some economic development policies are sound, and whether such policies, in fact, affect the locational decisions of firms.

Some observers have argued that none of the business inducements have any impact on job creation and puzzle over why state legislatures continue to enact business incentives. Dennis O. Grady attempts to resolve the issue empirically. In his article "State Economic Development Incentives: Why Do States Compete?," which is reprinted in this chapter as Reading 20, Grady spells out the various explanations for state economic development incentives and indicates that only one has any basis in fact. He then suggests a solution to what he sees as the fundamental problem of state economic development policies.

NOTES

1. Ann O'M. Bowman and Richard C. Kearney, *State and Local Government.* (Boston: Houghton Mifflin, 1990), p. 455.

2. See Alan Beals, "The Role of U.S. Local Governments in Economic Development," *Planning and Administration* 13, No. 2 (Autumn 1986), p. 68.

3. Ibid.

4. See Susan A. MacManus, "Linking State Employment and Training and Economic Development Programs: A 20-State Analysis," *Public Administration Review* 46 (November/December 1986), p. 640.

SENSIBLE STATE AND LOCAL ECONOMIC DEVELOPMENT

Barry M. Rubin and C. Kurt Zorn

Economic development initiatives have become common in recent years as states and localities have sought to attract jobs and increase economic activity. However, it is not always true that policies adopted to promote economic development are efficient or effective. Many economic initiatives undertaken by state and local governments have considerable hidden costs associated with them. The authors note an example wherein a city put together an incentive package to attract a truck assembly plant. In addition to a host of other incentives, the city granted personal and real property tax abatements to the truck assembly plant. The authors argue that it is questionable, first, whether the tax abatement status was a sound economic decision and, second, whether the tax abatement status affected the truck assembly's company decision to locate in that city.

Barry M. Rubin and C. Kurt Zorn question whether, given the other incentives to the assembly company to locate in the city, the tax abatement status had any impact on the company's decision to do so. They argue that corporate enterprises seeking to relocate usually make investment decisions based on factors other than tax abatement. These factors, termed *uncontrollable business costs,* include transportation, energy, and labor costs. While it is generally recognized that the three uncontrollables loom largest in corporate locational decisions, states and cities concentrate their efforts on factors under their control, such as grants of land, issuance of industrial revenue bonds, land use privileges, and tax concessions. The authors aver that taxes do not play a significant role in a firm's choice of location *among* regions, but do play a role if the emphasis by the firm on geographical location decreases.

Rubin and Zorn contend that states and cities need to understand that industrial expansion across states can be best explained by uncontrollable factors and that controllables gain in a firm's locational decision only as differentials in uncontrollables diminish. Accordingly, many states and cities may be offering development incentives which are excessive and have little or no impact on a firm's decision to locate or not locate in their respective jurisdictions. However, there is a solution to the problem: state and local economic development policymakers should concentrate their efforts on firms that find the controllable factors significant at the margin. In short, *economic development efforts should be focused on attracting firms that would find their state or city competitive in terms of uncontrollable costs.*

Hardly a day goes by without the media's reporting new economic development initiatives by states and localities in the United States. Competition is keen and the stakes are high because officials and the electorate view a "successful" economic development policy as being essential. One of the best recent examples, underscoring the intensity and importance of this issue, was the bidding war that the states of Indiana and Ohio waged in 1982 over the International Harvester Corporation.

It is generally accepted that economic development initiatives are an important component of state and local public policy, and the electorate expects its elected officials to succeed in promoting economic development. Unfortunately, it is not always true that the policies adopted to promote development are efficient or effective.

Many of the economic development initiatives undertaken by state and local governments have sizable hidden costs associated with them. It is not difficult to find examples of industrial development incentive packages offered by states and localities that fail to stand up to even the most rudimentary scrutiny. For example, in the summer of 1984 Fort Wayne, Indiana, announced that it had attracted a large General Motors truck assembly plant. The city and state put together a $26.4 million incentive package that included interstate highway construction and renovation, sewer and water service to the plant site, and renovation and improvement to nearby roads and railroad lines.[1] In addition, the city and county granted personal and real property tax abatement status to the GM plant.

Despite the fact that the plant will create jobs, increase personal income, and increase retail sales in Fort Wayne, it is not clear that the city's granting of tax abatement status was a sound economic decision. First, the local tax structure makes it virtually impossible for the locality to

Source: Barry M. Rubin and C. Kurt Zorn, "Sensible State and Local Economic Development," *Public Administration Review* 45 (March/April, 1985), pp. 333–39. Reprinted with permission from *Public Administration Review* © by the American Society for Public Administration (ASPA), 1120 G Street NW, Suite 700, Washington DC 20005. All rights reserved.

raise sizable revenues from taxation of the increased area income or retail sales that are expected to occur. Second, and more importantly, it is questionable whether the granting of tax abatement status affected GM's decision on the plant site.

To even the most unseasoned eye, it is clear that substantial competition exists among regions, states, and localities for new business and industry. The intensity of the efforts is such that it has been labeled the "second war between the states."[2] As regions, states, and localities watch their neighbors attract jobs and economic activity, the desire is to get a piece of the action. As more and more governmental units offer industrial location incentives to help tip business location decisions in their favor, support is lent to the belief that these incentives are necessary and that they significantly affect choices.[3]

The authors do not share the view, which is apparently widespread in the U.S., that all policies which nurture economic development are constructive. At a minimum, more careful thought should be given before the decision is made to offer firms industrial location incentives. To develop this argument, the economic rationale behind economic development policy is reviewed next. Then section three discusses the current state of economic development policymaking, and an alternative approach to economic development is formulated in section four. A summary and conclusion are contained in the final section.

WHAT ECONOMIC RATIONALE UNDERLIES ECONOMIC DEVELOPMENT?

Public finance theory suggests that, at a very basic level, most economic development policies are flawed. Three major economic functions of government are generally accepted in the United States: distribution of income, stabilization of the economy, and resource allocation.[4] In the U.S. federal system of government it is most appropriate for the national level to concern itself with stabilization and distribution while state and local levels of government are best suited, in terms of equity and efficiency considerations, for resource allocation. Stabilization and distribution policies by the subnational levels of government generally are not effective because these policies can be easily circumvented. Some constituents are mobile, particularly commercial and industrial interests, and over the long run they will choose those governments whose fiscal policies suit them best.

Economic development policy, as it is currently structured in the U.S., attempts to affect the distribution of income and provide economic stability by attracting jobs and economic activity to the region, state, or locality. Success or failure of this policy usually is determined by whether or not the firm decides to locate in the area, instead of whether the benefits realized from attracting the firm are greater than the costs incurred. Many policymakers are not cognizant of the fact that the industrial location incentives being offered are not costless and thus focus on the benefits alone. This biased perspective results in an overstatement of the advantages of success.

When incentives are offered to attract economic activity, whether it is in the form of industrial or commercial development, it is implicitly assumed that increased revenues arising from tax levies on the new economic activity will pay for the incentives. But as the bidding wars among states and localities heat up, it is not certain that the increased economic activity which the industrial location incentives attract pays its own way. If this is the case, what looked like a good decision in the short run may turn out to be counterproductive. In the long run, the mobile segments of the citizenry choose to move to another location to avoid the increased revenue demands placed on them to support the new economic activity.

Even if the new firm "pays its own way" by providing sources of revenue sufficient to cover the cost of the incentives used to attract it, the new firm may be costly to the jurisdiction's taxpayers. By attracting the firm, the city may gain a reputation for economic vitality, and thus experience ancillary growth beyond that which was anticipated. The end result can be unmanageable population density, congested transportation networks, and strained public services. As this occurs, tax burdens will rise and the quality of life will diminish leading to the same type of population loss described above. Thus, in the long run, no net gain for the community may occur.

This discussion has so far assumed that the incentives are successful in attracting desired industry. The process of creating, packaging, and promoting these incentives is by no means costless. As such, the short run costs become even greater when one adds the cost of those incentives which failed to attract the sought after industries.

When seen from a national perspective, economic development policymakers are involved in a zero sum game. When one state wins by convincing a firm to locate within its boundaries, the other 49 states lose. When state A attracts a firm that is located in state B, state A clearly benefits at state B's expense. The movement of firms in response to state and local economic development policies has, at best, no effect on the total welfare of society. When the cost of providing and collecting information, arriving at a decision, and relocating are considered, it is difficult to imagine that the cost of economic development policies, in terms of societal welfare, does not exceed the benefits.

At best, it appears that subnational economic development policy considers the short-run results enjoyed by a specific geographical location, disregarding societal welfare or the long-run effects. Policymakers are afraid that if they do not participate in the economic development bidding game, their jurisdiction will lose jobs, economic stability, and the appearance of vitality and robustness. There apparently is disregard for the fact that, in most cases, the marketplace will determine the most efficient location for firms.[5]

Although present economic development practices lack a sound economic foundation, it is politically naive to expect policymakers to stop using them, absent alternatives. Therefore, it is important to devise other approaches to encourage desired economic development. Although offering of industrial location incentives appears illogical in terms of the economic rationale for government, location theory and comparative cost analysis provide a basis to construct an alternative approach to state and local economic development.

THE STATE OF ECONOMIC DEVELOPMENT POLICYMAKING

It is apparent that the intent of the industrial location incentives being offered by state and local governments is to influence a firm's locational decision. Although it is recognized that many factors enter into a firm's decision, the basic assumption is that a firm is a profit maximizer—the location chosen will provide the greatest margin between revenues and costs.[6] Because the state or locality has little control over demand for the firm's product, efforts tend to focus on the costs of producing and marketing the firm's product.

It is generally recognized that firms consider three major cost components when making locational decisions—transportation, labor, and energy.[7] All three components can be quantified and thus the decision becomes, more or less, a mathematical exercise. At the same time, all three of these cost components tend to be uncontrollable from the viewpoint of policymakers. No doubt state and local governments may act to improve the attractiveness of their location in terms of transportation, labor, and energy costs, but the overall impact will be minimal.

Logically, state and local government efforts have concentrated on other factors more directly under their control. State and local industrial location incentives that focus on these controllables can be categorized as financial incentives, including grants of land and the issuance of industrial revenue bonds; tax concessions; labor related incentives, including right to work laws and programs to increase labor productivity; and land use incentives.[8] The variety and extent of industrial location incentives offered have been characterized as a well-stocked candy store.[9]

Of all state and local industrial location incentives, taxes are the most visible of the controllables. They are an important cost of doing business,[10] and much attention has been focused on how taxes affect industrial location.[11] Despite the perception among policymakers that taxes matter and therefore a good incentive package should contain tax concessions, the overriding conclusion from previous research is that taxes do not play a significant role in a firm's choice of location *among regions*.[12] Research also has shown that the other nontax controllables contained in state and local industrial incentive packages play little or no role in a firm's *interregional* choice of location.[13] But as the geographical area diminishes, the importance of taxes and fiscal incentives increase. Transportation, energy, labor cost, and market differentials tend to decrease as the area under consideration diminishes, making taxes a more significant locational determinant.

Although fiscal incentives do not have a significant effect on firms' locational decisions, it does not follow that states and localities should forego offering industrial incentive packages in their effort to attract new and retain existing industry. The presence of fiscal incentives is interwined in the ambiguous concept of business climate, and thus the elimination or omission of incentives can bode ill for the governmental unit. If a state or locality fails to offer fiscal incentives to industry while its peers do, it may appear that the governmental unit is not concerned or aware that its policies affect the business community. Thus, the omission may portend a bad business climate.

The problem with the business climate concept is that it is nebulous and inexact, open to individual definition and interpretation.[14] The subjectivity of the business climate measure has not deterred a number of consulting firms from using the measure and it appears, at least on the surface, that firms considering relocation take business climate into consideration.[15] Recent analyses, however, do not support this appearance, and suggest that the impact which business climate has on industrial location and growth is not significant.[16]

AN ALTERNATIVE ECONOMIC DEVELOPMENT APPROACH

Industrial expansion across states can be best explained by uncontrollable factors.[17] On the whole, controllable factors (industrial location incentives) have little or no effect on firms' locational decisions.[18] Controllable factors gain in significance only as the differentials in uncontrollables—transportation, energy, and labor costs—diminish. Thus, the present practice of state and local governments of offering a wide selection of incentives may be misguided, even from a second best point of view.

Presently, states and localities offer industrial location incentives indiscriminately. Indications are that many do not consider how they fare relative to their peers in terms of uncontrollable costs before offering location incentives. If a firm bases its decision on factors outside the control of the policymakers, it makes no sense to offer incentives which will not affect the decision. State and local economic development policymakers should concentrate their efforts on firms that find the controllable factors significant on the margin. In other words, if a firm can be identified that would find the state or locality competitive in terms of uncontrollable costs, economic development efforts should be focused on attracting that firm.

To identify those firms that should be targeted for economic development efforts on the state level, a procedure was developed to estimate uncontrollable costs. Specifically, the methodology facilitates the estimate of transportation, energy, and labor costs for 20 manufacturing industries in each of the 48 continental states.[19] The 20 manufacturing categories defined at the two-digit level by the Standard Industrial Classification System (SIC) of the U.S. Department of Commerce form the basis for the cost variation analysis.

Since a firm's structure, operations, and location affect its cost of doing business, a representative firm was constructed for each manufacturing industry. The representative firm for each of the 20 SIC categories was defined as the median size firm in the industry, as determined from data provided by the Internal Revenue Service in its *Sourcebook of Statistics of Income*. Balance sheets and income statements for each of the representative firms were derived from these data.

The representative firm approach is necessary for a quantitative analysis of variations in manufacturing costs across states. It allows for total uniformity in corporation structure and operations, thus highlighting variations in costs due to location.[20]

Table 1 shows the 1982 aggregate uncontrollable costs encountered by representative firms in each of the 20 SIC categories in the 48 continental United States. Aggregate uncontrollable costs are the total of individually estimated transportation, energy, and labor cost components. A wide variation exists in the absolute magnitude of total costs across SIC categories, but more importantly, substantial variation is present across states within a SIC category. This underscores the fact that all locations are not equal in the comparative cost advantage they can offer firms. Thus, the profit maximizing firm will not consider all locations as equal substitutes.

TABLE 1 1982 Aggregate Uncontrollable Costs (Thousands of 1982 Dollars)

State	SIC 20	SIC 21	SIC 22	SIC 23	SIC 24	SIC 25	SIC 26	SIC 27	SIC 28	SIC 29	SIC 30	SIC 31	SIC 32	SIC 33	SIC 34	SIC 35	SIC 36	SIC 37	SIC 38	SIC 39
New England																				
Maine	189.31	----	285.70	247.55	868.08	----	677.49	49.11	160.32	496.47	127.57	41.12	----	776.91	155.94	105.84	105.34	370.02	----	141.84
New Hampshire	246.19	----	292.65	225.20	861.23	549.71	634.53	45.61	160.64	----	143.75	41.64	1516.09	776.63	155.25	103.69	122.34	352.90	36.89	140.73
Vermont	213.18	----	322.76	269.28	822.17	481.73	598.29	57.49	146.46	524.28	147.52	45.46	1524.64	815.62	155.04	109.90	154.54	390.46	41.60	159.75
Massachusetts	209.42	----	321.36	248.43	878.61	581.83	630.32	52.09	166.98	----	----	33.52	----	792.40	161.62	118.86	129.14	430.69	35.29	149.24
Rhode Island	----	----	----	274.85	----	----	622.01	52.09	164.58	534.38	152.80	----	1426.11	817.20	154.34	114.97	114.03	408.69	37.74	176.36
Connecticut	----	----	----	----	----	556.33	663.19	50.90	----	----	----	----	----	----	152.69	118.70	----	----	----	----
Middle Atlantic																				
New York	204.30	----	294.94	264.07	817.38	531.26	587.60	56.22	143.42	525.99	133.62	40.05	1443.55	770.10	156.52	125.50	130.42	474.47	46.39	157.72
New Jersey	214.08	----	318.14	261.08	785.46	510.89	610.37	49.24	158.61	523.45	144.53	42.09	----	779.30	161.92	118.88	144.68	449.42	42.87	152.07
Pennsylvania	214.92	51.42	289.86	258.40	792.59	530.77	569.46	52.02	147.79	499.93	148.76	39.20	1369.58	782.07	157.09	121.41	127.27	390.38	39.88	175.32
East North Central																				
Ohio	179.73	----	308.40	294.37	697.34	531.08	525.99	50.80	142.97	491.33	149.46	40.54	1199.40	734.08	153.94	123.02	133.66	437.16	42.40	----
Indiana	170.55	----	275.64	231.08	653.51	475.86	518.77	47.37	135.77	447.40	136.71	37.22	----	710.45	120.79	121.50	141.52	404.48	35.01	174.18
Illinois	184.15	----	318.56	256.93	680.48	542.38	511.85	53.76	130.03	448.67	134.61	42.62	----	710.81	144.06	134.44	119.85	391.19	39.31	163.10
Michigan	197.23	----	416.46	484.71	723.11	612.46	560.20	52.82	134.69	443.50	145.74	44.11	1232.78	725.14	159.11	136.35	143.85	505.62	42.46	174.04
Wisconsin	184.53	----	312.85	257.58	699.36	512.17	556.84	52.83	133.74	481.70	138.32	45.91	----	657.93	146.30	126.65	128.85	412.21	37.05	154.68
West North Central																				
Minnesota	196.08	----	304.76	243.66	790.00	553.85	632.01	55.35	136.43	456.93	141.70	56.57	1307.89	693.69	155.81	114.44	125.45	359.34	39.90	149.84
Iowa	203.79	----	302.15	227.00	687.77	605.12	540.02	47.31	128.47	----	158.15	----	1151.41	703.34	138.12	141.78	127.96	----	39.82	160.32
Missouri	176.96	----	258.17	228.58	593.88	455.06	568.40	47.22	123.26	376.71	----	40.12	----	686.13	140.71	111.59	112.19	415.55	34.05	127.39
North Dakota	191.20	----	----	----	----	----	----	----	136.69	----	----	----	1360.54	----	----	----	----	----	----	----
South Dakota	215.82	----	----	231.52	665.84	555.13	----	44.55	126.28	432.12	----	----	1239.03	----	----	88.22	----	290.74	----	136.76
Nebraska	186.05	----	----	----	----	----	----	----	----	----	----	----	1114.12	747.04	137.82	105.48	122.34	296.80	35.06	127.27
Kansas	185.58	----	----	217.87	628.99	507.02	547.80	47.07	123.99	414.57	160.52	37.56	1078.28	650.74	130.49	98.96	104.61	339.36	29.43	152.32
South Atlantic																				
Delaware	207.48	----	307.18	265.00	693.28	464.25	506.30	49.12	156.69	----	153.69	29.19	1332.33	687.89	132.95	98.45	133.11	451.06	----	155.33
Maryland	184.24	74.91	239.59	224.18	750.59	420.68	554.48	51.14	142.67	444.28	146.27	35.57	1329.36	733.73	154.05	129.34	142.61	376.34	36.81	138.90
Virginia	170.19	----	280.62	236.11	662.51	441.00	603.91	46.82	137.66	457.27	136.21	38.98	1149.01	795.61	138.40	108.09	115.77	393.33	36.05	145.95
West Virginia	153.12	61.97	274.96	216.00	692.66	441.86	524.52	44.29	132.26	----	138.18	39.44	1170.61	627.00	134.72	106.89	135.89	284.73	----	143.43
North Carolina	160.99	----	286.20	217.74	686.06	460.72	560.54	43.02	130.94	465.61	----	----	1149.87	667.77	126.22	99.69	108.65	401.65	30.41	137.19
South Carolina	150.43	----	275.75	220.00	653.09	480.17	571.70	47.43	126.88	----	145.51	37.56	1082.45	674.15	129.51	92.71	95.92	345.83	33.05	122.07
Georgia	161.20	----	272.29	235.98	----	----	625.21	48.06	132.25	----	----	----	1270.59	738.79	125.22	96.92	110.36	----	----	132.59
Florida	185.84	41.28	----	----	724.33	----	----	----	140.12	----	----	----	----	----	146.10	102.71	112.87	----	----	----
East South Central																				
Kentucky	173.35	70.17	288.15	240.37	650.03	449.57	530.95	44.51	140.92	484.45	140.75	40.13	1063.71	725.67	125.85	117.46	125.89	412.18	33.60	131.71
Tennessee	164.20	48.06	275.93	226.46	593.88	434.34	549.26	44.23	133.45	----	143.53	41.04	1084.75	749.21	129.18	110.97	100.57	311.42	30.87	139.75
Alabama	151.05	----	276.88	221.96	621.15	440.26	585.96	44.00	136.41	414.90	178.52	----	785.14	785.14	129.84	89.44	105.29	358.97	31.12	139.45
Mississippi	149.22	----	280.26	223.44	611.04	445.99	559.46	39.40	118.69	----	----	38.93	1063.56	644.45	128.02	93.72	100.00	355.03	23.56	144.98
West South Central																				
Arkansas	149.58	----	296.05	224.49	610.00	453.39	577.58	36.44	126.95	412.14	134.99	43.34	1008.67	643.96	122.10	93.60	106.18	275.38	30.08	133.79
Louisiana	169.13	----	262.63	237.16	648.56	520.75	612.43	47.32	134.14	455.34	166.47	----	1125.40	586.00	145.93	102.68	143.81	373.91	35.82	147.91
Oklahoma	178.42	----	328.72	218.27	627.45	474.66	563.04	47.83	119.45	423.31	----	36.92	----	663.25	142.19	100.02	130.02	356.74	33.19	141.23
Texas	188.01	----	295.27	230.81	566.54	470.05	585.87	48.00	140.81	----	146.60	----	1163.03	786.38	148.59	111.53	118.56	319.66	----	----
Mountain																				
Montana	----	----	----	----	832.16	----	----	----	209.34	484.10	----	----	1535.47	----	----	----	----	----	----	----
Idaho	230.67	----	----	----	----	----	----	----	152.40	489.96	----	----	1635.38	----	----	113.97	----	298.71	----	----
Wyoming	----	----	----	----	----	----	----	----	----	----	----	----	1285.42	----	----	----	----	----	----	----
Colorado	206.14	----	----	251.01	620.58	502.61	619.91	51.55	163.05	465.47	160.18	----	----	841.85	157.30	114.06	122.63	439.89	44.82	156.17
New Mexico	----	----	----	241.33	----	----	----	50.31	232.61	472.38	----	----	1478.04	----	323.17	----	106.24	386.40	----	233.30
Arizona	245.58	----	----	425.70	648.31	----	766.97	56.15	189.13	----	----	----	1556.70	876.71	168.99	111.85	122.40	485.53	32.19	163.17
Utah	220.06	----	----	----	653.41	----	640.17	51.59	----	478.78	----	----	1533.74	----	174.08	113.48	122.72	378.90	----	143.24
Nevada	----	----	----	----	----	----	----	----	181.33	----	----	----	----	928.30	----	----	----	----	----	176.46
Pacific																				
Washington	270.20	----	384.48	284.90	966.07	711.39	867.30	68.82	241.82	674.92	190.33	----	2015.95	1013.80	206.39	147.39	133.75	528.47	43.66	----
Oregon	270.75	----	----	----	985.24	676.18	918.93	67.47	215.07	612.83	----	----	----	1078.86	----	133.96	126.27	536.05	----	----
California	255.00	----	384.49	268.51	727.76	618.59	817.25	62.29	200.92	575.57	187.38	46.96	1726.53	1055.16	192.20	131.73	138.96	506.14	40.75	165.36

335

The comparative cost advantage that an individual state has in a specific SIC category can be more easily seen in Table 2. For example, if a state economic development policymaker in Indiana were interested in which manufacturing industries would find Indiana attractive relative to other states in terms of uncontrollable costs, the information could be obtained from the table. Indiana's total costs are under the national average for all but four of the 18 SIC categories for which complete data exist.[21] Indiana's comparative advantage looks especially strong in SIC 20, 22, 23, 26, 28, 30, 31, and 34.

It is sensible for a state's economic development efforts to be concentrated on firms in SIC categories for which the state has a relatively low index. The index suggests that manufacturing firms in these industries would find location within the state attractive in terms of low uncontrollable costs—transportation, energy, and labor. Because firms in these SIC categories would be likely to consider a location in the state, the state can more effectively focus its industrial location incentives on them and make the location even more attractive in terms of both uncontrollables and controllables. By concentrating economic development efforts on these firms by offering industrial location incentives, state governments are more likely to have an impact on the locational decision, tipping the balance against a competing state that has similar uncontrollable costs. Using this strategy, a state is less likely to offer industrial location incentives to firms that would locate in the state regardless of the incentive package offered, or it may avoid setting an expensive precedent by offering lucrative incentives to a firm that has no serious intention of locating there.

The example above illustrates the usefulness of a targeting strategy based on this methodology. Admittedly, it only provides an aggressive analysis of the variation in manufacturing business costs across states, but that does not diminish its usefulness in contributing to a more rational approach to state and local economic development policymaking. By first looking at the three major components of manufacturing business costs, it can be determined in which SIC category a state has a comparative advantage in terms of uncontrollable costs.

SUMMARY

Economic development activities are generally key components of state and local policy. Often, however, these policies are not efficient or effective in achieving their purposes.

Public finance theory suggests that attempts by state and local governments to promote economic growth and to affect the distribution of

TABLE 2 1982 Aggregate Uncontrollable Costs Indices (U.S. Average = 1.00)

State	SIC 20	SIC 21	SIC 22	SIC 23	SIC 24	SIC 25	SIC 26	SIC 27	SIC 28	SIC 29	SIC 30	SIC 31	SIC 32	SIC 33	SIC 34	SIC 35	SIC 36	SIC 37	SIC 38	SIC 39
New England																				
Maine	0.97	--	0.95	0.98	1.21	--	1.12	0.98	1.07	1.04	0.85	1.01	--	1.02	1.03	0.94	0.86	0.95	--	0.93
New Hampshire	1.27	--	0.97	0.89	1.21	1.07	1.04	0.91	1.07	--	0.96	1.02	1.15	1.02	1.02	0.92	0.99	0.90	1.01	0.93
Vermont	--	--	1.07	1.06	1.15	0.94	0.98	1.15	0.97	--	--	1.12	1.16	1.07	1.02	0.97	1.26	0.99	1.14	--
Massachusetts	1.10	--	1.07	0.98	1.23	1.13	1.04	1.05	1.11	1.10	0.99	0.82	--	1.04	1.07	1.05	1.05	1.10	0.97	1.05
Rhode Island	1.04	--	1.07	1.08	--	1.08	1.02	1.04	1.10	1.12	1.02	--	1.08	1.08	1.02	1.02	0.93	1.04	1.04	0.98
Connecticut	--	--	--	--	--	--	1.09	1.01	1.10	--	--	--	--	1.01	1.03	1.05	--	--	--	1.16
Middle Atlantic																				
New York	1.05	--	0.98	1.04	1.14	1.03	0.97	1.12	0.95	1.10	0.89	0.98	1.10	1.01	1.07	1.11	1.06	1.21	1.27	1.04
New Jersey	1.10	--	1.06	1.03	1.10	0.99	1.00	0.98	1.06	1.09	0.97	1.03	1.03	1.03	1.04	1.05	1.18	1.15	1.18	1.00
Pennsylvania	1.12	0.89	0.96	1.02	1.11	1.03	0.94	1.04	0.98	1.05	1.00	0.96	1.04	0.97	1.01	1.07	1.03	0.99	1.09	1.16
East North Central																				
Ohio	0.92	--	1.02	1.16	0.98	1.07	0.87	1.01	0.95	1.03	1.00	1.00	0.91	0.94	0.85	1.09	1.09	1.11	1.16	1.16
Indiana	0.88	--	0.92	0.91	0.91	0.92	0.85	0.94	0.90	0.93	0.92	0.91	0.91	0.94	0.95	1.06	1.15	1.03	0.96	1.15
Illinois	0.95	--	1.06	1.01	0.95	1.05	0.84	1.07	0.87	0.94	0.90	1.05	--	0.95	1.05	1.19	0.97	1.00	1.08	1.08
Michigan	1.01	--	1.38	1.91	1.01	1.19	0.92	1.05	0.90	0.93	0.98	1.08	0.94	0.87	0.96	1.21	1.17	1.29	1.17	1.15
Wisconsin	0.95	--	1.04	1.02	0.98	0.99	0.92	1.05	0.89	1.01	0.93	1.13	--	0.91	1.03	1.12	1.05	1.05	1.02	1.02
West North Central																				
Minnesota	1.01	--	1.01	0.96	1.11	1.06	1.04	1.10	0.91	0.96	0.95	1.39	0.99	0.93	0.91	1.01	1.02	0.92	1.10	0.99
Iowa	1.05	--	1.00	0.90	0.96	1.18	0.89	0.94	0.86	0.86	1.06	--	0.88	0.90	0.93	1.25	1.04	--	1.09	1.06
Missouri	0.91	--	0.86	0.90	0.83	0.88	0.94	0.94	0.91	0.79	--	0.99	--	--	0.97	0.99	0.91	1.06	0.93	0.84
North Dakota	0.98	--	--	--	--	--	--	--	--	--	--	--	1.03	--	--	--	--	--	--	--
South Dakota	1.11	--	--	--	0.93	1.08	--	0.89	0.84	0.90	--	--	0.94	0.98	0.91	0.78	0.99	0.74	--	0.90
Nebraska	0.96	--	--	0.91	--	0.98	--	0.94	0.83	0.87	--	--	0.85	0.86	0.86	0.93	0.85	0.76	0.96	0.84
Kansas	0.95	--	--	0.86	0.88	--	0.90	--	--	--	1.07	--	0.82	0.91	0.88	0.88	--	0.86	0.81	1.00
South Atlantic																				
Delaware	1.07	--	1.02	1.05	0.97	0.90	0.83	0.98	1.04	0.93	1.03	--	1.01	0.91	0.88	0.87	1.08	--	1.01	1.02
Maryland	0.95	--	0.80	0.88	1.05	0.82	0.91	1.02	0.95	--	0.98	0.72	1.01	0.97	1.02	1.14	1.16	1.15	0.99	0.92
Virginia	0.88	1.29	0.93	0.93	0.93	--	0.99	0.93	0.92	0.96	--	0.87	--	1.05	0.91	0.96	0.94	0.96	--	0.96
West Virginia	0.79	--	0.91	0.86	0.97	0.86	0.86	0.88	0.88	--	0.91	0.96	0.87	0.83	0.89	0.95	1.10	1.00	0.95	0.95
North Carolina	0.83	1.07	0.95	0.86	0.96	0.86	0.92	0.86	0.87	--	0.92	0.97	0.89	0.88	0.85	0.88	0.88	0.73	0.83	0.90
South Carolina	0.77	--	0.95	0.87	0.91	0.89	0.94	0.95	0.84	--	--	--	0.87	0.89	0.83	0.82	0.78	--	0.91	0.80
Georgia	0.83	--	0.92	0.93	1.01	0.93	1.03	0.96	0.88	0.97	--	0.92	0.82	--	0.80	0.86	0.90	1.02	0.91	0.87
Florida	0.96	0.71	0.90	0.86	0.88	0.93	--	--	0.93	0.87	0.97	--	0.97	0.96	0.98	0.91	0.92	0.88	--	--
East South Central																				
Kentucky	0.89	1.21	0.96	0.95	0.91	0.87	0.87	0.89	0.94	1.01	0.94	0.99	0.81	0.96	0.94	1.04	1.02	1.05	0.92	0.87
Tennessee	0.84	0.83	0.92	0.89	0.83	0.84	0.90	0.88	0.89	0.87	0.96	1.01	0.82	0.99	0.98	0.89	0.82	0.79	0.85	0.92
Alabama	0.78	--	0.92	0.88	0.87	0.86	0.96	0.94	0.91	--	1.19	--	0.81	1.03	--	0.79	0.86	0.91	0.85	0.92
Mississippi	0.77	--	0.93	0.88	0.86	0.87	0.92	0.79	0.79	--	--	0.96	--	0.85	0.84	0.83	0.81	0.90	0.65	0.96
West South Central																				
Arkansas	0.77	--	0.98	0.89	0.85	0.88	0.95	0.73	0.85	0.86	0.90	1.06	0.77	0.85	0.80	0.83	0.86	0.70	0.83	0.88
Louisiana	0.87	--	0.87	0.94	0.91	1.01	1.01	0.94	0.89	0.95	--	--	0.86	0.77	2.13	0.91	1.17	0.95	--	0.97
Oklahoma	0.92	--	1.09	0.86	0.88	0.92	0.93	0.95	0.80	0.89	1.11	--	--	0.87	1.11	0.96	1.06	0.91	0.98	0.93
Texas	0.97	--	0.98	0.91	0.79	0.91	0.96	0.96	0.94	0.83	0.98	1.06	0.88	1.03	1.15	0.99	0.96	0.81	0.91	--
Mountain																				
Montana	1.19	--	--	--	--	--	--	--	1.39	1.01	--	--	1.17	--	--	--	--	--	--	--
Idaho	--	--	--	--	1.16	--	--	--	1.01	1.02	--	--	1.24	--	--	1.01	--	0.76	--	--
Wyoming	1.07	--	--	--	--	0.98	1.02	1.03	1.09	0.97	--	--	0.98	1.11	--	--	1.00	--	--	1.03
Colorado	--	--	--	0.99	0.87	--	--	1.00	1.55	0.99	1.07	--	--	--	1.36	1.01	0.86	1.12	1.23	1.54
New Mexico	1.26	--	--	0.95	--	--	1.26	1.12	1.26	--	--	--	1.12	1.15	--	--	0.99	0.98	--	1.08
Arizona	1.13	--	--	1.68	0.91	--	1.05	1.03	--	1.00	--	--	1.18	--	1.27	0.99	1.00	1.24	0.88	0.94
Utah	--	--	--	--	0.91	--	--	--	1.21	--	--	--	1.17	1.22	--	1.00	--	0.97	--	1.16
Nevada	--	--	--	--	--	--	--	--	--	--	--	0.91	--	--	--	--	--	--	--	--
Pacific																				
Washington	1.39	--	1.28	1.12	1.35	1.38	1.43	1.37	1.43	1.41	1.27	--	1.53	1.33	1.36	1.30	1.09	1.35	1.20	--
Oregon	1.39	--	--	--	1.38	1.31	1.51	1.34	1.43	1.28	--	--	--	1.42	1.19	1.19	1.03	1.37	--	--
California	1.32	--	1.28	1.06	1.02	1.20	1.35	1.24	1.34	1.20	1.25	1.15	1.31	1.39	1.27	1.17	1.13	1.29	1.12	1.09

income are doomed in the long run. At best, economic development, measured in terms of nation-wide societal welfare, is a zero sum game, and evidence exists to demonstrate that it may actually be a losing proposition. But, it would be naive to think that states and localities will cease their efforts to promote their own economic growth. Thus, an approach is needed to minimize counterproductive efforts and to optimize gains.

The purpose of economic development policies is to attract jobs and economic activity. It is recognized that three business costs are at the heart of a firm's locational decision—transportation, energy, and labor costs. Presently, it appears that policymakers all but ignore these uncontrollable costs and focus on controllables such as taxes and amenities. Unfortunately, this approach may lead to an inefficient economic decision.

By first looking at the comparative advantage (or disadvantage) that a state has in terms of uncontrollable costs, industrial location incentives can be better focused. This methodology provides a way to quantify these costs in a consistent and reproducible manner. Once it has been determined in which industry a state has a comparative advantage or is competitive, the economic development policymaker can tailor the variety of incentives to best suit the subject. The end result should be a more cost effective use of industrial location incentives.

NOTES

1. "GM Says Yes to City," *Fort Wayne News Sentinel* (August 31, 1984), sec. 1-1, 4.

2. "Second War between the States: A Bitter Struggle for Jobs, Capital, and People," *Business Week* (May 17, 1976), 92.

3. An exhaustive summary of interstate variations in industrial development incentives is provided in John Gray and Dean Spina, "State and Local Industrial Location Incentives—A Well-Stocked Candy Store," *Journal of Corporation Law* 5 (Spring 1980), 517–687.

4. Richard A. Musgrave, *The Theory of Public Finance* (New York: McGraw-Hill, 1959), 3.

5. It is not being argued that government has no role in the marketplace. The distinction that is being made is that, in the absence of market failure, economic development policies that attempt to redistribute income and stabilize state and local economies reduce efficiency.

6. For a taste of the myriad of factors that enter into a corporation's locational decision-making process see Roger Schmenner, *Making Business Location Decisions* (Englewood Cliffs, N.J.: Prentice-Hall, 1982).

7. Walter Isard, *Introduction to Regional Science* (Englewood Cliffs, N.J.: Prentice-Hall, 1975), 80–84.

8. Gray and Spina, op. cit., 517–687.

9. Ibid., 517–687.

10. Ibid., 556–557.

11. For example, see Advisory Commission on Intergovernmental Relations, *Regional Growth: Interstate Tax Competition* (Washington, D.C.: ACIR, March 1981); Arthur Andersen and Co., *Comparative Study of State and Local Taxes* (Columbus, Ohio: Arthur Andersen, April 1977); John F. Due, "Studies of State-Local Tax Differences on Location of Industry," *National Tax Journal* 14 (June 1961), 163–173; Wisconsin Department of Revenue, Division of Research and Analysis, *Corporate Tax Climates: A Comparison of Sixteen States* (Madison: Wisconsin Department of Revenue, December 1979); and *The Fourth Study of General Manufacturing Business Climates* (Chicago: Alexander Grant and Company, 1982).

12. Michael Wasylenko, "The Location of Firms: The Role of Taxes and Fiscal Incentives," in *Urban Government Finance*, Roy Bahl, ed. (Newbury Park, Calif.: Sage Publications, 1981), 155–190.

13. Ibid., 186; Gray and Spina, op. cit., 517–687; and Steven R. Kale, "U.S. Industrial Development Incentives and Manufacturing Growth during the 1970s," *Growth and Change* 15 (January 1984), 26–34.

14. A good discussion of the elusive business climate concept is contained in Donald M. Steinnes, "Business Climate, Tax Incentives, and Regional Economic Development," *Growth and Change* 15 (April 1984), 38–39.

15. See, for example, "State Rankings of Business Climate" (Chicago: Fantus Company, 1975) and *The Fourth Study of General Manufacturing Business Climates* (Chicago: Alexander Grant and Company, 1982).

16. T. R. Plaut and J. E. Pluta, "Business Climate, Taxes and Expenditures, and State Industrial Growth in the United States," *Southern Economic Journal* 50 (July 1983), 99–119; and Steinnes, op. cit., 38–47.

17. Plaut and Pluta, op. cit., 114–115.

18. It should be noted that although fiscal incentives gain in importance as the geographical area diminishes, most local economic development efforts are intertwined with state economic development policies. Thus, the case of intrastate local competition for economic activity is relatively unimportant.

19. Barry M. Rubin and C. Kurt Zorn, "A Comparative Analysis of Interstate Variations in Manufacturing Industry Business Costs," report to the Division of Economic Analysis, Indiana Department of Commerce, Indianapolis, Indiana, 1983.

20. The description of the methodology used to derive each of the cost components is lengthy and thus beyond the scope of this paper. For details see ibid.

21. The appendix lists the names of the 20 SIC categories.

Appendix

SIC category	Category name
20	Food and kindred products
21	Tobacco manufacturers
22	Textile mill products
23	Apparel and other textile products
24	Lumber and wood products
25	Furniture and fixtures
26	Paper and allied products
27	Printing and publishing
28	Chemicals and allied products
29	Petroleum and coal products
30	Rubber and miscellaneous products
31	Leather and related products
32	Stone, clay, and glass products
33	Primary metal industries
34	Fabricated metal products
35	Machinery, except electrical
36	Electrical and electric machinery
37	Transportation and motor vehicle equipment
38	Instruments and related products
39	Miscellaneous manufacturing

STATE ECONOMIC DEVELOPMENT INCENTIVES: WHY DO STATES COMPETE?

Dennis O. Grady

Dennis O. Grady avers that a war continues to be fought among the fifty state governments over the issues of jobs and business climates. He notes that states have made available numerous incentives, especially a mixture of taxes and subsidies, to attract and maintain businesses and industries. Yet economic development research reveals that such incentives rarely make much difference despite the fact that they cost taxpayers a lot of money. Why, then, do states continue to compete among themselves through enacting ever higher business incentives when it appears clear that such competition is counterproductive?

According to Grady, the literature provides three explanations purporting to show why competition among the states continues: (1) states become involved in the incentive war because of declining employment within their borders; (2) an iron triangle or subgovernment (i.e., business interests working in conjunction with the state development agency) push incentives through a receptive and compliant legislature; and (3) states engage in an arms race by matching and raising incentives as they compete with other states for a limited number of businesses and industries. Let us now examine briefly the three arguments advanced by Grady to explain this competition:

1. If business incentives are voted by state legislatures as a response to declining employment in their states, there should be a correlation between indicators of declining employment and legislative increases in incentive offerings. Conversely, Grady contends one would expect state legislatures to reduce such incentives when employment increases. To test the declining employment argument, Grady examined state employment data and changes in manufacturing employment for the fifty states from 1974 to 1979. He also calculated changes in state incentive scores for the fifty states over the same period of time. Using simple correlational analysis, he found that decisions by state legislatures to increase or decrease business

incentives were unrelated to employment indicators. Grady, therefore, dismisses the declining employment argument as driving business incentives competition.

2. If an iron triangle is operating, that is, a business lobby is working in cooperation with the state development bureaucracy to persuade the legislature to enact incentives, then one should expect states with (a) strong business lobbies, (b) large economic development bureaucracies, and (c) relatively uninformed legislatures to offer more incentives to lure business and industry. To test the iron triangle explanation, Grady assessed the relationship between business interest group strength and economic development incentives enacted by the legislatures in the fifty states. His findings indicated no correlation between the strength of business groups in the states and legislative economic development effort. Furthermore, Grady did not find even the slightest correlation between economic development agency size and legislatively enacted development incentives.

3. A third explanation for the growth and spread of legislatively enacted incentives, called by some the *arms race explanation,* holds that business incentives offered by other states, especially states in one's region, have to be matched. Using a series of rank-order correlations for the period 1976 to 1983, Grady found general support for the arms race explanation for each of the regions in the United States. In short, Grady's research revealed that there is great likelihood that a state will adopt a new economic development incentives program if other states within the region have already adopted this idea.

In conclusion, Grady believes that states enact economic development incentives without regard to economic conditions. The arms race which all the states follow (whether they do so explicitly or implicitly) is mainly a defense measure against intraregional competition. Grady proposes interstate agreements that would permit states to concentrate on proactive economic development programs rather than on the reactive ones now in fashion.

State governments are actively involved in enacting policies to enhance their relative comparative advantage in attracting and maintaining business and industry. While states have encouraged private enterpreneurial activities within their borders since our nation's birth (Eichner 1970), recent highly publicized efforts to compete for the General Motors Saturn assembly plant and other capital intensive developments have made the general citizenry more aware of this traditionally unglamorous aspect of state policy. This emerging awareness has lagged behind the concern among state policymakers who have considered economic development policy a priority for the past decade (Herzig 1983). The significance of this policy area was demonstrated within the business community in a special report of *Business Week* (1976) which described a "Second War Between the States" over the issues of jobs and business climates. This war continues to be fought among the 50 state governments with little prospect for a cease-fire. Like much current warfare, it most closely resembles a guerrilla war where victories are sporadic, frequently Pyrrhic, and battle lines are difficult to discern.

The battle among states for economic growth has not gone unnoticed nor unstudied by state government analysts. Several studies have identified the numerous incentives states make available to business and industry (Eichner 1970; Reinshuttle 1983; Kieschnick 1981; Hansen 1984; Conway 1966–85). These reports indicate that, while each state places different emphasis on particular incentives, all states provide a mixture of tax, locational, labor force, and expenditure subsidies to attract and maintain industry. For a listing of specific business incentives most commonly used see Table 1. Another major strain of research in this area deals with the economic impact of these incentives. Works by the Advisory Commission on Intergovernmental Relations (ACIR) (1981), Harrison and Kanter (1978), Kale (1984), Litvak and Daniels (1983), Rubin and Zorn (1985), and Peretz (1986) fall into this category of analysis. The general consensus of this research is captured by Litvak and Daniels.

> Most state policies thought to promote economic growth do not work— they just cost the taxpayers money. The preponderance of evidence is clear: state taxes represent a small cost of doing business; state tax incentives and subsidies do not change business decisions (26).

Source: Dennis O. Grady, "State Economic Development Incentives: Why Do States Compete?" Reprinted from STATE AND LOCAL GOVERNMENT REVIEW, Vol. 19, No. 3 (Fall 1987). By permission of the author and the Carl Vinson Institute of Government, University of Georgia.

The reason incentives have little impact on job creation centers on the process of business location decision making and the dynamics of the job creation process. From a location perspective, businesses are more concerned about access to markets, labor force characteristics, and the availability of natural and energy resources than they are about differentials in state taxes (ACIR 1981). From the job creation perspective, the majority of new jobs are created by firms with fewer than 50 employees, yet the incentives are typically targeted to large firms (Jacobs 1979). Some evidence exists (Kale 1984; Hansen 1984) that incentives have the potential to move jobs from one state to another intraregionally; but no evidence exists that the incentives actually create new jobs. This intraregional job heist has been dubbed the "begger thy neighbor" strategy by Timothy Schellhardt of the *Wall Street Journal* (1983).

The fact that states continue to compete among themselves through business inducements despite the evidence that the competition is generally counterproductive is an obvious anomaly for students of state government and policy. Furthermore, this competition is more than a theoretical concern since these inducements represent a substantial investment of state resources. For example, in the 1980 competition over a new Volkswagen plant, the winning bidder, Pennsylvania, provided $40 million in direct state expenditures, $27 million in bonds, and a loss of property tax revenue for the first five years of the plant's operation (Hansen 1984). In addition, because of the established precedent of direct business subsidization, companies can essentially blackmail states with the threat of leaving or generate competitive bidding between states over a new investment.

Within the literature, implicit assumptions are made regarding the causes for the competition without specifically testing whether these causes are actually valid. Three distinct origins for the conflict are posited. The first is that states become involved in the incentive war because of declining employment within the state (*Business Week* 1976; Carroll, Hyde, and Hudson 1985). This appears intuitively reasonable given that the economic development programs are supposed to create jobs. A second hypothesis follows the tradition of explaining many policy areas and can be termed the subgovernment explanation wherein business interests working in conjunction with the state development agency push incentives through a receptive legislature (Harrison and Kanter 1978; Jacobs 1979). The third hypothesis has been termed the "arms race model" (Peretz 1986) and represents a variation of Walker's (1969) well-known policy diffusion theory explaining the spread of many state policies within our federal system. As its name implies, this theory posits a process of matching and raising incentives as states compete for a limited number of capital expansion opportunities.

All of these explanations are reasonable and each implies a different process for the development and expansion of business incentives. This paper will test each of these potential explanations for the tremendous growth of incentives over the past decade. By coming to terms with why the Second War between the States continues, perhaps we may begin the process of winding it down.

MEASURING THE STATES' BUSINESS INCENTIVE EFFORT

Since 1966, a private consulting firm, Conway Data, Inc., has systematically surveyed business incentive legislation across the 50 states and published its findings in its trade publication, *Industrial Development*. This periodical is targeted to industrial site-location specialists and provides the only annual, comprehensive, cross-sectional reporting of industrial incentives in the United States. These data are also reported in the "Economic Development" section of the *Book of the States*, a major information source for comparative state policy research published by the Council of State Governments (CSG) (1980).

Conway identifies 57 unique legislatively enacted programs and 18 specific industrial revenue bond financing programs used by the states to lure industry. While the published tables have had a few minor changes over the 18 years that the survey has been conducted, these minor additions and deletions do not materially affect the consistency of the data base over time. One way to view this data set is simply as the tabulation of the number of these different incentives made available by states over the years. However, as Kale points out, "The total number of incentives for a state, however, does not accurately reflect differences in their relative importance to prospective recruits" (1984, 27). Fortunately, this issue has been addressed through a survey of professional industrial facility planners conducted by the Industrial Development Research Council (IDRC) in 1977. The IDRC asked the facility planners to prioritize the top 10 incentives from the Conway inventory of 57 incentives and 18 bonding programs. The incentives were then weighted based upon their relative rankings with 10 points for a first place vote, 9 points for a second place vote, etc. Table 1 presents the top 20 incentives and their respective weights reported by the IDRC.[1]

For the following analysis a state's business incentive effort for any given year will be measured by summing its weighted scores on the top 20 programs it offers in that year. For example, State A offers in 1979 only

TABLE 1   The 20 Most Important Industrial Incentives

Rank	Incentive	Weight
1	Property tax exemption or moratorium on land, capital improvements	207
2	State right-to-work law	202
3	Property tax exemption on manufacturing inventory	199
4	Corporate income tax exemption	197
5	Industrial bond financing	191
6	Property tax exemption on equipment	181
7	Accelerated depreciation	174
8	Sales tax exemption—new equipment	141
9	State-supported training	117
10	Property tax exemption—materials used in manufacturing	98
11	Inventory tax exemption—goods in transit	96
12	License or excise tax exemption	59
13	State-supported recruiting, screening of industrial employees	55
14	Statewide uniform property tax law	51
15	Wage incentive program	44
16	Tax stabilization for specified industries	36
17	Tax exemption for research and development	35
18	State or local loans for plant construction	31
19	State program to promote research and development	20
20	State incentives to establish plants in high unemployment areas	12

Source: *The Industrial Facility Planner's View of Special Incentives* (Atlanta: Industrial Development Research Council, 1977), 12–13.

the top five incentives and receives an incentive effort score of 996 (*207 + 202 + 199 + 197 + 191 = 996*). State B offers in 1979 only the 6th-through 11th-ranked incentives and receives a score of 807 (*181 + 174 + 141 + 117 + 98 + 96 = 807*). State A is considered to provide greater incentive effort than State B. This measure of incentive effort, variations of which have been used in previous research (Kale 1984; Grady 1986; Blair, Fichtenbaum, and Swaney 1984; Ambrosius 1986), serves as the dependent variable for testing the hypotheses.

THE EMPLOYMENT PROBLEM EXPLANATION

If business incentives are the way state legislatures respond to employment problems in their states, we would expect to find an association between indicators of declining employment and increases in incentive offerings. Conversely, as the employment picture brightens, we would expect state legislatures to reduce the states' incentives.

To examine whether such an association is present, two variables were calculated measuring changes in relative state unemployment and marginal percentage changes in manufacturing employment for the 50 states over the 1974–79 period.[2] Relative state unemployment is the state's unemployment rate in comparison to the national rate for any given year.[3] This measure is used rather than actual state unemployment because actual state unemployment is meaningless without some benchmark for comparison. For example, a state rate of 6.0 percent in 1974 when the national rate was 5.6 percent would indicate a relatively bad employment situation whereas that same state rate in 1975 when the national rate was 8.5 percent would indicate a relatively good employment picture. We are dealing with the legislature's perception of employment problems, so these perceptions are stated in terms relative to the performance of the national economy.

The marginal percentage change in manufacturing employment is simply the net percentage gain or loss of manufacturing jobs in a state from one year to the next.[4] The variable is calculated in this fashion to account for the wide variation among states in manufacturing employment. For example, Pennsylvania reported 1.34 million manufacturing jobs in 1977 while Maine reported approximately 100,000 manufacturing jobs (Department of Labor 1982). If both states lost 10,000 manufacturing jobs from one year to the next, both the political and economic impact would be much greater in Maine than in Pennsylvania. We would therefore expect Maine to respond more vigorously than Pennsylvania to the same actual decline in manufacturing employment.

Marginal changes in state incentive scores were also calculated for the 50 states over the period with the same procedures used to calculate manufacturing employment changes.[5] The logic of the calculation also follows the logic of the previous calculations. We are not concerned with the actual level of the states' incentive effort in testing this hypothesis, but rather we are interested in what accounts for changes in the effort. Since the states' incentive scores vary considerably both across states at any particular year and across years for any given state (Grady 1986), we need some way to standardize the absolute change in a state's score for each year under investigation. For example, Missouri's incentive score was 941 in 1977, while Oklahoma's was 1,401. If both states added incentives in 1978 which increased their scores by 300 points, Missouri would have produced a 32 percent increase whereas Oklahoma's would be a more modest 21 percent increase. In relative terms, Missouri's legislature

TABLE 2 Pearson's Correlation Coefficients between Measures of Unemployment Change and Changes in Incentive Effort

		Employment measures	
		Relative unemployment changes	Manufacturing employment changes
Incentive score change	1-year lag	−.0180	−.0110
	2-year lag	.0002	.0011

would have provided more incentive effort than Oklahoma's from 1977 to 1978.

To assess the relationship between relative changes in unemployment rates and marginal percentage changes in incentive scores, simple correlational analysis was used. The states' relative incentive effort scores were lagged one year and two years to allow time for legislatures to react to previous years' employment figures. The lagging procedure takes into account the timing of reporting annual unemployment rates and the cycle of legislative sessions. Annual unemployment rates are typically reported in February of the succeeding year (annual figures for 1977 were reported in February of 1978). Some legislatures meet annually and could respond in the 1978 session. This situation is captured by the one-year lag. Other legislatures meet biennially and some controversial incentive proposals could take two years to be enacted. These situations are captured by the two-year lag. In other words, the state's relative unemployment rate and its marginal percentage change in manufacturing employment for 1973 were correlated with the marginal incentive score changes in both 1974 and 1975, while the employment figures for 1974 were correlated with incentive changes in 1975 and 1976, etc. Lagging the dependent variable is necessary since we could hardly expect legislatures to react to information before it is available or when they are not in session. The results of the analyses are presented in Table 2.

The results indicate absolutely no relationship between measures of employment change and changes in incentive effort for either one or two years after the employment changes. This indicates that neither bad nor good news about the states' employment is associated with changes in incentive offerings. The two concepts appear to be totally independent. This analysis provides fairly convincing evidence that during the 1974–79 period decisions by the legislatures to increase or decrease incentives were not related to employment indicators in any systematic fashion. These results nicely round the circle regarding the relationship between economic incentives and jobs. Previous research has repeatedly found that these incentives do not lead to employment growth. This analysis indicates that lack of jobs does not lead to incentives. We cannot, therefore, lay the blame for incentive competition on the doorstep of economic necessity (assuming leaders think the incentives will work) or symbolic politics (assuming leaders know the incentives do not work). It appears that something else is driving the business incentive competition.

THE POLICY SUBSYSTEM EXPLANATION

Another plausible source for the growth in business incentives is the business lobby in the state working in conjunction with the state development bureaucracy pushing incentives through a receptive legislature. Harrison and Kanter (1978) offer this explanation.

> Not surprisingly, capitalists are constantly trying to resist the redistribution (of wealth) and to reverse it whenever possible. To assist them in this process, business firms employ paid lobbyists....But firms can also count on the assistance of many of the officials of the government agencies administering the many programs that affect business, and the legislators who vote upon them (433).

This rationale describes the policymaking process from the subgovernment or iron triangle perspective (Ripley and Franklin 1984). Following this rationale we would expect states with strong business lobbies, large economic development bureaucracies, and relatively uninformed legislatures to offer more incentives. The following three sections take each of these factors in turn and assess the influence of business lobbies, state development agencies, and legislative professionalism on incentive effort.

BUSINESS INTEREST GROUP STRENGTH AND ECONOMIC INCENTIVES

Examining the influence of state interest groups is a difficult enterprise primarily because so little information exists concerning their activities. Typically, analysts either examine the significance of interest group influence in one state (Patterson 1963) or examine the influence of one group in a limited number of states (Browne 1985). Within the state politics literature, only one analyst has attempted a 50-state comparison of various interest groups and assessed their relative influence within each state (Morehouse 1981).[6]

In her study, Morehouse classified the states according to the strength of the interest group system in general and identified for each state those interests reported to be most influential. Her research indicates that business interests are considered the strongest despite variations in the strength of the interest group system. As Zeigler (1983) reports after examining Morehouse's data,

> However, no matter what the nature of the business, and irrespective of whether groups are generally strong, moderately strong, or weak, business organizations have no peers in reputed influence. In strong lobby states, 75 percent of the powerful groups are business; in states with moderately strong groups, 71 percent of the influential organizations are affiliated with business interests; in states with a weak pressure group system, 58 percent of the groups nominated as powerful are from business (99).

Given the above, we can use the categorizations provided by Morehouse regarding state influence group strength as a proximate measure of business influence within state legislative chambers. She divides the states into three categories—22 states with strong pressure groups, 18 states with moderately strong interests, and 10 weak interest group systems. Footnote 6 contains the states by her classifications. Assuming her classifications are accurate, we may assess the relationship between business interest group strength and economic development programming. In so doing, we would expect to find that those states with strong business interests would provide greater business incentive packages. We would also expect that strong interest group states would be fairly stable over time in offering incentives.

Table 3 examines the relationship between Morehouse's categories and economic development effort measured by the states' weighted incentive scores and their consistency, measured by the states' standard deviations over the period 1966–84. The cutoff points for incentive effort and stability are the states' aggregate mean effort score for the 1966–84 period (1,057) and the standard deviation for the population over the 18 years (332). States with 18-year averages above 1,057 are classified as high effort states and states with standard deviations below 332 across the 18 years are considered stable in programming terms.

Table 3 indicates absolutely no relationship between Morehouse's classifications and economic development effort or stability. In fact, the results indicate almost the reverse of what was expected given the evolutionary theory offered by Harrison and Kanter (1978). While strong inter-

TABLE 3 Economic Incentive Effort and Stability by Interest Group Strength

	Stability	
	Stable	Unstable
High effort	North Dakota, Mississippi, New York, South Carolina, Tennessee, Kentucky, Pennsylvania, Wisconsin, Maryland, Arizona, Connecticut, Wyoming (4 strong, 4 moderate, 4 weak)	Alabama, Minnesota, Louisiana, Kansas, Delaware, South Dakota, Michigan, Iowa, Florida, New Jersey, Oklahoma, Virginia, Oregon (6 strong, 4 moderate, 3 weak)
Low effort	Texas, Rhode Island, Massachusetts, Idaho, Nebraska, North Carolina, Nevada, Utah, California, West Virginia, Colorado (4 strong, 4 moderate, 3 weak)	Indiana, Missouri, Montana, Ohio, Georgia, Washington, Arkansas, New Hampshire, Maine, Hawaii, Illinois, Vermont, New Mexico, Alaska (8 strong, 6 moderate, 0 weak)

est group states were expected to score high on effort and be stable over the period, only 4 of the 22 such states did so. In addition, none of the 10 weak interest group states possessed the expected characteristics of low effort and lack of stability. To explore further the relationship between interest group strength and economic development programming, a number of ordinal level associations were run on the data to see if interest groups had any particular influence on different types of programming. None of the associations were statistically significant or meaningful. The Kendall's tau b between Morehouse's classifications and the states' weighted incentive score is –.05044, for tax incentive programming tau b is –.09070, for financial assistance programming tau b is –.09822. In each relationship, there is little reason to suspect that business interests systematically influence the amount or type of programming a state undertakes.

While little evidence appears to support the notion of systematic business influence on economic development programming, this analysis does not rule out the possibility (probability) that in certain situations business groups are responsible for particular legislative enactments. To specify further the linkage between business interests and economic programming requires additional information regarding the interest group influence structure within each state (e.g., replicating Browne's study on a 50-state basis with a focus on business interests rather than aging interests) and a clear theoretical specification of the political and economic conditions which increase or decrease the likelihood that a particular state will adopt a particular program. Without such a design, it is impossible to nullify Harrison and Kanter's theory. We can state, however, that business group influence on economic development programming is more complex and multifaceted than posited by their theory.

ECONOMIC DEVELOPMENT AGENCY SIZE AND ECONOMIC INCENTIVES

Each state has an agency responsible for economic development planning and promotion with policy direction coming from the governor's office (Reinshuttle 1983). The economic development staffs are the foot soldiers in the war among the states for new capital investments. As part of their arsenal of weapons, the economic development professionals employ incentives to lure businesses. It is therefore within the self-interest of the economic development agency to push for incentives which enhance its competitive advantage in attracting industry.

One might expect that states which devote considerable resources to the economic development agency would also supply the agency with numerous incentives with which to work. However, the relationship between state development agency budgets and state incentive effort is nonexistent. To assess this relationship, the analysis used data provided by the National Association of State Development Agencies (NASDA). On a periodic basis, NASDA surveys its membership and collects information on each state's economic development budget. These budget figures were correlated with the states' incentive score for the years 1977, 1979, and 1982. The simple correlation between budgets and incentives for these years is .0065 indicating absolutely no relationship between these measures.

Because states differ radically in the operation of their state development agencies, direct comparison of budget figures across states can be misleading. Even with that caveat, if incentives were a result of bureaucratic muscle (as the subgovernment theory implies) one would expect to see at least some slight association between agency budget and incentive offerings. The fact that there is none casts further doubt on the subgovernment explanation.

LEGISLATIVE PROFESSIONALISM AND ECONOMIC INCENTIVES

The standard subgovernment explanation for the development and enlargement of particular policy areas usually implies a strong, well-informed policy committee dedicated to pursuing its agenda through the chamber. However, when dealing with economic incentives, the traditional assumption of the well-informed legislative committee is not an accurate depiction. As the ACIR (1981) observes:

> Econometricians have not been able to develop the methodology that would enable them to say whether taxes really count in industrial location decisions. The likelihood that taxes weigh heavily in some manufacturing location decisions, but not at all in others—along with the inability to distinguish between these two circumstances—have left the policymaker free to follow personal advice, intuition, and inclinations (26).

This view of legislative decision making on economic incentives has been suported by Dewar's (1986) case study of industrial policymaking by the Minnesota legislature. "The political leaders failed to use economic development analysis in choosing goals partly because no one involved had either the background or the inclination to analyze an economy that way" (292).

These analyses would indicate that economic development policy is a result of ignorance rather than information since, as previously noted, most information concerning the economic utility of the incentives indicates that they do not work. One would think that a well-informed legislature, confronted with evidence that a particular incentive might cost the state more in foregone revenue than it could hope to recoup in future taxes, would weigh the evidence carefully and refuse to enact the incentive. Following this logic we would expect a better-informed legislature to be less prone to enact business incentives.

Three measures of an "informed" legislature were developed following the tradition of comparative legislative research (ACIR 1985): annual legislative salaries and turnover rate for the lower chamber (CSG 1978); and staff-to-legislator ratios (National Conference of State Legislatures 1979). We would expect that higher salaries, higher staff ratios, and lower turnover would be inversely related to incentive offerings. The correlation coefficients for these measures during the 1977–78 biennium are as follows:

	Salaries	Staff ratio	% Turnover
Incentive effort	.01882	−.10209	−.02672

The relationships between incentives and these measures of an informed legislature are totally random for the biennium analyzed.

If a policy subsystem is in operation around the economic incentive system, it does not operate in any systematic manner across the 50 states. Had there been even the slightest suggestion that one of the actors in the subsystem had influence on the level of incentives offered, it would be worthwhile to investigate further the possibility of some form of subsystem in operation. However, neither business interest group strength in the legislature nor agency size nor legislative professionalism measures are even slightly related to incentives. If subsystems operate in this policy area, they are probably temporary alliances within particular states over specific legislation. A case study approach would be required to tap that dimension of economic development policymaking.

THE ARMS RACE EXPLANATION

Peretz (1986) offers a third potential explanation for the growth and spread of economic incentives which he terms the "arms race model."

> The spread appears to be largely the result of risk averse behavior by development officers, combined with genuine ignorance among legislators. The result is a general feeling that incentives offered by other states have to be matched (630).

This hypothesis is a variation of Walker's (1969) innovation diffusion theory.

> ...the likelihood of a state adopting a new program is higher if other states have already adopted the idea. The likelihood becomes higher still if the innovation has been adopted by a state viewed by key decision makers as a point of legitimate comparison....Emerging from this study is a picture of a national system of emulation and competition. The states are grouped into regions based on both geographical contiguity and their place in the specialized set of communication channels through which flow new ideas, information and policy cues (897–98).

States generally compete for industry intraregionally due to the dynamics of the industrial site location process (Rubin and Zorn 1985, 335). This intraregional arms race analysis requires the specification of regional competitors. A number of regional configurations are available, each with their own particular weaknesses. Perhaps the most sophisticated exercise in grouping states into regions has been offered by Foster (1978) who employed regression procedures on Walker's innovation scores for each state and organized the states by their models' resulting residuals. Foster's regions are employed for testing the arms race hypothesis.[7]

If the arms race model describes the economic incentive process of growth and spread, we would expect to see considerable movement within regions among the states' rank orderings on their incentive scores. In other words, if a state ranked low on its incentive score relative

TABLE 4 Rank Order Correlations for Economic Incentives by Region for Selected Years

	Regions						
Pair	1	2	3	4	5	6	7
1976–77	.7143	.5636	.8000	.3333	.6429	.9444	.3333
1976–78	.8571	.8441	.8000	.0000	.4286	.8733	1.0000
1976–79	.2857	.7340	.6000	–.6667	.1429	.6111	.3333
1976–80	.2857	.5138	.6000	–.6667	.1429	.1667	.3333
1976–81	.5000	.4182	.6000	–.6667	.2143	.2778	.3333
1976–82	.5000	.2364	.0000	–.3333	.0714	.2535	.3333
1976–83	.4286	.0909	.0000	.3333	.1429	.2222	.3333

Regions (number of states)
1. Northeast (8)
2. South (11)
3. Border (5)
4. Lower Great Lakes (4)
5. Upper Midwest and Plains (8)
6. Mountains and Southwest (9)
7. Pacific (3, Alaska and Hawaii excluded)

to its regional competitors in any given year, the state would increase its offerings the following year in order to improve its regional standing. The other states in the region would see themselves slip in the rankings and take corrective action in succeeding years. This process would continue indefinitely with the rank orderings of the states becoming more dissimilar from the base year as time progressed. We can see if this is the case by running a series of rank order correlations (Kendall's tau b) within Foster's seven regions over time. The results of this analysis for the period 1976 to 1983, using 1976 as the baseline rank ordering, are displayed in Table 4.

The data indicate general support for the arms race hypothesis for each of the regions. One would expect to find relatively high coefficients for the most proximate pairs (1976–77, 1976–78) with the tau's approaching .0 as time progresses. This indicates a significant volatility among states within regions as each attempts to match and raise a competitor's incentive offerings. Through the process, a state's relative position within the region fluctuates. Region 4, the Lower Great Lakes states, illustrates the process in its purest form. Table 5 examines that region more closely.

Pennsylvania was the regional inducement leader in 1976. Two years

TABLE 5 Ranking of Lower Great Lakes States by Incentive Effort for Selected Years

State	1976	Rank	1978	Rank	1980	Rank	1982	Rank	1984	Rank
Pennsylvania	1079	1	898	2	1345	3	1200	4	1571	2
Indiana	837	2	837	3	1339	4	1339	3	1657	1
Ohio	789	3	1397	1	1366	2	1456	1	1100	4
Illinois	642	4	642	4	1382	1	1382	2	1394	3

later it had eliminated (according to the Conway data) some of its incentives, in the process dropping behind Ohio which had virtually doubled its offerings during the same period. By 1980, Pennsylvania had added numerous incentives (almost 450 points worth) but dropped another position because its competitors had been even more active. Pennsylvania's 1982 score drops again placing the state in last position. Over the next biennium the Pennsylvania legislature enacted numerous incentives allowing the state to climb into second place while Ohio tumbled during the same period from first to last.

The decline in incentive scores for Pennsylvania and Ohio at points in the series raises interesting questions. The arms race model assumes a continual escalation which is true in general across all regions: however, it does not account for any reduction in a state's incentive effort. Since 44 states reduced their effort for at least one year during the 1966–84 period (according to the Conway data), it is not unusual for a reduction to take place despite the overall trend toward growth. Examining the dynamics of reducing incentives could well lead to a more comprehensive and sophisticated understanding of the business incentive process. This would require a case study approach. Nonetheless, from the comparative and longitudinal perspective, it appears that the arms race model comes closest to explaining the dynamics of the growth and spread of business incentives across the states.

DISCUSSION

The purpose of the analysis has been to identify the forces driving the competition among states for jobs and industry. This analysis indicates that states enact incentives irrespective of employment problems—the purported rationale for the incentives. We cannot, therefore, lay the blame for the competition on economic forces. Nor can we accuse an insidious policy subsystem where powerful interest groups work in conjunction with an avaricious bureaucracy to pull the wool over the eyes of an unknowing public. These explanations simply do not seem to account for the systematic growth and spread of incentives across the states. It appears that states enact incentives generally as a defensive measure against regional competitors.

If competition among states for jobs improved the average citizen's quality of life or resulted in a more competitive national economy, the incentive competition would be to everyone's benefit. Unfortunately, neither of these desirable outcomes are obtained (ACIR 1981). Instead, because of the states' balanced budget requirements, reducing business taxation requires decreasing services or increasing other consumer-based taxes, actions which raise serious questions about the social equity of the entire business incentive system. To the extent that policymakers are concerned about tax equity, the escalation of business tax incentives is a policy problem requiring attention. What options are available?

Hellman, Wassall, and Falk (1976) offer three potential scenarios for the policymaker concerned about business incentives. One suggestion is to let the programs run their course which will lead eventually to a neutralization of incentives as each state adopts "...similar programs so that, in the end, there will be no impact on location choice. The only impact would be a reduction in federal revenues and a shifting of capital from nonsubsidized sectors into manufacturing" (99). A second alternative is for the federal government to forbid the states to offer incentives, "[s]ince the federal government bears the cost, at least in part, of the interest subsidy incentive programs" (100). This alternative is undesirable from the political perspective as well as from the constitutional federalism perspective. The third alternative is for states to negotiate interstate agreements within regions to coordinate industrial inducement policies. This, in effect, would neutralize intraregional inducement advantages and allow states to concentrate on more proactive economic development programs rather than the reactive incentives we currently see in operation. Regional mechanisms are in place to facilitate such an effort. This recommendation is also offered by the nonprofit think tank, the Committee for Economic Development (CED) in its review of the issue (1986, 36). If states were not constantly looking over their shoulders to see what new business giveaway their regional competitors were offering, they could concentrate on enhancing their own economic development potentials based on an honest assessment of their relative strengths and weaknesses.

Competition among states is not unhealthy. It leads to innovation, increased productivity, and more creative use of resources. The competition, however, should not be over tax codes, but rather, over the quality of the states' education, infrastructure, environment, and the productivity of the labor force. With incentive competition, the beneficiaries are the stockholders of the corporations receiving the tax breaks, free land, and cheap credit. If the competition were over the quality of traditional state services, every citizen would benefit.

NOTES

1. Since the right-to-work law has implications beyond business recruitment, the following analyses were run both with and without that policy in the dependent variable. Results were virtually identical since the correlation between the two measures is 96. The ensuing analyses include "right to work" in the dependent variable.

2. The states' unemployment rates data are from the U.S. Department of Labor 1980, while data for manufacturing employment come from the U.S. Department of Labor 1982.

3. Calculating relative state unemployment (RSU) for any given year is straightforward. It is simply the difference between the state unemployment rate and the national unemployment rate in a given year.

4. Marginal percentage change in manufacturing employment is calculated as follows:

$$\Delta ME\%_{tt} = \frac{ME_{tt} - ME_{t-l}}{ME_{t-l}} \quad \begin{aligned} where: \; & \Delta ME\%_{tt} = marginal\ \%\ change \\ & ME_{tt} = manuf.\ employ\ any\ year \\ & ME_{t-l} = previous\ year \end{aligned}$$

5. Marginal percentage change in incentive effort (Δ IE%) is calculated as follows:

$$\Delta IE\%_{tt} = \frac{IE_{tt} - IE_{t-l}}{IE_{t-l}}$$

6. Morehouse's (1981) Classification of States by Reputed Interest Group Strength—

Strong: Alabama, Alaska, Arkansas, Florida, Georgia, Hawaii, Iowa, Kentucky, Louisiana, Mississippi, Montana, Nebraska, New Hampshire, New Mexico, North Carolina, Oklahoma, Oregon, South Carolina, Tennessee, Texas, Washington, and West Virginia.

Moderate: Arizona, California, Delaware, Idaho, Illinois, Indiana, Kansas, Maine, Maryland, Missouri, Nevada, Ohio, Pennsylvania, South Dakota, Utah, Vermont, Virginia, and Wyoming.

Weak: Colorado, Connecticut, Massachusetts, Michigan, Minnesota, New Jersey, New York, North Dakota, Rhode Island, and Wisconsin.

7. Foster's (1976) Regional Classifications—

Northeast: Massachusetts, Connecticut, New York, New Jersey, Maine, New Hampshire, Vermont, and Rhode Island.

South: Georgia, Alabama, North Carolina, Florida, Arkansas, Virginia, Tennessee, Mississippi, Louisiana, South Carolina, and Texas.

Border: Kentucky, Maryland, West Virginia, Delaware, and Missouri.

Lower Great Lakes: Pennsylvania, Indiana, Ohio, and Illinois.

Upper Midwest and Plains: Minnesota, North Dakota, Kansas, Michigan, Iowa, Wisconsin, Nebraska, and South Dakota.

Mountains and Southwest: Colorado, Idaho, New Mexico, Montana, Oklahoma, Utah, Arizona, Wyoming, and Nevada.

Pacific: Oregon, California, and Washington.

REFERENCES

Advisory Commission on Intergovernmental Relations (ACIR). 1981. *Interstate tax competition.* Washington, D.C.: U.S. Government Printing Office (US GPO).

_____ . 1985. *The question of state government capability.* Washington, D.C.: US GPO.

Ambrosius, Margery. 1986. Effects of state development policies on the health of state economies: A time series regression analysis. Paper delivered at the annual meeting of the Midwest Political Science Association, Chicago, April 10–12.

Blair, John, Rudy Fichtenbaum, and James Swaney. 1984. The market for jobs: Location decisions and the competition for economic development. *Urban Affairs Quarterly* (September) 64–77.

Browne, William P. 1985. Variations in the behavior and style of state lobbyists and interest groups. *Journal of Politics* 47:450–67.

Business Week. 1976. See The second war between the states.

Carroll, John, Mark Hyde, and William Hudson. 1985. Economic development policy: Why Rhode Islanders rejected the Greenhouse Compact. *State Government* 58, no. 3:110–12.

Committee for Economic Development (CED). 1986. *Leadership for dynamic state economies.* New York: CED Press.

Conway, McKinley. 1966–1985. The fifty legislative climates. *Industrial Development and Site Location.* Atlanta: Conway Data, Inc.

Council of State Governments (CSG). 1978. *Book of the states, 1978–79.* Lexington, Ky.: CSG Press.

Dewar, Margaret. 1986. Development analysis confronts politics: Industrial policy on Minnesota's Iron Range. *APA Journal* (Summer): 290–98.

Eichner, Alfred S. 1970. *State development agencies and employment expansion.* Ann Arbor: University of Michigan Press.

Foster, John L. 1978. Regionalism and innovation in the American states. *The Journal of Politics* 40:179–87.

Grady, Dennis. 1986. The evolution of state economic development policy. Paper presented at annual meeting of the Midwest Political Science Association, Chicago, April 10–12.

Hansen, Susan B. 1984. The effects of state industrial policies on economic growth. Paper presented at the annual meeting of the American Political Science Association, Washington, D.C., August 30–September 2.

Harrison, Bennett, and Sandra Kanter. 1978. The political economy of states' job creation business incentives. *AIP Journal* (October): 424–35.

Heilman, D. A., G. W. Wassall, and L. H. Falk. 1976. *State financial incentives to industry.* Lexington, Mass.: D.C. Heath and Co.

Herzig, Eric. 1983. Governors and issues. A typology of concerns. *State Government* 56: 58–64.

Jacobs, Jerry. 1979. *Bidding for business: Corporate auctions and the 50 disunited states.* Washington, D.C.: Public Interest Research Group.

Kale, Steven R. 1984. U.S. industrial development incentives and manufacturing growth during the 1970s. *Growth and Change* (January): 26–34.

Kieschnick, Michael. 1981. *Taxes and growth: Business incentives and economic development.* Washington, D.C.: Council of State Planning Agencies.

Litvak, Lawrence, and Blenden Daniels. 1983. Innovation in development finance. In *Financing state and local economic development.* Michael Barker, ed. Durham, N.C.: Duke University Press.

Morehouse, Sarah. 1981. *State politics, parties and policy.* New York, N.Y.: Holt, Rinehart and Winston, Inc.

National Conference of State Legislatures (NCSL). 1979. *A legislator's guide to staffing patterns.* Denver: NCSL Press.

Patterson, Sam. 1963. The role of the lobbyist: The case of Oklahoma. *Journal of Politics* 25: 75–92.

Peretz, Paul. 1986. The market for incentives: Where angels fear to tread? *Policy Studies Journal* 5, no. 3: 624–33.

Reinshuttle, Robert. 1983. *Economic development: A survey of state activities.* Lexington, Ky.: CSG press.

Ripley, Randall, and Grace Franklin. 1984. *Congress, the bureaucracy, and public policy.* 3d ed. Homewood, Ill.: Dorsey Press.

Rubin, Barry M., and C. Kurt Zorn. 1985. Sensible state and local economic development. *Public Administration Review* (March/April): 333–39.

Schellhardt, Timothy. 1984. War among states for jobs and business becomes ever fiercer. *The Wall Street Journal* February 14:1A.

The second war between the states: A bitter struggle for jobs, capital, and people. 1976. *Business Week* May 17: 92–114.

U.S. Department of Labor. 1982. *Employment and earnings, states and areas.* Washington, D.C.: U.S. GPO.

———. 1980. *Manpower Reports.* Washington, D.C.: US GPO.

Walker, Jack L. 1969. The diffusion of innovations among the American states. *American Political Science Review* 63: 880–900.

Zeigler, L. Harmon. 1983. Interest groups in the states. In *Politics in the American States: A comparative perspective.* Virginia Gray, Hubert Jacob, and Kenneth N. Vines, eds. Boston: Little, Brown.

STATE AND LOCAL GOVERNMENT AND POLITICS: ESSENTIAL READINGS
Edited by Robert J. Cunningham, Lake Forest, Illinois
Production supervision by Kim Vander Steen, Palatine, Illinois
Cover design by Lesiak/Crampton Design, Inc., Chicago, Illinois
Composition by Point West, Inc., Carol Stream, Illinois
Printed and bound by Braun-Brumfield, Inc., Ann Arbor, Michigan
Paper, Glatfelter
The text is set in Palatino